Lecture Notes in Computer Science   8636

Commenced Publication in 1973
Founding and Former Series Editors:
Gerhard Goos, Juris Hartmanis, and Jan van J ̄ ̄ ̄ ̄ ̄ ̄

T0255087

Claire Le Goues   Shin Yoo (Eds.)

Search-Based Software Engineering

6th International Symposium, SSBSE 2014
Fortaleza, Brazil, August 26-29, 2014
Proceedings

 Springer

Volume Editors

Claire Le Goues
Carnegie Mellon University
School of Computer Science
Institute for Software Research
5000 Forbes Avenue, Pittsburgh, PA 15213, USA
E-mail: clegoues@cs.cmu.edu

Shin Yoo
University College London
Department of Computer Science
Gower Street, London WC1E 6BT, UK
E-mail: shin.yoo@ucl.ac.uk

ISSN 0302-9743   e-ISSN 1611-3349
ISBN 978-3-319-09939-2   e-ISBN 978-3-319-09940-8
DOI 10.1007/978-3-319-09940-8
Springer Cham Heidelberg New York Dordrecht London

Library of Congress Control Number: 2014945224

LNCS Sublibrary: SL 2 – Programming and Software Engineering

Typesetting: Camera-ready by author, data conversion by Scientific Publishing Services, Chennai, India

Printed on acid-free paper

Springer is part of Springer Science+Business Media (www.springer.com)

Preface

Message from the SSBSE 2014 General Chair

SBSE is growing up! In its sixth edition, the conference left home and expanded its reach in a process of becoming a truly global forum. Brazil was proudly chosen to kick off this process, mainly in recognition of its strong and still growing SBSE community. Besides innovating in its location, SSBSE 2014 implemented a series of novelties. First, it stood alone once again. As a test of maturity, this decision sheds light on how independent and solid the SBSE field has become. Second, it brought an all-inclusive experience, allowing for a much higher level of integration among participants, in turn strengthening the community and helping create a much more cooperative environment. Finally, it implemented a double-blind submission and review process for the first time, providing as fair and objective an evaluation of the submitted papers as possible.

Obviously, this historical event would not have been possible without the help of many people, who I would like to recognize and thank. First of all, I would like to thank our program chairs, Shin Yoo (University College London, UK) and Claire Le Goues (Carnegie Mellon University, USA). They led the review process with great competence and dedication and put together a very rich and high-quality scientific program. I extend this recognition to all members of our Program Committee, for the dedicated work in the review and selection of our papers. Next, I thank our Graduate Student Track chair, Nadia Alshahwan (University College London, UK), and our SBSE Challenge Track chair (Márcio de Oliveira Barros, Federal University of the State of Rio de Janeiro, Brazil), for their hard work on organizing those two special tracks. I would also like to give special thanks to my friend Allysson Araújo (State University of Ceará, Brazil), our Web chair, for accepting the important challenge of creating and maintaining our website and operating this task with perfection. Also, I thank our publicity chair, Sina Shamshiri (University of Sheffield, UK), for the important job of keeping everybody informed about our event. Finally, I also thank the SSBSE Steering Committee, chaired by Mark Harman (University College London, UK), for their vote of confidence in giving us the privilege of organizing SSBSE 2014.

I must also mention and thank our long list of sponsors, who believed in our proposal and provided confidence in me and in the field of SBSE. Without their support, SSBSE 2014 would not have been nearly so special.

I hope you enjoy reading these proceedings as much as I enjoyed organizing the event.

August 2014   Jerffeson Teixeira de Souza

Message from the SSBSE 2014 Program Chairs

On behalf of the SSBSE 2014 Program Committee, we are pleased to present the proceedings of the 6th International Symposium on Search-Based Software Engineering. This year brought SSBSE to South America for the first time, in the oceanside paradise of Fortaleza, Brazil! SSBSE 2014 continued to bring together the international community of SSBSE researchers to exchange and discuss ideas and celebrate the latest progress in this rapidly advancing field.

We are delighted to report that we had a record-breaking 51 submissions to our four tracks: 32 Full Research Track submissions, eight Graduate Student Track submissions, three Fast Abstract submissions, and eight SBSE Challenge Track submissions. Submissions came from 19 different countries: Argentina, Austria, Brazil, Canada, China, the Czech Republic, France, Germany, India, Ireland, Italy, Luxembourg, Norway, the Russian Federation, Sweden, Switzerland, Tunisia, the UK, and the USA. After each submission was reviewed by at least three members of the Program Committee, we accepted 14 Full Research Track papers, one Fast Abstract track paper, three Graduate Student Track papers, and four SBSE Challenge Track papers.

We would like to thank the members of the SSBSE 2014 Program Committee. Without their continued support, we would not have been able to further improve the quality of the submissions and maintain the symposium's tradition of a high-quality technical program. The general chair, Jerffeson Teixeira de Souza, deserves a special mention for leading an excellent team, especially locally, to make the conference an unforgettable experience for everyone. In addition, Márcio Barros worked hard to manage the fast-growing SBSE Challenge Track, while Nadia Alshahwan oversaw the process of handling the Graduate Student Track. The technical program would not have been the same without their effort, for which we especially want to thank them.

As an experiment, this year we implemented a double-blind review procedure for the main research track of the SSBSE program. Our intention was to enable as fair a review process as possible, and recent evidence suggests that removing information like institutional affiliation, country of origin, and author name from submissions under review can contribute to this goal. We want to thank both the Program Committee and our submitting authors for their patience with a new and largely unfamiliar system, and for allowing us to experiment with our review procedure. We encourage those who participated to continue sharing their perspectives on this and other issues related to review and feedback quality. Peer review remains a collaborative and work-in-progress system, and we are interested in the community's experience to help inform future decisions for both this conference and others like it.

The symposium has an excellent tradition of hearing and learning from world experts in both software engineering and meta-heuristic optimization, and we are glad to report that this year was not an exception. We had the honor of having a keynote from Prof. Mauro Pezzè, whose research on software redundancy bears a strong connection to SBSE. Furthermore, we also had a keynote from Dr. Marc Schoenauer, who brought us up to date with progress in adaptive learning research. Finally, the Brazilian SBSE community warmly and enthusiastically invited Prof. Mark Harman to present a review of the field.

We would like to thank all the authors who submitted papers to SSBSE 2014, regardless of the outcome, and everyone who attended the symposium. We hope that, with these proceedings, anyone who did not have a chance to be at Fortaleza will have the opportunity to experience the exuberance of the SBSE community.

August 2014   Claire Le Goues
                                                                  Shin Yoo

Conference Organization

General Chair

Jerffeson Teixeira de Souza   Universidade Estadual do Ceará, Brazil

Program Chairs

Claire Le Goues   Carnegie Mellon University, USA
Shin Yoo   University College London, UK

Graduate Students Track Chair

Nadia Alshahwan   University College London, UK

SBSE Challenge Track Chair

Márcio de Oliveira Barros   Universidade Federal do Estado do Rio de Janeiro, Brazil

Organizing Committee

Sina Shamshiri   University of Sheffield, UK
Allysson Allex de Paula Araújo   Universidade Estadual do Ceará, Brazil

Program Committee

Enrique Alba	University of Málaga, Spain
Shaukat Ali	Simula Research Laboratory, Norway
Giuliano Antoniol	Ecole Polytechnique de Montréal, Canada
Andrea Arcuri	Schlumberger & Simula Research Laboratory, Norway
Leonardo Bottaci	University of Hull, UK
Betty Cheng	Michigan State University, USA
Francisco Chicano	University of Málaga, Spain
Myra Cohen	University of Nebraska-Lincoln, USA
Massimiliano Di Penta	University of Sannio, Italy
Arilo Claudio Dias-Neto	Universidade Federal do Amazonas, Brazil

Robert Feldt	Blekinge Institute of Technology, Sweden
Gordon Fraser	University of Sheffield, UK
Mathew Hall	University of Sheffield, UK
Mark Harman	University College London, UK
Colin Johnson	University of Kent, UK
Gregory Kapfhammer	Allegheny College, USA
Marouane Kessentini	University of Michigan, USA
Dongsun Kim	University of Luxembourg, Luxembourg
Yvan Labiche	Carleton University, Canada
Raluca Lefticaru	University of Bucharest, Romania
Zheng Li	Beijing University of Chemical Technology, China
Spiros Mancoridis	Drexel University, USA
Auri Marcelo Rizzo Vincenzi	Universidade Federal de Goiás, Brazil
Tim Menzies	North Carolina State University, USA
Fitsum Meshesha Kifetew	Fondazione Bruno Kessler - IRST, Italy
Leandro Minku	University of Birmingham, UK
Martin Monperrus	University of Lille, France
Mel Ó Cinnéide	University College Dublin, Ireland
Justyna Petke	University College London, UK
Pasqualina Potena	University of Alcalá, Spain
Simon Poulding	University of York, UK
Xiao Qu	ABB Corporate Research, USA
Marc Roper	University of Strathclyde, UK
Federica Sarro	University College London, UK
Chris Simon	University of the West of England, UK
Lee Spector	Hampshire College, USA
Angelo Susi	Fondazione Bruno Kessler - IRST, Italy
Jerry Swan	University of Stirling, UK
Paolo Tonella	Fondazione Bruno Kessler - IRST, Italy
Silvia Vergilio	Universidade Federal do Paraná, Brazil
Tanja E.J. Vos	Universidad Politècnica de València, Spain
David White	University of Glasgow, UK
Xin Yao	University of Birmingham, UK

External Reviewers

Kenyo Faria	Universidade Federal de Goiás, Brazil
Eduardo Freitas	Universidade Federal de Goiás, Brazil
Damiano Torre	Carleton University, Canada
Shuai Wang	Simula Research Laboratory, Norway
Zhihong Xu	University of Nebraska Lincoln, USA

Steering Committee

Mark Harman (Chair)	University College London, UK
Andrea Arcuri	Schlumberger & Simula Research Laboratory, Norway
Massimiliano Di Penta	University of Sannio, Italy
Gordon Fraser	University of Sheffield, UK
Mel Ó Cinnéide	University College Dublin, Ireland
Jerffeson Teixeira de Souza	Universidade Estadual do Ceará, Brazil
Joachim Wegener	Berner and Mattner, Germany
David White	University of Glasgow, UK
Yuanyuan Zhang	University College London, UK

Sponsors

Keynote Addresses

Intrinsic Software Redundancy: Applications and Challenges (Extended Abstract)

Mauro Pezzè

University of Lugano, Switzerland and University of Milano Bicocca, Italy
mauro.pezze@usi.ch

Abstract. Search-based software engineering has many important applications. Here, we identify a novel use of search-based techniques to identify redundant components. Modern software systems are intrinsically redundant, and such redundancy finds many applications. In this paper we introduce the concept of intrinsic redundancy, and we present some important applications to develop self-healing systems and automatically generate semantically relevant oracles. We then illustrate how search-based software engineering can be used to automatically identify redundant methods in software systems, thus paving the road to an efficient exploitation of intrinsic redundancy, and opening new research frontiers for search-based software engineering.

Reliability is becoming a necessity for many software systems and redundancy is its cornerstone. Well defined processes, efficient design approaches, careful coding and pervasive testing and analysis can build excellent software products, but cannot completely eliminate failures in the field, and the software products may not meet a sufficient reliability level.

The classic way of improving the reliability of systems of different kinds exploits some form of redundancy. RAID disks (Redundant Array of Independent Disks) are a successful example of the use of redundancy for improving hardware reliability [1], the HDFS (Hadoop Distributed File System) is a popular example of the use of redundancy for improving data reliability [2], N-version programming is a classic approach that exploits redundancy for improving software reliability [3].

In these different approaches, redundancy is *deliberately* added to the system to improve reliability, and comes with additional costs that depend on the goals. In hardware systems, redundancy aims to reduce the impact of production defects, and is added at the production level, thus impacts mostly on production costs. In database systems, redundancy is added at the server level and impacts mostly on infrastructure costs. N-version programming targets design errors and is added at the design level, where the impact on costs is relevant.

We point to a different kind of software redundancy that is *intrinsically* present in software systems, and is thus available without additional design or production costs. Our empirical investigation indicates that such form of redundancy is widely spread in modern software systems and is a consequence of good design practice. Our work shows that this form of redundancy can be automatically synthetized by means of search-based techniques [4], and can be successfully exploited in many ways, including the automatic generation of self-healing mechanisms [5] and of semantic oracles [6].

Redundancy is present at many abstraction levels, here we discuss it referring to redundancy at method call level. We say that two methods are redundant when their execution is both different and produces equivalent results. Results are equivalent when both the output and the final state are indistinguishable from an external observer viewpoint, as formalised with the concept of observational equivalence [7]. Executions are different when they involve different statements or the same statements but in different order.

Redundancy is intrinsically present in software systems due to modern design practice. Design for reusability often leads to the same functionality implemented in different methods to improve compatibility with different uses, as it happened in containers that provide different methods to add one or more elements to the container. Performance optimisation frequently results in different methods implementing the same functionality, albeit with different, optimised code, like the *trove4J* library that duplicates many of the functionalities offered by the standard Java containers. Backward compatibility is obtained by keeping the old versions of the reimplemented functionalities thus offering redundant methods. Redundancy is massively present in modern software systems: Our manual inspection of several popular libraries including Apache Ant, Google Guava, Joda Time, Eclipse SWT, graphstream and Lucene identified over 4,700 redundant methods, with an average of 5 redundant methods per class.

Intrinsic redundancy can be exploited to build self-healing mechanisms. Once identified a set of redundant methods, we can automatically deploy a mechanism that substitutes a failing method with a redundant one to avoid the failure. We call such approach *automatic workaround*. The design of automatic workarounds requires a mechanism to reveal failures, we rely on assertions embedded in the code, a method to roll back to a correct state, we rely on an optimised rollback mechanism, and a method to execute a redundant method, we rely on a source to source code transformation [8,5].

Another interesting application of intrinsic redundancy is the automatic synthesis of semantically relevant test oracles. The increasing availability of automated test cases exacerbates the need of automated oracles, and the cost pressure of software development calls for automatically generated oracles. Oracles that can be easily generated automatically, such as implicit oracles, can only reveal simple failures, like unhandled exceptions, while oracles derived from formal specifications can reveal failures that depend on the program semantics, but require formal specifications that are expensive to produce. We exploit the intrinsic redundancy of software systems to automatically generate test oracles that can reveal failures related to the program semantics by cloning the program state before executing a method call, executing the original call on the original state and the corresponding redundant call on the cloned state, and comparing the results. In this way we can reveal discrepancies between the executions of methods that should produce equivalent results and reveal failures related to the program semantics. We call such oracles *cross-checking oracles* [6].

The automatic synthesis of both self-healing mechanisms and automated oracles requires a set of redundant program elements as input. We can automatically synthetize redundant methods without expensive formal specifications by exploiting search-based techniques. We use a genetic algorithm for synthetizing a method call equivalent to a given method for an initial scenario (usually one or few test cases). We then look for a counterexample that, if found, gives us a new scenario to search for a redundant method, and, if not found, confirms the redundancy of the original and the identified method. We can automatically synthetize a large amount of redundant methods by applying the approach to all methods in the target software system.

Acknowledgement. We would like to acknowledge the Swiss National Foundation (SNF) for supporting this work through the projects Perseos (SNF 200021_116287), Wash (SNF 200020_124918) and Shade (SNF 200021_138006), and the many people who contributed to the work, Antonio Carzaniga, Alberto Goffi, Alessandra Gorla, Andrea Mattavelli, Nicolò Perino and Paolo Tonella.

References

1. Patterson, D., Gibson, G., Katz, R.: A case for redundant arrays of inexpensive disks (RAID). SIGMOD Record 17(3), 109–116 (1988)
2. Shvachko, K., Kuang, H., Radia, S., Chansler, R.: The hadoop distributed file system. In: Proceedings of the IEEE 26th Symposium on Mass Storage Systems and Technologies (MSST), pp. 1–10. IEEE Computer Society (2010)
3. Avizienis, A.: The N-version approach to fault-tolerant software. IEEE Transactions on Software Engineering 11(12), 1491–1501 (1985)
4. Goffi, A., Gorla, A., Mattavelli, A., Pezzè, M., Tonella, P.: Search-based synthesis of equivalent method sequences. In: Proceedings of the 2014 ACM Sigsoft Conference on the Foundations of Software Engineering (ACM FSE). ACM (2014)
5. Carzaniga, A., Gorla, A., Mattavelli, A., Perino, N., Pezzè, M.: Automatic recovery from runtime failures. In: Proceedings of the 2013 International Conference on Software Engineering (ICSE), pp. 782–791. IEEE Press (2013)
6. Carzaniga, A., Goffi, A., Gorla, A., Mattavelli, A., Pezzè, M.: Cross-checking oracles from intrinsic software redundancy. In: Proceedings of the 2014 International Conference on Software Engineering (ICSE). IEEE Press (2014)
7. Hennessy, M., Milner, R.: On observing nondeterminism and concurrency. In: de Bakker, J., van Leeuwen, J. (eds.) ICALP 1980. LNCS, vol. 85, pp. 299–309. Springer, Heidelberg (1980)
8. Carzaniga, A., Gorla, A., Perino, N., Pezzè, M.: Automatic workarounds for web applications. In: Proceedings of the 2010 ACM Sigsoft Conference on the Foundations of Software Engineering (ACM FSE), pp. 237–246. ACM (2010)

Programming by Ranking
(Extended Abstract)

Marc Schoenauer[1,2] and Michèle Sebag[2,1]

[1] TAO Project-team, INRIA Saclay - Île-de-France
[2] Laboratoire de Recherche en Informatique (UMR CNRS 8623)
Université Paris-Sud, 91128 Orsay Cedex, France
FirstName.LastName@inria.fr

As early as 1904, Spearman [19] proposed to use ranks rather than actual values to unveil correlations between data of unknown distribution. This was the beginning of rank statistics and non-parametric tests. Still, in practice non-parametric statistics are generally less accurate than their parametric counterparts (even though more widely applicable), and the latter are often used even though the underlying hypotheses (normally distributed data, size of sample) are not satisfied.

In the context of optimization and programming however, rank-based approaches might prove more beneficial that value-based approaches even in cases where both approaches apply. Three test cases related to Algorithm Engineering will be surveyed here, dealing with Black-Box Optimization (Section 1), Algorithm Selection using ideas from recommender systems (Section 2) and robot programming by weak experts (Section 3).

1 Rank-SVM Surrogate Models for CMA-ES

In the general framework of (black-box) continuous optimization, the human mind cannot always easily grasp quantified measures to assess the quality of a potential solution. In a famous example of interactive optimization [8], when the coffee maker asks some coffee experts how close the taste of a coffee is from a targeted coffee taste, there does not even exist a scale that could be used by all experts to put a number on taste proximity. However, every expert can assess whether a coffee is closer or farther than another one with respect to the target taste.

Quantifying differences might be a problem even when there is no human being in the loop. More generally, the optimization of a given real-valued function $\mathcal{F}$ is unchanged if $\mathcal{F}$ undergoes any monotonous transformation (from preconditioning to non-linear regularization), although this can have a huge impact on the efficiency of most optimization algorithms. Comparison-based algorithms de facto possess such invariance w.r.t. monotonous transformations. In the case of expensive optimization problems, the usual strategy is to learn an approximation a.k.a. surrogate model of $\mathcal{F}$ by numerical regression; this strategy however destroys the invariance property as the surrogate model depends on the *values* of $\mathcal{F}$. Ordinal regression, aka rank-based learning, instead defines a surrogate model which only preserves the ranks of the $\mathcal{F}$ values [10]. The use of such rank-based surrogates preserves the invariance property in comparison-based optimization [17]. Interestingly, the Covariance Matrix Adaptation Evolution Strategy [7] (CMA-ES, considered today the state-of-the-art method in Black-Box optimization) can be tightly integrated with rank-based learning, thus preserving all invariance properties of CMA-ES [14], while enforcing the control and adaptation of the learning hyper-parameters [15]. The resulting surrogate-augmented algorithm further improves the performance of the basic variants of CMA-ES on the BBOB (Black-Box Optimization Benchmarking [5]) platform.

2   Algorithm Selection as a Collaborative Filtering

In the domain of recommendation algorithms, similarly, movie rating can vary a lot from user to user, clearly raising a scaling issue in recommendation systems [4]. On the opposite, any user is able to rank the movies he has seen. The CofiRank method [21] uses the Maximal Margin Matrix Factorization to approximate rankings rather than ratings, bringing more robustness in the recommender system.

Similar issues arise in algorithm selection, a key issue to get peak performance from algorithm portfolios. It turns out that algorithm selection can be formalized as a collaborative filtering problem [20], by considering that a problem instance "prefers" the algorithms with better performance on this particular instance. Learning the *rating*, i.e. the actual performance of the algorithm on the problem instance raises significant difficulties, as the performance of an algorithm can vary by orders of magnitude depending on the problem instance. Learning how to rank algorithms depending on the problem instance can instead be achieved efficiently [16].

A main difficulty in algorithm selection is the handling of the so-called 'cold start' problem: how to choose an algorithm for a brand-new instance? Former algorithm selection methods relied on known features describing the problem instances – however with mixed results [12]. But the Matrix Factorization method amounts to identify latent features that are by construction well suited to the algorithm selection problem. Supervised learning of a mapping between known features and those latent features is the key to solving the cold-start problem, as demonstrated in [16] on three problem domains (the 2008 CSP and 2011 SAT competitions, and the BBOB platform).

3   Programming by Feedback

In the context of adapting software or hardware agents (e.g., a companion robot) to the precise requirements or preferences of their human users, the limitation comes from both the quantity and the quality of what can be asked to the user. Whereas you can ask experts to demonstrate the desired behavior to the robot, as in Inverse Reinforcement Learning approaches [1, 11], you can only ask limited amount of feedback to the average user. On the one hand, the feedback is uneasily provided through numbers; on the other hand, even a preference feedback (it is better, it is worse) can be noisy and inconsistent.

Preference-based reinforcement learning, hybridizing reinforcement learning and learning to rank, has been proposed to handle domains with no numerical rewards [6], allowing the user to compare and rank the agent behaviors [22, 2]. The key issues are to deliver a good performance with a limited number of comparison queries, and particularly to stand the comparison errors and the possible user inconsistencies. These issues have been addressed in [3], enabling the agent to model the user's competence; indeed the cooperation between two intelligent partners is better supported by each partner having a model of the other one (see e.g. [13]).

From the user point of view, the game is similar to the well-known children's game "Hot-and-Cold": she only has to tell the robot whether each new demonstrated behavior is better or worse than the previous one – and she can be inconsistent (or her goal can evolve). From the robot perspective, the idea is to gradually learn the user's utility function in the demonstration space, accounting for the user's estimated competence, and, based on the current utility function, to optimize in the solution space the behavior with respect to some maximal posterior utility, demonstrating the best one to the user. Experimental results on artificial RL benchmark problems favorably compare to the state of the art [22], and proof-of-principle results are obtained on a real NAO robot, though on elementary tasks: 5 (resp. 24) interactions with the user are required to solve problems involving 13 (resp. 20) states spaces.

4 Conclusion

There is emerging evidence that the art of programming could be revisited in the light of the current state of the art in Machine Learning and Optimization. While the notion of formal specifications has been at the core of software sciences for over three decades, the relevance of ML-based approaches has been demonstrated in the domain of pattern recognition since the early 90s.

Along this line, a new trend dubbed *Programming by Optimization* advocates algorithm portfolios endowed with a control layer such that *determining what works best in a given use context [could be] performed automatically, substituting human labor by computation* [9]. Similarly, it has been suggested that *the state of the art can be improved by configuring existing techniques better rather than inventing new learning paradigms* [18].

Going further, we propose the *Programming by Ranking* paradigm, extending the above *Programming by Feedback*; several proofs of principle thereof in different domains have been described, related to expensive optimization, algorithm selection and policy design. Ultimately, our claim is that learning-to-rank Machine Learning algorithms, based on minimal and possibly noisy specification/information/feedback from the user, have today reached the come-of-age and should be considered whenever optimization at large is at stake.

References

1. Abbeel, P.: Apprenticeship Learning and Reinforcement Learning with Application to Robotic Control. PhD thesis, Stanford University (2008)
2. Akrour, R., Schoenauer, M., Sebag, M.: April: Active preference learning-based reinforcement learning. In: Flach, P.A., De Bie, T., Cristianini, N. (eds.) ECML PKDD 2012, Part II. LNCS, vol. 7524, pp. 116–131. Springer, Heidelberg (2012)
3. Akrour, R., Schoenauer, M., Sebag, M., Souplet, J.-C.: Programming by feedback. In: ICML. volume to appear of ACM Int. Conf. Proc. Series (2014)
4. Bennett, J., Lanning, S.: The netflix prize. In: Proc. 13th Intl Conf. on Knowledge Discovery and Data Mining (KDD) Cup and Workshop (2007)
5. Finck, S., Hansen, N., Ros, R., Auger, A.: Real-parameter black-box optimization benchmarking 2010: Experimental setup. Technical Report 2009/21, Research Center PPE (2010)
6. Fürnkranz, J., Hüllermeier, E., Cheng, W., Park, S.-H.: Preference-based reinforcement learning. Machine Learning 89(1-2), 123–156 (2012)
7. Hansen, N., Müller, S., Koumoutsakos, P.: Reducing the time complexity of the derandomized evolution strategy with covariance matrix adaptation (CMA-ES). Evolutionary Computation 11(1), 1–18 (2003)
8. Herdy, M.: Evolution strategies with subjective selection. In: Ebeling, W., Rechenberg, I., Voigt, H.-M., Schwefel, H.-P. (eds.) PPSN IV. LNCS, vol. 1141, pp. 22–31. Springer, Heidelberg (1996)
9. Hoos, H.H.: Programming by optimization. Commun. ACM 55(2), 70–80 (2012)
10. Joachims, T.: A support vector method for multivariate performance measures. In: Proceedings of the 22nd International Conference on Machine Learning, pp. 377–384. ACM (2005)
11. Konidaris, G., Kuindersma, S., Barto, A., Grupen, R.: Constructing skill trees for reinforcement learning agents from demonstration trajectories. In: NIPS 23, pp. 1162–1170 (2010)
12. Kotthoff, L.: Hybrid regression-classification models for algorithm selection. In: De Raedt, L., et al. (eds.) Proc. ECAI 2012, pp. 480–485. IOS Press (2012)
13. Lőrincz, A., Gyenes, V., Kiszlinger, M., Szita, I.: Mind model seems necessary for the emergence of communication. Neural Information Processing - Letters and Reviews 11(4-6), 109–121 (2007)
14. Loshchilov, I., Schoenauer, M., Sebag, M.: Comparison-Based Optimizers Need Comparison-Based Surrogates. In: Schaefer, R., Cotta, C., Kołodziej, J., Rudolph, G. (eds.) PPSN XI. LNCS, vol. 6238, pp. 364–373. Springer, Heidelberg (2010)
15. Loshchilov, I., Schoenauer, M., Sebag, M.: Self-Adaptive Surrogate-Assisted cma-es. In: ACM-GECCO, pp. 321–328. ACM Press (July 2012)
16. Misir, M., Sebag, M.: Algorithm selection as a collaborative filtering problem. Technical report, INRIA (December 2013)
17. Runarsson, T.P.: Ordinal Regression in Evolutionary Computation. In: Runarsson, T.P., Beyer, H.-G., Burke, E., Merelo-Guervós, J.J., Whitley, L.D., Yao, X. (eds.) PPSN IX. LNCS, vol. 4193, pp. 1048–1057. Springer, Heidelberg (2006)
18. Snoek, J., Larochelle, H., Adams, R.P.: Practical Bayesian optimization of machine learning algorithms. In: NIPS, pp. 2960–2968 (2012)

19. Spearman, C.: The proof and measurement of association between two things. The American Journal of Psychology 100(3-4), 441–471 (1904)
20. Stern, D., Herbrich, R., Graepel, T., Samulowitz, H., Pulina, L., Tacchella, A.: Collaborative expert portfolio management. In: AAAI, pp. 179–184 (2010)
21. Weimer, M., Karatzoglou, A., Le, Q., Smola, A.: COFI-RANK: Maximum Margin Matrix Factorization for Collaborative Ranking. In: NIPS 2007, pp. 222–230 (2007)
22. Wilson, A., Fern, A., Tadepalli, P.: A Bayesian approach for policy learning from trajectory preference queries. In: NIPS, pp. 1142–1150 (2012)

Invited Talk

SBSE: Introduction, Motivation, Results and Directions

Mark Harman

University College London, CREST Centre, UK

Abstract. This talk at SSBSE 2014 will provide an introduction to SBSE [4, 6, 14, 18], drawing on results from recent work and the many surveys of SBSE for requirements [30], predictive modelling [1, 8] software project management [5], cloud engineering [15], design [27], maintenance [25], testing [2, 22], refactoring [7, 23] and repair [20]. The talk will be partly interactive, discussing the motivation for computational search in software engineering. We will also explore why it is that, among all engineering disciplines, it is software engineering for which computational search finds its most compelling and promising application [9]. This theme will be developed by considering recent work that optimises the engineering material at the heart of all software systems: the source code itself. We will focus, in particular, on recent developments in Dynamic Adaptive SBSE [10, 11, 13] and genetic improvement for repair [21, 20], non-functional enhancement [3, 16, 19, 24, 28, 29], source code transplantation [17, 26] and Software Product Line optimisation [12].

References

1. Abbeel, P.: Apprenticeship Learning and Reinforcement Learning with Application to Robotic Control. PhD thesis, Stanford University (2008)
2. Afzal, W., Torkar, R., Feldt, R.: A systematic review of search-based testing for non-functional system properties. Information and Software Technology 51(6), 957–976 (2009)
3. Arcuri, A., White, D.R., Clark, J.A., Yao, X.: Multi-objective improvement of software using co-evolution and smart seeding. In: 7th SEAL, pp. 61–70 (2008)
4. Colanzi, T.E., Vergilio, S.R., Assuncao, W.K.G., Pozo, A.: Search based software engineering: Review and analysis of the field in Brazil. Journal of Systems and Software 86(4), 970–984 (2013)
5. Ferrucci, F., Harman, M., Sarro, F.: Search based software project management. In: Software Project Management in a Changing World. Springer (to appear, 2014)
6. de Freitas, F.G., de Souza, J.T.: Ten years of search based software engineering: A bibliometric analysis. In: Cohen, M.B., Ó Cinnéide, M. (eds.) SSBSE 2011. LNCS, vol. 6956, pp. 18–32. Springer, Heidelberg (2011)
7. Ghannem, A., El Boussaidi, G., Kessentini, M.: Model refactoring using interactive genetic algorithm. In: Ruhe, G., Zhang, Y. (eds.) SSBSE 2013. LNCS, vol. 8084, pp. 96–110. Springer, Heidelberg (2013)
8. Harman, M.: How SBSE can support construction and analysis of predictive models (keynote paper). In: 6th PROMISE (2010)
9. Harman, M.: Search based software engineering (keynote paper). In: 13th FASE (2010)

10. Harman, M., Burke, E., Clark, J.A., Yao, X.: Dynamic adaptive search based software engineering (keynote paper). In: 6th ESEM, pp. 1–8 (2012)

11. Harman, M., Clark, J.: Dynamic adaptive search based software engineering needs fast approximate metrics (keynote paper). In: 4th WeTSOM (2013)

12. Harman, M., Jia, Y., Krinke, J., Langdon, B., Petke, J., Zhang, Y.: Search based software engineering for software product line engineering: A survey and directions for future work (keynote paper). In: 15th SPLC (2014)

13. Harman, M., Jia, Y., Langdon, W.B., Petke, J., Moghadam, I.H., Yoo, S., Wu, F.: Genetic improvement for adaptive software engineering (keynote paper). In: 9th SEAMS, pp. 1–4 (2014)

14. Harman, M., Jones, B.F.: Search based software engineering. Information and Software Technology 43(14), 833–839 (2001)

15. Harman, M., Lakhotia, K., Singer, J., White, D., Yoo, S.: Cloud engineering is search based software engineering too. Journal of Systems and Software 86(9), 2225–2241 (2013)

16. Harman, M., Langdon, W.B., Jia, Y., White, D.R., Arcuri, A., Clark, J.A.: The GISMOE challenge: Constructing the pareto program surface using genetic programming to find better programs (keynote paper). In: 27th ASE, pp. 1–14 (2012)

17. Harman, M., Langdon, W.B., Weimer, W.: Genetic programming for reverse engineering (keynote paper). In: 20th WCRE (2013)

18. Harman, M., Mansouri, A., Zhang, Y.: Search based software engineering: Trends, techniques and applications. ACM Computing Surveys 45(1), 11:1–11:61 (2012)

19. Langdon, W.B., Harman, M.: Optimising existing software with genetic programming. IEEE Transactions on Evolutionary Computation (to appear, 2014)

20. Le Goues, C., Forrest, S., Weimer, W.: Current challenges in automatic software repair. Software Quality Journal 21(3), 421–443 (2013)

21. Le Goues, C., Nguyen, T., Forrest, S., Weimer, W.: GenProg: A generic method for automatic software repair. IEEE Transactions on Software Engineering 38(1), 54–72 (2012)

22. McMinn, P.: Search-based software testing: Past, present and future (keynote paper). In: SBST, pp. 153–163 (2011)

23. Cinnéde, Ó., Tratt, M., Harman, L., Counsell, M., Moghadam, S.,, I.H.: Experimental assessment of software metrics using automated refactoring. In: 6th ESEM, pp. 49–58 (2012)

24. Orlov, M., Sipper, M.: Flight of the FINCH through the java wilderness. IEEE Transactions Evolutionary Computation 15(2), 166–182 (2011)

25. Di Penta, M.: SBSE meets software maintenance: Achievements and open problems. In: Fraser, G., Teixeira de Souza, J. (eds.) SSBSE 2012. LNCS, vol. 7515, pp. 27–28. Springer, Heidelberg (2012)

26. Petke, J., Cohen, M.B., Harman, M., Yoo, S.: Efficiency and early fault detection with lower and higher strength combinatorial interaction testing. In: ESEC/FSE, pp. 26–36 (2013)

27. Räihä, O.: A survey on search–based software design. Computer Science Review 4(4), 203–249 (2010)

28. Swan, J., Epitropakis, M.G., Woodward, J.R.: Gen-o-fix: An embeddable framework for dynamic adaptive genetic improvement programming. Tech. Rep. CSM-195, Computing Science and Mathematics, University of Stirling (2014)

29. White, D.R., Arcuri, A., Clark, J.A.: Evolutionary improvement of programs. IEEE Transactions on Evolutionary Computation 15(4), 515–538 (2011)

30. Zhang, Y.-Y., Finkelstein, A., Harman, M.: Search based requirements optimisation: Existing work and challenges. In: Paech, B., Rolland, C. (eds.) REFSQ 2008. LNCS, vol. 5025, pp. 88–94. Springer, Heidelberg (2008)

Table of Contents

Full Research Papers

Short Papers

Graduate Student Track Papers

SBSE Challenge Track Papers

On the Effectiveness
of Whole Test Suite Generation

Andrea Arcuri[1] and Gordon Fraser[2]

[1] Simula Research Laboratory, P.O. Box 134, 1325 Lysaker, Norway
arcuri@simula.no,
[2] University of Sheffield, Dep. of Computer Science, Sheffield, UK
gordon.fraser@sheffield.ac.uk

Abstract. A common application of search-based software testing is to generate test cases for all goals defined by a coverage criterion (e.g., statements, branches, mutants). Rather than generating one test case at a time for each of these goals individually, *whole test suite generation* optimizes entire test suites towards satisfying all goals at the same time. There is evidence that the overall coverage achieved with this approach is superior to that of targeting individual coverage goals. Nevertheless, there remains some uncertainty on whether the whole test suite approach might be inferior to a more focused search in the case of particularly difficult coverage goals. In this paper, we perform an in-depth analysis to study if this is the case. An empirical study on 100 Java classes reveals that indeed there are some testing goals that are easier to cover with the traditional approach. However, their number is not only very small in comparison with those which are only covered by the whole test suite approach, but also those coverage goals appear in small classes for which both approaches already obtain high coverage.

Keywords: automated test generation, unit testing, search-based testing, EvoSuite.

1 Introduction

Search-based software engineering has been applied to numerous different tasks in software development [15], and software testing is one of the most successful of these [1, 19]. One particular task in software testing for which search-based techniques are well suited is the task of automated generation of unit tests. For example, there are search-based tools like AUSTIN for C programs [18] or EvoSuite for Java programs [8].

In search-based software testing, the testing problem is cast as a search problem. For example, a common scenario is to generate a set of test cases such that their code coverage is maximized. A code coverage criterion describes a set of typically structural aspects of the system under test (SUT) which should be exercised by a test suite, for example all statements or branches. Here, the search space would consist of all possible data inputs for the SUT. A search algorithm

C. Le Goues and S. Yoo (Eds.): SSBSE 2014, LNCS 8636, pp. 1–15, 2014.

(e.g., a genetic algorithm) is then used to explore this search space to find the input data that maximize the given objective (e.g., cover as many branches as possible).

Traditionally, to achieve this goal a search is carried out on each individual coverage goal [19] (e.g., a branch). To guide the search, the fitness function exploits information like the approach level [24] and branch distance [17]. It may happen that during the search for a coverage goal there are others goals that can be "accidentally" covered, and by keeping such test data one does not need to perform search for those accidentally covered goals. However, there are several potential issues with such an approach:

- *Search budget distribution:* If a coverage goal is infeasible, then all search effort to try to cover it would be wasted (except for any other coverage goals accidentally covered during the search). Unfortunately, determining whether a goal is feasible or not is an undecidable problem. If a coverage goal is trivial, then it will typically be covered by the first random input. Given a set of coverage goals and an overall available budget of computational resources (e.g., time), how to assign a search budget to the individual goals to maximise the overall coverage?
- *Coverage goal ordering:* Unless some smart strategies are designed, the search for each coverage goal is typically independent, and potentially useful information is not shared between individual searches. For example, to cover a nested branch one first needs to cover its parent branch, and test data for this latter could be use to help the search for the nested branch (instead of starting from scratch). In this regard, the order in which coverage goals are sought can have a large impact on final performance.

To overcome these issues, in previous work we introduced the *whole test suite approach* [11, 12]. Instead of searching for a test for each individual coverage goal in sequence, the search problem is changed to a search for a set of tests that covers all coverage goals at the same time; accordingly, the fitness function guides to cover all goals. The advantage of such an approach is that both the questions of how to distribute the available search budget between the individual coverage goals, and in which order to target those goals, disappear. With the whole test suite approach, large improvements have been reported for both branch coverage [11] and mutation testing [12].

Despite this evidence of higher overall coverage, there remains the question of how the use of whole test suite generation influences individual coverage goals. Even if the whole test suite approach covers more goals, those are not necessarily going to be a superset of those that the traditional approach would cover. Is the higher coverage due to more *easy* goals being covered? Is the coverage of *difficult* goals adversely affected? Although higher coverage might lead to better regression test suites, for testing purposes the difficult coverage goals might be more "valuable" than the others. So, from a practical point of view, preferring the whole test suite approach over the traditional one may not necessarily be better for practitioners in industry.

In this paper, we aim to empirically study in detail how the whole test suite approach compares to the traditional one. In particular, we aim at studying whether there are specific coverage goals for which the traditional approach is better and, if that is the case, we want to characterise those scenarios. Based on an empirical study performed on 100 Java classes, our study shows that indeed there are cases in which the traditional approach provides better results. However, those cases are very rare (nearly one hundred times less) compared to the cases in which only the whole test suite approach is able to cover the goals. Furthermore, those cases happen for small classes for which average branch coverage is relatively high.

This paper is organised as follows. Section 2 provides background information, whereas the whole test suite approach is discussed in details in Section 3. The performed empirical study is presented in Section 4. A discussion on the threats to the validity of the study follows in Section 5. Finally, Section 6 concludes the paper.

2   Background

Search-based techniques have been successfully used for test data generation (see [1, 19] for surveys on this topic). The application of search for test data generation can be traced back to the 70s [20], and later the key concepts of *branch distance* [17] and *approach level* [24] were introduced to help search techniques in generating the right test data.

More recently, search-based techniques have also been applied to test object-oriented software (e.g., [13, 21–23]). One specific issue that arises in this context is that test cases are sequences of calls, and their length needs to be controlled by the search. Since the early work of Tonella [22], researchers have tried to deal with this problem, for example by penalizing the length directly in the fitness function. However, longer test sequences can lead to achieve higher code coverage [2], yet properly handling their growth/reduction during the search requires special care [10].

Most approaches described in the literature aim at generating test suites that achieve as high as possible branch coverage. In principle, any other coverage criterion is amenable to automated test generation. For example, mutation testing [16] is often considered a worthwhile test goal, and has been used in a search-based test generation environment [13].

When test cases are sought for individual goals in such coverage based approaches, it is important to keep track of the accidental collateral coverage of the remaining goals. Otherwise, it has been proven that random testing would fare better under some scalability models [5]. Recently, Harman et al. [14] proposed a search-based multi-objective approach in which, although each coverage goal is still targeted individually, there is the secondary objective of maximizing the number of collateral goals that are accidentally covered. However, no particular heuristic is used to help covering these other coverage goals.

All approaches mentioned so far target a single test goal at a time – this is the predominant method. There are some notable exceptions in search-based software testing. The works of Arcuri and Yao [6] and Baresi et al. [7] use a single sequence of function calls to maximize the number of covered branches while minimizing the length of such a test case. A drawback of such an approach is that there can be conflicting testing goals, and it might be impossible to cover all of them with a single test sequence regardless of its length.

To overcome those issues, in previous work we proposed the whole test suite approach [11,12]. In this approach, instead of evolving individual tests, whole test suites are evolved, with a fitness function that considers all the coverage goals at the same time. Promising results were obtained for both branch coverage [11] and mutation testing [12].

3   Whole Test Suite Generation

To make this paper self-contained, in this section we provide a summarised description of the traditional approach used in search-based software testing and the whole test suite approach. For more details on the traditional approach, the reader can for example refer to [19, 24]. For the whole test suite approach, the reader can refer to [11, 12].

Given a SUT, assume X to be the set of coverage goals we want to automatically cover with a set of test cases (i.e., a test suite) T. Coverage goals could be for example branches if we are aiming at branch coverage, or any other element depending on the chosen coverage criterion (e.g., mutants in mutation testing).

3.1   Generating Tests for Individual Coverage Goals

Given $|X| = n$ coverage goals, traditionally there would be one search for each of them. To give more gradient to the search (instead of just counting "yes/no" on whether a goal is covered), usually the approach level $\mathcal{A}(t,x)$ and branch distance $d(t,x)$ are employed for the fitness function [19, 24]. The approach level $\mathcal{A}(t,x)$ for a given test t on a coverage goal $x \in X$ is used to guide the search toward such target branch. It is determined as the minimal number of control dependent edges in the control dependency graph between the target branch and the control flow represented by the test case. The branch distance $d(t,x)$ is used to heuristically quantify how far a predicate in a branch x is from being evaluated as true. In this context, the considered predicate x_c is taken for the closest control dependent branch where the control flow diverges from the target branch. Finally, the resulting fitness function to minimize for a coverage goal x will be:

$$f(t,x) = \mathcal{A}(t,x) + \nu(d(t,x_c)) \ ,$$

where ν is any normalizing function in [0,1] (see [3]). For example, consider this trivial function:

```
public static void foo(int z){
    if(z > 0)
        if(z > 100)
            if(z > 200)
                ; //target
}
```

With a test case t_{50} having the value $z = 50$, the execution would diverge at the second if-condition, and so the resulting fitness function for the target $x_{z>200}$ would be

$$f(t_{50}, x_{z>200}) = 1 + \nu(|50 - 100| + 1) = 1 + \nu(51) ,$$

which would be higher (i.e., worse) than a test case having $z = 101$:

$$f(t_{101}, x_{z>200}) = 0 + \nu(|101 - 200| + 1) = 0 + \nu(100) .$$

While implementing this traditional approach, we tried to derive a faithful representation of current practice, which means that there are some optimizations proposed in the literature which we did not include:

- New test cases are only generated for branches that have not already been covered through collateral coverage of previously created test cases. However, we do not evaluate the collateral coverage of all individuals during the search, as this would add a significant overhead, and it is not clear what effects this would have given the fixed timeout we used in our experiments.
- When applying the one goal at a time approach, a possible improvement could be to use a *seeding* strategy [24]. During the search, we could store the test data that have good fitness values on coverage goals that are not covered yet. These test data can then be used as starting point (i.e., for seeding the first generation of a genetic algorithm) in the successive searches for those uncovered goals. However, we decided not to implement this, as reference [24] does not provide sufficient details to reimplement the technique, and there is no conclusive data regarding several open questions; for example, potentially a seeding strategy could reduce diversity in the population, and so in some cases it might in fact reduce the overall performance of the search algorithm.
- The order in which coverage goals are selected might also influence the result. As in the literature usually no order is specified (e.g., [14, 22]), we selected the branches in random order. However, in the context of procedural code approaches to prioritize coverage goals have been proposed, e.g., based on dynamic information [24]. However, the goal of this paper is neither to study the impact of different orders, nor to adapt these prioritization techniques to object-oriented code.
- In practice, when applying a single goal strategy, one might also bootstrap an initial random test suite to identify the trivial test goals, and then use a more sophisticated technique to address the difficult goals; here, a difficult, unanswered question is when to stop the random phase and start the search.

3.2   Whole Test Suite Generation

For the whole test suite approach, we used exactly the same implementation as in [11, 12]. In the *Whole* approach, the approach level $\mathcal{A}(t,x)$ is not needed in the fitness function, as all branches are considered at the same time. In particular, the resulting fitness function to minimize for a set of test cases T on a set of branches X is:

$$w(T,X) = \sum_{x \in X} d(T,x) \; ,$$

where $d(T,x)$ is defined as:

$$d(T,x) = \begin{cases} 0 & \text{if the branch has been covered,} \\ \nu(d_{min}(t \in T,x)) & \text{if the predicate has been} \\ & \text{executed at least twice,} \\ 1 & \text{otherwise.} \end{cases}$$

Note that these X coverage goals could be considered as different objectives. Instead of linearly combining them in a single fitness score, a multi-objective algorithm could be used. However, a typical class can have hundreds if not thousands of objectives (e.g., branches), making a multi-objective algorithm not ideal due to scalability problems.

4   Empirical Study

In this paper, we carried out an empirical study to compare the whole test suite approach (*Whole*) with the traditional one branch at a time approach (*OneBranch*). In particular, we aim at answering the following research questions:

RQ1: Are there coverage goals in which *OneBranch* performs better?

RQ2: How many coverage goals found by *Whole* get missed by *OneBranch*?

RQ3: Which factors influence the relative performance between *Whole* and *OneBranch*?

4.1   Experimental Setup

In this paper, for the case study we randomly chose 100 Java classes from the SF100 corpus [9], which is a collection of 100 projects randomly selected from the SourceForge open source software repository. We randomly selected from SF100 to avoid possible bias in the selection procedure, and to have higher confidence to generalize our results to other Java classes as well. In total, the selected 100 classes contain 2,383 branches, which we consider as test goals.

The SF100 currently contains more than 11,000 Java classes. We only used 100 classes instead of the entire SF100 corpus due to the type of experiments we carried out. In particular, on the selected case study, for each class we ran EVOSUITE in two modes: one using the traditional one branch at a time approach (*OneBranch*), and the other using the whole test suite approach (*Whole*). To take randomness into account, each experiments was repeated 1,000 times, for a total of $100 \times 2 \times 1,000 = 200,000$ runs of EvoSuite.

When choosing how many classes to use in a case study, there is always a tradeoff between the number of classes and the number of repeated experiments. On one hand, a higher number of classes helps to generalize the results. On the other hand, a higher number of repetitions helps to better study in detail the differences on specific classes. For example, given the same budget to run the experiments, we could have used 10,000 classes and 10 repetitions. However, as we want to study the "corner cases" (i.e., when one technique completely fails while the other compared one does produce results), we gave more emphasis on the number of repetitions to reduce the random noise in the final results.

Each experiment was run for up to three minutes (the search on a class was also stopped once 100% coverage was achieved). Therefore, in total the entire case study took up to $600,000/(24 \times 60) = 416$ days of computational resources, which required a large cluster to run. When running the *OneBranch* approach, the search budget (i.e., the three minutes) is equally distributed among the coverage goals in the SUT. When the search for a coverage goal finishs earlier (or a goal is accidentally covered by a previous search), the remaining budget is redistributed among the other goals still to cover.

To properly analyse the randomized algorithms used in this paper, we followed the guidelines in [4]. In particular, when branch coverage values were compared, statistical differences were measured with the Wilcoxon-Mann-Whitney U-test, where the effect size was measured with the Vargha-Delany $\hat{A}_{12}$. A $\hat{A}_{12} = 0.5$ means no difference between the two compared algorithms.

When checking how often a goal was covered, because it is a binary variable, we used the Fisher exact test. As effect size, we used the odds ratios, with a $\delta = 1$ correction to handle the zero occurrences. When there is no difference between two algorithms, then the odds ratio is equal to one. Note, in some of the graphs we rather show the natural logarithm of the odds ratios, and this is done only to simplify their representation.

4.2 Results

Table 1 shows the average coverage obtained for each of the 100 Java classes. The results in Table 1 confirm our previous results in [11]: the whole test suite approach leads to higher code coverage. In this case, the average branch coverage increases from 67% to 76%, with a 0.62 effect size. However, there are two classes in which the *Whole* approach leads to significantly worse results: RecordingEvent and BlockThread. Two cases out of 100 could be due to the randomness of the algorithm, although having 1,000 repetitions does reduce the probability of this. However, in both cases the *Whole* approach does achieve relatively high coverage (i.e, 84% and 90%).

Looking at RecordingEvent in detail, we see that there are some branches that are never covered by the *Whole* approach, but sometimes by *OneBranch* (see Figure 1). Specifically, there is a disjunction of two conditions on two static variables ourJVMLocalObjectFlavor and ourFlavors. As EvoSuite works at

Table 1. For each class, the table reports the average branch coverage obtained by the *OneBranch* approach and by the *Whole* approach. Effect sizes and p-values of the comparisons are in bold when the p-values are lower than 0.05.

Class	OneB.	Whole	$\hat{A}_{12}$	p-value
MapCell	1.00	1.00	0.50	-
br.com.jnfe.base.CST_COFINS	0.99	1.00	**0.53**	**< 0.001**
ch.bfh.egov.nutzenportfolio.service.kategorie.KategorieDaoService	0.00	0.01	**0.97**	**< 0.001**
com.browsersoft.aacs.User	0.51	0.87	**1.00**	**< 0.001**
com.browsersoft.openhre.hl7.impl.config.HL7SegmentMapImpl	0.04	0.99	**0.99**	**< 0.001**
com.gbshape.dbe.sql.Select	0.06	0.08	**0.57**	**< 0.001**
com.lts.caloriecount.ui.budget.BudgetWin	0.11	0.12	**0.64**	**< 0.001**
com.lts.io.ArchiveScanner	0.07	0.45	**0.99**	**< 0.001**
com.lts.pest.tree.ApplicationTree	0.00	0.00	0.50	-
com.lts.swing.table.dragndrop.test.RecordingEvent	0.95	0.84	**0.03**	**< 0.001**
com.lts.swing.thread.BlockThread	0.98	0.90	**0.27**	**< 0.001**
com.werken.saxpath.XPathLexer	0.51	0.73	**1.00**	**< 0.001**
corina.formats.TRML	0.03	0.21	**0.99**	**< 0.001**
corina.map.SiteListPanel	0.00	0.00	0.50	-
de.huxhorn.lilith.data.eventsource.EventIdentifier	0.99	1.00	**0.51**	**< 0.001**
de.huxhorn.lilith.debug.LogDateRunnable	0.60	0.60	0.50	-
de.huxhorn.lilith.engine.impl.eventproducer.SerializingMessageBasedEventProducer	0.99	1.00	0.50	0.316
de.outstare.fortbattleplayer.gui.battlefield.BattlefieldCell	0.17	0.21	**0.64**	**< 0.001**
de.outstare.fortbattleplayer.statistics.CriticalHit	1.00	1.00	0.50	-
de.paragon.explorer.util.LoggerFactory	1.00	1.00	0.50	-
de.progra.charting.render.InterpolationChartRenderer	0.12	0.55	**0.96**	**< 0.001**
edu.uiuc.ndiipp.hubandspoke.workflow.PackageDissemination	0.02	0.09	**0.99**	**< 0.001**
falselight	1.00	1.00	0.50	-
fi.vtt.noen.mfw.bundle.common.DataType	1.00	1.00	0.50	-
fi.vtt.noen.mfw.bundle.probe.plugins.measurement.WatchDog	0.03	0.31	**0.86**	**< 0.001**
fi.vtt.noen.mfw.bundle.probe.shared.MeasurementReport	0.09	1.00	**0.99**	**< 0.001**
fi.vtt.noen.mfw.bundle.server.plugins.webui.sacservice.OperationResult	1.00	1.00	0.50	-
fps370.MouseMoveBehavior	0.19	0.55	**0.98**	**< 0.001**
geo.google.mapping.AddressToUsAddressFunctor	0.04	0.52	**0.98**	**< 0.001**
httpanalyzer.ScreenInputFilter	0.73	0.83	**0.64**	**< 0.001**
jigl.gui.SignalCanvas	0.85	0.95	**0.89**	**< 0.001**
jigl.image.io.ImageOutputStreamJAI	0.21	0.54	**0.94**	**< 0.001**
jigl.image.utils.LocalDifferentialGeometry	0.04	0.43	**0.99**	**< 0.001**
lotus.core.phases.Phase	0.50	0.50	0.50	-
macaw.presentationLayer.CategoryStateEditor	0.00	0.00	0.50	-
messages.round.RoundTimeOverMsg	0.99	1.00	**0.50**	**0.007**
module.ModuleBrowserDialog	0.00	0.00	0.50	-
net.sf.xbus.base.bytearraylist.ByteArrayConverterAS400	0.00	0.00	0.50	-
net.sourceforge.beanbin.command.RemoveEntity	1.00	1.00	0.50	-
net.virtualinfinity.atrobots.robot.RobotScoreKeeper	1.00	1.00	0.50	-
nu.staldal.lagoon.util.Wildcard	0.99	1.00	**0.50**	**< 0.001**
oasis.names.tc.ciq.xsdschema.xal._2.PremiseNumberSuffix	1.00	1.00	0.50	-
org.apache.lucene.search.exposed.facet.FacetMapSinglePackedFactory	0.00	0.18	**0.99**	**< 0.001**
org.databene.jdbacl.dialect.H2Util	1.00	0.99	**0.49**	**< 0.001**
org.databene.jdbacl.identity.mem.AbstractTableMapper	0.20	0.71	**0.99**	**< 0.001**
org.dom4j.io.STAXEventReader	0.14	0.28	**0.99**	**< 0.001**
org.dom4j.tree.CloneHelper	1.00	1.00	0.50	-
org.dom4j.util.PerThreadSingleton	0.85	0.85	0.49	0.165
org.exolab.jms.config.GarbageCollectionConfigurationLowWaterThresholdType	1.00	1.00	0.50	-
org.exolab.jms.config.SecurityConfigurationDescriptor	0.62	0.62	**0.47**	**< 0.001**
org.exolab.jms.selector.And	0.87	0.99	**0.77**	**< 0.001**
org.exolab.jms.selector.BetweenExpression	0.33	0.75	**0.94**	**< 0.001**
org.fixsuite.message.view.ListView	0.10	0.10	0.50	0.312
org.jcvi.jillion.assembly.consed.phd.PhdFileDataStoreBuilder	0.43	0.83	**0.99**	**< 0.001**
org.jcvi.jillion.fasta.FastaRecordDataStoreAdapter	0.00	0.00	0.50	-
org.jsecurity.authc.credential.Md2CredentialsMatcher	1.00	1.00	0.50	-
org.jsecurity.io.IniResource	0.40	0.82	**0.99**	**< 0.001**
org.jsecurity.io.ResourceUtils	0.32	0.79	**0.99**	**< 0.001**
org.jsecurity.web.DefaultWebSecurityManager	0.07	0.37	**0.99**	**< 0.001**
org.quickserver.net.qsadmin.gui.SimpleCommandSet	0.83	0.83	0.50	-
org.quickserver.net.server.AuthStatus	0.33	0.33	0.50	-
org.sourceforge.ifx.framework.complextype.ChkAcceptAddRs_Type	1.00	1.00	0.50	-
org.sourceforge.ifx.framework.complextype.ChkInfo_Type	1.00	1.00	0.50	-
org.sourceforge.ifx.framework.complextype.ChkOrdInqRs_Type	0.99	1.00	0.50	0.080
org.sourceforge.ifx.framework.complextype.CreditAdviseRs_Type	0.99	1.00	0.50	0.315
org.sourceforge.ifx.framework.complextype.DepAcctStmtInqRq_Type	1.00	1.00	0.50	-
org.sourceforge.ifx.framework.complextype.EMVCardAdviseRs_Type	1.00	1.00	0.50	-
org.sourceforge.ifx.framework.complextype.ForExDealMsgRec_Type	1.00	1.00	0.50	-
org.sourceforge.ifx.framework.complextype.PassbkItemInqRs_Type	0.99	1.00	0.50	0.312
org.sourceforge.ifx.framework.complextype.RecPmtCanRq_Type	1.00	1.00	0.50	-
org.sourceforge.ifx.framework.complextype.StdPayeeId_Type	1.00	1.00	0.50	-
org.sourceforge.ifx.framework.complextype.SvcAcctStatus_Type	1.00	1.00	0.50	-
org.sourceforge.ifx.framework.complextype.TINInfo_Type	1.00	1.00	0.50	-
org.sourceforge.ifx.framework.element.AllocateAllowed	1.00	1.00	0.50	-
org.sourceforge.ifx.framework.element.BillInqRs	1.00	1.00	0.50	-
org.sourceforge.ifx.framework.element.ChksumModRq	1.00	1.00	0.50	-
org.sourceforge.ifx.framework.element.ChksumStatusCode	1.00	1.00	0.50	-
org.sourceforge.ifx.framework.element.CompositeCurAmtId	1.00	1.00	0.50	-
org.sourceforge.ifx.framework.element.CurAmt	1.00	1.00	0.50	-
org.sourceforge.ifx.framework.element.CustAddRs	1.00	1.00	0.50	-
org.sourceforge.ifx.framework.element.CustId	1.00	1.00	0.50	-
org.sourceforge.ifx.framework.element.CustPayeeRec	1.00	1.00	0.50	-
org.sourceforge.ifx.framework.element.DepBkOrdAddRs	1.00	1.00	0.50	-
org.sourceforge.ifx.framework.element.DevCimTransport	1.00	1.00	0.50	-
org.sourceforge.ifx.framework.element.FSPayee	1.00	1.00	0.50	-
org.sourceforge.ifx.framework.element.Gender	1.00	1.00	0.50	-
org.sourceforge.ifx.framework.element.Language	1.00	1.00	0.50	-
org.sourceforge.ifx.framework.element.StdPayeeRevRs	1.00	1.00	0.50	-
org.sourceforge.ifx.framework.element.TerminalSPObjAdviseRq	1.00	1.00	0.50	-
org.sourceforge.ifx.framework.element.URL	1.00	1.00	0.50	-
org.sourceforge.ifx.framework.pain001.simpletype.BatchBookingIndicator	1.00	1.00	0.50	-
org.sourceforge.ifx.framework.pain001.simpletype.CashClearingSystem2Code	1.00	1.00	0.50	-
org.sourceforge.ifx.framework.pain004.simpletype.CashClearingSystem2Code	1.00	1.00	0.50	-
org.sourceforge.ifx.framework.simpletype.DevName_Type	1.00	1.00	0.50	-
teder.Teder	1.00	1.00	0.50	-
umd.cs.shop.JSListSubstitution	0.97	0.99	**0.53**	**< 0.001**
wheel.components.Block	0.04	0.16	**0.56**	**< 0.001**
wheel.json.JSONStringer	0.99	1.00	**0.50**	**< 0.001**
Average	0.67	0.76	0.62	

```
class RecordingEvent {
  static protected DataFlavor ourJVMLocalObjectFlavor;
  static protected DataFlavor[] ourFlavors;

  static protected void initializeConstants() {
    if (null != ourJVMLocalObjectFlavor || null !=
        ourFlavors)
      return;

    ourJVMLocalObjectFlavor = ...
    ourFlavors = new DataFlavor[] {
        ourJVMLocalObjectFlavor };
    // ...
  }
  // ...
}
```

Fig. 1. Static behavior in `RecordingEvent`: If the test independence assumption is not satisfied, then results become unpredictable

the level of bytecode, this disjunction results in four branches – two for each of the conditions. The *Whole* approach only succeeds in covering one out of these four branches, i.e., when `outJVMLocalObjectFlavor` is non-null and the return statement is taken. This is because in the default configuration of EvoSuite the static state of a class is not reset, and so once the `initializeConstants` method has been executed, the two static variables are non-null. In the case of *OneBranch*, if the first chosen coverage goal is to make either of the two conditions false, then this will be covered in the first test executed by EvoSuite, and thus the two true-branches will have a covering test. If, however, `initializeConstants` is executed as part of the search for any other branch, then the coverage will be the same as for *Whole*. This is a known effect of static states, and so EvoSuite has an experimental feature to reset static states after test execution. When this feature is enabled, then both *Whole* and *OneBranch* succeed in covering three out of the four branches. (To cover the fourth branch, the assignment to `ourJVMLocalObjectFlavor` would need to throw an exception such that only one of the two variables is initialized). However, even when static state is reset, the overall coverage achieved by *Whole* is significantly lower than for *OneBranch*. The "difficult" branches are cases of a `switch` statement, and branches inside a loop over array elements. These branches are sometimes covered by *Whole*, but less reliably so than by *OneBranch*.

`BlockThread` only has a single conditional branch, all other methods contain just sequences of statements (in EvoSuite, a method without conditional statements is counted as a single branch, based on the control flow graph interpretation). However, the class spawns a new thread, and several of the methods synchronize on this thread (e.g., by calling `wait()` on the thread). EvoSuite uses

Table 2. For each branch, we report how often the *Whole* approach is better (higher effect size) than the *OneBranch*, when they are equivalent, and when it is *OneBranch* that is better. We also report the number of comparisons that are statistically significant at 0.05 level, and when only one of the two techniques ever managed to cover a goal out of the 1,000 repeated experiments.

	# of Branches	Statistically at 0.05	Never Covered by the Other
Whole Approach is better:	1631	1402	246
Equivalent:	671	–	–
OneBranch is better:	81	58	3
Total:	2383		

a timeout of five seconds for each test execution, and any test case or test suite that contains a timeout is assigned the maximum (worst) fitness value, and not considered as a valid solution in the final coverage analysis. In `BlockThread`, many tests lead to such timeouts, and a possible conjecture for the worse performance of the *Whole* approach may be that the chances of having an individual test case without timeout are simply higher than the chances of having an entire test *suite* without timeouts.

To study the difference between *OneBranch* and *Whole* at a finer grained level, Table 2 shows on how many coverage goals (i.e., branches) one technique is better than the other. There are 58 cases in which *OneBranch* led to better results. Three of them, *Whole* never manages to cover.

> **RQ1**: *There are 58 coverage goals in which OneBranch obtained better results. Three of them were never covered by Whole.*

On the other hand, there are 1,402 cases (out of 2,383) in which *Whole* gives better results. For 246 of them, the *OneBranch* approach *never* managed to generate any results in any of the 1,000 runs. In other words, even if there are some (i.e., three) difficult goals that only *OneBranch* can cover, there are many more ($246/3 = 82$ times) difficult branches that only *Whole* does cover.

> **RQ2**: *Whole test suite generation is able to handle 82 times more difficult branches than OneBranch.*

Once assessed that the *Whole* approach leads to higher coverage, even for the difficult branches, it is important to study what are the conditions in which this improvement is obtained. For each coverage goal (2,383 in total), we calculated the odds ratio between *Whole* and *OneBranch* (i.e., we quantified what are the odds that *Whole* has higher chances to cover the goal compared to *OneBranch*). For each odds ratio, we studied its correlation with three different properties: (1) the $\hat{A}_{12}$ effect size between *Whole* and *OneBranch* on the class the goal belongs to; (2) the raw average branch coverage obtained by *OneBranch* on the class the

Table 3. Correlation analyses between the odds ratios for each coverage goal and three different properties. For each analysis, we report the obtained correlation value, its confidence interval at 0.05 level and the obtained p-value (of the test whether the correlation is different from zero).

Property	Correlation	Confidence Interval	p-value
$\hat{A}_{12}$ Whole vs. OneBranch	0.275	[0.238, 0.312]	< 0.001
OneBranch Coverage	0.016	[-0.024, 0.056]	0.433
# of Branches	0.051	[0.011, 0.091]	0.012

goal belongs to; and, finally, (3) the size of the class, measured as number of branches in it. Table 3 shows the results of these correlation analyses.

There is correlation between the odds ratios and the $\hat{A}_{12}$ effect sizes. This is expected: on a class in which the *Whole* approach obtains higher coverage on average, then it is more likely that on each branch in isolation it will have higher chances to cover those branches. However, this correlation is weak, at only 27%.

On classes with many infeasible branches (or too difficult to cover for both *Whole* and *OneBranch*), one could expect higher results for *Whole* (as it is not negatively affected by infeasible branches [11]). It is not possible to determine if branches are feasible or not. However, we can somehow quantify the difficulty of a class by the obtained branch coverage. Furthermore, one would expect better results of the *Whole* approach on larger, more complex classes. But the results in Table 3 show no significant correlation of the odds ratios with the obtained average branch coverage, and only very small (just 5%) with the class size. In other words, the fact that *Whole* approach has higher chances of covering a particular goal seems irrelevant from the overall coverage obtained on such class and its size.

The analysis presented in Table 3 numerically quantifies the correlations between the odds ratios and the different studied properties. To study them in more details, we present scatter plots: Figure 2 for the $\hat{A}_{12}$ effect sizes, Figure 3 for the *OneBranch* average coverage and, finally Figure 4 for class sizes.

Figure 2 is in line with the 27% correlation value shown in Table 3. There are two main clusters, where low odds ratios lead to low $\hat{A}_{12}$ effect sizes, and the other way round for high values. There is also a further cluster of values around $\hat{A}_{12} = 0.5$ for which higher odds are obtained.

Although there is no clear correlation between the odds ratios and the obtained coverage of *OneBranch* (only 1% in Table 3), Figure 3 shows an interesting trend: the only coverage goals for which *Whole* perform worse (i.e., logarithms of the odds ratios are lower than zero) are in classes for which *OneBranch* obtains high coverage (mostly close to 100%). This is visible in the top-left corner in Figure 3. There are coverage goals for which *Whole* approach has much higher odds (logarithms above 30), and those appear only in classes for which the *OneBranch* approach obtains an overall low branch coverage (see the rightmost values in Figure 3).

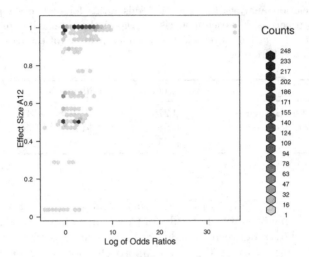

Fig. 2. Scatter plot of the (logarithm of) odds ratios compared to the $\hat{A}_{12}$ effect sizes

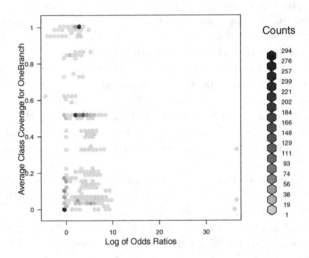

Fig. 3. Scatter plot of the (logarithm of) odds ratios compared to average class coverage obtained by *OneBranch*

When looking at the effects of size, in Figure 4 we can see that the only cases in which *OneBranch* has better odds ratios are when the SUTs are small. This is visible in the bottom-left corner of Figure 4.

> **RQ3:** *Our data does not point to a factor that strongly influences the relative performance between Whole and OneBranch.*

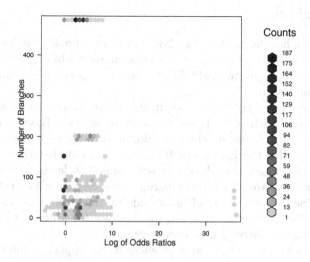

Fig. 4. Scatter plot of the (logarithm of) odds ratios compared to the sizes of the classes

Interestingly, the few cases in which *OneBranch* obtains better results seem located in small classes in which both approaches obtain relatively high code coverage.

5   Threats to Validity

Threats to *internal validity* might come from how the empirical study was carried out. To reduce the probability of having faults in our testing framework, it has been carefully tested. But it is well known that testing alone cannot prove the absence of defects. Furthermore, randomized algorithms are affected by chance. To cope with this problem, we ran each experiment 1,000 times, and we followed rigorous statistical procedures to evaluate their results. For the comparisons between the *Whole* approach and the *OneBranch* approach, both were implemented in the same tool (i.e., EVOSUITE) to avoid possible confounding factors when different tools are used.

There is the threat to *external validity* regarding the generalization to other types of software, which is common for any empirical analysis. Because of the large number of experiments required (in the order of hundreds of days of computational resources), we only used 100 classes for our in depth evaluations. These classes were randomly chosen from the SF100 corpus, which is a random selection of 100 projects from SourceForge. We only experimented for branch coverage and Java software. Whether our results do generalise to other programming languages and testing criteria is a matter of future research.

6   Conclusions

Existing research has shown that the whole test suite approach can lead to higher code coverage [11,12]. However, there was a reasonable doubt on whether it would still perform better on particularly difficult coverage goals when compared to a more focused approach.

To shed light on this potential issue, in this paper we performed an in-depth analysis to study if such cases do indeed occur in practice. Based on a random selection of 100 Java classes in which we aim at automating test generation for branch coverage with the EVOSUITE tool, we found out that there are indeed coverage goals for which the whole test suite approach leads to worse results. However, these cases are very few compared to the cases in which better results are obtained (nearly two orders of magnitude in difference), and they are also located in less "interesting" classes: i.e., small classes for which both approaches can already achieve relatively high code coverage.

The results presented in this paper provides more support to the validity and usefulness of the whole test suite approach in the context of test data generation. Whether such an approach could be successfully adapted also to other search-based software engineering problems will be a matter of future research.

To learn more about EVOSUITE, visit our website at:

http://www.evosuite.org/study

Acknowledgments. This project has been funded by the EPSRC project "EX-OGEN" (EP/K030353/1), a Google Focused Research Award on "Test Amplification", and the Norwegian Research Council.

References

1. Ali, S., Briand, L., Hemmati, H., Panesar-Walawege, R.: A systematic review of the application and empirical investigation of search-based test-case generation. IEEE Transactions on Software Engineering (TSE) 36(6), 742–762 (2010)
2. Arcuri, A.: A theoretical and empirical analysis of the role of test sequence length in software testing for structural coverage. IEEE Transactions on Software Engineering (TSE) 38(3), 497–519 (2012)
3. Arcuri, A.: It really does matter how you normalize the branch distance in search-based software testing. Software Testing, Verification and Reliability (STVR) 23(2), 119–147 (2013)
4. Arcuri, A., Briand, L.: A hitchhiker's guide to statistical tests for assessing randomized algorithms in software engineering. Software Testing, Verification and Reliability, STVR (2012), doi:10.1002/stvr.1486
5. Arcuri, A., Iqbal, M.Z., Briand, L.: Random testing: Theoretical results and practical implications. IEEE Transactions on Software Engineering (TSE) 38(2), 258–277 (2012)
6. Arcuri, A., Yao, X.: Search based software testing of object-oriented containers. Inform. Sciences 178(15), 3075–3095 (2008)
7. Baresi, L., Lanzi, P.L., Miraz, M.: Testful: An evolutionary test approach for java. In: IEEE International Conference on Software Testing, Verification and Validation (ICST), pp. 185–194 (2010)

8. Fraser, G., Arcuri, A.: EvoSuite: Automatic test suite generation for object-oriented software. In: ACM Symposium on the Foundations of Software Engineering (FSE), pp. 416–419 (2011)
9. Fraser, G., Arcuri, A.: Sound empirical evidence in software testing. In: ACM/IEEE International Conference on Software Engineering (ICSE), pp. 178–188 (2012)
10. Fraser, G., Arcuri, A.: Handling test length bloat. Software Testing, Verification and Reliability, STVR (2013), doi:10.1002/stvr.1495
11. Fraser, G., Arcuri, A.: Whole test suite generation. IEEE Transactions on Software Engineering 39(2), 276–291 (2013)
12. Fraser, G., Arcuri, A.: Achieving scalable mutation-based generation of whole test suites. Empirical Software Engineering (EMSE) (to appear, 2014)
13. Fraser, G., Zeller, A.: Mutation-driven generation of unit tests and oracles. IEEE Transactions on Software Engineering (TSE) 28(2), 278–292 (2012)
14. Harman, M., Kim, S.G., Lakhotia, K., McMinn, P., Yoo, S.: Optimizing for the number of tests generated in search based test data generation with an application to the oracle cost problem. In: International Workshop on Search-Based Software Testing, SBST (2010)
15. Harman, M., Mansouri, S.A., Zhang, Y.: Search-based software engineering: Trends, techniques and applications. ACM Computing Surveys (CSUR) 45(1), 11 (2012)
16. Jia, Y., Harman, M.: An analysis and survey of the development of mutation testing. Technical Report TR-09-06, CREST Centre, King's College London, London, UK (September 2009)
17. Korel, B.: Automated software test data generation. IEEE Transactions on Software Engineering, 870–879 (1990)
18. Lakhotia, K., McMinn, P., Harman, M.: An empirical investigation into branch coverage for c programs using cute and austin. J. Syst. Softw. 83(12) (December 2010)
19. McMinn, P.: Search-based software test data generation: A survey. Software Testing, Verification and Reliability 14(2), 105–156 (2004)
20. Miller, W., Spooner, D.L.: Automatic generation of floating-point test data. IEEE Transactions on Software Engineering 2(3), 223–226 (1976)
21. Ribeiro, J.C.B.: Search-based test case generation for object-oriented Java software using strongly-typed genetic programming. In: Genetic and Evolutionary Computation Conference (GECCO), pp. 1819–1822. ACM (2008)
22. Tonella, P.: Evolutionary testing of classes. In: ACM Int. Symposium on Software Testing and Analysis (ISSTA), pp. 119–128 (2004)
23. Wappler, S., Lammermann, F.: Using evolutionary algorithms for the unit testing of object-oriented software. In: Genetic and Evolutionary Computation Conference (GECCO), pp. 1053–1060. ACM (2005)
24. Wegener, J., Baresel, A., Sthamer, H.: Evolutionary test environment for automatic structural testing. Information and Software Technology 43(14), 841–854 (2001)

Detecting Program Execution Phases
Using Heuristic Search

Omar Benomar, Houari Sahraoui, and Pierre Poulin

Dept. I.R.O., Université de Montréal, Canada
{benomaro,sahraouh,poulin}@iro.umontreal.ca

Abstract. Understanding a program from its execution traces is extremely difficult because a trace consists of thousands to millions of events, such as method calls, object creation and destruction, etc. Nonetheless, execution traces can provide valuable information, once abstracted from their low-level events. We propose to identify feature-level phases based on events collected from traces of the program execution. We cast our approach in an optimization problem, searching through the dynamic information provided by the program's execution traces to form a set of phases that minimizes coupling while maximizing cohesion. We applied and evaluated our search algorithms on different execution scenarios of *JHotDraw* and *Pooka*.

Keywords: Execution phase, execution trace, dynamic analysis, genetic algorithm.

1 Introduction

There is a consensus today that program comprehension is a major challenge in software maintenance [3]. However, understanding a program is a considerable resource-consuming activity [12]. To address this issue, a growing program-comprehension research community actively develops techniques and tools to support maintenance. One such family of techniques deals with dynamic analysis, which helps in understanding behavioral aspects of the analyzed program.

Dynamic analysis shows to developers information from a different perspective to better grasp how a program executes. This execution comprehension is crucial when analyzing a program because for many problems, it is more precise than static analysis, which relies on the source code. However, this comes at a much higher cost in complexity. Typically, a program execution produces an execution trace that records execution events such as method calls and returns, object creations and destructions, etc. Usually, an execution generates thousands to millions of such events. This is prohibitively too large for a developer to even just look at, in order to gain a better understanding of the program. Fortunately, not all execution events need to be considered to grasp the dynamic behavior of the program. In fact, developers get a better idea of the execution when they get the "big picture" of the run-time information. For all these reasons, one should focus directly on useful parts of execution traces that relate to system functionality in

C. Le Goues and S. Yoo (Eds.): SSBSE 2014, LNCS 8636, pp. 16–30, 2014.
© Springer International Publishing Switzerland 2014

order to reduce such complexity. Ideally, this abstraction should be computed automatically by identifying in the execution, the phases that correspond to program functionalities.

Some approaches (e.g., [13]) have addressed the problem of phase identification, but they lack scalability by considering executions containing only a few thousands of events. Another issue with existing approaches is the online processing, i.e., the program run-time information is processed on the fly instead of being collected in files and treated offline. While online processing benefits from lower memory usage (for large execution traces), one can question the pertinence of detecting high-level phases from the developer's perspective if the developer is performing the execution phases online [13,16]. An additional limitation is that most high-level phase detection techniques make use of several parameters or thresholds in their algorithms, such as the estimated number of execution phases [19]. The determination of appropriate values for these parameters can be difficult and may vary between programs. Furthermore, the results can be very sensitive to the modification of such parameters.

We propose an automatic approach for the detection of high-level execution phases from previously recorded execution traces, based on object lives, and without the specification of parameters or thresholds. Our technique is simple and based on the heuristic that, to a certain extent, different phases involve different objects. We apply a metaheuristic to implement our heuristic. We utilize in particular a genetic algorithm to search for the best decomposition of an execution trace into high-level phases according to the objects triggered during the program execution. To the best of our knowledge, it is novel to use a search-based approach for high-level phase detection. We used *JHotDraw* and *Pooka* as case studies for the evaluation of our approach, and identified execution phases on seven use-case scenarios of these two open source software systems.

The rest of the paper is organized as follows. Section 2 details our phase-identification technique and explains the underlying heuristic and the search algorithm. The settings and results of the evaluation appear in Section 3, and Section 4 discusses the achieved results and their impact. Section 5 introduces related work and contributions that are comparable to our work. Finally, Section 6 summarizes the content of this paper and exposes limitations of our approach and future research directions.

2   Phase Identification

A program execution typically involves various functionalities. Knowing which part of the execution (phase) belongs to which functionality helps maintainers to focus on this part during their comprehension and maintenance tasks. However, there are no explicit links in a program (source code or execution) between functionalities and execution events. The goal of our work is to explore various heuristics that approximate this link. Before introducing these heuristics, we first define the related concepts. Then we present the implementation of heuristics using a genetic algorithm to search for program execution phases.

2.1 Basic Definitions

Event: An event is an action that occurs periodically during the execution, e.g., a method call, a method return, an object creation. It encapsulates information such as the class of the triggered method, the instance of the class, and the method name.

Object: An object is the instance of the class concerned by the execution event. Objects are uniquely identified.

Object life: An object begins its life when it is created and the end of its life is approximated by its last appearance (reference) in the execution trace.

Trace: A trace is the sequence of all execution events representing the entire execution scenario.

Phase: A phase is a sequence of consecutive execution events; it is a portion of the trace.

Cut position: A cut position is the location of the first event of a phase in the trace.

Phase identification solution: A solution is a set of cut positions that decomposes the trace into phases.

2.2 Heuristics

Our approach for phase identification stands on assumptions concerning the activities of objects during their lifetime. Our rationale is based on the role of objects during program execution and is outlined as follows:

- Two successive execution phases should not have many active objects in common, otherwise it could suggest that the program is still within the same phase.
- Not all objects active in a phase are representative of this phase. Such objects are more general and are indifferently used during the execution. Other objects characterize the phase as they are only triggered during this particular phase.
- A phase does not begin between two successive method calls, between two successive method returns, or even between a method call and a method return. A phase switch occurs only when the program's execution exits a method and enters a method.

2.3 Detection Algorithm

We approach phase identification as an optimization problem. We consider phases as subsets of the execution events contained in the execution trace. The phase detection problem then becomes one of determining the best decomposition of the execution trace's events.

Considering that an execution trace contains n events (possibly in the order of hundreds of thousands), and that a particular execution contains any number m of phases, the number of possible solutions is C_k^l, where $0 \leq l \leq (n/2) - 2$, $k = m-1$ is the number phase shifts in the trace, and l is the number of positions in the execution trace where a phase shift can occur. The number C_k^l depends on the shape of the call tree. The wider the tree is, the larger l will be.

To understand the effect on l, consider two extreme cases. First, a call tree with one branch coming out of the root node, this branch consisting of a series of method calls followed by a series of method returns; then $l = 0$ because there is no method return followed by a method entry in the entire trace. Second, a call tree with a depth of 1, and each method call is immediately followed by a method return; then $l = (n/2) - 2$ because there are as many potential phase shifting positions as the number of pairs of method return/call (in this order), minus the root method call (at the beginning of the trace) and the root method return (at the end of the trace).

The number k of phase switches during execution is the number of phases minus 1. For instance, an execution phase containing two phases has one phase switch. The problem of phase detection considers therefore the number of possible combinations of k from l. As mentioned before, the number of events n can be very large and despite the fact that $l \leq (n/2) - 2$, l remains also large. This results in an exceedingly large search space to investigate exhaustively. Hence, we rely on a metaheuristic search, in our case a genetic algorithm, to find a solution to our phase identification problem.

The algorithm starts by creating an initial population of solutions, i.e., different trace decompositions. In the first generation, these solutions are generated randomly. Then in an iterative process, every iteration produces a new generation of solutions derived from the previous ones. For each iteration, we push the fittest candidates to the next generation (elitism), and then we generate the rest of the solutions composing the next generation by combining/modifying existing solutions using crossover and/or mutation operators. The fitness of a solution is computed using a function implementing the heuristics stated earlier.

The details about the main aspects of our algorithm are presented in the following subsections.

Solution Encoding. A solution is a decomposition of the execution trace into different chunks representing phases. Our algorithm searches for the best cut positions to decompose the execution trace into phases. These cut positions in the trace are events where a phase shift occurs. Figure 2 (left) schematizes two solutions: A and B. The rectangle represents the entire trace, that is divided in two phases in solution A with one cut position (dashed line), and in four phases in solution B with three cut positions. As all solutions are decompositions of the same execution trace, we simply represent a solution by a vector of integers containing the cut positions. Each cut position consists of a valid potential phase switching event position in the trace, according to heuristics in Section 2.2. This vector representation of our solution maps perfectly with the genomic representation solutions in genetic algorithms, where each vector position corresponds to a chromosome of our solution or phenotype. The vector size indicates the number of execution phases, and therefore, it can have different sizes as we do not limit our search to a fixed number of phases.

Initial Population. At the beginning of the search algorithm, we create an initial population of solutions, i.e., integer vectors containing phase cut positions. In order to diversify the population's individuals, we generate N solutions as follows (in our experiments, N was set to 100):

1. We randomly choose cut positions in the trace, within the number of events in the trace. The positions must be valid phase shifting positions, i.e., a cut position is a method call (start of a phase) AND its preceding event must be a method return (end of a phase).
2. The random cut positions are sorted in ascending order because events are ordered in time, and phases are successive. Two equal cut positions are merged, and only one of them is conserved.
3. In order to vary the number of phases in an initial population of N individuals, we generate $N/10$ solutions with two phases, $N/10$ other solutions with three phases, and so on. In total, we produce solutions containing two to eleven phases. Again, our technique is not bound by a fixed number of phases or even a subset of phases' numbers, and therefore the number of phases can exceed eleven during the search.

Fitness Function. The fitness function is the most important element of our approach. It encodes our phase detection heuristics explained in Section 2.2, and thus, guides the search process. There are different ways to translate the proposed heuristics into measurable properties that allow evaluating the quality of a phase detection solution. We propose three metrics that are combined to define fitness functions for our problem.

1) Phase Coupling: Two successive phases are coupled if they share objects. An object is shared by phases if its lifetime covers them. Figure 1 illustrates eight different cases that can occur when computing coupling over two phases. These cases differ in the way object lifetimes are distributed over the two successive phases. Some of them are more desirable than others, and therefore, are given larger weights when computing the result. The latter is a linear combination of the number of objects per category. Here are the details and rationale behind our weight affectation starting from the most desirable to the less desirable distribution of object lifetimes. We illustrate the different cases using the examples of Figure 1. We refer to consecutive phases as the first phase and the second phase (phase i and phase j in Figure 1).

First, objects that are included in one phase have a weight of 6, i.e., they are created and destroyed within each phase. This is the ideal case since each phase would involve a different set of objects, e.g., *Obj*1 and *Obj*2.

Second, we assign a weight of 5 to objects that are destroyed in the first phase or are created in the second phase, e.g., *Obj*6 and *Obj*7. This resembles the first category, except for the fact that objects are not created/destroyed within the first/second phase respectively. It is a good category because the two successive phases do not share objects.

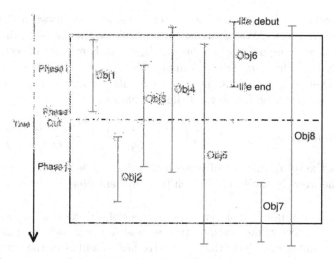

Fig. 1. Phase coupling with object's lives

Third, there are objects that are created in the first phase and destroyed after the second phase, such as *Obj*5. Here we have two sub-categories, one of which is more desirable than the other. If the object is not active in the second phase, i.e., the object is not involved in any event, we assign a weight of 4. Although the two phases share the object, according to our earlier definition, the second phase does not use it. However, if the object is involved in the second phase, we assign to it a weight of 2 because the object is active in the two consecutive phases, which probably means that the cut position is not appropriate. There is also the contraposition of the previous case, in which we used the same weights' values, where an object is destroyed in the second phase and created previous to the first phase, e.g., *Obj*4.

Then, there is the case of an object created before the first phase and destroyed after the second phase, such as *Obj*8. The object could be involved in the first phase only, the second phase only, or both. Following the same principle as the two previous cases, we assign a weight of 3 when the object is involved in one phase only, and a weight of 2 if it is active in both phases.

Finally, the less desirable case is when the object is created in the first phase and destroyed in the second phase, such as *Obj*3. Here we assign the lowest weight of 1 because we probably should merge the two phases and hence remove the cut position.

The coupling between two successive phases is computed as the number objects in each category, multiplied by its corresponding weight. Formally:

$$Coup(phase_i, phase_j) = \frac{\sum_k (w_k |OC_k|) - [\min (\{w_k\}) \sum_k (|OC_k|)]}{[\max (\{w_k\}) - \min (\{w_k\})] \sum_k (|OC_k|)} \quad (1)$$

where OC_k is the set of objects of category k, and w_k is the weight affected to the objects of category k. The coupling for a solution is the average coupling on the successive phase pairs.

2) Object Similarity: This metric calculates the similarity between the objects of two successive phases. We construct for each phase the list of distinct active objects. Then, we compute the number of objects in common between the two successive phases. The number of common objects in each phase is divided by its total number of the objects. The object similarity is taken as the average between the two resulting numbers of the two phases

$$Obj(phase_i, phase_j) = 1 - \frac{1}{2} \left(\frac{|DO_i \cap DO_j|}{|DO_i|} + \frac{|DO_i \cap DO_j|}{|DO_j|} \right) \qquad (2)$$

where DO is the set of distinct objects in the phase. The object similarity of a solution is the average similarity of each two adjacent phases.

3) Thin Cut: The thin cut represents the number of objects that are divided, in terms of their respective lifetimes, by the cut position. For each cut position, we compute the number of objects that are active before and after the cut position. The resulting number is then normalized by the number of objects in the entire trace. For example in Figure 1, there are four objects divided by the cut position: $Obj3$, $Obj4$, $Obj5$, and $Obj8$. Therefore, the result would be $4/M$, where M is the number objects created before the given cut. Formally:

$$Cut(position_i) = 1 - \frac{|CO_i|}{|TO|} \qquad (3)$$

where CO is the set of objects that are created before cut position i and destroyed after it, and TO is the set of all objects in the execution trace. The thin cut of a given solution is simply the average score of each position.

Finally, the fitness function of a solution is defined as follows:

$$fitness(sol) = \frac{a \times Coup(sol) + b \times Obj(sol) + c \times Cut(sol)}{a + b + c} \qquad (4)$$

where solution *sol* to be evaluated consists of cut positions in the execution trace, and a, b, and c are the weights affected to each component.

Genetic Operators. To create the new population in a given generation, we first automatically add the two fittest solutions. Then to complete the $N - 2$ solutions, we select $(N - 2)/2$ pairs of solutions, and for each pair, we produce two offspring solutions. We use the roulette-wheel strategy to select the parent solutions for reproduction. For each pair, a given solution has a probability to be selected, proportional to its fitness. When two-parent solutions are selected, we apply the crossover and mutation operators with certain probabilities.

A) Crossover: We use a single-point crossover. To perform a crossover between two solutions, we randomly pick a new cut position independently from the two solutions' cut positions. The new cut position at the same location in both solutions produces two parts for each. The upper part of solution A is combined

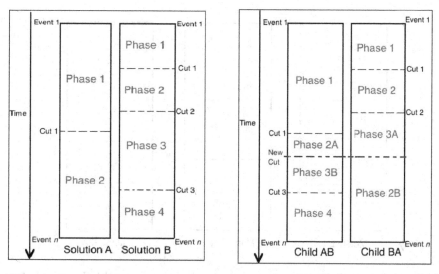

Fig. 2. The result of the crossover operator (right) applied to the solutions (left)

with the lower part of solution B to form a child solution (AB). Conversely, the upper part of solution B is combined with the lower part of solution A (BA). Figure 2 (right) illustrates the resulting children from the application of the crossover on solutions A and B from Figure 2 (left). The new random cut position is shown as a dashed blue line dividing both solutions. According to the cut position, child AB is formed from phase 1 and part of phase 2 of solution A, and part of phase 3 and phase 4 of solution B. The child BA is a result of combining phase 1, phase 2, and a portion of phase 3 of solution B, and the remaining portion of phase 2 of solution A. The two siblings share the new random position, and receive portions of their parents other chromosomes.

B) Mutation: We mutate an individual in three different manners depending on a certain probability. The first mutation strategy consists in merging two successive phases into a single one, where we randomly select one of the cut positions and discard it. The second mutation strategy splits one phase into two, by generating randomly a new cut position and inserting it at the correct location in the solution. Finally, the third mutation strategy randomly changes a cut position, i.e., the boundary between two consecutive phases is repositioned. The third mutation is applied twice.

This results in the alteration of three existing phases (the previous, selected, and subsequent phases) without changing the number of phases in the solution. Figure 3 illustrates the three mutation strategies applied to solution B from Figure 2 (left). Mutant B1 is the result of removing the 3rd cut position of solution B, which resulted in the merging of phase 2 and phase 3. Phase 3 in solution B was subdivided into two phases with the insertion of a new cut position to produce mutant B1'. The first and second cut positions of solution B

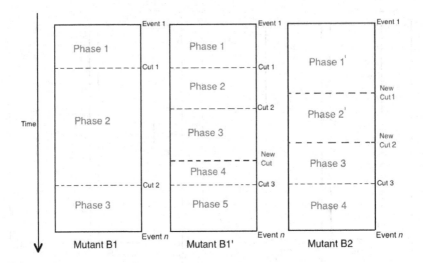

Fig. 3. The result of the mutation operator applied to solution B in Figure 2 (left)

were altered resulting in the modification of phase 1 and phase 2 in mutant B2 (phase 1' and phase 2').

3   Evaluation

To assess our approach, we apply our phase detection algorithm on three scenarios of the *JHotDraw* system and four scenarios of the *Pooka* system. This section introduces the settings of our case studies and the choices made while evaluating our approach. In particular, we evaluate the accuracy of our technique in detecting high-level execution phases based on object usage and lifetime.

3.1   Settings

Trace Extraction. Our phase detection technique takes as input an execution trace. This trace is constructed by monitoring the execution of a program and by recording its events. We use an implementation in C of the JVMTI API to listen to the JVM for method entries and exits. Each execution event is described by its type (method entry or exit), the class name with the method triggered, a timestamp, the method arguments, the return type, the object unique id, and the dynamic object in the case of polymorphism or dynamic dispatch. To determine the reference which our solutions will be compared to, the tracer allows us to record event ids on demand. These serve to determine the beginning and ending events of each external functionality, i.e., boundaries of their corresponding phases.

Execution Scenarios. We extracted three execution traces, one for each of three scenarios of *JHotDraw* [7], an open source Java GUI framework for technical and structured graphics. It contains 585 classes distributed over 30 packages. We also executed four scenarios of *Pooka* [14], an open source email client written in Java, using the Javamail API. It contains 301 classes organized in 32 packages.

The execution traces differ in size and in performed tasks. For each scenario, we defined the beginning and ending events of each phase in the trace, as explained above. These events serve as reference for evaluating our phase detection approach. The following table summarizes the information about the extracted execution scenarios, which were used during the evaluation.

Scenario	Description	# events
J1	Init ; New file ; Draw round rectangle;	66983
J2	Init ; Open file ; Animation ; New file; Window tile;	100151
J3	Init ; Open file ; Delete figure ; Write html text area;	105069
P1	Init ; Open email ; Reply to sender ; Consult Help;	79506
P2	Init ; Change theme ; Send new email;	101710
P3	Init ; Search inbox ; Delete email;	99128
P4	Init ; Get new emails; Window tile;	63162

For example, execution scenario J1 contains three execution phases: an initialization phase, a phase representing the opening of a new file, and a phase representing the drawing of a rectangle with round edges. In the second phase ('New file'), *JHotDraw* opens a window canvas for drawing, on which we draw a round rectangle figure. In terms of cut positions, an ideal solution for this scenario would be to have two cut positions: one at the end of the initialization phase, and the other at the end of the 'New file' phase.

Algorithm Parameters. Our genetic algorithm uses parameters that may influence the resulting solution. We present here the values chosen for our evaluation.

The **initial-population size**, which stays constant throughout the iterative process, affects both the algorithm's performance and efficiency [6]. We start our search with a population of 100 solutions. Solutions are generated randomly (see Section 2.3), but only those having a fitness value $\geq 50\%$ are incorporated in the initial population. This starts with a population of a reasonable quality.

For the **selection strategy**, the roulette-wheel technique is used. We also use the **elitist strategy** that incorporates the two fittest solutions directly to the next generation. Regarding the **genetic operators' probabilities**, we use a crossover probability of 90% and a mutation probability of 10%. As a **termination criterion**, we fixed the number of generations to be produced to 10× the size of a population, i.e., 1000 generations. Finally, for the **fitness function definition**, we utilized a combination of three metrics (see Section 2.3). We investigated several other metrics, such as common methods between phases, phase cohesion where objects in a phase collaborate together, etc. In Section 3.2

we show results for the combination that produces the best solutions for most execution scenarios (coupling, object similarity, and thin cut metrics).

3.2   Results

We ran our algorithm on the seven described scenarios. As our algorithm is probabilistic, each scenario was processed six times; the best solution was retained.

As discussed in Section 3.1, the beginning and end positions (i.e., events) of each phase is recorded during the tracing process. We used these positions as an oracle to evaluate our solutions. Precision and recall were used to assess our solutions. We computed the precision in terms of events as explained by Asadi et al. [1], as well as recall. They are defined formally as:

$$precision_{event}(DE, AE) = \frac{|DE \cap AE|}{|DE|} \qquad recall_{event}(DE, AE) = \frac{|DE \cap AE|}{|AE|}$$

(5)

where DE is the set of detected phase events and AE the set of actual phase events. The event precision and recall of a solution are simply the averages of the phases precision and recall, respectively.

We computed precision and recall by comparing the detected phases with the actual phases, as done by Watanabe et al. [19]. A phase is considered detected if it has $\geq 75\%$ event precision with the corresponding oracle phase.

$$precision_{phase} = \frac{|Detected \cap Actual|}{|Detected|} \qquad recall_{phase} = \frac{|Detected \cap Actual|}{|Actual|}$$

(6)

Table 1. Summary of the evaluation results of the seven scenarios

Scenario	$precision_{event}$	$recall_{event}$	$precision_{phase}$	$recall_{phase}$
J1	.85 (.94)	.38 (.57)	.66 (1)	.50 (.66)
J2	.89 (.96)	.58 (.59)	.80 (1)	.60 (.75)
J3	.82 (.92)	.64 (.64)	.66 (1)	.20 (.50)
P1	.91 (.95)	.71 (.71)	1 (1)	.60 (.75)
P2	.93 (.96)	.69 (.61)	1 (1)	.75 (.66)
P3	.94 (.99)	.32 (.32)	.83 (1)	.33 (1)
P4	.96 (.99)	.37 (.37)	1 (1)	.66 (1)

All the execution scenarios include an initialization phase. There are many object creations during this phase, many of them remain active in subsequent phases. Our approach is based on the objects' lifetimes, hence, it fails to detect the initialization phase of several scenarios. The results of Table 1 take into consideration the initialization phase, which penalizes them. The results between parentheses do not include the initialization phase in the calculations and are clearly higher, which suggests that the rest of the phases are correctly detected (see $precision_{phase}$). This suggests a further investigation of this special phase.

Finally, for sanity check, we compared our results to random search. To have a similar setup than our algorithm, we generated the same number of solutions (100 individuals × 1000 generations), i.e., 100000 random solutions for each scenario. Each time, we selected the best solutions from these, according to the same fitness function. The results of the Wilcoxon test showed that our algorithm performs significantly better than random search for $precision_{event}$ ($p = .018$), $precision_{phase}$ ($p = .027$), and $recall_{phase}$ ($p = .043$). However, the difference for $recall_{event}$ is not statistically significant ($p = .271$).

4 Discussion

When developing our approach, we made several decisions concerning the detection heuristics and their implementation. The results of our experiments showed that these decisions could still be improved.

We considered that all objects utilized by a program to accomplish an execution phase contribute equally to phase detection. However, objects are different in terms of lifetime, number of uses, and execution pattern. Some objects are created at the beginning and destroyed at the end of the execution, others are more specialized and have shorter lifetimes. Apart from their lifetimes, objects also differ in the way they are used in the execution. An object may be executed sparsely from its creation to its destruction, or it can be used in a dense manner. Another aspect of object execution is the regularity with which it appears in the execution trace. These object execution properties should be further investigated to define object execution profiles that will be much more representative of execution phases.

Our single-point crossover strategy also introduces some mutation in the form of the new common cut position of two-parent individuals. This strategy preserves most of the parents' phases and possibly creates new phases. This crossover strategy is consistent with our execution phase definition, which states that a phase is a portion of the trace. Another possible crossover strategy is a uniform one, where we generate two child solutions from two parents by selecting their cut points. Here no new cut position is introduced, and all the parents cut points are inherited. However, the resulting individuals may end up with no phases from the parents since these latters could be further segmented by cut positions from the other parent. Although we opted for our first strategy, we believe that more sophisticated crossover operations could reduce the mutation factor while preserving the completeness and consistency of trace decomposition.

The choice of the fitness function metrics is an important decision when using the approach. We tried several metrics to evaluate the fitness of our solutions. Some of them gave better results in some particular scenarios. We chose the metrics configuration that gave the best results in average for all scenarios. Therefore, we believe it is important to investigate the relationship between the nature of the functionalities involved in a scenario and the metrics. For example, some metrics favor solutions with few phases while others tend to orient the search towards solutions with more phases.

Finally, the fitness function is computed as a combination of three metrics (Equation (4)). The factors were weighted equally, on the same domain ([0, 1]), but they have in practice different magnitudes. Taking the simple average could favor some metrics over others. To alleviate this, we can use a multi-objective search algorithm for which the magnitude of single objectives is not important.

5   Related Work

Techniques for execution phase detection can be divided in two groups. First, there are techniques concerned with detecting program execution phases at a low level of granularity, such as program instructions, conditional branches, etc. These techniques (e.g., [10,11,4]) are typically used for hardware configuration, compiler optimization, and dynamic optimization in general. The detected phases represent portions of execution where the program is stable, i.e., where there is a certain repetition in the executed instructions.

The second group of phase detection techniques is concerned with the identification of execution phases at a higher level. Phases are related to what the program is doing from the user's perspective, e.g., initializing, database connection, performing computations [17]. Our approach belongs to this group of techniques. Compared to the first group where there is extensive work on low-level phase detection, there is much less research on the identification of high-level phases.

One contribution that addresses high-level phase detection comes from Watanabe et al. [19]. They employ information from the objects to detect phase transition by keeping an updated list of recently used objects. A steep increase in change frequency is interpreted as entering a new phase. An execution trace is collected according to a use-case scenario and processed to retrieve the objects' information used to identify feature-level phases. In summary, their work uses the assumption that different functionalities use different sets of objects. However, it also makes the assumption that the number of phases is known. Our method has the clear advantage of not making this assumption.

Pirzadeh et al. [13] exploit the sequence of method calls during program execution to reveal phase shifting within an execution trace. They claim that executed methods tend to disappear as the program enters a new execution phase. They construct a set of methods invoked as the program executes. The methods are ranked according to their prevalence, which is used to decide if they are disappearing from the execution, i.e., if phase shifting is occurring.

Reiss [17] uses dynamic information online, i.e., dynamic data is collected and processed during program execution. Periodically, he gathers counters for classes and packages, such as the number of method calls and object allocations, in addition to the threads' states. Reiss determines a phase switch when the similarity value between successive periods' data exceeds a threshold. The phases are then displayed using *JIVE* [16].

Several contributions treat dynamic behavior visualization. Cornelissen et al. [2] propose two views to visualize execution traces: a massive sequence view as a UML-based view, and a circular bundle view. The massive sequence view permits the visual identification of the major execution phases. Similarly, *Jinsight* [4] provides views for exploring and understanding a program's run-time behavior. Execution patterns can be identified using its execution view.

Furthermore, there are contributions in program slicing [18] and feature location [5], that correlate parts of the source code to program functionality. Asadi et al. [1] identify concepts in execution traces using genetic algorithms. The authors segment an execution trace according to the conceptual cohesion of the methods' source code. Their work tries to solve a different problem, i.e., feature location, using genetic algorithms. However, the heuristics involved in the search are different since we use object collaborations and lifetimes. Medini et al. [8] compare genetic algorithms and dynamic programming in terms of efficiency and precision, in the identification of concepts in execution traces. Although their work suggests that dynamic programming increases performance, the application to our approach and its success are not guaranteed because of the difference in problem representation and heuristics in the two methods.

Finally, some methods in search-based software engineering on module clustering [9,15] use search algorithms to automatically re-modularize a software system. The module clustering problem is related to our work as it can be seen as a clustering of objects according to their lifetimes.

Our phase-identification approach automatically detects periods of the program's execution that abstract the external behavior. Typically, we correlate the program's execution information with observable actions from the users.

6 Conclusion

We presented an automatic approach for identifying program execution phases. Our technique is based on object lifetimes and object collaborations. We cast the problem of finding execution phases as an optimization problem and utilize a genetic algorithm to search for a good solution. We evaluated our automatic results by comparing with phases manually detected. We ran our algorithm on three different scenarios of *JHotDraw* and four scenarios of *Pooka*.

Although the computed results are satisfactory, there is still room for improvement. In addition to the future research directions mentioned in Section 4, we will consider other heuristics for the search algorithm, such as the structure of the call graph or the linguistic similarity between phases to improve our detection. We also intend to use our approach at a different level of granularity, i.e., on program instruction, where rather than analyzing only the method calls, we could consider the control flow (instruction). However, considering the amount of data and their nature, we have to redesign a large portion of our approach.

References

1. Asadi, F., Di Penta, M., Antoniol, G., Guéhéneuc, Y.-G.: A heuristic-based approach to identify concepts in execution traces. In: Conf. on Software Maintenance and Reengineering, CSMR, pp. 31–40 (2010)

2. Cornelissen, B., Holten, D., Zaidman, A., Moonen, L., van Wijk, J.J., van Deursen, A.: Understanding execution traces using massive sequence and circular bundle views. In: Proc. Intl. Conf. on Program Comprehension, ICPC, pp. 49–58. IEEE (2007)

3. Cornelissen, B., Zaidman, A., van Rompaey, B., van Deursen, A.: Trace visualization for program comprehension: A controlled experiment. In: Proc. Int. Conf. on Program Comprehension, pp. 100–109. IEEE (2009)

4. De Pauw, W., Jensen, E., Mitchell, N., Sevitsky, G., Vlissides, J.M., Yang, J.: Visualizing the Execution of Java Programs. In: Diehl, S. (ed.) Dagstuhl Seminar 2001. LNCS, vol. 2269, pp. 151–162. Springer, Heidelberg (2002)

5. Eisenbarth, T., Koschke, R., Simon, D.: Locating features in source code. IEEE Trans. Softw. Eng. 29(3), 210–224 (2003)

6. Grefenstette, J.J.: Optimization of control parameters for genetic algorithms. IEEE Trans. Systems, Man and Cybernetics 16(1), 122–128 (1986)

7. JHotDraw. A Java GUI framework, http://www.jhotdraw.org

8. Medini, S., Galinier, P., Di Penta, M., Guéhéneuc, Y.-G., Antoniol, G.: A fast algorithm to locate concepts in execution traces. In: Cohen, M.B., Ó Cinnéide, M. (eds.) SSBSE 2011. LNCS, vol. 6956, pp. 252–266. Springer, Heidelberg (2011)

9. Mitchell, B.S., Mancoridis, S.: On the automatic modularization of software systems using the Bunch tool. IEEE Trans. Softw. Eng. 32(3), 193–208 (2006)

10. Nagpurkar, P., Hind, M., Krintz, C., Sweeney, P.F., Rajan, V.T.: Online phase detection algorithms. In: Intl. Symp. on Code Generation and Optimization, CGO, pp. 111–123 (2006)

11. Nagpurkar, P., Krintz, C.: Visualization and analysis of phased behavior in Java programs. In: Proc. Intl. Symp. on Principles and Practice of Programming in Java, PPPJ, pp. 27–33. Trinity College Dublin (2004)

12. Pigoski, T.M.: Practical Software Maintenance: Best Practices for Managing Your Software Investment. Wiley (1996)

13. Pirzadeh, H., Agarwal, A., Hamou-Lhadj, A.: An approach for detecting execution phases of a system for the purpose of program comprehension. In: Proc. ACIS Intl. Conf. on Software Engineering Research, Management and Applications, SERA, pp. 207–214. IEEE (2010)

14. Pooka. An email client written in JAVA

15. Praditwong, K., Harman, M., Yao, X.: Software module clustering as a multi-objective search problem. IEEE Trans. Softw. Eng. 37(2), 264–282 (2011)

16. Reiss, S.P.: Visualizing Java in action. In: Proc. ACM Symp. on Software Visualization, SoftVis, p. 57. ACM (2003)

17. Reiss, S.P.: Dynamic detection and visualization of software phases. In: Proc. Intl. Work. on Dynamic Analysis, WODA, pp. 1–6. ACM (2005)

18. Wang, T., Roychoudhury, A.: Hierarchical dynamic slicing. In: Proc. Intl. Symp. on Software Testing and Analysis, ISSTA, pp. 228–238. ACM (2007)

19. Watanabe, Y., Ishio, T., Inoue, K.: Feature-level phase detection for execution trace using object cache. In: Proc. Intl. Work. on Dynamic Analysis, WODA, pp. 8–14. ACM (2008)

On the Use of Machine Learning
and Search-Based Software Engineering for Ill-Defined
Fitness Function: A Case Study on Software Refactoring

Boukhdhir Amal[1], Marouane Kessentini[1], Slim Bechikh[1], Josselin Dea[1],
and Lamjed Ben Said[2]

[1] University of Michigan, MI, USA
`firstname@umich.edu`
[2] University of Tunis, Tunisia
`lamjed.bensaid@isg.rnu.tn`

Abstract. The most challenging step when adapting a search-based technique for a software engineering problem is the definition of the fitness function. For several software engineering problems, a fitness function is ill-defined, subjective, or difficult to quantify. For example, the evaluation of a software design is subjective. This paper introduces the use of a neural network-based fitness function for the problem of software refactoring. The software engineers evaluate manually the suggested refactoring solutions by a Genetic Algorithm (GA) for few iterations then an Artificial Neural Network (ANN) uses these training examples to evaluate the refactoring solutions for the remaining iterations. We evaluate the efficiency of our approach using six different open-source systems through an empirical study and compare the performance of our technique with several existing refactoring studies.

1 Introduction

Large scale software systems exhibit high complexity and become difficult to maintain. In fact, it has been reported that software cost dedicated to maintenance and evolution activities is more than 80% of total software costs [16]. To facilitate maintenance tasks, one of the widely used techniques is refactoring which improves design structure while preserving the overall functionalities and behavior [28, 29].

SBSE was applied successfully to reformulate software refactoring as a search problem using metaheuristics [8, 22, 25, 24, 21, 19]. In the majority of these studies, refactoring solutions are evaluated based on the use of quality metrics. However, the evaluation of the design quality is subjective and difficult to formalize using quality metrics with the appropriate threshold values due to several reasons. First, there is no general consensus about the definition of design defects [29], also called code-smells, due to the various programming behaviors and contexts. Thus, it is difficult to formalize the definitions of these design violations in terms of quality metrics then use them to evaluate the quality of a refactoring solution. Second, the majority of existing refactoring studies do not include the developer in the loop to analyze the suggested refactoring solutions and give their feed-back during the optimization

C. Le Goues and S. Yoo (Eds.): SSBSE 2014, LNCS 8636, pp. 31–45, 2014.
© Springer International Publishing Switzerland 2014

process. In [5], the authors used an interactive genetic algorithm to estimate the quality of refactoring solutions but it is fastidious task for developers to evaluate every refactoring solution at each iteration. Third, the calculation of some quality metrics is expensive thus the defined fitness function to evaluate refactoring solutions can be expensive. Finally, quality metrics can just evaluate the structural improvements of the design after applying the suggested refactorings but it is difficult to evaluate the semantic coherence of the design without an interactive user interpretation.

The paper tackles a problem that is faced a lot of search based software engineering (SBSE) research: how do we define fitness when the computation of fitness is an inherently subjective and aesthetic judgment that can only really be properly made by human?

We propose, in this paper, a GA-based interactive learning algorithm of software refactoring based on Artificial Neural Networks (ANN) [27]. Harman [9] noticed that fully automated search-based software engineering solutions, sometimes, are not very desired due to the fact that the developers/designers are not considered in the loop during the optimization process. He stressed that the contribution of the decision maker (DM) is important to guide the search through, for example, predictive models. Predictive models have been, recently, the subject of a Harman's paper [9]. He claimed that there are many unexplored areas including both predictive models (Artificial Neural Networks, Bayesian Networks, etc.) and SBSE. In this paper, we are interested in modeling DM's refactoring preferences using ANN as a predictive model to approximate the fitness function for the evaluation of software refactoring solutions. The developer is asked to evaluate manually refactoring solutions suggested by a Genetic Algorithm (GA) for few iterations then these examples are used as a training set for the ANNs to evaluate the solutions of the GA in the next iterations. We evaluated our approach on open-source systems using an existing benchmark [22, 23, 4]. We report the results on the efficiency and effectiveness of our approach, compared to existing approaches [5, 14, 19, 18].

The rest of this paper is outlined as follows. Section 2 is dedicated to the problem statement. Section 3 presents the proposed approach. Section 4 presents results of experimentations. Finally, section 5 summarizes our findings.

2   Related Work

Several studies are proposed in the literature to address the refactoring problem. We focus mainly in this related work on existing search-based refactoring work. These studies are based on the use of mono, multi and many-objective optimization techniques. The GA was the most used metaheuristic search algorithm according to a recent survey [8] and recently there has been also many other algorithms such as NSGA-II [25] and NSGA-III [22]. Hence, we classify those approaches into two main categories: (1) mono-objective approaches, and (2) multi/many-objective ones.

In the first category, the majority of existing work combines several metrics in a single fitness function to find the best sequence of refactorings. Seng et al. [24] have proposed a single-objective optimization based-approach using genetic algorithms to suggest a list of refactorings to improve software quality. The search process uses a single fitness function to maximize a weighted sum of several quality metrics. The used metrics are mainly related to various class level properties such as coupling, cohesion, complexity and stability. Furthermore, there is another similar work of Simons et al. [31] have used interactive evolution in various software design problems but their approach requires a fastidious and high number of interactions with the designer. O'Keeffe et al. [21] that have used different local search-based techniques such as hill climbing and simulated annealing to provide an automated refactoring support. Eleven weighted object-oriented design metrics have been used to evaluate the quality improvements. In [3], Qayum et al. considered the problem of refactoring scheduling as a graph transformation problem. They expressed refactorings as a search for an optimal path, using Ant colony optimization, in the graph where nodes and edges represent respectively refactoring candidates and dependencies between them. Recently, Kessentini et al. [14] have proposed a single-objective combinatorial optimization using genetic algorithms to find the best sequence of refactoring operations that improve the quality of the code by minimizing as much as possible the number of design defects detected on the source code. Jensen et al. [1] have proposed an approach that supports composition of design changes and makes the introduction of design patterns a primary goal of the refactoring process. They used genetic programming and software metrics to identify the most suitable set of refactorings to apply to a software design. Kilic et al. [6] explore the use of a variety of population-based approaches to search-based parallel refactoring, finding that local beam search could find the best solutions.

In the second category of work, Harman et al. [19] have proposed a search-based approach using Pareto optimality that combines two quality metrics, CBO (coupling between objects) and SDMPC (standard deviation of methods per class), in two separate fitness functions. The authors start from the assumption that good design quality results from good distribution of features (methods) among classes. Their Pareto optimality-based algorithm succeeded in finding good sequence of move method refactorings that should provide the best compromise between CBO and SDMPC to improve code quality. Ó Cinnéide et al. [20] have proposed a multi-objective search-based refactoring to conduct an empirical investigation to assess some structural metrics and to explore relationships between them. To this end, they have used a variety of search techniques (Pareto-optimal search, semi-random search) guided by a set of cohesion metrics. Furthermore, Ouni et al. [25] have proposed a new multi-objective refactoring to find the best compromise between quality improvement and semantic coherence using two heuristics related to the vocabulary similarity and structural coupling.

Overall, most of refactoring studies are based on the use of quality metrics as a fitness function to evaluate the quality of the design after applying refactorings. However, these metrics can only evaluate the structural improvements. Furthermore, the efficient evaluation of the suggested refactoring from a semantic perspective requires an interaction with the designer. In addition, the symptoms of design defects are difficult to formalize using quality metrics due to the very subjective process to identify them that depends on the programming context and the preferences of developers (programming behavior). Finally, the definition of a fitness function based on quality metrics can be expensive. To address these challenges, we describe in the next section our approach based on machine learning and search-based techniques to evaluate the refactoring solutions without the need to explicitly define a fitness function. There were very few works that combine those two fields (SBSE and ML) as mentioned recently by Harman [9] and Zang [30]. This work represents one of the first studies in this area.

3   Refactoring as an Interactive Search-Based Learning Problem

3.1   Approach Overview

As described in Figure 1, our technique takes as input the system to refactor, an exhaustive list of possible refactoring types and the number of DM's interactions during the search process. It generates as output the best refactoring sequence that improves the quality of the system. Our approach is composed of two main components: the interactive component (IGA) and the learning module (LGA).

The algorithm starts first by executing the IGA component where the designer evaluates the refactoring solutions manually generated by GA for a number of iterations. The designer (DM) evaluates the feasibility and the efficiency/quality of the suggested refactorings one by one since each refactoring solution is a sequence of refactoring operations. Thus, the designer classifies all the suggested refactorings as good or not one by one based on his preferences.

After executing the IGA component for a number of iterations, all the evaluated solutions by the developer are considered as training set for the second component LGA of the algorithm. The LGA component executes an ANN to generate a predictive model in order to approximate the evaluation of the refactoring solutions in the next iteration of the GA. Thus, our approach does not requires the definition of a fitness function. Alternatively, the LGA incorporates many components to approximate the unknown target function f. Those components are the training set, the learning algorithm and the predictive model. For each new sequence of refactoring X_{k+1} , the goal of learning is to maximize the accuracy of the evaluation y_{k+1}. We applied the ANN as being among the most reliable predictive models, especially, in the case of noisy and incomplete data. Its architecture is chosen to be a multilayered architecture in which all neurons are fully connected; weights of connections have been, randomly, set at the beginning of the training. Regarding the activation function, the sigmoid function is applied [17] as being adequate in the case of continuous data. The network is composed of three layers: the first layer is composed of p input neurons. Each neuron is assigned the value x_{kt}. The hidden layer is composed of a set of hidden neurons. The learning algorithm is an iterative algorithm that allows the training of the network. Its performance is controlled by two parameters. The first parameter is the momentum factor that tries to avoid local minima by stabilizing weights. The second factor is the learning rate which is responsible of the rapidity of the adjustment of weights.

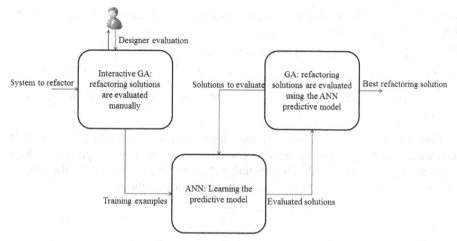

Fig. 1. Approach overview

3.2   Algorithm Adaptation

3.2.1 Solution Representation

To represent a candidate solution (individual), we used a vector representation. Each vector's dimension represents a refactoring operation. Thus, a solution is defined as a long sequence of refactorings applied to different parts of the system to fix design defects. When created, the order of applying these refactorings corresponds to their positions in the vector. In addition, for each refactoring, a set of controlling parameters (stored in the vector), e.g., actors and roles are randomly picked from the program to be refactored and stored in the same vector.

Moreover, when creating a sequence of refactorings (individuals), it is important to guarantee that they are feasible and that they can be legally applied. The first work in the literature was proposed by Opdyke [29] who introduced a way of formalizing the preconditions that must be imposed before a refactoring can be applied in order to preserve the behavior of the system. Opdyke created functions which could be used to formalise constraints. These constraints are similar to the Analysis Functions used later by Ó Cinneide [21] and Roberts [2] who developed an automatic refactoring tool to reduce program analysis. In our approach, we used a system to check a set of simple conditions, taking inspiration from the work proposed by Ó Cinnéide [21]. Although we suggest a recommendation system and we do not apply refactorings automatically, we verify the applicability of the suggested refactorings. Similarly to [2], our search-based refactoring tool simulates refactorings using pre and post conditions that are expressed in terms of conditions on a code model.

3.2.2 Training Set and Data Normalization

Before the learning process, the data used in the training set should be normalized. In our case, we choose to apply the Min-max technique since it is among the most accurate techniques according to [10]. We used the following data representation to the GA-based learning problem using ANN for software refactoring. Let us denote by

E the training set of the ANN. It is composed of a set of couples that represent the refactoring sequence and its evaluation.

$$E = \{(X_1, y_1), (X_2, y_2), (X_3, y_3), ..., (X_k, y_k), ..., (X_n, y_n)\}, k \in [1..n]$$

X_k is a refactoring sequence represented as $X_k = [x_{k1}, x_{k2}, ..., x_{kt}, ..., x_{kp}], t \in [1..p]$.

y_k is the evaluation associated to the kth refactoring sequence in the range $y_k \in [0..1]$.

Let's denote by O the matrix that includes numerical values related to the set of refactorings and by Y the vector that contains numerical values representing X_k's evaluations. O is composed of n lines and p columns where n is equal to the number of refactoring sequences and p is equal to the number of solutions.

$$O = \begin{bmatrix} x_{11} & x_{12} & ... & x_{1p} \\ x_{21} & x_{22} & ... & x_{2p} \\ . & . & . & . \\ . & . & . & . \\ . & . & . & . \\ x_{n1} & x_{n2} & ... & x_{np} \end{bmatrix} \qquad Y = \begin{bmatrix} y1 \\ y2 \\ . \\ . \\ . \\ y_n \end{bmatrix}$$

3.2.3 Change Operators

To better explore the search space, the crossover and mutation operators are defined. For crossover, we use a single, random, cut-point crossover. It starts by selecting and splitting at random two parent solutions. Then crossover creates two child solutions by putting, for the first child, the first part of the first parent with the second part of the second parent, and, for the second child, the first part of the second parent with the second part of the first parent. This operator must ensure that the length limits are respected by eliminating randomly some refactoring operations. Each child combines some of the refactoring operations of the first parent with some ones of the second one. In any given generation, each solution will be the parent in at most one crossover operation. The mutation operator picks randomly one or more operations from a sequence and replaces them by other ones from the initial list of possible refactorings. After applying genetic operators (mutation and crossover), we verify the feasibility of the generated sequence of refactoring by checking the pre and post conditions. Each refactoring operation that is not feasible due to unsatisfied preconditions will be removed from the generated refactoring sequence.

4   Validation

4.1   Research Questions

In our study, we assess the performance of our refactoring approach by finding out whether it could generate meaningful sequences of refactorings that fix design defects while reducing the number of code changes, preserving the semantic coherence of the design, and reusing as much as possible a base of recorded refactoring operations applied in the past in similar contexts. Our study aims at addressing the research questions outlined below.

RQ1: To what extent can the proposed approach improve the design quality and propose efficient refactoring solutions?

RQ2: How does the proposed approach perform compared to other existing search-based refactoring approaches and other search algorithms?

RQ3: How does the proposed approach perform comparing to existing approaches not based on heuristic search?

To answer **RQ1**, we use two different validation methods: manual validation and automatic validation to evaluate the efficiency of the proposed refactorings. For the manual validation, we asked groups of potential users of our refactoring tool to evaluate, manually, whether the suggested refactorings are feasible and efficient. We define the metric "refactoring efficiency" (RE) which corresponds to the number of meaningful refactoring operations over the total number of suggested refactoring operations. For the automatic validation we compare the proposed refactorings with the expected ones using an existing benchmark [22, 23, 4]. In terms of recall and precision. The expected refactorings are those applied by the software development team to the next software release. To collect these expected refactorings, we use Ref-Finder [13], an Eclipse plug-in designed to detect refactorings between two program versions. Ref-Finder allows us to detect the list of refactorings applied to the current version we use in our experiments to suggest refactorings to obtain the next software version.

To answer **RQ2**, we compare our approach to two other existing search-based refactoring approaches: Kessentini et al. [14] and Harman et al. [19] that consider the refactoring suggestion task using fitness function as a combination of quality metrics (single objective). We also assessed the performance of our proposal with the IGA technique proposed by Ghannem et al. [5] where the developer evaluates all the solutions manually.

To answer **RQ3**, we compared our refactoring results with a popular design defects detection and correction tool JDeodorant [18] that do not use heuristic search techniques in terms precision, recall and RE. The current version of JDeodorant is implemented as an Eclipse plug-in that identifies some types of design defects using quality metrics and then proposes a list of refactoring strategies to fix them.

4.2   Experimental Settings

The goal of the study is to evaluate the usefulness and the effectiveness of our refactoring tool in practice. We conducted a non-subjective evaluation with potential developers who can use our refactoring tool. Our study involved a total number of 16 subjects. All the subjects are volunteers and familiar with Java development. The experience of these subjects on Java programming ranged from 2 to 15 years including two undergraduate students, four master students, six PhD students, one faculty member, and three junior software developers. Subjects were very familiar with the practice of refactoring.

We used a set of well-known and well-commented open-source Java projects. We applied our approach to six open-source Java projects: Xerces-J, JFreeChart, GanttProject, AntApache, JHotDraw, and Rhino. Xerces-J is a family of software packages for parsing XML. JFreeChart is a powerful and flexible Java library for generating charts. GanttProject is a cross-platform tool for project scheduling. AntApache is a build tool and library specifically conceived for Java applications. JHotDraw is a GUI framework for drawing editors. Finally, Rhino is a JavaScript interpreter and compiler written in Java and developed for the Mozilla/Firefox browser. We selected these systems for our validation because they range from medium to large-sized open-source projects, which have been actively developed over the past 10 years, and their design has not been responsible for a slowdown of their developments. Table 1 provides some descriptive statistics about these six programs.

Table 1. Studied systems

Systems	Release	# classes	KLOC
Xerces-J	v2.7.0	991	240
JFreeChart	v1.0.9	521	170
GanttProject	v1.10.2	245	41
AntApache	v1.8.2	1191	255
JHotDraw	v6.1	585	21
Rhino	v1.7R1	305	42

To collect the expected refactorings applied to next version of studied systems, we use Ref-Finder [13]. Ref-Finder, implemented as an Eclipse plug-in, can identify refactoring operations applied between two releases of a software system. Table 2 shows the analyzed versions and the number of refactoring operations, identified by Ref-Finder, between each subsequent couple of analyzed versions, after the manual validation.

Table 2. Expected refactorings collected using Ref-Finder

Systems	Expected refactorings	
	Next release	# Refactorings
Xerces-J	v2.8.1	39
JFreeChart	v1.0.11	31
GanttProject	v1.11.2	46
AntApache	v1.8.4	78
JHotDraw	v6.2	27
Rhino	1.7R4	46

In our experiments, we use and compare different refactoring techniques. For each algorithm, to generate an initial population, we start by defining the maximum vector length (maximum number of operations per solution). The vector length is proportional to the number of refactorings that are considered and the size of the program to be refactored. During the creation, the solutions have random sizes inside the allowed range. For all algorithms, we fixed the maximum vector length to 150 refactorings,. We consider a list of 11 possible refactorings to restructure the design of the original program. Table 3 presents the parameter setting used in our experiments.

Table 3. Parameter setting

Parameter	Our approach	Ghannem	Harman et al.	Kessentini et al.
Population size	50	50	50	50
Termination criterion	10000	10000	10000	10000
Crossover probability	0.8	0.8	0.8	0.8
Mutation probability	0.2	0.2	0.2	0.2
Individual size	150	150	150	150
Number of interactions	35	90	N/A	N/A
Interaction sample size	4	4	N/A	N/A

Our approach, like the others search-based approaches (Harman et al., Ghannem et al. and Kessentini et al.), is stochastic by nature, i.e., two different executions of the same algorithm with the same parameters on the same systems generally leads to different sets of suggested refactorings. To confirm the validity of the results, we executed each of the three algorithm 31 times and tested statistically the differences in terms of precision, recall, and RE. To compare two algorithms based on these metrics, we record the obtained metric's values for both algorithms over 51 runs. After that, we compute the metric's median value for each algorithm. Besides, we execute the Wilcoxon test with a 99% confidence level ($\alpha = 0.01$) on the recorded metric's values using the Wilcoxon MATLAB routine. If the returned p-value is less than 0.01 than, we reject H0 and we can state that one algorithm outperforms the other, otherwise we cannot say anything in terms of performance difference between the two algorithms. In table 4, we have performed multiple pairwise comparisons using the Wilcoxon test. Thus, we have to adjust the p-values. To achieve this task, we used Holm method which is reported to be more accurate than the Bonferroni one [1].

Table 4. Multiple pairwise comparisons using the Wilcoxon test

	ILGA	Kessentini et al.	Harman et al.	Ghannem et al.
Xerces-J	0.00341 (Kessentini) 0.00072 (Harman) 0.00491 (Ghannem) 0.00327 (JDeodorant)	0.00030 (Harman) 0.00283 (Ghannem) 0.00352 (JDeodorant)	0.00163 (Ghannem) 0.00039 (JDeodorant)	0.00324 (JDeodorant)
JFreeChart	0.00602 (Kessentini) 0.00521 (Harman) 0.00746 (Ghannem) 0.00364 (JDeodorant)	0.00063 (Harman) 0.00392 (Ghannem) 0.00162 (JDeodorant)	0.00149 (Ghannem) 0.00062 (JDeodorant)	0.00422 (JDeodorant)
GanttProject	0.00453 (Kessentini) 0.00136 (Harman) 0.00947 (Ghannem) 0.00243 (JDeodorant)	0.00172 (Harman) 0.00042 (Ghannem) 0.00152 (JDeodorant)	0.00139 (Ghannem) 0.00372 (JDeodorant)	0.00892 (JDeodorant)
AntApache	0.00361(Kessentini) 0.00141Harman) 0.00275 (Ghannem) 0.00561 (JDeodorant)	0.00384(Harman) 0.00029 (Ghannem) 0.00186 (JDeodorant)	0.00286 (Ghannem) 0.00158 (JDeodorant)	0.00672 (JDeodorant)
JHotDraw	0.00368(Kessentini) 0.00272 (Harman) 0.00571 (Ghannem) 0.00372 (JDeodorant)	0.00054 (Harman) 0.00132 (Ghannem) 0.00293 (JDeodorant)	0.00281 (Ghannem) 0.00427 (JDeodorant)	0.00427 (JDeodorant)
Rhino	0.00623 (Kessentini) 0.00105(Harman) 0.00041 (Ghannem) 0.00254(JDeodorant)	0.00052 (Harman) 0.00182 (Ghannem) 0.00037 (JDeodorant)	0.00274 (Ghannem) 0.00081(JDeodorant)	0.00358 (JDeodorant)

As interesting observation from the results that will be detailed in the next section is that the medians are close, the results are statistically different but the effect size which quantifies the difference is small for most of the systems and techniques considered in our experiments.

4.3   Results and Discussions

Results for RQ1: To answer RQ1, we need to assess the correctness/meaningfulness of the suggested refactorings from developers' stand point. We reported the results of our empirical evaluation in Figure 2. We found that the majority of the suggested refactorings, with an average of more than 85% of RE, are considered by potential users as feasible, efficient in terms of improving the quality of the design and make sense.

In addition to the empirical evaluation performed manually by developers to evaluate the suggested refactorings, we automatically evaluate our approach without using the feedback of potential users to give more quantitative evaluation to answer RQ1. Thus, we compare the proposed refactorings with the expected ones. The expected refactorings are those applied by the software development team to the next software release as described in Table 2. We use Ref-Finder to identify refactoring operations that are applied between the program version under analysis and the next version. Figures 3 and 4 summarizes our results. We found that a considerable number of proposed refactorings (an average of more than 80% for all studied systems in terms of recall) are already applied to the next version by software development team which is considered as a good recommendation score, especially that not all refactorings applied to next version are related to quality improvement, but also to add new functionalities, increase security, fix bugs, etc.

To conclude, we found that our approach produces good refactoring based on potential users of our refactoring tool and expected refactorings applied to the next program version.

Results for RQ2: To answer RQ2, we evaluate the efficiency of our approach comparing to three existing search-based refactoring contributions Harman et al. [19] Kessentini et al. [14] and Ghannem et al. [5]. In [19], Harman et al. proposed a multi-objective approach that uses two quality metrics to improve (coupling between objects CBO, and standard deviation of methods per class SDMPC) after applying the refactorings sequence. In [14], a single-objective genetic algorithm is used to correct defects by finding the best refactoring sequence that reduces the number of defects. In [5], Ghannem et al. proposed an interactive Genetic Algorithm (IGA) for software refactoring where the user manually evaluates the suggested solutions by the GA. The comparison is performed through three metrics of Precision, Recall and RE. Figures 2, 3 and 4 summarize our findings and report the median values of each of our evaluation metrics obtained for 31 simulation runs of all projects.

We found that a considerable number of proposed refactorings (an average of 80% for all studied systems in terms of precision and recall) are already applied to the next version by software development team comparing to other existing approaches having only 65% and 74% for respectively Harman et al. and Kessentini et al. The precision and recall scores of the interactive approach proposed by Ghannem et al. are very similar to our approach (ILGA). However, our proposal requires much less effort and interactions with the designer to evaluate the solutions since the ANN replace the DM after a number of iterations/interactions. The same observations are also valid for RE where developers evaluated manually the best refactoring suggestions on all systems as described in Figure 2.

Results for RQ3: JDeodorant uses only structural information/improvements to suggest refactorings. Figures 2, 3 and 4 summarize our finding. It is clear that our proposal outperforms JDeodorant, in average, on all the systems in terms of RE, precision and recall. This is can be explained by the fact that JDeodorant use only structural metrics to evaluate the impact of suggested and do consider the designer preferences and the programming context.

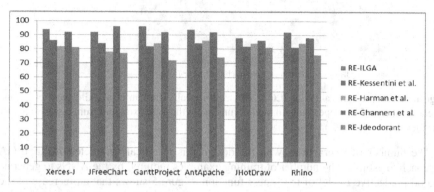

Fig. 2. RE median values of ILGA, Kessentini et al., Harman et al., Ghannem et al. and JDeodorant over 31 independent simulation runs using the Wilcoxon rank sum test with a 99% confidence level ($\alpha < 1\%$)

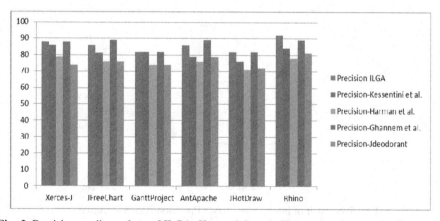

Fig. 3. Precision median values of ILGA, Kessentini et al., Harman et al., Ghannem et al. and JDeodorant over 31 independent simulation runs using the Wilcoxon rank sum test with a 99% confidence level ($\alpha < 1\%$)

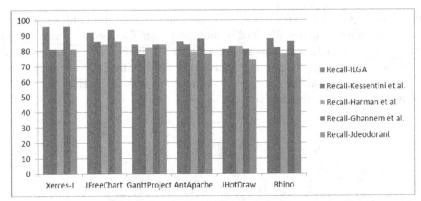

Fig. 4. Recall median values of ILGA, Kessentini et al., Harman et al., Ghannem et al. and JDeodorant over 31 independent simulation runs using the Wilcoxon rank sum test with a 99% confidence level ($\alpha < 1\%$)

The number of interactions with the designer is a critical parameter of our ILGA approach to estimate the number of training examples required by the ANNs to generate a good predictive model of the fitness function. Figure 5 shows that an increase of the number of interactions improve the quality of the results on Xerces however after around 35 interactions (iterations) the precison and recall scores become stable. At each iteration, the designer evaluates 4 refactoring solutions. Thus, we defined the number of interactions emprically in our experiments based on this observation.

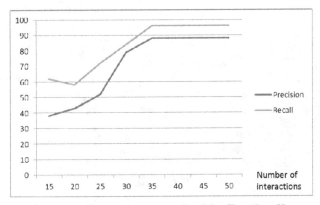

Fig. 5. Number of interactions versus Precision/Recall on Xerces

Usually in the optimization research field, the most time consuming operation is the evaluation step. Thus, we show how our ILGA algorithm is more efficient than existing search-based approaches from a CPU time (Computational Time) viewpoint. In fact, all the algorithms under comparison were executed on machines with Intel Xeon 3 GHz processors and 8 GB RAM. Figure 6 illustrates the obtained average CPU times of all algorithms on the systems. We note that the results presented in this figure were analyzed by using the same previously described statistical analysis methodology. In fact, based on the obtained p-values regarding CPU times, the ILGA is demonstrated to be faster than the remaining techniques as highlighted through

figure 6. The ILGA spends approximately the half amount of time required for IGA proposed by Ghannem et al. This observation could be explained by the fact that IGA requires a high number of interactions with the designer to evaluate the solutions which is a time consuming task. We can see that the use of an ANN to generate a surrogate fitness function seems to be an interesting approach to tackle software engineering problems where the individual evaluations are expensive like the case of software refactoring.

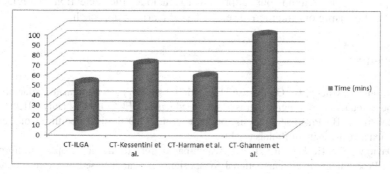

Fig. 6. Execution time

4.4   Threats to Validity

In our experiments, construct validity threats are related to the absence of similar work that uses interactive search-based learning techniques for software refactoring. For that reason we compare our proposal with several other refactoring techniques. Another construct threat can be related to the corpus of manually applied refactorings since developers do not all agree if a candidate is a code smell or not. We will ask some new experts to extend the existing corpus and provide additional feedback regarding the suggested refactorings. In addition, the parameter tuning of the different algorithms can be another threat related to our experiments that should be addressed in the future by further experiments with different parameters.

We take into consideration the internal threats to validity in the use of stochastic algorithms since our experimental study is performed based on 31 independent simulation runs for each problem instance and the obtained results are statistically analyzed by using the Wilcoxon rank sum test [15] with a 95% confidence level ($\alpha = 5\%$). However, the parameter tuning of the different optimization algorithms used in our experiments creates another internal threat that we need to evaluate in our future work.

External validity refers to the generalizability of our findings. In this study, we performed our experiments on seven different widely-used open-source systems belonging to different domains and with different sizes. However, we cannot assert that our results can be generalized to industrial applications, other programming languages, and to other practitioners. Future replications of this study are necessary to confirm the generalizability of our findings.

5   Conclusion

This paper presented a novel interactive search-based learning refactoring approach that does not require the definition of a fitness function. The developer is asked to evaluate manually refactoring solutions suggested by a Genetic Algorithm (GA) for few iterations then these examples are used as a training set for the ANNs to evaluate the solutions of the GA in the next iterations. We evaluated our approach on open-source systems. We report the results on the efficiency and effectiveness of our approach, compared to existing approaches.

In future work, we are planning to investigate an empirical study to consider additional systems and larger set of refactoring operations in our experiments. We are also planning to extend our approach to include the detection of refactoring opportunities using our interactive search-based learning approach.

References

1. Jensen, A., Cheng, B.: On the use of genetic programming for automated refactoring and the introduction of design patterns. In: Proceedings of GECCO. ACM (July 2010)
2. Roberts, D.B.: Practical Analysis for Refactoring. PhD thesis, Department of Computer Science, University of Illinois (1999)
3. Qayum., F., Heckel, R.: Local search-based refactoring as graph transformation. In: Proceedings of 1st International Symposium on Search Based Software Engineering, pp. 43–46 (2009)
4. Palomba, F., Bavota, G., Penta, M.D., Oliveto, R., Lucia, A.D., Poshyvanyk, D.: Detecting bad smells in source code using change history information. In: ASE, pp. 268–278 (2013)
5. Ghannem, A., El Boussaidi, G., Kessentini, M.: Model refactoring using interactive genetic algorithm. In: Ruhe, G., Zhang, Y. (eds.) SSBSE 2013. LNCS, vol. 8084, pp. 96–110. Springer, Heidelberg (2013)
6. Kilic, H., Koc, E., Cereci, I.: Search-based parallel refactoring using population-based direct approaches. In: Cohen, M.B., Ó Cinnéide, M. (eds.) SSBSE 2011. LNCS, vol. 6956, pp. 271–272. Springer, Heidelberg (2011)
7. Harman, M., Clark, J.A.: Metrics are fitness functions too. In: Proc. of the IEEE International Symposium on Software Metrics, pp. 58–69 (2004)
8. Harman, M., Mansouri, S.A., Zhang, Y.: Search-based software engineering: Trends, techniques and applications. ACM Computing Surveys 45(1), 11 (2012)
9. Harman, M.: The Relationship between search based software engineering and predictive modeling. In: Proc. of the International Conference on Predictive Models in Software Engineering, pp. 1–13 (2013)
10. Hecht-Nielsen, R.: Neurocomputing. Addison- Wesley, CA (1990) ISBN 0201093553
11. Idri, A., Khoshgoftaar, T.M., Abran, A.: Can neural networks be easily interpreted in software cost estimation. In: Proc. of the IEEE International Conference on Fuzzy Systems, pp. 1162–1167 (2002)
12. Jayalakshmi, T., Santhakumaran, A.: Statistical normalization and back propagation for classification. International Journal of Computer Theory and Engineering 3(1), 1793–8201 (2011)
13. Prete, K., Rachatasumrit, N., Sudan, N., Kim, M.: Template-based reconstruction of complex refactorings. In: Proceedings of the ICSM 2010, pp. 1–10 (2010)
14. Kessentini, M., Kessentini, W., Sahraoui, H., Boukadoum, M., Ouni, A.: Design defects detection and correction by example. In: Proc. of the IEEE International Conference on Program Comprehension, pp. 81–90 (2011)
15. Kruskal, W.H., Wallis, W.A.: Use of ranks in one-criterion variance analysis. Journal of the American Statistical Association 47(260), 583–621 (1952)

16. Erlikh, L.: Leveraging legacy system dollars for e-business. IT Professional 02(3), 17–23 (2000)
17. Lars, W., Yaochu, J.: Comparing neural networks and kriging for fitness approximation in evolutionary optimization. In: Proc. of the IEEE Congress on Evolutionary Computation, pp. 663–670 (2003)
18. Fokaefs, M., Tsantalis, N., Stroulia, E., Chatzigeorgiou, A.: JDeodorant: identification and application of extract class refactorings. In: International Conference on Software Engineering (ICSE), pp. 1037–1039 (2011)
19. Harman, M., Tratt, L.: Pareto optimal search based refactoring at the design level. In: Proceedings of the Genetic and Evolutionary Computation Conference (GECCO 2007), pp. 1106–1113 (2007)
20. Ó Cinnéide, M., Tratt, L., Harman, M., Counsell, S., Moghadam, I.H.: Experimental Assessment of Software Metrics Using Automated Refactoring. In: Proc. Empirical Software Engineering and Management (ESEM), pp. 49–58 (September 2012)
21. O'Keeffe, M., Cinnéide, M.O.: Search-based Refactoring for Software Maintenance. J. of Systems and Software 81(4), 502–516
22. Mkaouer, W., Kessentini, M., Bechikh, S., Deb, K.: High dimensional search-based software engineering: Finding tradeoffs among 15 objectives for automating software refactoring using NSGA-III. In: Proc. of the Genetic and Evolutionary Computation Conference (accepted, 2014)
23. Moha, N., Guéhéneuc, Y.-G., Duchien, L., Meur, A.-F.L.: DECOR: A method for the specification and detection of code and design smells. IEEE Trans. Softw. Eng. 36, 20–36 (2009)
24. Seng, O., Stammel, J., Burkhart, D.: Search-based determination of refactorings for improving the class structure of object-oriented systems. In: Proceedings of the Genetic and Evolutionary Computation Conference (GECCO 2006), pp. 1909–1916 (2006)
25. Ouni, A., Kessentini, M., Sahraoui, H., Hamdi, M.S.: The use of development history in software refactoring using a multi-objective. In: Proc. the Genetic and Evolutionary Computation Conference, pp. 1461–1468 (2013)
26. Shukla, K.K.: Neuro-genetic prediction of software development effort. Information and Software Technology 42(10), 701–713 (2000)
27. Sibo Yang, T.O.T., Man, K.L., Guan, S.U.: Investigation of neural networks for function approximation. In: Proc. of the International Conference on Information Technology and Quantitative Management, pp. 586–594 (2013)
28. Mens, T., Tourwé, T.: A Survey of Software Refactoring. IEEE Trans. Software Eng. 30(2), 126–139 (2004)
29. Opdyke, W.F.: Refactoring: A Program Restructuring Aid in Designing Object-Oriented Application Frameworks, Ph.D. thesis, University of Illinois at Urbana-Champaign (1992)
30. Zhang, D.: Machine Learning and software engineering. In: Proc. of the International Conference on Tools with Artificial Intelligence, pp. 87–119 (2002)
31. Simons, C.L., Parmee, I.C., Gwynllyw, R.: Interactive, Evolutionary Search in Upstream Object-Oriented Class Design. IEEE Trans. Software Eng. 36(6), 798–816 (2010)
32. Holm, S.: A simple sequentially rejective multiple test procedure. Scandinavian Journal of Statistics 6, 65–70 (1979)

Producing Just Enough Documentation: The Next SAD Version Problem

J. Andres Diaz-Pace, Matias Nicoletti, Silvia Schiaffino, and Santiago Vidal

ISISTAN Research Institute, CONICET-UNICEN, Campus Universitario, Paraje
Arroyo Seco (B7001BBO) Tandil, Buenos Aires, Argentina
{adiaz,mnicolet,sschia,svidal}@exa.unicen.edu.ar

Abstract. Software architecture knowledge is an important asset in today's projects, as it serves to share the main design decisions among the
project stakeholders. Architectural knowledge is commonly captured by
the Software Architecture Document (SAD), an artifact that is useful
but can also be costly to produce and maintain. In practice, the SAD
often fails to fulfill its mission of addressing the stakeholders' information needs, due to factors such as: detailed or high-level contents that
do not consider all stakeholders, outdated documentation, or documentation generated late in the lifecycle, among others. To alleviate this
problem, we propose a documentation strategy that seeks to balance the
stakeholders' interests in the SAD against the efforts of producing it.
Our strategy is cast as an optimization problem called "the next SAD
version problem" (NSVP) and several search-based techniques for it are
discussed. A preliminary evaluation of our approach has shown its potential for exploring cost-benefit tradeoffs in documentation production.

Keywords: architecture documentation model, stakeholders, information needs, combinatorial optimization, search-based techniques.

1 Introduction

As software systems grow large and complex, the reliance on some form of documentation becomes a necessity in many projects [1]. Since producing documentation does not come without cost, software engineers must carefully consider how
this process plays out in the development lifecycle (e.g., artifacts, techniques,
tools), and furthermore, identify the goals of the project stakeholders. In particular, a useful model for describing the high-level structure of a system is the
software architecture [2], which is the main domain explored in this work. The
architecture is typically captured by the so-called *Software Architecture Document (or SAD)*, as an information repository that enables knowledge sharing
among the architecture stakeholders [3]. The SAD is structured into sections that
contain text and design diagrams, known as *architectural views*, which permit to
reason about the architectural solution from different perspectives.

Documenting an architecture with multiple stakeholders poses challenges for
the SAD. A first challenge is that the SAD contents target readers that might

C. Le Goues and S. Yoo (Eds.): SSBSE 2014, LNCS 8636, pp. 46–60, 2014.

have different backgrounds and information needs [4]. For example, project managers are mainly interested in high-level module views and allocation views, whereas developers need extensive information about module views and behavioral views. Many times, the SAD is loaded with development-oriented contents that only consider a few (internal) stakeholders. In practice, the documentation usefulness decreases as more information is added, because finding relevant information in a large set of documents becomes difficult [1]. A second challenge is the effort necessary for creating (and updating) the SAD, an expenditure that developers and managers do not wish to bear, mainly because of budget constraints, tight schedules, or pressures on developing user-visible features. As a result, the architecture knowledge ends up informally captured. Besides the stakeholders' dissatisfaction, the problem of ineffective documentation brings hidden costs such as: knowledge vaporization, re-work, and poor quality [5].

Recently, some works have investigated the practices and value of architecture documentation [6]. In this context, we argue that the SAD should be produced in incremental versions and concurrently with the design work. Thus, the main question becomes: how much documentation is good enough for the next SAD release? Answering this question involves a tradeoff between documenting those aspects being useful to the stakeholders and keeping the documentation efforts low. To deal with this tradeoff, we previously proposed [7] an optimization tool that, for a given SAD version, is able to assist the documenter in choosing a set of SAD updates that brings high value for the stakeholders. The tool is based on the Views & Beyond (V&B) method [8,3], which explicitly links the candidate architectural views for the SAD to the needs of its stakeholders. The optimization was treated as a knapsack problem that maximizes the stakeholders' utility without exceeding a cost constraint. Yet, considering that documentation is more a business decision than a technical one, we believe that alternative optimizations can be required, depending on cost-benefit concerns of the project.

In this work, we provide a general formulation of the SAD documentation strategy and its associated optimization problem(s), that we call the Next SAD Version Problem (NSVP), by analogy with the well-known Next Release Problem (NRP) [9,10]. As its main contribution, our proposal considers two variants for NSVP: a single-objective cost minimization and a bi-objective optimization (cost versus utility), in addition to the single-objective utility maximization of [7]. We also investigate different satisfaction functions for stakeholders. The experimental results, although preliminary, show that the NSVP optimization approach helps to explore alternative documentation strategies with reduced costs.

The article is organized as follows. Section 2 provides background about architecture documentation. Section 3 formally defines the NSVP as an optimization problem. Section 4 discusses exact and heuristic algorithms for NSVP. Section 5 reports on an empirical evaluation with a SAD case-study. Section 6 discusses related work. Finally, Section 7 gives the conclusions and future work.

2   Background

The software architecture is the set of structures needed to reason about a computing system, comprising software elements, their relations, and properties of both [2]. Design decisions are part of the architecture, as they record the rationale behind the architects' solution [11]. An example of decisions is the use of certain patterns, such as layers or client-server, to meet stakeholders' goals, such as modifiability or performance qualities, among others. Thus, the architecture acts as a blueprint in which the main stakeholders' concerns can be discussed. By *stakeholder* [12], we mean any person, group or organization that is interested in or affected by the architecture (e.g., managers, architects, developers, testers, end-users, contractors, auditors). In order to share the architecture knowledge among the stakeholders, it must be adequately documented and communicated. The SAD is the usual "knowledge radiator" and can take a variety of formats, for instance: Word documents, UML diagrams, or Web pages in a Wiki [13,14].

The notion of *architectural views* is key in the organization of architectural documentation, and it is part of most current documentation methods [3]. A view presents an aspect or viewpoint of the system (e.g., static aspects, runtime aspects, allocation hardware, etc.). Typical views include: module views (the units of implementation and their dependencies), component-and-connector views (the elements having runtime presence and their interactions), or allocation views (the mappings of software elements to hardware). In addition, these views include text describing the design elements and decisions that pertain to the views. Therefore, we can see a SAD as a collection of documents with textual and graphical contents. Figure 1 shows a snapshot of a Wiki-based SAD[1], in which their documents (Wiki pages) adhere to the V&B templates[2].

In architecture-centric projects, the SAD usually emerges as a by-product of the architects' design work. The stakeholders (both internal and external ones) are the main SAD consumers. Moreover, a SAD is useful as long as its contents satisfy the *stakeholders' information needs*. A good strategy to ensure this goal is to deliver the SAD in incremental versions along with the (iterative & incremental) development of the architecture itself [15,1]. In the documentation process, the documenter must decide what should be added (or updated) in a given SAD version. She is expected to follow the well-known rule: "write the SAD contents from the reader's perspective rather than from writer's" [3], but also consider the so-called TAGRI principle[3]: "They [the stakeholders] Ain't Gonna Read It", which advocates for documenting only what reflects true needs. To realize these ideas, a model of stakeholders' interests regarding the architectural contents of the SAD is needed. For instance, we can have a matrix of S stakeholders (or stakeholder roles) and D SAD documents (or view types), in which a cell indicates that stakeholder S_i is interested in the information of document D_j.

---

[1] SEI example:
   https://wiki.sei.cmu.edu/sad/index.php/The_Adventure_Builder_SAD
[2] V&B templates:
   http://www.sei.cmu.edu/downloads/sad/SAD_template_05Feb2006.dot
[3] Scott Ambler's website: http://www.agilemodeling.com/essays/tagri.htm

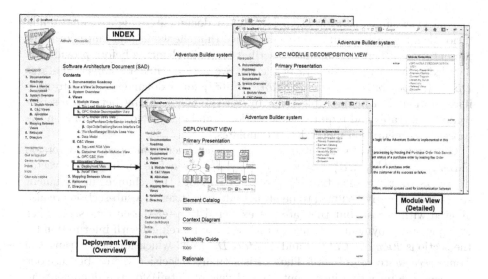

Fig. 1. Example of a Wiki-based SAD with architectural views of the V&B method

In fact, some documentation methods, and specifically V&B, provide guidance for generating the SAD contents according to such a model [8,16].

In an ideal situation, one would analyze the matrix and produce a SAD version addressing all stakeholders' interests. Unfortunately, this is seldom the case in practice, either because the documentation resources are scarce or because of conflicts between stakeholders' interests. Empirical studies [17] have shown that individual stakeholder's concerns are met by a SAD fraction (less than 25%), but for each stakeholder a different (sometimes overlapping) fraction is needed. Therefore, determining the "delta" of SAD contents that brings most utility (or benefit) to the stakeholders as a whole is not a straightforward decision.

3   The Next SAD Version Problem (NSVP)

We see the SAD as an artifact that contains n documents, each one associated to a predefined view template[4]. In this work, we assume the usage of the V&B views and templates, although other view-centric methods are equally possible. Let $SAD_t = <d_1^t, ..., d_n^t>$ be a SAD version at time t, in which each vector position corresponds to a document and d_k ($1 \leq k \leq n$) is its level of detail (at time t). We assume a discretization of the possible completion states of a document k, based on the sub-sections prescribed by the V&B templates. Figure 2 depicts how a view document of V&B can be filled with new contents over time. This should not be interpreted as a strict documentation progression for the documenter, but rather as a guideline based on the relative importance of the sub-sections

---

[4] Admittedly, other documents with no architectural views are usually part of a SAD (e.g., system context, main stakeholders, architectural drivers, or glossary). These documents are out of the current NSVP scope, but still considered in our evaluation.

for the view under consideration [8] (e.g., a documenter might begin adding rationale information, but it is recommended that she works first on the primary presentation of her solution and describes its main elements before providing a detailed solution rationale). In particular, we here assume 4 completion states $DS = \{empty, overview, someDetail, detailed\}$ for a document, so as to keep its evolution at a manageable level. In general, the mapping between discrete completion states and required view sections can be adjusted, depending on the chosen documentation method and templates.

Given a partially-documented SAD_t, let us consider an arbitrary next version $SAD_{t+1} =< d_1^{t+1}, ..., d_n^{t+1} >$ with $d_i^{t+1} \geq d_i^t$. We define an increment vector $\Delta =< x_1, ..., x_n >$ such that $d_i^t + x_i = d_i^{t+1}$. Note that changes in document states are currently assumed to be always additive (fixes to a sub-section are also allowed with a cost, but they are not expected to alter the current state). For example, a deployment view like in Figure 1 can be refined with information for the sections *Element Catalog* and *Context Diagram*, which implies a transition from *overview* to *someDetail*. Thus, Δ is actually a decision vector, because one can choose alternative increments (i.e., levels of detail) for the documents in order to fulfill objectives related to stakeholders' satisfaction and cost.

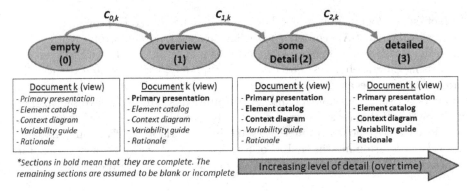

Fig. 2. Evolution of the contents of a document (based on *View* template of V&B)

The cost of a document state change $d_k \rightarrowtail d_k'$ is assumed to be a fixed quantity. Then, we have a cost vector $C_\Delta =< c_1, ..., c_n >$ with $c_k = cost(d_k, d_k')$, and the total cost of an increment Δ, denoted by $Cost(\Delta)$, is the sum of the individual costs of changing document. If $d_k = d_k'$, a zero cost is assigned, unless fixes were applied to the document (without altering its completion level). We refer to $Cost(\Delta)$ as the *production cost* for the next SAD version.

The expected utility of an increment Δ is a function of the vectors SAD_t and SAD_{t+1}, but it also depends on the stakeholders' preferences on those two state vectors. Similarly to the cost formulation, we assume a benefit vector $B_\Delta =< b_1, ..., b_n >$ with $b_k = benefit(d_k, d_k', satisfaction_k(S))$ in the range $[0, 1]$ (0 means no utility, and 1 means high utility). Given a set of m stakeholders $S = \{S_1, ..., S_m\}$, $satisfaction_k(S)$ captures the combined preferences of all stakeholders on the document state transition $d_k \rightarrowtail d_k'$. For example, stakeholder X might prefer a deployment view D in *overview*, while stakeholder Y

might instead prefer the same document in *detailed*. In other words, b_k is the "happiness" of the stakeholders group with an increased detail in document k, and $Benefit(\Delta)$ is computed as the sum of the utilities through all documents. $Benefit(\Delta)$ is a measure of the *stakeholders' utility* with the next SAD version.

The NSVP consists of *choosing an increment Δ for a SAD_t such that both $Cost(\Delta)$ and $Benefit(\Delta)$ are optimized*. Specifically, 3 variants are possible: (i) NSVP-B, in which $Benefit(\Delta)$ is maximized with $Cost(\Delta)$ lower than a threshold C; (ii) NSVP-C, in which $Cost(\Delta)$ is minimized with $Benefit(\Delta)$ above a threshold B; or (iii) NSVP-BC, in which $Benefit(\Delta)$ is maximized while $Cost(\Delta)$ is minimized. The first two variants are constrained, mono-objective optimizations, whereas the third variant is a bi-objective optimization. In the latter, we are interested in the *non-dominated solutions* of the benefit-cost space.

3.1 Determining Production Costs

The production cost of the next SAD version is $Cost(\Delta) = \sum_{k=1}^{n} cost(x_k) = \sum_{k=1}^{n} cost(d_k^t, d_k^{t+1})$. In our 4-state model the detail level of a document increases according to the sequence $empty\,(0) \rightarrow overview\,(1) \rightarrow someDetail\,(2) \rightarrow detailed\,(3)$. Thus, we assume an "atomic" cost associated to each transition in the sequence (see Figure 2). An atomic cost $c_{i,k}$ denotes the (documenter's) effort of updating document k with current detail i to its next consecutive level $i+1$. For a transition between not-consecutive states, we use a "composite" cost equal to the sum of the atomic costs across the transition.

Certainly, estimating the costs of writing SAD sections is a subjective activity. One proxy for estimating such costs is the number of words. For instance, if a document has 1000 words and is considered to have a 100% of completeness, its atomic costs can be $c_0 = c_1 = c_2 \simeq 333$. This estimation is crude, since costs are affected by the document type (e.g., architectural view, template used, typical amount of text required, or need of design diagrams). In practice, the final length of a SAD document can be unknown. Nonetheless, it is possible for the documenter to provide ballpark estimates (often, in collaboration with the manager or experienced architects), based on: historical effort information, importance of certain views, or number of design decisions involved, among others.

3.2 Assessing Stakeholders' Utility

The benefit of the next SAD is given by $Benefit(\Delta) = \sum_{k=1}^{n} benefit(x_k) = \sum_{k=1}^{n} benefit(d_k^t, d_k^{t+1}, satisfaction_k(S))$. Computing $benefit(d_k, d_k'$, $satisfaction_k(S))$ for a document k requires the specification of: i) the satisfaction information $satisfaction_k(S)$, and ii) a procedure to combine individual satisfactions into one single value. For every SAD document, a stakeholder can prefer any state in $DS = \{empty, overview, someDetail, detailed\}$. Note here that *empty* is interpreted as the stakeholder being "not interested" in the document. This model of preferences is derived from the V&B method [8,3]. In order to translate preferences to satisfaction values, we introduce the notion of *satisfaction function*. We depart from the assumption that a stakeholder somehow knows her "perfect" level of detail for a document, based on her own information needs and the expected information to be conveyed by an architectural view. This knowledge is modeled by functions of the form $sf : DS \times DS \to [0,1]$, which depend on both the actual and preferred completion states of a document and also on the view type. Based on our experience with architectural documentation projects, we propose three candidate functions that can be assigned to stakeholders, as described in Figure 3. Anyway, other satisfaction functions that take into account the semantics of document changes are also possible.

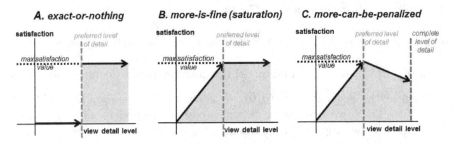

Fig. 3. Satisfaction functions for stakeholders' preferences on detail of documents

Document k (someDetail)	S_1	S_2	S_3	S_4	S_5
Preference	overview	detailed	detailed	someDetail	empty
function A →	0.00	0.00	0.00	1.00	0.00
function B →	1.00	0.75	0.75	1.00	1.00
function C →	0.33	0.75	0.75	1.00	0.00

Fig. 4. Example of converting stakeholder preferences to satisfaction values

Function A (exact-or-nothing) gives maximal satisfaction (1.0) when the current detail of the document matches exactly the stakeholder preference, and 0.0 satisfaction otherwise. Function B (more-is-fine) proportionally increases the satisfaction value as the current detail of the document gets closer to the stakeholder preference, and beyond that point the satisfaction gets the maximal value (1.0). This reflects the situation in which the stakeholder does not care having more detail than required. Function C (more-can-be-penalized) is a variant of Function B. It begins with a proportional increase until the document detail matches the stakeholder preference, but for higher detail than required the satisfaction value decreases slightly. This situation would happen when the stakeholder is overwhelmed by an excess of information. In all functions, we set $\varepsilon = 0.1$ as the "allowed difference" for a matching between a preference $pref_k$ and a document state d_k, that is, $pref_k \approx d_k \Rightarrow | pref_k - d_k | \leq \varepsilon$. Eliciting the right satisfaction function of a stakeholder is not trivial, and it is out of the scope of this work.

In the end, after applying this kind of satisfaction functions, we obtain a vector $satisfaction_k(S) = < s_k(S_1), ..., s(S_m) >$ with $s_k(S_i) \in [0, 1]$. Examples of satisfaction vectors computed with functions A, B, and C are shown in Figure 4. Note that two (or more) stakeholders might have competing preferences on the same document, which cannot be solved by means of the satisfaction functions (except perhaps when Function B is used). This tradeoff situation means that selecting a detail level for a document might satisfy some stakeholders but might just partially satisfy others. In our model, the aggregation of the stakeholder satisfaction is based on a weighted average schema. Specifically, we assign each stakeholder S_i a priority p_i in the range $[0, 10]$, where 0 is the lowest priority and 10 is the highest one. This priority can be defined by the role that the stakeholder plays in the project. Along this line, the average utility of all stakeholders with document k is $benefit(d_k , d'_k, satisfaction_k(S)) = (\sum_{i=1}^{m} u_k(S_i) * p_i) / \sum_{i=1}^{m} p_i$.

4   Exact and Heuristic Algorithms for NSVP

To solve NSVP instances (i.e., find a "good" SAD documentation strategy), discrete optimization techniques can be applied [18], based either on exact or heuristic algorithms. In our case, the number of SAD documents (N) is the main contributor to problem size, affecting the choice between exact or heuristic algorithms. Real-life SAD sizes have typically 15-40 documents, depending on how critical the architecture is for the system (and hence, its documentation). In this work, we explored 2 exact and 2 heuristic implementations, namely: i) Backtracking, ii) SAT4J [19], iii) Random Search, and iv) the NSGA-II algorithm [20]. The goal here was to assess their performance and optimality (of results) using synthetic data for SAD state vectors, costs, and stakeholders' preferences. The goodness (or score) of a solution is tied to the NSVP variant, namely: highest benefit (NSVP-B), lowest cost (NSVP-C), or non-dominated cost-benefit pairs (NSVP-BC). Figure 5 shows outputs of SAT4J, NSGA-II and RandomSearch for NSVP-BC. The points represent the Pareto front of pairs *(benefit, cost)*.

The 4 implementations are summarized next. First, *Backtracking* is a algorithm that progressively generates and evaluates all valid decision vectors Δ that derive from SAD_t. We used backtracking as a baseline for the SAT4J algorithm, knowing in advance that backtracking would have trouble with medium-to-large instances (e.g., SADs with $N \geq 20$). Second, *SAT4J* treats the document state representation as if it were a *0-1 Knapsack Problem* [7]. The tasks model the transitions between document states, like in Figure 2. With this representation, we took advantage of the state-of-the-art Pseudo-boolean (PB) solver of SAT4J [19]. The PB solver only deals with single-objective minimization subject to constraints (NSVP-C), but its adaptation to single-objective maximization

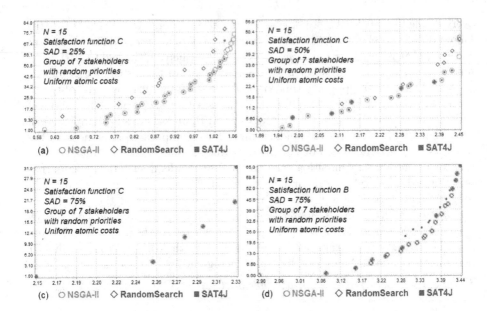

Fig. 5. Sample of Pareto fronts (cost versus benefit) using exact/heuristic algorithms

(NSVP-B) is straightforward. In NSVP-BC, we iterate over all possible costs, defining each one as a constraint and then invoking the solver with an NSVP-B instance. Non-dominated solutions are returned. This schema adds some overhead, but still capitalizes on the SAT4J performance.

Third, the *Random Search* implementation takes the current SAD_t and then randomly generates vectors Δ leading to SAD_{t+1}. It was built on top of an implementation provided by the MOEA framework[5], as a baseline for the NSGA-II algorithm. Despite the low execution times of Random Search for the 3 NSVP variants, the solutions are seldom optimal (see Figures 5a and 5b), and sometimes they even violate the cost (or benefit) constraints. Fourth, *NSGA-II* is a well-known genetic algorithm for multi-objective optimization [20]. Our implementation was based on the NSGA-II version of MOEA, and solves any of the NSVP variants. In short, NSGA-II uses an evolutionary process with operators such as selection, genetic crossover and genetic mutation, applied to the document state representation of NSVP. An initial population of vectors Δ is evolved through several generations.

For the sake of brevity, we focus our analysis on the NSVP-BC formulation. From Figure 5 (and other Pareto fronts, not included here), we observed that the percentage of SAD completion affects the number of non-dominated solutions: the higher the percentage the fewer the solutions. Also, the differences in solution quality (cost and benefit) for the 3 algorithms get smaller, as the completion percentage increases. A possible explanation for this trend is that the

---

[5] http://www.moeaframework.org/

optimization problem gets "easier" for SAD percentages greater than 70% (because the potential solution space to search for is small). Nonetheless, there were differences between the solutions of NSGA-II and Random Search for NSVP-BC, particularly for large SADs ($N \geq 30$), as NSGA-II produced Pareto fronts closer to the reference front of SAT4J. In addition, the SAD completion influenced the costs attainable by the NSVP-BC solutions, with wider cost fluctuations in the Pareto sets for SAD instances with completion lower than 30%. Along this line, we can say that the completion range 25-50% offers the best opportunities for the documenter to find diverse cost-benefit solutions.

Another interesting observation is how the satisfaction functions modulate the Pareto solutions. The choice of function B (more-is-fine) leads to more solutions than the other functions (see Figures 5c and 5d), because function B is more likely to accommodate many stakeholder preferences, even if the stakeholders have different priorities. Function A (exact-or-nothing) showed the opposite behavior, with a very "strict" preference satisfaction that generates a sort of competition among stakeholders, which ultimately leads to few solution alternatives.

A performance analysis of the SAT4J and NSGA-II showed that their scalability varies, as expected, depending on the SAD sizes. For example, Figure 6 presents execution times of the 3 algorithms for a range of N (15-40) and incremental SAD completions (25%, 50%, and 75%). Overall, NSGA-II came out as an efficient alternative for the 3 NSVP variants. On one hand, NSGA-II showed bound execution times, with a slight increase at $N \simeq 30$, independently of the SAD completion. This behavior can be attributed to the evolutionary process of the genetic algorithm. On the other hand, SAT4J performed well for small SADs ($N \leq 30$), with a fast response for SADs above 50%. Its execution times started to degrade beyond $N = 30$ but only for incomplete SADs (completion around 25%). Although more experiments are needed, this finding suggests that SAT4J is very competitive for NSVP instances involving small-to-medium SADs and medium-to-high completion levels. For a general setting (or future, more complex NSVPs), we conclude that NSGA-II should be the solver of choice.

N	SAT4J			NSGA-II			RandomSearch		
	SAD 25%	SAD 50%	SAD 75%	SAD 25%	SAD 50%	SAD 75%	SAD 25%	SAD 50%	SAD 75%
15	319	5	2	799	503	488	130	95	91
20	488	10	3	1184	704	636	175	125	128
25	2624	11	3	937	629	591	195	145	141
30	2995	23	3	990	693	677	203*	176*	169
35	19089	34	4	1415	909	743	302*	200*	183
40	50938	50	7	1307	881	835	283*	227*	218

Group of 7 stakeholders with random priorities - Uniform atomic costs
NSVP-B with C <= 50 (*) solutions with cost <=50 might (randomly) appear

Fig. 6. Performance (in ms.) of exact/heuristic algorithms for different SAD sizes

5   Case-Study

In addition to the experiments with synthetic data, we evaluated our approach on Wiki-based SADs being accessed by groups of (simulated) stakeholders. The main goal was to compare SAD increments produced by the SAT4J (or NSGA-II) algorithm against SAD versions generated in a usual manner (i.e., with no content optimization whatsoever). The objects of the study were incremental SAD versions, and we measured the cost of producing those increments as well as their benefit for predefined stakeholders. The subjects (stakeholders) were undergraduate students from a Software Architecture course taught at UNICEN University (Tandil, Argentina), with 2-4 years of developing experience. We organized these students into 11 groups of 7 members, each member playing a distinctive stakeholder role: 3 members took the architect role, whereas the other 4 members were divided into: 1 manager, 1 evaluator (responsible for design reviews) and 2 clients (e.g., representatives of external companies). Their priorities were as follows: $p_{manager} = 10$, $p_{architect} = 6$, $p_{client1} = 6$, $p_{evaluator} = 2$, $p_{client2} = 2$.

The architects (of each group) were asked to: i) design an architecture solution for a model problem called CTAS[6], and ii) use V&B to produce SADs (one per group) that should satisfy the concerns of the other roles of the group. The stakeholders' preferences were derived from the view-role matrix of [3]. Both the design and documentation work had to be done in 3 iterations of 3 weeks, with 2 (partial) SAD versions for the first 2 iterations and a final release after 9 weeks. The managers, clients, and evaluators periodically assessed the solution and documentation quality, and gave feedback to the architects. We refer to these documentation versions as *normal SADs*, because their production strategy was only based on architects' criteria (and not steered by optimization techniques).

Once all the groups were finished, we obtained 3 normal SAD versions (or slices) per group with the different completion percentages: 10-25% after the 1st iteration (slice 1), 40-60% after the 2nd iteration (slice 2), and 75-85% after the 3rd iteration (final SAD). The final SADs were not considered as 100% complete, because some sections were unfinished or lacked details. These percentages were estimated by counting the number of words and images per document (an image ≈ 200 words). The same metric was also used to estimate the cost of producing a SAD document, by considering a word as a unit of effort. We established the costs and utilities of the normal SAD slices as references for the optimization counterparts. Under a NSVP-BC formulation, we initially executed the optimization algorithms on slice 1 of every group (transition to slice 2). The same procedure was then repeated for slice 2 (transition to final SAD). We refer to the SAD versions produced by our algorithms as *optimized SADs*. Based on the Pareto fronts, we analyzed two situations: i) the best benefit reachable for each slice (and its corresponding cost), and ii) the cost for having the same benefit shown by the (next) normal slice.

---

[6] http://people.cs.clemson.edu/~johnmc/courses/cpsc875/resources/ Telematics.pdf

Figure 7 shows the evolution of the average values of costs and benefits across the normal SAD versions, and the vectors represent *what-if* optimization analyzes (for the 3 satisfaction functions). The Utility Evolution chart (left side) compares utility values of normal SADs against optimized SADs. For instance, at slice 2, *normal-Fa* (normal SAD for function A) reached a utility of 5.52, whereas *opt-optimal-Fa* (best solution of optimized SAD for function A) reached a utility of 6. The Cost Evolution chart (right side) compares the costs of producing normal SADs against: i) optimized SADs with maximum benefit, and ii) optimized SADs with the same benefit as normal SADs. For instance, at slice 2, the cost of having a normal SAD was 98, while the costs of *opt-optimal-Fa* and *opt-same-utility-normal-Fa* were 103 and 78 respectively. In *opt-optimal-Fa* we had a slightly higher cost than that of normal SADs but the utility was better. In *opt-same-utility-normal-Fa,* the optimization helped to reach a utility of 5.52 (*normal-Fa* at slice 2 in Utility Evolution chart) but with a lower effort.

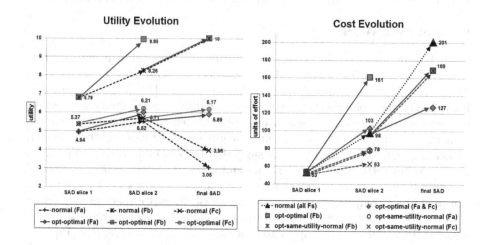

Fig. 7. Evolution of utility and cost over different SAD versions

From the results of Figure 7, we noticed that the optimized SADs achieved higher benefits for the 3 satisfactions functions, ranging between 9-20% of improvement for slice 2 and 55-93% for slice 3. Although, the costs to compute optimal solutions increased by 11%. However, for the same utility values of the normal SADs, we observed lower costs when applying optimization with savings of 44-78%. These savings mean that our algorithms produced smaller SADs with comparable utilities. Furthermore, it would suggest that the normal SADs had unnecessary contents for the stakeholder's needs.

We applied a Mann-Whitney-Wilcoxon (MWW) test to statistically validate results of this case-study. We tested the null hypothesis H_0 : *individual utility values of normal SADs are equal to those of optimized SADs,* for slice 2 and the final SAD. With a significance level of 0.05, we verified a significant difference between utility values in favor of optimized SADs, except for function C at slice 2 and function B at the final SAD. Nevertheless, in those cases the average utility values of optimized SADs were still higher. Furthermore, in order to get insights on why optimized SADs outperformed normal ones, we manually inspected a sample of manual SADs in terms of satisfaction values. We realized that documenters who produced normal SADs tended to satisfy all stakeholders alike. On the contrary, the optimized SADs clearly favored high-priority stakeholders. These observations also support our conjecture about the complexity of producing satisfying documentation for stakeholders with competing interests.

At last, the evaluation has some validity threats. First, the results of our case-study cannot be generalized, as we used students in an academic environment, which might differ from an industrial context with seasoned practitioners. However, many students were actually working for software companies. Second, our effort unit for SAD production costs (amount of words of documents) is a simplification, and a better estimation proxy should be applied in real scenarios.

6   Related Work

In the last decade, several methods for software architecture documentation have emerged, namely: *Kruchten's 4+1 View Model, Siemens Four Views, Software Systems Architecture* and *SEI Views & Beyond* (V&B) [3,16]. A common aspect is the prescription of a SAD structure (i.e., templates) and the usage of views for different system viewpoints, which might be related to stakeholders' concerns. Nonetheless, these methods do not provide guidelines for creating the documentation package, except for the steps suggested by V&B [3]. V&B also proposes basic rules for relating stakeholder roles and views. The documenter is expected to apply these rules when determining the contents of a SAD release, but still this might be a complex and time-consuming task. This drawback motivated our NSVP work as a semi-automated aid to the documenter. However, our approach is not tied to V&B and can apply to other strategies, such as ACDM [15].

Optimization techniques have been used in several Software Engineering fields [21]. In particular, the Next Release Problem (NRP) is initially due to Bagnall et al. [9]. In the NRP formulation, a software company has to determine a subset of features that should be included in the next product release, in such a way the overall satisfaction of the company customers is maximized. Every customer is interested in a given subset of features and her satisfaction is proportional to the percentage of relevant features being included in the next release. Each feature is associated to a cost, and the total cost of the scheduled features must not exceed the available resources. The NRP was lately extended to a multi-objective formulation, known as MONRP (Multi-Objective Next Release Problem) [10,22], which treats the cost as a minimization objective. Along this line, MONRP has admits several solutions. Experiments with synthetic data [10,22] to solve (large) MONRP instances have shown that NSGA-II algorithms outperformed other ones with acceptable execution times. Nonetheless, the application of these ideas to other domains is still a topic of research.

7   Conclusions and Future Work

In this article, we have formalized the NSVP as an optimization problem for the production of software architecture documentation. A novel aspect of NSVP is that it seeks to balance the multiple stakeholders' interests in the SAD contents against the efforts of producing them. To do so, we characterize common stakeholder profiles and relate them to architectural views prescribed by SAD templates. The stakeholders' benefits were quantified by means of possible satisfaction functions. Our NSVP formulation admits 3 optimization variants. The project context should inform the selection of the most suitable variant. Two algorithms (SAT4J and NSGA-II) for efficiently solving the NSVP were discussed, although other algorithms are also possible. This kind of algorithms supports the documenter's tasks, assisting her to explore alternative solutions (e.g., the Pareto fronts). We actually envision a practical scenario where she can quickly identify "unnecessary" architectural information (with the consequent effort savings), and then prioritize relevant contents for the next SAD version.

A preliminary evaluation of the NSVP algorithms with both synthetic data and a case-study showed encouraging results. We observed a clear improvement in the quality of the optimized SAD versions, when compared to SAD counterparts generated in the usual manner. Regarding the satisfaction functions, we corroborated that, beyond a certain completion ($\approx$ 75%), the addition of more documentation reduces the SAD global utility. There is a "sweet spot" for applying optimized documentation when the SAD has a 25-40% of completion.

The current NSVP formulation still has shortcomings, mostly related to the assumptions of our model, such us stakeholders' interests on views, the completion actions for templates, the satisfaction functions, and the cost measures. These assumptions are either based on the authors' experience or taken from the literature, but they must be further validated (e.g., with user studies). We need to empirically investigate the correlations between the satisfaction computed by the functions and the actual stakeholders' satisfaction [6]. Regarding the SAD structure, some aspects ignored in today's model include: dependencies between SAD sections, or varied documentation actions (e.g., updating a section due to system refactoring, or deleting a section). These extensions to the NSVP pose a more complex optimization problem, and might emphasize the role of heuristic solvers. As for the V&B schema of stakeholder preferences, we will enhance it with user profiling techniques that incorporate personal dynamic interests, instead of using just predefined roles. Finally, we plan to consider stakeholders' concerns that might crosscut the SAD with the support of document processing/recognition techniques. For instance, interests on topics, such us system features or quality attributes, that affect more than one view or document.

Acknowledgments. This work was supported by PICT Project 2011-0366 (ANPCyT) and also by PIP Project 112-201101-00078 (CONICET) - Argentina.

References

1. Ruping, A.: Agile Documentation: A Pattern Guide to Producing Lightweight Documents for Software Projects. John Wiley & Sons (2003)
2. Bass, L., Clements, P., Kazman, R.: Software Architecture in Practice, 3rd edn. Addison-Wesley Professional (2012)
3. Clements, P., Bachmann, F., Bass, L., Garlan, D., Ivers, J., Little, R., Merson, P., Nord, R., Stafford, J.: Documenting Software Architectures: Views and Beyond, 2nd edn. Addison-Wesley Professional (2010)
4. ISO/IEC/IEEE: ISO/IEC/IEEE 42010: Systems and software engineering - architecture description. C/S2ESC. IEEE Computer Society (2011)
5. Parnas, D.L.: Precise documentation: The key to better software. In: Nanz, S. (ed.) The Future of Software Engineering, Springer, pp. 125–148. Springer (2010)
6. Falessi, D., Briand, L.C., Cantone, G., Capilla, R., Kruchten, P.: The value of design rationale information. ACM Trans. Softw. Eng. Methodol. 22(3), 21 (2013)
7. Diaz-Pace, J.A., Nicoletti, M., Schiaffino, S., Villavicencio, C., Sanchez, L.E.: A stakeholder-centric optimization strategy for architectural documentation. In: Cuzzocrea, A., Maabout, S. (eds.) MEDI 2013. LNCS, vol. 8216, pp. 104–117. Springer, Heidelberg (2013)
8. Clements, P., Bachmann, F., Bass, L., Garlan, D., Ivers, J., Little, R., Nord, R., Stafford, J.: A practical method for documenting software architectures. In: Proceedings of the 25th ICSE (2003)
9. Bagnall, A., Rayward-Smith, V., Whittley, I.: The next release problem. Information and Software Technology 43(14), 883–890 (2001)
10. Zhang, Y., Harman, M., Mansouri, S.A.: The multi-objective next release problem. In: Proceedings of the 9th GECCO, pp. 1129–1137. ACM, New York (2007)
11. Jansen, A., Bosch, J.: Software architecture as a set of architectural design decisions. In: Proceedings Working Conf. on Software Architecture, pp. 109–120 (2005)
12. Mitchell, R.K., Agle, B.R., Wood, D.J.: Toward a theory of stakeholder identification and salience: Defining the principle of who and what really counts. Academy of Management Review 22, 853 (1997)
13. Farenhorst, R., van Vliet, H.: Experiences with a wiki to support architectural knowledge sharing. In: Proc. 3rd Wikis4SE, Portugal (2008)
14. Bachmann, F., Merson, P.: Experience using the web-based tool wiki for architecture documentation. Technical Report CMU/SEI-2005-TN-041, SEI, CMU (2005)
15. Lattanze, A.: Architecting Software Intensive Systems: A Practitioners Guide. Taylor & Francis (2008)
16. Rozanski, N., Woods, E.: Software Systems Architecture: Working With Stakeholders Using Viewpoints and Perspectives, 2nd edn. Addison-Wesley (2011)
17. Koning, H., Vliet, H.V.: Real-life it architecture design reports and their relation to ieee std 1471 stakeholders and concerns. Auto. Soft. Eng. 13, 201–223 (2006)
18. Diwekar, U.: Introduction to Applied Optimization, 2nd edn. Springer Publishing Company, Incorporated (2010)
19. Berre, D.L., Parrain, A.: The SAT4J library, release 2.2. JSAT 7(2-3), 59–64 (2010)
20. Deb, K., Pratap, A., Agarwal, S., Meyarivan, T.: A fast and elitist multiobjective genetic algorithm: NSGA-II. Trans. Evol. Comp. 6(2), 182–197 (2002)
21. Harman, M., Mansouri, S.A., Zhang, Y.: Search-based software engineering: Trends, techniques and applications. ACM Comput. Surv. 45(1), 1–11 (2012)
22. Durillo, J.J., Zhang, Y., Alba, E., Harman, M., Nebro, A.J.: A study of the bi-objective next release problem. Empirical Softw. Eng. 16(1), 29–60 (2011)

A Multi-model Optimization Framework for the Model Driven Design of Cloud Applications

Danilo Ardagna, Giovanni Paolo Gibilisco,
Michele Ciavotta, and Alexander Lavrentev

Politecnico di Milano, Dipartimento di Elettronica e Informazione, Milano, Italy
{danilo.ardagna,giovannipaolo.gibilisco,
michele.ciavotta}@polimi.it,
alexander.lavrentev@mail.polimi.it

Abstract. The rise and adoption of the Cloud computing paradigm had a strong impact on the ICT world in the last few years; this technology has now reached maturity and Cloud providers offer a variety of solutions and services to their customers. However, beside the advantages, Cloud computing introduced new issues and challenges. In particular, the heterogeneity of the Cloud services offered and their relative pricing models makes the identification of a deployment solution that minimizes costs and guarantees QoS very complex. Performance assessment of Cloud based application needs for new models and tools to take into consideration the dynamism and multi-tenancy intrinsic of the Cloud environment. The aim of this work is to provide a novel mixed integer linear program (MILP) approach to find a minimum cost feasible cloud configuration for a given cloud based application. The feasibility of the solution is considered with respect to some non-functional requirements that are analyzed through multiple performance models with different levels of accuracy. The initial solution is further improved by a local search based procedure. The quality of the initial feasible solution is compared against first principle heuristics currently adopted by practitioners and Cloud providers.

1 Introduction

The rise and consolidation of the Cloud computing paradigm had a significant impact on the ICT world in recent years. Cloud has now reached maturity; many are the technologies and services supplied by various providers, resulting in an already highly diversified market. Tools for fast prototyping, enterprise developing, testing and integration are offered, delegating to Cloud providers all the intensive tasks of management and maintenance of the underlying infrastructure. However, besides the unquestionable advantages, Cloud computing introduced new issues and important challenges in application development. In fact, current Cloud technologies and pricing models can be so different and complex that looking for the solution that minimizes costs while guaranteeing an adequate performance, might result in a tremendous task. To carry out such a labor, application designer should consider multiple architectures at once and be able to evaluate costs and performance for each of them. Moreover, while information on architectures and costs are openly available, the performance assessment aspect turns

C. Le Goues and S. Yoo (Eds.): SSBSE 2014, LNCS 8636, pp. 61–76, 2014.

out to be a far more complicated concern because Cloud environments are often multi-tenant and their performance can vary over time, according to the congestion level and the competition for resources among the different applications. Although some analytical performance models have been proposed to attain an approximate assessment of software systems performance, there is, until now, no attempt to extend those models for taking into account the specificity of Cloud solutions. Consider, for example, Palladio Component Model (PCM) and Palladio Bench [10] for Quality of Service (QoS) evaluation. PCM is a Domain Specific Language (DSL) for the description of software architecture, resource and analysis of non-functional requirements but it is limited to enterprise systems, QoS can be assessed only for the peak workload, and it lacks support for Cloud systems. On the contrary, Cloud based systems are dynamic and time-dependent parameters have to be considered to assess performance and costs. It should also be noticed that cost and performance assessments are just one side of the coin. On the other side, the problem of quickly and efficiently explore the space of possible Cloud configurations in automatic or semi-automatic way also exists.

The aim of this work is to propose and validate a novel Mixed Integer Linear Program (MILP) designed to quickly find a minimum-cost Cloud configuration for a certain application, where the feasibility of a solution is considered according to some non-functional constraints expressed in the model. To realize an accurate model, the most common Cloud systems have been analyzed deriving general meta-models and parameter values. Those meta-models have been expressed by means of a Cloud-based extension of the PCM. This extension, presented for the first time here, is able to express different kinds of QoS constraints and time-dependent profiles for most important performance parameters. The proposed MILP is finally validated against a local search based metaheuristic also designed to explore the space of alternative Cloud configurations. The MILP solution is also compared with first principle heuristics currently adopted by practitioners and Cloud providers.

The remainder of the paper is organized as follows. In Section 2 the PCM proposed extension is briefly introduced. The optimization model is introduced in Section 3, whereas Section 4 illustrates the experimental campaign the optimization model underwent and analyzes the outcomes. The State-of-the-art analysis is reported in Section 5; conclusions are finally drawn in Section 6.

2   Background: Architecture Modeling and Analyses

In order to model the application under analysis, we extended the Palladio Component Model [10]. The PCM language allows developers to represent different aspects of the application by building specific diagrams. Figure 1 shows the main components of Apache Open For Business (OfBiz), our case study application; the figure is a summary of the information that can be expressed via our PCM extension, represented in a UML-like notation.

OfBiz [1] is an enterprise open source automation software developed by the Apache software foundation and adopted by many companies. We focus here on the E-Commerce

---

[1] http://ofbiz.apache.org/

functionality of OfBiz since it is a good candidate to be implemented with Cloud technology. The left most activity diagram models the behavior of users of the system, in this example on average 70% of users will access the application to purchase some product while the remaining 30% will check the status of a scheduled order. The incoming workload is expressed in number of requests per second. Our extension allows to specify a workload profile of 24 hours. All requests generated by users are served by the *Request Handler* component. The behavior of the *checkout* functionality is described by the activity diagram associated with the request handler. To serve a checkout request, the front-end needs to perform some internal computation (e.g., calculate the shipping price), whose impact on physical resources hosting the system is shown as *Demand*, and interact with some components hosted on the back-end. In particular the request handler interacts with the *Database* component to check the availability of the desired item and with the *Payment* component to check the validity of the credit card information specified by the user. The topmost part of the diagram shows that the request handler component is deployed alone in the front-end tier while the database and the payment service are co-located in the same back-end tier.

The standard PCM allows application designers to build diagrams with this kind of information and derive (for every time slot) a Layered Queuing Network (LQN) model from them. LQN models can then be solved analytically or by means of a simulation in order to derive performance metrics. As opposed to [26] we suppose that the component allocation to application tiers has already been chosen by the software developer therefore will not be changed by the optimization process. Multiple QoS metrics can

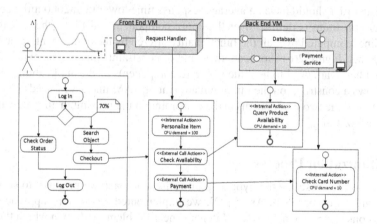

Fig. 1. OfBiz Application Example

be derived from the analysis of LQN models, in this work our focus is on response time and cost.

In a Cloud environment, infrastructural *Costs* are also difficult to compute, since the pricing policy offered by Cloud providers is very heterogeneous. In this work we refer to cost as to the sum of the prices of allocated resources, charged on a per-hour basis. This kind of pricing policy is a common denominator of all the most important Cloud provider offers, the main objective of this cost modeling is to show that cost related aspects can be included in the optimization process, not to provide a comprehensive description of the costs related to any specific Cloud environment.

As main performance metric we consider server side request *response time*. We also suppose that all Virtual Machines (VMs) hosting the application components are located inside the same local network (e.g., the same availability zone in Amazon EC2) so that the communication between the different application layers does not cause a bottleneck.

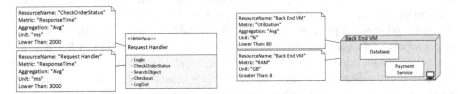

(a) QoS constraints defined over an interface   (b) Architectural constraints defined over an auto-scaling group

Fig. 2. Examples of different type of constraints that can be specified on the modeled application

In order to describe the Cloud environment the modeled application will run in, we made use of the meta models presented in [16]. We also extended those models in order to express constraints over the application QoS to drive the optimization process. Figure 2(a) shows two examples of QoS constraints that can be defined on a component. The topmost constraint expresses the fact that the functionality in charge of checking the status of an order should have an average response time lower than 2000 milliseconds. The other constraint is defined over the entire component and limits the average response time, computed over all the functionality offered by the component, to be lower than 3000 ms. Figure 2(b) shows another kind of constraints that can be expressed on the virtual hardware used to host the software components of the application. The example shows a constraint on the minimum amount of RAM that a VM needs to feature in order to run the two components and a constraint on the maximum allowed value of the CPU utilization.

3   Optimization Process

In this section we describe the hybrid optimization approach we propose, to solve the capacity allocation problem. As in [22], we implemented a two-steps approach. The first step consists in solving a Mixed Integer Linear Problem (MILP) in which the QoS associated to a deployment solution is calculated by means of an M/G/1 queuing model with processor sharing policy. Such performance model allows to calculate the average response time of a request in closed form. Our goal is to determine quickly an approximated initial solution through the MILP solution process which is then further improved by a local search based optimization algorithm (step 2). The aim of this algorithm is to iteratively improve the starting Cloud deployment exploring several application configurations. A more expressive performance model (LQN) is employed to derive more accurate estimations of the QoS by means of the LQNS tool [17]. Figure 3 shows the workflow of the optimization process. As explained in Section 2 the specification of

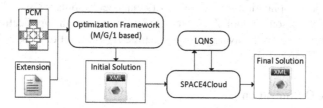

Fig. 3. Solution generation workflow

the application design is given in form of a PCM with an accompanying extension. The information contained in these models constitutes the input of the optimization problem and is passed to the optimization framework, which is the main object of this work, in order to derive an initial solution. This solution is then passed to the SPACE4Cloud tool [5], which performs an assessment of the solution using the more accurate LQN model and an heuristic optimization to derive an optimized solution.

In the remainder of the paper, Section 3.1 describes in details the capacity allocation problem faced in this work, Section 3.2 provides its MILP formulation, while Section 3.3 outlines the heuristic local search approach.

3.1   Search Problem Formulation

The aim of the optimal selection and capacity allocation problem for Cloud applications is to minimize the usage cost of Cloud resources, while satisfying some user-defined constraints. As discussed in Section 2, an application can be described as a composition of several components $\mathcal{C}$, each of them implementing a particular set of functionalities $\mathcal{K}$ with a certain resources demand. Each component is deployed into a resource pool, or application tier, $\mathcal{I}$ composed by a set of homogeneous VMs. Such a set is not static but can scale to handle variations of the incoming workload. Since, the daily workload is periodic for many applications [11], we decided to limit our analysis to a single day horizon. Many Cloud providers charge the use of VMs per hour (e.g., Amazon EC2 *on-demand* pricing scheme[2]), hence it is reasonable to split the time horizon into 24 time slots $\mathcal{T}$ of one hour each . For the sake of simplicity, in the following we consider QoS constraints predicating on application response time. In a nutshell, the problem we deal with presents two main decision aspects, first is the selection of a certain VM type $\mathcal{V}$ for each resource pool, while the second faces the way the application has to scale in order to meet the constraints, i.e., aims at determining the optimum number of VMs to be devoted to each pool at every hour of the day. The overall workload of an application is described in terms of requests per second Λ_t.

Users interact with the application by making requests, the set of possible requests is referred to as $\mathcal{K}$. Moreover, each class of requests is characterized with a probability to be executed (α_k specified in the model, see Figure 1) and by a set of components supporting its execution (i.e., its execution path [6]). Finally, we assume that requests are served according to the processor sharing scheduling policy, a typical scheduling

---

[2] http://aws.amazon.com/ec2/pricing

policy in Web and application server containers that evenly splits the workload among all the VMs of the resource pool. As for the QoS requirements the application designer can define a threshold on the average response time $\overline{R}_k$ for a set of classes $\mathcal{K}_{Avg} \subseteq \mathcal{K}$ (as depicted in Figure 2(a)).

3.2 Analytic Optimization

In the light of the considerations made so far, the optimal capacity allocation problem can be formulated as follows:

$$\min_{z,\mathcal{V}} \sum_{i \in \mathcal{I}} \sum_{v \in \mathcal{V}} \sum_{t \in \mathcal{T}} C_{v,t} z_{i,v,t} \tag{1}$$

Subject to:

$$\sum_{v \in \mathcal{V}} w_{i,v} = 1 \qquad\qquad \forall i \in \mathcal{I} \tag{2}$$

$$w_{i,v} \leq z_{i,v,t} \qquad\qquad \forall i \in \mathcal{I}, \forall v \in \mathcal{V}, \forall t \in \mathcal{T} \tag{3}$$

$$z_{i,v,t} \leq N w_{i,v} \qquad\qquad \forall i \in \mathcal{I}, \forall v \in \mathcal{V}, \forall t \in \mathcal{T} \tag{4}$$

$$\sum_{v \in \mathcal{V}} M_v w_{i,v} \geq \overline{M}_i \qquad\qquad \forall i \in \mathcal{I} \tag{5}$$

$$\sum_{v \in \mathcal{V}} (1 - \mu_{k,c} \overline{R}_{k,c} S_v) z_{i_c,v,t} \leq \mu_{k,c} G_{k,c,t} \overline{R}_{k,c} \qquad \forall k \in \mathcal{K}, \forall c \in \mathcal{C}, \forall t \in \mathcal{T} \tag{6}$$

$$\sum_{v \in \mathcal{V}} S_v z_{i_c,v,t} > G_{k,c,t} \qquad\qquad \forall k \in \mathcal{K}, \forall c \in \mathcal{C}, \forall t \in \mathcal{T} \tag{7}$$

$$z_{i,v,t} \ Integer \qquad\qquad \forall i \in \mathcal{I}, \forall t \in \mathcal{T} \tag{8}$$

$$w_{i,v} \in \{0,1\} \qquad\qquad \forall i \in \mathcal{I}, \forall v \in \mathcal{V} \tag{9}$$

Where $\mathcal{T} = \{1 \dots 24\}$ and $G_{k,c,t} = \Lambda_t \sum_{\tilde{c} \in I_c} \sum_{\tilde{k} \in \mathcal{K}} \frac{\alpha_k p_{k,\tilde{c}}}{\mu_{\tilde{k},\tilde{c}}}$.
Table 1 summarizes the list of parameters of our optimization model and Table 2 reports the decision variables.

The value expressed by (1) represents the total usage cost of the Cloud application and it is the objective function to minimize. As $w_{i,v}$ are binary decision variables (eq. 9) equal to 1 if the VM type v is assigned to the i-th resource pool, condition (2) guarantees that exactly one type can be selected for each resource pool. Equation (8) defines a set of integer variables $z_{i,v,t}$ that represent the number of VMs of type v assigned to resource pool i at time t. Condition (3) in combination with (2) and (9) guarantees that a nonempty set of VMs is assigned to each resource pool. Moreover, condition (4) imposes the set of VMs assigned to each resource pool to be homogeneous. Indeed, if $w_{i,v} = 0$ the total number of VMs of type v assigned to resource pool i is forced to be zero as well and this happens for all $v \in \mathcal{V}$ but one (eq. (2)). Besides, if $w_{i,v} = 1$ the number of VMs assigned to the resource pool i is at least 1, for eq. (3), and at most N, which is an arbitrary large integer number. Finally, equations (5) and (6)

Table 1. Optimization model parameters

System parameters

Index	
$t \in T$	time interval
$i \in \mathcal{I}$	resource pool or application tiers
$k \in \mathcal{K}$	class of request
$v \in \mathcal{V}$	type of virtual machine
Parameters	
Λ_t	number of incoming requests (workload) at time t
α_k	proportion of requests of class k in the workload
$p_{k,c}$	probability of request of class k to be served by component c
$\mu_{k,c}^v$	maximum service rate of requests of class k on component c hosted on a VM of type v
U_k	set of components serving request k
I_c	set of components that are co-located with c
$C_{v,t}$	cost of a single machine of type v at time t
M_v	memory of a virtual machine of type v
$\overline{M}_i$	memory constraint for tier i
$\overline{R}_{k,c}$	maximum average response time for the k-class of requests on component c

Table 2. Optimization model decision variables

Optimization model decision variables.

$w_{i,v}$	binary variable that is equal to 1 if the VMs type v is assigned to the i-th tier and equal to 0 otherwise
$z_{i,v,t}$	number of virtual machines of type v assigned to the i-th resource pool at time t

represent memory and QoS constraints, respectively, while (7) is the M/G/1 equilibrium condition.

As previously discussed, to evaluate the average response time of the Cloud application we model each VM container as an M/G/1 queue. However, in general, a request of class k is processed by more than a single component. Let $\Lambda_{k,t} = \alpha_k \Lambda_t$ be the incoming workload at time t for request class k and $\Lambda_{k,c,t} = p_{k,c} \Lambda_{k,t}$ the arrival rate of request class k at component c. The response time of requests in class k can then be obtained by:

$$R_{k,t} = \sum_{c \in U_k} p_{k,c} R_{k,c,t} = \sum_{c \in U_k} p_{k,c} \frac{\frac{1}{\mu_{k,c}^{\tilde{v}}}}{1 - \sum_{\tilde{c} \in I_c} \sum_{\tilde{k} \in K} \frac{\Lambda_{\tilde{k},\tilde{c},t}}{\mu_{\tilde{k},\tilde{c}}^{\tilde{v}} z_{i_c,\tilde{v},t}}} \qquad (10)$$

where U_k is the set of components serving class k requests and I_c represents the set of components that are co-located with c on the same VM (I_c can be obtained by standard PCM allocation diagrams, see Figure 1). In other words, the average response time is obtained by summing up the time spent by the request in each component weighted by the probability of the request to actually be processed by that component. Notice that $R_{k,c,t}$ depends on the type and number of VMs ($\tilde{v}$ and $z_{i_c,\tilde{v},t}$, respectively) the component c is allocated in at time t.

In order to simplify expression (10) we consider the lowest CPU machine a reference machine and calculate the maximum service rates for each request class and component, $\mu_{k,c}$. In this way $\mu_{k,c}^v$ can be written as:

$$\mu_{k,c}^v = \mu_{k,c} \, S_{i_c} = \mu_{k,c} \sum_v S_v \, w_{i_c,v} \tag{11}$$

where S_v is the speed ratio between the reference machine and a VM of type v, while i_c is the index of the resource pool where component c is allocated.

Let $z_{i,t} = \sum_v z_{i,v,t}$ be the number of VMs of the selected type (only one type can be selected (eq.2)) for resource pool i at time t. Therefore the following expression holds:

$$\mu_{k,c}^v \, z_{i_c,v,t} = \mu_{k,c} \, S_{i_c} \, z_{i_c,t} = \mu_{k,c} \sum_v S_v \, z_{i_c,v,t} \tag{12}$$

Under M/G/1 assumptions the response time of a request of class k processed by component c hosted on a VM of type v is given by:

$$R_{k,c,t} = \frac{\dfrac{1}{\mu_{k,c} S_{i_c}}}{1 - \displaystyle\sum_{\bar{c} \in I_c} \sum_{\bar{k} \in \mathcal{K}} \frac{\Lambda_{\bar{k},\bar{c},t}}{\mu_{\bar{k},\bar{c}} S_{i_c} z_{i_c,t}}} \tag{13}$$

By replacing (11) and (12) in (10) we can write the following constraint on the response time of requests of class k:

$$R_{k,t} = \sum_{c \in U_k} p_{k,c} \, R_{k,c,t} = \sum_{c \in U_k} p_{k,c} \frac{\dfrac{1}{\mu_{k,c} S_{i_c}}}{1 - \dfrac{\Lambda_t}{S_{i_c} z_{i_c,t}} \displaystyle\sum_{\bar{c} \in I_c} \sum_{\bar{k} \in \mathcal{K}} \frac{\alpha_{\bar{k}} p_{\bar{k},\bar{c}}}{\mu_{\bar{k},\bar{c}}}} \leq \overline{R_k}, \tag{14}$$

Equation (14) is non-linear due to the presence of product $S_i z_{i,t}$ in the denominator; in order derive a linear model, which can be solved efficiently by MILP solvers, we explode it into a set of stricter constraints defined over the average response time of each component traversed by the request.

To do so we split the response time constraint among components of a path and take the most stringent constraint among the conditions generated by all the possible paths that the request can traverse. In other words, let:

$$r_{k,c,u} = \begin{cases} \dfrac{\dfrac{1}{\mu_{k,c}}}{\displaystyle\sum_{c \in u} \dfrac{1}{\mu_{k,c}}} & \text{if } c \text{ belongs to path } u \\[2em] 0 & \text{otherwise} \end{cases} \tag{15}$$

and let: $\overline{R}_{k,c} = \min_u r_{k,c,u} \, \overline{R}_k$. Instead of using constraint (13) for the response time we introduce the constraint family: $R_{k,c,t} \leq \overline{R}_{k,c}$ and after some algebra we get constraint (6).

Finally, constraint (7) represents the M/G/1 equilibrium condition obtained from (13) imposing the denominator to be greater than zero.

3.3 Local Search Optimization

The aim of this section is to provide a brief description of the optimization algorithm implemented by the SPACE4Cloud [5] tool that we used to further optimize the solution obtained by the MILP optimization problem. One of the key differences between the two optimization processes is the fact that the performance model used by SPACE4Cloud, the LQN model, is more complex and accurate than the M/G/1 models used in the analytic formulation of the optimization problem. Another differentiating factor is the way SPACE4Cloud explores the free space, in fact it uses an heuristic approach that divides the problem into two levels delegating the assignment of the type of VMs to the first (upper) level and the definition of the number of replicas to the second (lower) level. The first level implements a stochastic local search with tabu memory, at each iteration the type of the VMs used for a particular tier is changed randomly from all the available VMs, according to the architectural constraints. The tabu memory is used to store recent moves and avoid cycling of the candidate solutions around the same configurations. Once the VM size is fixed the solution may enter in a repair phase during which the number of VMs is increased until the feasibility is restored (switching to slower VMs can make the current system configuration unfeasible). The solution is then refined by gradually reducing the number of VMs until the optimal allocation is found. This whole process is repeated for a pre-defined number of iterations updating the final solution each time a feasible and cheaper one is found.

4 Experimental Results

The proposed optimization approach has been evaluated for a variety of system and workload configurations. Our solution will be compared with current approaches for capacity allocation and according to threshold based the auto-scaling policies that can be implemented at IaaS providers.

Analysis performed in this Section are intended to be representative of real Cloud applications. We have used a very large set of randomly generated instances, obtained varying the performance model parameters according to the ranges used by other literature approaches [4], [3], [36], [39] and from real system [7] (see Table 3). VMs costs and capacities have been taken from Amazon EC2, Microsoft Azure, and Flexiscale.

As, in [8,4], the request class service time threshold has been set equal to:

$$\overline{R}_k = 10 \sum_{c \in U_k} \frac{p_{k,c}}{\mu_{k,c}^{\overline{v}}}$$

where we considered as reference VM, the Amazon EC2 small with index $\overline{v}$.

Workloads have been generated by considering the trace of a large Web system including almost 100 servers. The trace contains the number of sessions, on a per-hour basis, over a one year period. The trace follows a bimodal distribution with two peaks around 11.00 and 16.00. Multiple workloads have been obtained by adding random

Table 3. Ranges of model parameters

Parameter	Range
α_k	$[0.1; 1]$ %
$p_{k,c}$	$[0.01; 0.5]$
$\mu_{k,c}^v$	$[50; 2800]$ req/sec
$C_{v_{p,i}}$	$[0.06; 1.06]$ \$ per hour
M_i	$[1;4]$ GB
N	5000 VMs
$\overline{R}_{k,c}$	$[0.005; 0.01]$ sec

Table 4. MILP sets cardinalities

Description	Variation range
Number of resource containers $|\mathcal{I}|$	$[1; 9]$
Time Intervals $|\mathcal{T}|$	$[4; 24]$
Number of Requests Classes $|\mathcal{K}|$	$[1; 10]$
Number of VM types $|\mathcal{V}|$	$[1; 12]$

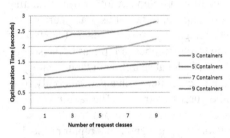

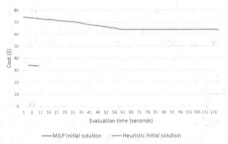

(a) CPLEX optimization time varying the number of containers and request classes.

(b) Example of SPACE4Cloud execution trace.

white noise to each sample as in [4] and [24]. The MILP optimization model sets cardinality has been varied as reported in Table 4. The number of applications components has been varied between 1 and 10.

The next Section reports the results of the scalability of the MILP formulation. The quality of the MILP solution is evaluated in Section 4.2.

4.1 Scalability Analysis

Tests have been performed on a VirtualBox virtual machine based on Ubuntu 12.10 server running on an Intel Xeon Nehalem dual socket quad-core system with 32 GB of RAM. CPLEX 12.2.0.0 [3] has been used as MILP solver.

In order to guarantee statistical independence of our scalability results, for each test we considered ten different instances with the same size. The results reported here have been obtained by considering 10,000 total runs.

Figure 4(a) reports a representative example and shows how CPLEX optimization time (i.e., the time required to optimally solve the model) for optimizing a system with 10 components varies by changing the number of containers and request classes. On average CPLEX is able to find a solution in 0.5-3 seconds. In the very worst case, considering a system including 5 containers, 9 requests classes and 9 components the optimization time was 8.72 seconds.

---

[3] http://www-01.ibm.com/software/commerce/optimization/cplex-optimizer/

Table 5. Results comparison

First Feas. Time Savings	Final Opt. Time Savings	First Feas. Cost Savings	Final Opt. Cost Savings	MILP Feas. Initial Sol.	HEU Feas. Initial Sol.
-57.2%	414.5%	130.7%	98.5%	78.5%	82.0%

4.2 Initial Solution Quality Evaluation

In general the performance of a heuristic based optimization approach is measured by assessing final local solutions values and the time needed to generate such solutions. We evaluate the benefits of the MILP formulation by comparing the final solution that can be obtained by SPACE4Cloud considering as initial solution the MILP configuration and the one obtained by the following heuristic:

– for all containers, the cheapest VM type available at the Cloud provider satisfying also the memory constraint (5) is adopted;
– as in other literature approaches [36,39] and coherently to the auto-scaling policies that can be implemented by current IaaS providers[4], the number of VMs of each resource pool is determined such that the average CPU utilization is lower than a given threshold $\bar{\rho}$.

In our experiments we set $\bar{\rho} = 0.6$ as in [39]. More in details, the performance metrics we considered in our comparison are:

– the time required by SPACE4Cloud to find the first feasible solution;
– the time required by SPACE4Cloud to converge to the final local optimum;
– the cost of the first feasible solution;
– the cost of the final local optimum;
– the percentage of initial feasible solutions obtained by the MILP and heuristic approach.

Table 5 summarizes the results achieved. The results reported here have been obtained by considering 100 total runs. Figures report the average percentage improvements that can be obtained by adopting the MILP formulation. The precentages have been evaluated by considering the ratio $(Y - X)/X$, where X and Y are the MILP and heuristic performance, respectively (negative values means that the heuristic solution performs better). The first two columns report the percentage time saving obtained to identify the first feasible solution and the final local optimum. The third and fourth columns report the percentage of cost reduction of the first feasible and final local optimum solution, while the last two columns report the average percentage of QoS constraints that are satisfied by the two initial solutions. Even if the MILP approach introduces an overhead to find the first feasible solution (the first feasible solution is obtained by the heuristic with around 57% lower time), the hybrid approach outperforms the heuristic, reducing the time to converge to the final local optimum and improving significantly the cost of the final optimum solution.

---

[4] http://aws.amazon.com/elasticbeanstalk/

As an example, Figure 4(b) reports the execution trace of SPACE4Cloud for optimising a system including 5 containers, 9 request classes, and 9 components. On the x axis the overall optimization time is reported (including the time required to determine the initial solution by the MILP or the heuristic and the local search execution time), while the y axis reports the Cloud daily resource cost. The blue and red lines are the costs of the best current solution obtained by considering as initial solution the MILP and the heuristic solution, respectively. The initial gap shows the time required by identifying the first initial solution (which is more evident for the MILP trace where around 3 seconds are needed). Even if the evaluation of the MILP solution introduces an initial delay, the local search performance are significantly improved. In this specific case the final solution is around 88% cheaper, while the time required by the local search to identify the final local optimum is reduced by almost an order of magnitude.

5   Related Work

In the last two decades prediction and assessment of QoS characteristics of complex software systems has emerged as an important requirement. An effective way of dealing with this requirement is to integrate non functional properties prediction techniques into the software development process by means of appropriate tools and techniques. In these kind of approaches a model of the software architecture is annotated with non functional elements that are used to predict the performance of the application. The output of this analysis is used by application designers as feedback to modify the architecture in order to meet the requirements.

The Model-Driven Quality Prediction (MDQP) approach is to model the application with UML models, in order to support the specification of non functional properties the Object Management Group (OMG) introduced two profiles called *Schedulability, Performance and Time* (SPT) [31] and *Modeling and Analysis of Real-Time and Embedded Systems* MARTE [32]. This approach of extending UML is not the only one that deals with the analysis of non functional properties of software systems, Becker et al. developed the PCM [10], a language that can be used to model an application and its non functional properties and, with the support of the PCM-Bench tool, derive a LQN model to estimate the performance of the running system. The automated transformation of architecture-level models to predictive models is the second phase of the MDQP process (see, e.g., [37]). Many meta-models have been built to support performance prediction, some surveys of these models, their capability and their applicability to different scenarios can be found in [9,23,1]. The output of the performance analysis performed using these models is used to optimize the architecture of the application at design time in (semi-)automatic way.

We divide the most relevant approaches extending the classification presented by Martens et al. in [27]. The classes used to categorize the different solutions are: rulebase, meta-heuristic, generic Design Space exploration (DSE), quality-driven model transformations.

Rule-Based Approaches. Rule-based approaches use feedback rules to modify the architecture of the application. The QVT-Rational framework proposed in [13,14] extends the Query, View, Transformation language defined by OMG by adding the support for feedback rules for semi-automatic generation of system architectures. The PUMA [37] framework aims at filling the gap between the design model and the performance models and has been extended with support for feedback rules specification in JESS [38]. Other language-specific tools, like the one proposed by Parsons et al. [34] for Java EE, are able to identify performance anti-patterns in existing systems specified by a set of rules; the tool reconstruct the model of the application using different monitoring techniques and analyze the generated model against the stored rules. Rule-based model to model transformation approaches has been proposed by Kavimandan and Gokhale [20] to optimize real-time QoS configuration in distributed and embedded systems.

Meta-Heuristics. Meta-heuristics use particular algorithms that are specifically designed to efficiently explore the space of design alternatives and find solutions that are optimized with respect to some quality criteria. In [25], Li et al. propose the Automated Quality-driven Optimization of Software Architecture (AQOSA) toolkit that implements some advanced evolutionary optimization algorithms for multi-objective problems, the toolkit integrates modelling technologies with performance evaluation tools in order to evaluate the goodness of generated solution according to a cost function. Aleti et al. proposed a similar approach in [2]; they presented the ArcheOpterix framework that exploits evolutionary algorithms to derive Pareto optimal component deployment decisions with respect to multiple quality criteria. Meedeniva et al. developed a multi-objective optimization strategy on top of ArcheOpterix in [28] to find trade-off between reliability and energy consumption in embedded systems. PerOpteryx [21] use a similar approach to optimize software architectures modeled with the Palladio framework [10] according to performance, reliability and cost. Other approaches combine analytical optimization techniques with evolutionary algorithms to find Pareto optimal solutions, an example of this is presented by Koziolek et al. in [22] with a particular focus on availability, performance and cost. A tabu search (TS) heuristic has been used by Ouzineb et al. [33] to derive component allocation under availability constraints in the context of embedded systems. The SASSY [29] framework developed by Menascé et al. starts from a model of a service-oriented architecture, performs service selection and applies patterns like replication and load balancing in order to fulfill quality requirements. Finally, Frey et al. [18] proposed a combined metaheuristic-simulation approach based on a genetic algorithm to derive deployment architecture and runtime reconfiguration rules while moving a legacy application to the Cloud environment.

Generic Design Space Exploration (GDSE). Generic Design Space Exploration approaches encode feedback rules into a Constraint Satisfaction Problem (CSP) in order to explore the design space. The DeepCompass [12] framework proposed by Bondarev et al. perform design space exploration according to a performance analysis of component-based software on multiprocessors systems. The DESERT framework [30,15] performs a general exploration of design alternatives by modeling system variations in a tree structure and using Boolean constraints to cut branches without feasible solutions. The latest version of this framework, DESERT-FD [15] automates the constraint generation process and the design space exploration. The GDSE [35] framework proposed by Saxena et al.is a meta-programmable system domain-specific DSE problems, it provides a language to express constraints and support different solvers for candidate solution generation. A similar approach is proposed by Jackson et al. in the Formula [19] framework; Formula allows the specification of non-functional requirements, models and meta-models by first-order logic with arithmetic relations, the problem is solved by the Z3 Satisfiability Modulo Theory (SMT) solver to generate several design alternatives that comply with the specified requirements.

Most of the presented works are tailored to solve very particular problem and lack of generalization on the quality attributes supported for the design space exploration. Moreover, only one approach [18] tackles directly the problem of building architectures for the Cloud environment but it focuses on the migration of legacy applications.

6   Conclusions

In this paper, a hybrid approach for the cost minimization of Cloud based applications has been proposed. The MILP formulation that implements the first step of the hybrid approach is able to identify a promising initial solution for a local search optimization procedure which outperforms, both in terms of overall optimization time and final solution costs, first principles heuristics based on utilization thresholds. The proposed approach can lead to a reduction of Cloud application costs and to an improvement of the quality of the final system, because an automated and efficient search is able to identify more and better design alternatives.

Ongoing work focuses on the extension of the MILP formulation and the local search to multiple Cloud deployments and on QoS analyses of real case studies.

References

1. Aleti, A., Buhnova, B., Grunske, L., Koziolek, A., Meedeniya, I.: Software architecture optimization methods: A systematic literature review. IEEE Trans. Soft. Eng. 39(5), 658–683 (2013)
2. Aleti, A., Stefan Björnander, S., Grunske, L., Meedeniya, I.: Archeopterix: An extendable tool for architecture optimization of aadl models. In: MOMPES 2009 (2009)
3. Almeida, J., Almeida, V., Ardagna, D., Cunha, I., Francalanci, C., Trubian, M.: Joint admission control and resource allocation in virtualized servers. Journal of Parallel and Distributed Computing 70(4), 344 (2010)
4. Ardagna, D., Casolari, S., Colajanni, M., Panicucci, B.: Dual time-scale distributed capacity allocation and load redirect algorithms for cloud systems. Journal of Parallel and Distributed Computing 72(6), 796 (2012)
5. Ardagna, D., Ciavotta, M., Gibilisco, G.P., Casale, G., Pérez, J.: Prediction and cost assessment tool - proof of concept. Project deliverable (2013)
6. Ardagna, D., Mirandola, R.: Per-flow optimal service selection for web services based processes. Journal of Systems and Software 83(8), 1512–1523 (2010)
7. Ardagna, D., Panicucci, B., Trubian, M., Zhang, L.: Energy-aware autonomic resource allocation in multitier virtualized environments. IEEE Trans. Serv. Comp. 5(1), 2–19 (2012)
8. Ardagna, D., Pernici, B.: Adaptive service composition in flexible processes. IEEE Trans. Soft. Eng. 33(6), 369–384 (2007)
9. Balsamo, S., Di Marco, A., Inverardi, P., Simeoni, M.: Model-based performance prediction in software development: A survey. IEEE Trans. Soft. Eng. 30(5), 295–310 (2004)

10. Becker, S., Koziolek, H., Reussner, R.: The palladio component model for model-driven performance prediction. Journal of Systems and Software 82(1), 3–22 (2009)
11. Birke, R., Chen, L.Y., Smirni, E.: Data centers in the cloud: A large scale performance study. In: CLOUD 2012 (2012)
12. Bondarev, E., Chaudron, M.R.V., de Kock, E.A.: Exploring performance trade-offs of a jpeg decoder using the deepcompass framework. In: WOSP 2007 (2007)
13. Drago, M.L.: Quality Driven Model Transformations for Feedback Provisioning. PhD thesis, Italy (2012)
14. Drago, M.L., Ghezzi, C., Mirandola, R.: A quality driven extension to the qvt-relations transformation language. Computer Science - R&D 27(2) (2012)
15. Eames, B., Neema, S., Saraswat, R.: Desertfd: a finite-domain constraint based tool for design space exploration. Design Automation for Embedded Systems 14(1), 43–74 (2010)
16. Franceschelli, D., Ardagna, D., Ciavotta, M., Di Nitto, E.: Space4cloud: A tool for system performance and costevaluation of cloud systems. In: Multi-cloud 2013 (2013)
17. Franks, G., Hubbard, A., Majumdar, S., Neilson, J., Petriu, D., Rolia, J., Woodside, M.: A toolset for performance engineering and software design of client-server systems. Performance Evaluation 24, 1–2 (1996)
18. Frey, S., Fittkau, F., Hasselbring, W.: Search-based genetic optimization for deployment and reconfiguration of software in the cloud. In: ICSE 2013 (2013)
19. Jackson, E., Kang, E., Dahlweid, M., Seifert, D., Santen, T.: Components, platforms and possibilities: towards generic automation for mda. In: EMSOFT 2010 (2010)
20. Kavimandan, A., Gokhale, A.: Applying model transformations to optimizing real-time qos configurations in dre systems. Architectures for Adaptive Software Systems, 18–35 (2009)
21. Koziolek, A.: Automated Improvement of Software Architecture Models for Performance and Other Quality Attributes. PhD thesis, Germany (2011)
22. Koziolek, A., Ardagna, D., Mirandola, R.: Hybrid multi-attribute QoS optimization in component based software systems. Journal of Systems and Software 86(10), 2542–2558 (2013)
23. Koziolek, H.: Performance evaluation of component-based software systems: A survey. Performance evaluation 67(8), 634–658 (2010)
24. Kusic, D., Kephart, J.O., Hanson, J.E., Kandasamy, N., Jiang, G.: Power and performance management of virtualized computing environments via lookahead control. Cluster Computing 12(1), 1–15 (2009)
25. Li, R., Etemaadi, R., Emmerich, M.T.M., Chaudron, M.R.V.: An evolutionary multiobjective optimization approach to component-based software architecture design. In: CEC 2011 (2011)
26. Martens, A., Ardagna, D., Koziolek, H., Mirandola, R., Reussner, R.: A hybrid approach for multi-attribute qoS optimisation in component based software systems. In: Heineman, G.T., Kofron, J., Plasil, F. (eds.) QoSA 2010. LNCS, vol. 6093, pp. 84–101. Springer, Heidelberg (2010)
27. Martens, A., Koziolek, H., Becker, S., Reussner, R.: Automatically improve software architecture models for performance, reliability, and cost using evolutionary algorithms. In: WOSP/SIPEW 2010 (2010)
28. Meedeniya, I., Buhnova, B., Aleti, A., Grunske, L.: Architecture-driven reliability and energy optimization for complex embedded systems. In: Heineman, G.T., Kofron, J., Plasil, F. (eds.) QoSA 2010. LNCS, vol. 6093, pp. 52–67. Springer, Heidelberg (2010)
29. Menascé, D.A., Ewing, J.M., Gomaa, H., Malek, S., Sousa, J.P.: A framework for utility-based service oriented design in SASSY. In: WOSP/SIPEW 2010 (2010)
30. Neema, S., Sztipanovits, J., Karsai, G., Butts, K.: Constraint-based design-space exploration and model synthesis. In: Embedded Software, pp. 290–305 (2003)
31. OMG. UML Profile for Schedulability, Performance, and Time Specification (2005)

32. OMG. A uml profile for marte: Modeling and analysis of real-time embedded systems (2008)
33. Ouzineb, M., Nourelfath, M., Gendreau, M.: Tabu search for the redundancy allocation problem of homogenous series-parallel multi-state systems. Reliability Engineering & System Safety 93(8), 1257–1272 (2008)
34. Parsons, T., Murphy, J.: Detecting performance antipatterns in component based enterprise systems. Journal of Object Technology 7(3), 55–91 (2008)
35. Saxena, T., Karsai, G.: Mde-based approach for generalizing design space exploration. Model Driven Engineering Languages and Systems, 46–60 (2010)
36. Wolke, A., Meixner, G.: TwoSpot: A cloud platform for scaling out web applications dynamically. In: Di Nitto, E., Yahyapour, R. (eds.) ServiceWave 2010. LNCS, vol. 6481, pp. 13–24. Springer, Heidelberg (2010)
37. Woodside, M., Petriu, D.C., Petriu, D.B., Shen, H., Israr, T., Merseguer, J.: Performance by unified model analysis (puma). In: WOSP 2005 (2005)
38. Xu, J.: Rule-based automatic software performance diagnosis and improvement. In: WOSP 2008 (2008)
39. Zhu, X., Young, D., Watson, B., Wang, Z., Rolia, J., Singhal, S., McKee, B., Hyser, C., Gmach, D., Gardner, R., Christian, T., Cherkasova, L.: 1000 islands: An integrated approach to resource management for virtualized data centers. Journal of Cluster Computing 12(1), 45–57 (2009)

A Pattern-Driven Mutation Operator for Search-Based Product Line Architecture Design

Giovani Guizzo[1], Thelma Elita Colanzi[1,2], and Silvia Regina Vergilio[1,*]

[1] DInf - Federal University of Parana, CP: 19081, CEP 19031-970, Curitiba, Brazil
[2] DIN - State University of Maringa, Av. Colombo, 5790, Maringá, Brazil
{gguizzo,silvia}@inf.ufpr.br, thelma@din.uem.br

Abstract. The application of design patterns through mutation operators in search-based design may improve the quality of the architectures produced in the evolution process. However, we did not find, in the literature, works applying such patterns in the optimization of Product Line Architecture (PLA). Existing works offer manual approaches, which are not search-based, and only apply specific patterns in particular domains. Considering this fact, this paper introduces a meta-model and a mutation operator to allow the design patterns application in the search-based PLA design. The model represents suitable scopes, that is, set of architectural elements that are suitable to receive a pattern. The mutation operator is used with a multi-objective and evolutionary approach to obtain PLA alternatives. Quantitative and qualitative analysis of empirical results show an improvement in the quality of the obtained solutions.

Keywords: Software product line architecture, design patterns, search-based design.

1 Introduction

Software Product Line (SPL) encompasses commonality and variability that are present in several software products of a specific domain. Commonality refers to elements which are common to all products whereas variability comprises variable elements. Variabilities are represented by variation points and variants. Variation points are associated with variants that represent alternative designs. The Product Line Architecture (PLA) is a key asset that provides a common overall structure containing all the SPL commonalities and variabilities. The architecture of each product is derived from the PLA [19].

The PLA design is a crucial and people-intensive SPL engineering activity. This is due to the growing complexity of the software systems and, in general, there are different quality metrics to be considered by the architect, such as that ones related to modularity and extensibility. In addition to that, the application of design patterns is important to obtain higher quality solutions. Design

---

* The authors would like to thank CNPq and CAPES for financial support, and E. L. Féderle for developing the tool used in this work.

C. Le Goues and S. Yoo (Eds.): SSBSE 2014, LNCS 8636, pp. 77–91, 2014.

patterns, such as the ones grouped in the GoF catalog [13], document common solutions from several projects widely used among developers. Patterns lead to improve cohesion and coupling, which are directly connected to the software reusability. However, the use of metrics and the application of design patterns, in practice, are still hard tasks to many architects, mainly to novices.

We observe that the PLA design optimization is a problem that can be properly solved in the Search-Based Software Engineering (SBSE) field. In this sense, the work of Colanzi [6] introduces a multi-objective search-based approach for PLA optimization. The approach produces a set of good solutions with the best trade-off among different objectives, such as the SPL extensibility and modularity. The focus is the UML class diagrams, since this kind of model is commonly used to model software architectures in the detailed level [8]. A representation to the problem was proposed, as well as feature-driven search operators. Features are prominent characteristics of the products and plays an important role in the SPL context. However, the approach of Colanzi [6] does not address another important PLA design task, mentioned above, the application of design patterns.

The application of patterns has been focused by search-based design works [22]. Cinnéide and Nixon [4] investigate the use of patterns in the refactoring context, and Räihä et al. [23,24] in the synthesis of software architectures with Genetic Algorithms (GA). Although the ideas found in related work can be applied in the SPL context, they do not take into account specific PLA characteristics, such as variation points and variants. Works [18,27] considering such characteristics offer approaches that are not search-based, and, in many cases, present results from manual application of patterns, which are valid only in particular contexts. This lack of works is due to two main reasons. The definition of specific SPL patterns is a current research subject, not completely explored yet, and the search-based PLA design (SBPD) is an incipient field. Even though, there are evidences that, in intermediate or advanced PLA designs, mutation operators that apply design patterns or architectural styles would contribute to obtain better PLAs [7].

Another reason is that there are some challenges to be overcome to allow automatic application of patterns. It is necessary not only to know design patterns, but also to recognize and determine domain specific patterns based on the SPL requirements [20]. Coplien [9] stated that patterns are not meant to be executed by computers, but rather to be used by engineers with perception, taste, experience and aesthetics sense. Essentially, the idea is to use these virtues to analyze design patterns and to encapsulate the analytic results into algorithms capable of automatically identifying and applying them in software architectures.

Considering such challenges and the importance of design patterns, this paper contributes to the automatic application of design patterns in SBPD in three ways: i) introducing a metamodel to represent and automatically identify suitable scopes associated with design patterns in SBPD. A suitable scope is a part of a class diagram that has architectural elements satisfying minimum requirements for the application of a specific pattern; ii) defining a mutation operator to apply patterns only in suitable scopes, represented by the introduced model.

The operator includes verification and application methods to effectively apply the design patterns; and iii) presenting empirical results on the application of the proposed operator in three SPLs. The defined operator is implemented in the context of the search-based approach of Colanzi [6] and the empirical results show an improvement in the quality of the PLAs obtained.

The paper is organized as follows. Section 2 reviews the approach of Colanzi for SBPD [6]. Section 3 introduces the metamodel to represent suitable scopes. Section 4 describes the mutation operator. Section 5 presents empirical results with three real PLAs. Section 6 discusses related work. Finally, Section 7 concludes the paper.

2   A Search-Based Approach for PLA Design

Colanzi [6] proposed a multi-objective optimization approach for PLA design, which is used in this paper. The approach receives as input a PLA modeled in a UML class diagram containing the SPL variabilities. To this input a representation is generated, according to a metamodel defined in [8]. Such model represents architectural elements such as components, interfaces, operations and their inter-relationships. Each element is associated with features that it realizes by using UML stereotypes. A feature can be either common to all SPL products or variable being present only in some products. Variable elements are associated with variabilities that have variation points and their variants.

The PLA is optimized by using multi-objective algorithms. Two fitness functions are used [6]: i) CM (related to Conventional Metrics) is an aggregation of: cohesion, coupling and size of architectural elements; and ii) FM (related to Feature-driven Metrics, specific for SPL) is an aggregation of metrics that measure feature scattering, feature interaction and feature-based cohesion [25].

This approach also contains some mutation operators to improve the modularity and extensibility of PLA features [8]: Move Method; Move Attribute; Add Class; Move Operation; Add Component; and Feature-driven Mutation that aims at modularizing a feature tangled with others in a component. It selects a random component c_x, and if it has architectural elements assigned to different features, a random feature f_x is selected to be modularized in a new component c_z. All architectural elements from c_x assigned to f_x are moved to c_z, which in turn becomes client of c_x.

In addition to these operators, we acknowledge that the use of mutation operators to apply design patterns may contribute to obtain better solutions [7,23], which in turn are more flexible, understandable, and able to accommodate new features during the SPL maintenance or evolution. The application of design patterns in the approach described here is addressed in the next sections.

3   Representing Pattern Application Scopes

As mentioned before, to apply design patterns in SBPD it is necessary the automatic identification of suitable scopes. A suitable scope is a part of a class diagram that has architectural elements satisfying minimum requirements for the application of a pattern. Design patterns should be applied only in suitable scopes when the flexibility they provide is really needed, otherwise, an indiscriminately pattern application could result in the introduction of anomalies [13].

Guizzo *et al.* [15] analyzed GoF patterns [13] and determined their application feasibility in the approach of Colanzi [6]. The analysis considered the impact on metrics used in the fitness and the possibility of automatic identification of suitable scopes. Four design patterns were considered feasible: *Strategy*, *Bridge*, *Facade* and *Mediator*. The first two have specific applicability to SPL, and due to this they are focused in our work. Briefly, *Strategy* is used to freely interchange algorithms of an algorithm family, and *Bridge* to decouple the *abstraction* of its *implementation*, making both independent and interchangeable.

To allow automatic identification of suitable scopes, it is necessary to provide an easy way to deal with architectural elements associated with each pattern during the mutation process. To do this, Figure 1 presents a generic meta-model that represents suitable scopes. If a scope is suitable for the application of a design pattern, it is called "Pattern application Scope" (PS). The notation "PS<Pattern Name>" is used to designate a scope for a specific design pattern, e.g., PS<Strategy>. A scope may be a PS for more than one design pattern, thus any of the feasible pattern for this scope can be applied. In addition, there is a category of PS specific for SPL scopes: "Pattern application Scope in Product Line Architecture" (PS-PLA), denoted by "PS-PLA<Pattern Name>".

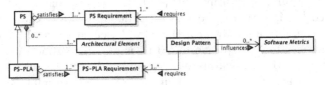

Fig. 1. Metamodel representing PS and PS-PLA

A PS/PS-PLA is a scope composed by at least one architectural element, which in turn may be present in multiple PSs/PSs-PLA. In fact, for a scope to be considered a PS to a particular design pattern, it needs to meet all the PS requirements that the design pattern requires. In addition to this, for a scope to be considered a PS-PLA, besides meeting all the PS requirements, it needs to meet also the PS-PLA requirements of the design pattern. These requirements are incorporated into verification methods (introduced in Section 4). Moreover, when a pattern is applied it influences some software metrics that are used by the evolutionary algorithms to evaluate the fitness of the achieved solutions.

Regarding the relation between PS and PS-PLA, we have: a) a PS-PLA<X> is obligatorily a PS<X>. If a scope is not a PS<X>, it cannot be in any circumstance a PS-PLA<X>; b) a PS<X> is not necessarily a PS-PLA<X>. If a scope is not a PS-PLA<X>, it can still be a PS<X>; and c) a design pattern X can be applied to any PS<X>, regardless the type of the architecture of the scope (conventional or PLA).

The PS and PS-PLA of each pattern are represented by instantiating the metamodel of Figure 1. The scope identification is given by some criteria. To exemplify the model instantiation, consider Figure 2, associated with the PS<Strategy> and PS-PLA<Strategy>. They include minimum requirements for the identification ("PS Requirement" and "PS-PLA Requirement" from Figure 1). The design pattern itself and the influenced software metrics were omitted. The architectural elements encompassed by PS and PS-PLA<Strategy> are a *Context*, which uses at least one *Class* or *Interface* that compose an *Algorithm Family*. For PS-PLA<Strategy>, *Context* must be a variation point and the *Classes/Interfaces* from the *Algorithm Family* must be variants.

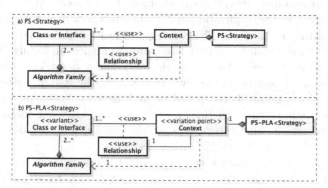

Fig. 2. Metamodel representing PS<Strategy> and PS-PLA<Strategy>

4   The Pattern-Driven Mutation Operator

Algorithm 1 presents the *Pattern-Driven Mutation Operator* proposed. First, a design pattern *DP* is randomly selected from the set of patterns (line 4). Then the mutation operator uses $f_s(A)$ to obtain a scope S from the architecture A (line 5). A possible implementation for $f_s(A)$ is to select a random number of random architectural elements (classes and interfaces) from A.

Algorithm 1. Pseudocode for the mutation operator

---
1   **Input:** A - Architecture to be mutated; $\rho_{mutation}$ - Mutation probability.
2   **Output:** The mutated architecture A
3   **begin**
4 | $DP \leftarrow$ randomly select a feasible design pattern;
5 | $S \leftarrow f_s(A)$;
6 | **if** $DP.verification(S, \rho_{pla})$ **and** $\rho_{mutation}$ *is achieved* **then**
7 | | $DP.apply(S)$;
8 | **end**
9 | **return** A;
10 **end**

The verification method *verify()* of *DP* checks whether the scope S is a PS/PS-PLA<*DP*> (line 6). The parameter ρ_{pla} is a random number to determine which verification method of *DP* will be used. If ρ_{pla} probability is not achieved, then the PS verification of DP is used, otherwise the PS-PLA verification is used. Therefore, if the verification method returns $true$ and the mutation probability $\rho_{mutation}$ is achieved, then the method $apply()$ applies DP to S (line 7). At the end, the architecture A is returned (line 9). Each design pattern has its own verification and application methods. In the next sections we present the verification and application methods of $Strategy$ and $Bridge$.

4.1 Verification Methods

Each pattern has a method named $verify()$ for PS verification. It receives a scope S as parameter and does several verifications on the elements of S to check if S is suitable to receive the application of DP, i.e., to check if S is a PS<DP>.

The verification method for PS<Strategy> checks if the scope has a set of architectural elements whih are part of a common algorithm family. After this, it verifies if at least one of the scope elements has a usage or a dependency relationship with an algorithm element, thus having the role of $context$. In this work, an algorithm family is composed by at least two classes/interfaces with: i) a common prefix or suffix in their names; or ii) at least one method with a common name and a same return type. Even though, different definitions for algorithm families could be used by other designers.

In SPL Engineering, a feature can be considered one concern to be realized. Concerns are used by the verification method of $Bridge$ to identify elements whose functionalities are related to some feature. In this work, concerns are associated with architectural elements by UML stereotypes.

The verification method for PS<Bridge> is similar to the method for PS<Strategy>, with an additional verification that checks if at least two elements from an algorithm family have at least one common concern assigned to them. Having a common concern assigned to a set of elements ensures their participation in a common functionality, so it can be abstracted by the $Bridge$ pattern. We assume a concern is: i) any feature directly assigned to a class or interface; and ii) any feature assigned to the methods of a class or interface.

Additionally, we also define PS-PLA verification methods for $Bridge$ and $Strategy$. The PS-PLA verification methods also check if the scope S is a PS-PLA for a specific pattern. The verification methods for PS-PLA<Strategy> and PS-PLA<Bridge> check if: i) $context$ is a variation point; and ii) all elements from the algorithm family are variants.

4.2 Application Methods

The method named $apply()$ performs the mutation. It applies the design pattern in the scope (PS or PS-PLA) by changing, removing and/or adding architectural elements. The application methods and some generic mutation examples are described below. Application methods identify the elements to be mutated in the scope and add a specific stereotype to the elements of the pattern structure, but these steps are implicit in the description. The attributes were suppressed in the diagrams due to lack of space and because they are not mutated by our operator.

The application methods first verify whether the respective design pattern is already applied to the scope. If yes, the method corrects, if necessary, any incoherence caused by other mutation operators in the elements associated with the pattern structure. Such corrections may be related to elements that should be part of the pattern structure or missing relationships.

Figure 3 presents an example of mutation performed by the method *apply()*. The architectural element "Client" in the PS<Strategy> has the role of *context*, whereas the concrete classes "AlgorithmA" and "AlgorithmB" are considered algorithms from an algorithm family because they have a common prefix in their names or a common method. The result of the mutation is shown in Figure 3.b.

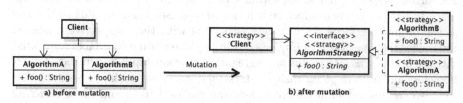

Fig. 3. Mutation example using the *Strategy* pattern

To reach this result, the *Strategy apply()* method either searches for any interface that has all the methods of the algorithm family and is implemented by any of the algorithm elements, or creates an interface *Strategy* for the algorithm family if such interface does not exist. After that, it declares in the *Strategy* interface all methods from the algorithm family elements and makes all algorithm elements to implement the *Strategy* interface and its methods. Then, it makes context and all other elements which use the elements from the algorithm family to use the *Strategy* interface instead. The relationship to the interface will be the same as before the mutation. If the architecture being mutated is a PLA and there is a variability whose variants are all part of an algorithm family, it moves this variability to the *Strategy* interface and defines it as variation point.

In the example, the *Strategy* interface "AlgorithmStrategy" was created to abstract all algorithms from the algorithm family: "AlgorithmA" and "AlgorithmB", which were decoupled from "Client" and can be interchanged dynamically. The method *foo()* is now declared and abstracted by the new interface.

In the same way, Figure 4 shows a mutation example for the *Bridge* pattern using its *apply()* method. "Client" has the role of *context*, whereas "ClassA" and "ClassB" are from an algorithm family and the concern x is assigned to them. These classes are considered algorithms from an algorithm family because they have a common prefix in their names or a common method (*foo()*).

To reach this result, the *Bridge apply()* method either searches for any abstract class (*abstraction*) that has all methods and concerns from the algorithm family and aggregates at least one interface of any algorithm element, or creates one if such class does not exist. After this, it declares in the *abstraction* class all methods from the algorithm elements and associates that class with all concerns of these elements. For each common concern assigned to the elements of the algorithm family, it either searches for an interface (*implementation*)

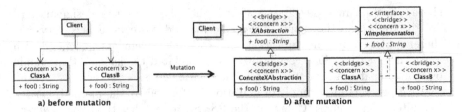

Fig. 4. Mutation example using the *Bridge* pattern

that: is aggregated by the *abstraction* class; is associated with the concern; and has all methods (from the algorithm elements) that are associated with the concern, or creates such interface if it does not exist. Then, it adds to the *implementation* interfaces the methods associated with their respective concerns, and makes the algorithms to implement the *implementation* interfaces associated with their concerns. It creates an aggregation relationship between the *abstraction* class and each *implementation* interface, if such relationships does not exist, and also creates a default concrete class and makes it to extend the *abstraction* class, if such class does not exist. At the end, it makes all elements which use the algorithms from the algorithm family to use the *abstraction* class instead. If the architecture being mutated is a PLA and there is a variability whose variants are all part of an algorithm family, then it moves this variability to the *implementation* interfaces and defines them as variation points.

The *Bridge* pattern has two main roles in its structure: *abstraction* ("XAbstraction" in the example) and *implementation* ("XImplementation"). The difference between them is that, whereas *implementation* defines which algorithm ("ClassA" or "ClassB") must be executed, *abstraction* defines how this execution is done. By detaching them, it is possible to vary them independently. For instance, if there were two concerns "X" and "Y", two *implementation* interfaces would have been created ("XImplementation" and "YImplementation"), then "ClassA" could be used to realize concern "X", while "ClassB" could be used to realize concern "Y". Furthermore, if only concern "X" was assigned to *foo()*, then it would be present in "XImplementation" and not in "YImplementation".

5   Empirical Study

An empirical study was conducted in order to answer the following research question: "Is the *Pattern-Driven Mutation Operator* beneficial for SBPD in terms of extensibility and modularity?". As mentioned before, the approach of Colanzi [6] aims at improving the PLA extensibility and modularity. The application of design patterns on PLA design by using the proposed *Pattern-Driven Mutation Operator* would obtain even better results with respect to these objectives.

In order to answer the research question, three experiments were configured, identified by: i) PLAM (*PLAMutation*) using only the operators of Colanzi's approach [8], named here traditional operators; ii) DPM (*DesignPatternMutation*) using only the *Pattern-Driven Mutation Operator*; and iii) PLADPM (*PLAandDesignPatternMutation*) using both kinds of operators. The results obtained in these three experiments were analyzed quantitatively, in terms of the fitness values (FM and CM values), and qualitatively, in terms of the solutions quality.

Three real PLAs were used. AGM (Arcade Game Maker [26]) encompasses three arcade games. MOS (Microwave Oven Software) [14] offers options from basic to top-of-the-line microwave ovens. The SSS (Service and Support System) [1] consists of applications with the purpose of letting a user or customer to request or receive technical assistance from a third party or computerized factor. Table 1 contains PLA information, such as the original *fitness* values (FM and CM), number of packages, interfaces, classes and variabilities.

Table 1. Characteristics of the PLAs

PLA	Fitness (FM, CM)	#Packages	#Interfaces	#Classes	#Variabilities
AGM	(789.0, 6.1)	9	15	31	5
MOS	(567.0, 0.1)	14	15	26	10
SSS	(118.0, 1.0)	6	0	30	11

We use NSGA-II [10], implemented by extending the framework jMetal [11]. NSGA-II is the algorithm generally used in related work [6,22]. No other algorithm was used because the goal of this study is only the proposed operator evaluation. Other algorithms can be evaluated in further studies.

The parameters were configured according to the experiments conducted by Colanzi. The maximum number of generations was set as 300 and it was used as stop criterion for all experiments. The population size value was 100. For the traditional mutation operators, used in the experiments PLAM and PLADPM, the mutation probability was 90%. For the *Pattern-Driven Mutation Operator* application, an empirical tuning [3] with the mutation values of 90%, 50% and 10% was conducted. Considering the hypervolume [28] of these three configurations, Friedman test [12] did not attest statistical difference among them. This can be explained by the capacity of *Pattern-Driven Mutation Operator* to encompass almost all elements that should be mutated in its operation and to correct the structures of design patterns. In this sense, a minimal quantity of mutation is enough to apply a design pattern or to correct it, while several mutations apply a design pattern only once in a scope, skip the next applications and only execute few corrections. We adopted the probability of 10%, since with this probability, the experiments were executed faster.

In the experiment PLADPM, first of all, a mutation operator was randomly selected and only after this the mutation probability was set. If the *Pattern-Driven Mutation Operator* were selected, the used mutation probability was 10%, otherwise, if a traditional operator were selected, the probability was 90%.

The initial population of each experiment is generated using one original instance of the used PLA and the remaining ones are obtained by applying a random mutation operator available in the experiment to the original PLA.

We performed 30 algorithm executions for each experiment and PLA. Each execution generated an *approximated Pareto front* (PF_a). Considering all solutions of each experiment, the *best-known Pareto front* (PF_k) [5] was obtained by joining the 30 PF_a and removing dominated and repeated solutions. Since the *true Pareto front* (PF_t) is not known, the PF_t for each PLA was obtained by the union of all sets PF_k and by removing dominated and repeated solutions.

We used hypervolume [28] to assess the quantitative quality of the generated solutions in our experiments. Briefly, hypervolume measures the area of the search space which is covered (dominated) by a Pareto front. Therefore, the higher the hypervolume value, the better the Pareto front. Besides using hypervolume as a quantitative indicator, we conducted a qualitative analysis to the solutions. We selected some solutions with the best Euclidean Distance to the ideal solution (ED) from each obtained Pareto front and analyzed them under the architects point of view to determine if they are coherent and anomaly free. ED measures how close a solution is to a fictional ideal solution (a solution with the best values for each objective), thus the solution with the lowest ED is the closest solution to the ideal one. It has the best trade-off between all solutions.

5.1   Results and Analysis

Table 2 presents quantitative results from each experiment. The second column shows the number of solutions in PF_t of each PLA. The third, fifth and seventh columns show the cardinality of each PF_k, and, between parenthesis, the number of solutions in PF_k that are part of PF_t. The fourth, sixth and eighth columns show the fitness values of each solution in PF_k. Solutions highlighted in bold are also in PF_t. For AGM, the solutions found by the PLAM experiment are the best ones and most numerous. These solutions dominated all other solutions found by the other two experiments. For MOS, the PLADPM experiment is better. It presents a greater number of optimal solutions, including most solutions of PF_t and both solutions found in PLAM (one of these solutions is the original MOS PLA). For SSS, the PLADPM and DPM experiments found the same two solutions (which are in PF_t), including the only one found by PLAM, which in this case is the original SSS PLA. The algorithm could not find many solutions because of the small search space of this PLA.

To evaluate the quality of each PF_k we used the hypervolume. Table 3 shows for each PLA in each experiment the mean hypervolume and the standard deviation in parenthesis (respectively, Columns 2, 3 and 4). The best hypervolume values are highlighted in bold. We used Friedman test at a 5% significance level [12] to perform a statistical comparison. For AGM, the PLAM experiment presented the best mean hypervolume, but Friedman test does not show difference between its results and PLADPM results. There is statistical difference only between PLAM and DPM results. For MOS, PLADPM is better than the other experiments, always with statistical significance. For SSS, PLADPM and DPM results are better than PLAM ones, with statistical difference. PLADM and DPM are statistically equivalent.

We observed that the PLADPM results are better than the DPM ones. A possible reason for this is that each operator of PLADPM (the pattern-driven operator and the traditional operators [8]) helps each other to trespass their local optimum, consequently bringing more diversity of solutions and improving the

Table 2. Experiments Results

PLA	PF$_t$	PLAM		PLADPM		DPM	
		PF$_k$	Fitness (FM, CM)	PF$_k$	Fitness (FM, CM)	PF$_k$	Fitness (FM, CM)
AGM	27	27 (27)	(657,2.059)(595,3.100) (605,3.091)(585,4.083) (831,2.025)(641,2.077) (730,2.031)(706,2.040) (717,2.034)(656,2.067) (698,2.042)(651,2.071) (631,3.059)(633,3.056) (770,2.026)(753,2.029) (762,2.026)(726,2.033) (684,2.045)(674,2.048) (670,2.053)(592,4.062) (567,4.111)(571,4.091) (640,2.111)(620,3.077) (625,3.067)	17 (0)	(925,2.053)(610,6.100) (611,6.083)(616,4.100) (684,2.083)(735,2.056) (734,2.059)(633,4.083) (673,2.111)(701,2.077) (681,2.100)(719,2.071) (729,2.062)(652,4.062) (646,4.067)(640,4.077) (622,4.091)	6 (0)	(789,6.143)(922,6.053) (892,6.067)(968,6.040) (936,6.048)(941,6.045)
MOS	10	2 (2)	(567,0.100)(543,0.125)	11 (9)	(543,0.125)(567,0.100) (737,0.067)(853,0.033) (847,0.034)(690,0.091) (812,0.045)(781,0.059) (708,0.083)(855,0.029) (784,0.048)	7 (3)	(543,0.125)(567,0.100) (878,0.059)(690,0.071) (1138,0.053)(1030,0.056) (831,0.067)
SSS	2	1 (1)	(118,1.000)	2 (2)	(118,1.000)(121,0.500)	2 (2)	(118,1.000)(121,0.500)

Table 3. Hypervolume Results

PLA	Mean Hypervolume (Standard Deviation)		
	PLAM	PLADPM	DPM
AGM	1098.4 (254.8)	683.8 (271.3)	23.7 (0.7)
MOS	73.8 (0.0)	94.4 (2.4)	84.8 (1.5)
SSS	0.31 (0.0)	0.36 (0.0)	0.36 (0.0)

evolutionary process and its results. Therefore, it seems that using both kinds of operators is a better choice than using only *Pattern-Driven Mutation Operator*.

In terms of solutions quality, a qualitative analysis shows the *Pattern-Driven Mutation Operator* does not introduce anomalies or incoherence in the generated PLAs. This happened because our operators are able to correct inconsistencies in the design patterns structures (as presented in Section 4.2). To illustrate this and how the operator works, Figure 5 presents an excerpt of a PLA design (solution) obtained in the PLADPM experiment with AGM. The picture shows the application of the *Strategy* design pattern.

Before the mutation, "PlayGameGUI" (*context*) was using the three algorithm elements "IPlayBrickles", "IPlayPong" and "IPlayBowling" directly with three dependency relationships. These algorithms had the same three methods before the mutation: *checkInstallation()*, *play()* and *checkDatePlayed()*. After the mutation, a *strategy* interface "IPlayStrategy" was created to abstract the three elements and *context* started using this interface instead. This mutation decouples *context* class from the algorithm elements and make them interchangeable. This mutation also improved the PLA extensibility, since the designer can add or remove algorithms without directly affecting the classes which use them. For the other PLAs, the results were similar, but involving more elements of different types and packages in the mutations.

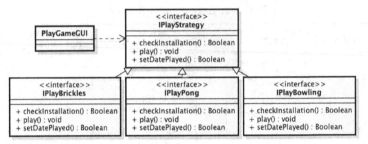

Fig. 5. PLA design achieved by applying *Strategy*

Figure 6 presents part of a solution obtained from PLADPM experiment with MOS PLA by applying *Bridge* design pattern.

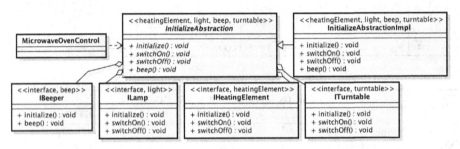

Fig. 6. PLA design achieved by applying *Bridge*

Before the experiment, in the original MOS PLA, the *context* class "MicrowaveOvenControl" was using the four *implementation* interfaces ("IBeeper", "ILamp", "IHeatingElement" and "ITurntable") directly. In fact, these interfaces are all from output components. After the mutation these interfaces were abstracted by two *abstraction* classes from *Bridge* pattern ("InitializeAbstraction" and "InitializeAbstractionImpl"). Now the designer can add new output elements by creating an aggregation between the *abstraction* class "InitializeAbstraction" and the new interface. With this mutation, the *Bridge* design pattern helps the *context* class to be decoupled from the *implementation* interfaces and to make these interfaces interchangeable. The solution is a coherent and anomaly-free application of the *Bridge* pattern. In addition, it is an architecture more extensible by making it able to easily accommodate new elements, and more modularized by keeping the elements in their components regarding their own operations.

It is hard to automatically determine if the flexibility of a pattern is needed in a scope. This decision is intellectual and should come from the designer. Our approach applies the patterns where they should be applied. When the final results are generated, the designer must choose architectures that fit for his/her purposes. In our experiment, there was only one instance of a design pattern by solution. In some cases the two design patterns were applied, but in different scopes of a same solution and not sharing elements.

As a conclusion of this study, and answering our research question, we observe that the application of design patterns helped to improve the design of the three PLAs presented in this section. The design patterns were applied in a coherent way, improved directly the hypervolume values and gave to the user a higher diversity of non-dominated solutions. Using the *Pattern-Driven Mutation Operator* contributed to find better solutions in terms of extensibility and modularity. It seems that the use of the proposed operator with the traditional ones is the best choice for a general case.

6 Related Work

We have not found in the literature works applying design patterns in the search-based optimization of PLA, maybe because SPL patterns is not a completely established research field. Works on this subject offer manual approaches and only apply specific patterns in particular domains [18,27]. Keepence and Mannion [18] developed a method that uses design patterns to model variabilities in object-oriented SPL models. They defined three patterns to model different variant types: (i) *Single Adapter* pattern, (ii) *Multiple Adapter* pattern and (iii) *Optional* pattern. The first two patterns allow modeling a group of mutually exclusive variants and a group of inclusive variants, respectively. The third pattern allows modeling optional variants. It is not possible to automatically apply these patterns in the context of our work, since they have some implementation details that cannot be identified in a class diagram. Ziadi *et al.* [27] proposed an approach based on the *Abstract Factory* design pattern to derive product models from a PLA modeled by UML. Their approach includes the usage specification of this pattern and an algorithm using OCL (Object Constraint Language) for the model derivation. However, the *Abstract Factory* was not used in our work, because it could not have its suitable scopes identified automatically.

Works most related to ours are from the search-based software design area [22]. However, they do not address specific characteristics of PLA design. Search-based algorithms have been used for finding optimal sequences of design pattern transformations to increase structural quality of software architectures [2,16,17,21]. Such works optimize the architectural design indirectly. Also, they do not find the appropriate place to apply the design patterns.

Cinnéide and Nixon [4] propose a semi-automated approach for applying patterns in systems using code refactoring. They assessed the approach application to the whole GoF catalog [13]. However, it delegates to the designer the decision of what pattern to apply and where. Räihä *et al.* [23,24] apply the design patterns *Facade, Adapter, Strategy, Template Method* and *Mediator* for synthesizing software architectures with genetic algorithms. The patterns are applied by mutation operators in order to build more modifiable and efficient solutions through the evolutionary process. Their approach ensures a valid automated application of design patterns. However, it does not necessarily mean that the design patterns are applied into suitable scopes. Furthermore, they adopted a different architecture representation from ours.

7 Concluding Remarks

This paper introduced an automatic way to apply design patterns in a search-based PLA design approach. We defined a metamodel to represent and identify suitable scopes associated with the design patterns, reducing probability of anomalies introduction. The model is used by a mutation operator, which includes verification and application methods to transform the PLA designs. The operator was implemented with NSGA-II and empirically evaluated.

The *Pattern-Driven Mutation Operator* contributed to find better solutions in terms of extensibility and modularity. For all SPLs, the use of the introduced operator with traditional operators obtained statistically better or equivalent results, considering the hypervolume. In a qualitative analysis, we observed coherent and anomaly-free application of design patterns in several scopes.

We intend to implement the mutation operator for other patterns, such as *Facade* and *Mediator*. We also intend to investigate the use of mini-patterns (such as the ones presented in [4]) to increase reuse, and the possibility of combining design patterns to improve the quality of the generated solutions. Future works can involve dynamic UML models, such as interaction and communication diagrams. Another possibility is to implement an interactive approach, so that the user can intervene directly with the approach to add his/her aesthetic experience in the evolution of PLAs and consequently to improve the results.

References

1. 3S Team: Service & Support Systems: UML Extentions - UML Profile for Software Product Line (2011), http://domainengineering.haifa.ac.il/seminar/Works/2011_ServiceAndSupportSystems/WebFiles/Pages/UML.html
2. Amoui, M., Mirarab, S., Ansari, S., Lucas, C.: A genetic algorithm approach to design evolution using design pattern transformation. International Journal of Information Technology and Intelligent Computing 1, 235–245 (2006)
3. Arcuri, A., Fraser, G.: On parameter tuning in search based software engineering. In: Cohen, M.B., Ó Cinnéide, M. (eds.) SSBSE 2011. LNCS, vol. 6956, pp. 33–47. Springer, Heidelberg (2011)
4. Cinnéide, M.Ó., Nixon, P.: Automated software evolution towards design patterns. In: Proceedings of the 4th International Workshop on Principles of Software Evolution, pp. 162–165 (2001)
5. Coello, C.A.C., Lamont, G.B., Veldhuizen, D.A.V.: Evolutionary Algorithms for Solving Multi-Objective Problems, 2nd edn. Springer Science and Business Media, LLC (2007)
6. Colanzi, T.E.: Search based design of software product lines architectures. In: 34th ICSE, Doctoral Symposium, pp. 1507–1510 (2012)
7. Colanzi, T.E., Vergilio, S.R.: Applying Search Based Optimization to Software Product Line Architectures: Lessons Learned. In: Fraser, G., Teixeira de Souza, J. (eds.) SSBSE 2012. LNCS, vol. 7515, pp. 259–266. Springer, Heidelberg (2012)
8. Colanzi, T.E., Vergilio, S.R.: Representation of Software Product Lines Architectures for Search-based Design. In: CMSBSE Workshop of ICSE (2013)

9. Coplien, J.O.: Software Design Patterns: Common Questions and Answers. In: Rising, L. (ed.) The Patterns Handbook: Techniques, Strategies, and Applications, pp. 311–320 (1998)

10. Deb, K., Pratap, A., Agarwal, S., Meyarivan, T.: A fast and elitist multiobjective genetic algorithm: NSGA-II. IEEE Transactions on Evolutionary Computation 6(2), 182–197 (2002)

11. Durillo, J.J., Nebro, A.J.: jMetal: A Java framework for multi-objective optimization. Advances in Engineering Software 42, 760–771 (2011)

12. Friedman, M.: The Use of Ranks to Avoid the Assumption of Normality Implicit in the Analysis of Variance. Journal of the American Statistical Association 32(200), 675–701 (1937)

13. Gamma, E., Helm, R., Johnson, R., Vlissides, J.: Design patterns: elements of reusable object-oriented software. Addison-Wesley Professional Computing Series, vol. 206 (1995)

14. Gomaa, H.: Designing Software Product Lines with UML: From Use Cases to Pattern-Based Software Architectures, vol. 8. Addison-Wesley Professional (2004)

15. Guizzo, G., Colanzi, T.E., Vergilio, S.R.: Applying design patterns in product line search-based design: feasibility analysis and implementation aspects. In: Proceedings of the 32nd SCCC (November 2013)

16. Harman, M., Tratt, L.: Pareto optimal search based refactoring at the design level. In: Proceedings of the 9th GECCO, pp. 1106–1113. ACM (2007)

17. Jensen, A.C., Cheng, B.H.C.: On the use of genetic programming for automated refactoring and the introduction of design patterns. In: Proceedings of the 12th GECCO, pp. 1341–1348 (2010)

18. Keepence, B., Mannion, M.: Using patterns to model variability in product families. IEEE Software, 102–108 (August, 1999)

19. van der Linden, F., Schmid, F., Rommes, E.: Software Product Lines in Action - The Best Industrial Practice in Product Line Engineering. Springer (2007)

20. Philippow, I., Streitferdt, D., Riebisch, M.: Design Pattern Recovery in Architectures for Supporting Product Line Development and Application. In: Modelling Variability for Object-Oriented Product Lines, pp. 42–57. Springer (2003)

21. Qayum, F., Heckel, R.: Local Search-Based Refactoring as Graph Transformation. In: Proceedings of the 1st SSBSE, pp. 43–46. IEEE Computer Society (2009)

22. Räihä, O.: A survey on search-based software design. Computer Science Review 4(4), 203–249 (2010)

23. Räihä, O., Koskimies, K., Mäkinen, E.: Generating software architecture spectrum with multi-objective genetic algorithms. In: Third World Congress NaBIC, pp. 29–36 (2011)

24. Räihä, O., Koskimies, K., Mäkinen, E.: Genetic synthesis of software architecture. In: Li, X., et al. (eds.) SEAL 2008. LNCS, vol. 5361, pp. 565–574. Springer, Heidelberg (2008)

25. Sant'Anna, C., Figueiredo, E., Garcia, A., Lucena, C.J.P.: On the modularity of software architectures: A concern-driven measurement framework. In: Oquendo, F. (ed.) ECSA 2007. LNCS, vol. 4758, pp. 207–224. Springer, Heidelberg (2007)

26. SEI: Arcade Game Maker pedagogical product line (2014), http://www.sei.cmu.edu/productlines/ppl/

27. Ziadi, T., Jézéquel, J., Fondement, F.: Product Line Derivation with UML. Tech. rep. (2003)

28. Zitzler, E., Thiele, L.: Multiobjective evolutionary algorithms: a comparative case study and the strength Pareto approach. IEEE Transactions on Evolutionary Computation 3(4), 257–271 (1999)

Mutation-Based Generation of Software Product Line Test Configurations

Christopher Henard, Mike Papadakis, and Yves Le Traon

Interdisciplinary Centre for Security, Reliability and Trust (SnT)
University of Luxembourg, Luxembourg
{christopher.henard,michail.papadakis,yves.letraon}@uni.lu

Abstract. Software Product Lines (SPLs) are families of software products that can be configured and managed through a combination of features. Such products are usually represented with a Feature Model (FM). Testing the entire SPL may not be conceivable due to economical or time constraints and, more simply, because of the large number of potential products. Thus, defining methods for generating test configurations is required, and is now a very active research topic for the testing community. In this context, mutation has recently being advertised as a promising technique. Mutation evaluates the ability of the test suite to detect defective versions of the FM, called mutants. In particular, it has been shown that existing test configurations achieving the mutation criterion correlate with fault detection. Despite the potential benefit of mutation, there is no approach which aims at generating test configurations for SPL with respect to the mutation criterion. In this direction, we introduce a search-based approach which explores the SPL product space to generate product test configurations with the aim of detecting mutants.

Keywords: Software Product Lines, Test Configuration Generation, Search-Based Software Engineering, Mutation, Feature Models.

1 Introduction

Software Product Lines (SPLs) extend the concept of reusability by allowing to configure and build tailored software product through a combination of different features [1]. Each feature represents a functionality or an abstraction of a functional requirement of the software product and is itself built from components, objects, modules or subroutines. Thus, an SPL is defined as a family of related software products that can easily be configured and managed, each product sharing common features while having specific ones. The possible products of an SPL are usually represented through a Feature Model (FM) which defines the legal combination between the features of the SPL, facilitates the derivation of new products and enables the automated analysis of the product line [2].

SPLs bring many benefits such as code resuability, a faster time to market, reduced costs and a flexible productivity [3]. However, SPLs are challenging to test due to the large amount of possible software that can be configured [4].

C. Le Goues and S. Yoo (Eds.): SSBSE 2014, LNCS 8636, pp. 92–106, 2014.
© Springer International Publishing Switzerland 2014

For instance, 20 optional features lead to 2^{20} possible products to configure, meaning more than a million of different software product that should be tested independently. Such a testing budget is usually unavailable for economic, technical or time reasons, preventing the SPL from being exhaustively tested. Thus, defining methods for generating test suites while giving enough confidence in what is tested is required, and is now a very active research topic for the testing community [5,6,7]. In this respect, Combinatorial Interaction Testing (CIT) [8] is a popular technique that has been applied to SPLs to reduce the size of the test suites. CIT operates by generating only the product configurations exercising feature interactions. While CIT has been shown to be effective for disclosing bugs [9,10], recent work has shown mutation as a promising alternative to the CIT criterion, also correlating with fault detection [11] for existing test suites.

Mutation evaluates the effectiveness of a test suite in terms of its ability to detect faults [12]. It operates by first creating defective versions of the artifact under test, called mutants and then by evaluating the ability of the test suite to detect the introduced mutants. Mutation has been identified as a powerful technique in several work, e.g., [13,14]. In this paper, defective versions of the FM are produced. A mutant is thus an altered version of the rules defining the legal feature associations. Such mutants are useful as they represent faulty implementations of the FMs that should be tested. Thus, while CIT measures the number of feature interactions of the FM exercised by the test suite, mutation measures the number of mutants detected by the test suite. However, and despite the potential benefit of mutation, there is no approach with the purpose of generating product configurations for SPL with respect to the mutation criterion.

Towards this direction, we devise the first approach which generates SPL test configurations using mutation of the FM. Since the SPL product space is too large to be exhaustively explored, we introduce a search-based technique based on the (1+1) Evolutionary Algorithm (EA) [15,16] in conjunction with a constraint solver in order to only deal with products that are conform to the FM. In order to guide the search towards the detection of mutants, four search operators are proposed to both add and remove test configurations from the test suite. The proposed approach solves the challenge of generating a test suite with respect to the mutation criterion. Experiments on 10 FMs show the ability of the proposed approach to generate test suites while with the purpose of mutation.

The remainder of this paper is organized as follows. Section 2 introduces the background concepts underlying the proposed approach. Section 3 describes the approach itself. Section 4 presents the conducted experiments. Finally, Section 5 discusses related work before Section 6 concludes the paper.

2   Background

2.1   Software Product Line Feature Models

A Feature Model (FM) encompasses the different features of the SPL and the constraints linking them. Thus, it defines the possible products that can be configured in an SPL. For instance, consider the FM of Figure 1. It contains 9 features. Some features are mandatory, which means included in every software product, e.g., `Draw`. There are other type of constraints for the features, such as implications or exclusion. For example, the presence of the `Color` feature in the software product requires the `Color Palette` one to be present too.

The FM can be represented as a boolean formula. In this paper, each constraint is represented in Conjunctive Normal Form (CNF). Such formulas are a conjunction of n clauses $C_1, ..., C_n$, where a clause is a disjunction of m literals. Here, a clause represents a constraint between features of the FM and a literal represent a feature that is selected (f_j) or not $(\overline{f_j})$:

$$FM = \bigwedge_{i=1}^{n} \underbrace{\left(\bigvee_{j=1}^{m} l_j \right)}_{\text{constraints}}, \text{ where } l_j = f_j \text{ or } \overline{f_j}.$$

For instance, the FM of Figure 1 encompasses $n = 18$ constraints represented as follows in Conjunctive Normal Form:

$f_1, (\overline{f_2} \vee f_1), (\overline{f_1} \vee f_2), (\overline{f_3} \vee f_1), (\overline{f_1} \vee f_3), (\overline{f_4} \vee f_1), (\overline{f_5} \vee f_1), (\overline{f_1} \vee f_5), (\overline{f_6} \vee f_3), (\overline{f_7} \vee f_3), (\overline{f_3} \vee f_6 \vee f_7), (\overline{f_8} \vee f_5), (\overline{f_9} \vee f_5), (\overline{f_5} \vee f_8 \vee f_9), (\overline{f_8} \vee \overline{f_9}), (\overline{f_7} \vee f_4), (\overline{f_4} \vee \overline{f_8}), (\overline{f_9} \vee f_4)$, where $RasterGraphicsEditor \mapsto f_1$, $Draw \mapsto f_2$, $Selection \mapsto f_3$, $ColorPalette \mapsto f_4$, $Rendering \mapsto f_5$, $Rectangular \mapsto f_6$, $ByColor \mapsto f_7$, $BlackWhite \mapsto f_8$, $Color \mapsto f_9$.

Thus, with respect to the FM of Figure 1, the corresponding boolean formula is a conjunction between all the constraints:

$$FM =$$
$f_1 \wedge (\overline{f_2} \vee f_1) \wedge (\overline{f_1} \vee f_2) \wedge (\overline{f_3} \vee f_1) \wedge (\overline{f_1} \vee f_3) \wedge (\overline{f_4} \vee f_1) \wedge (\overline{f_5} \vee f_1) \wedge (\overline{f_1} \vee f_5) \wedge (\overline{f_6} \vee f_3) \wedge (\overline{f_7} \vee f_3) \wedge (\overline{f_3} \vee f_6 \vee f_7) \wedge (\overline{f_8} \vee f_5) \wedge (\overline{f_9} \vee f_5) \wedge (\overline{f_5} \vee f_8 \vee f_9) \wedge (\overline{f_8} \vee \overline{f_9}) \wedge (\overline{f_7} \vee f_4) \wedge (\overline{f_4} \vee \overline{f_8}) \wedge (\overline{f_9} \vee f_4)$.

2.2   Software Product Line Test Configurations

We denote as a *test configuration* (TC) or *product configuration* to test the list of features of the FM that are present or not in a given product. For instance, with

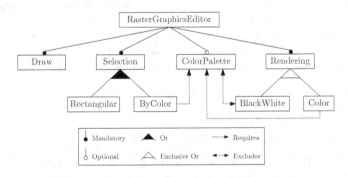

Fig. 1. A Feature Model of a raster graphic editor Software Product Line

respect to Figure 1, $TC_1 = \{f_1, f_2, f_3, f_4, f_5, \overline{f_6}, f_7, \overline{f_8}, f_9\}$ is a TC representing the software product proposing all the features except the rectangular selection and the black and white rendering. This TC satisfies the constraints of the FM that are described in the previous subsection. On the contrary, $TC_2 = \{f_1, \overline{f_2}, f_3, f_4, f_5, \overline{f_6}, f_7, \overline{f_8}, f_9\}$ violates the constraint which specifies that $f_2 =$ Draw is a mandatory feature. In the remainder of this paper, only TCs satisfying the constraints of the FM are considered. To this end, a satisfiability (SAT) solver is used. Finally, we denote as *test suite* (TS) a set of TCs.

3   Mutation-Based Generation of Software Product Line Test Configurations

The approach for generating TCs starts by creating mutants of the SPL FM. Then, a search-based process based on the (1+1) Evolutionary Algorithm (EA) [15,16] makes use of both the FM and the mutants to produce a set of test configurations. The (1+1) EA is a hill climbing approach which has been proven to be effective in several studies [17,18]. The overview of the approach is depicted in Figure 2. The following sections describe the different steps of the approach.

3.1   Creation of Mutants of the Feature Model

The first step of the approach creates altered versions of the FM. Each altered version is called a mutant and contains a defect within the boolean formula of the FM. For instance, the two following mutants are produced from the FM example of Figure 1:

$$M_1 =$$
$$\overline{f_1} \wedge (\overline{f_2} \vee f_1) \wedge (\overline{f_1} \vee f_2) \wedge (\overline{f_3} \vee f_1) \wedge (\overline{f_1} \vee f_3) \wedge (\overline{f_4} \vee f_1) \wedge (\overline{f_5} \vee f_1) \wedge (\overline{f_1} \vee f_5) \wedge (\overline{f_6} \vee f_3) \wedge (\overline{f_7} \vee f_3) \wedge (\overline{f_3} \vee f_6 \vee f_7) \wedge (\overline{f_8} \vee f_5) \wedge (\overline{f_9} \vee f_5) \wedge (\overline{f_5} \vee f_8 \vee f_9) \wedge (\overline{f_8} \vee \overline{f_9}) \wedge (\overline{f_7} \vee f_4) \wedge (\overline{f_4} \vee \overline{f_8}) \wedge (\overline{f_9} \vee f_4).$$

$$M_2 =$$
$$f_1 \wedge (\overline{f_2} \wedge f_1) \wedge (\overline{f_1} \vee f_2) \wedge (\overline{f_3} \vee f_1) \wedge (\overline{f_1} \vee f_3) \wedge (\overline{f_4} \vee f_1) \wedge (\overline{f_5} \vee f_1) \wedge (\overline{f_1} \vee f_5) \wedge (\overline{f_6} \vee f_3) \wedge (\overline{f_7} \vee f_3) \wedge (\overline{f_3} \vee f_6 \vee f_7) \wedge (\overline{f_8} \vee f_5) \wedge (\overline{f_9} \vee f_5) \wedge (\overline{f_5} \vee f_8 \vee f_9) \wedge (\overline{f_8} \vee \overline{f_9}) \wedge (\overline{f_7} \vee f_4) \wedge (\overline{f_4} \vee \overline{f_8}) \wedge (\overline{f_9} \vee f_4).$$

In M_1, a literal has been negated whereas in M_2, an operator OR has been replaced by an AND one. It should be noted that the proposed approach is independent from the way the mutants have been created and from the changes they operate compared to the original FM.

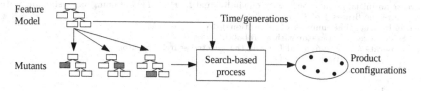

Fig. 2. Overview of the approach for generating test configurations

3.2   The Search-Based Process

Once the mutants are created, the search-based process starts to generate a set of test configurations. The different steps of the approach are described in Algorithm 1 and detailed in the following. First, an initial population is created and its fitness is evaluated (line 1 and 2). Then, the population is evolved (line 3 to 10): search-operators try to improve the population by adding or removing test configurations.

Individual. An individual I or potential solution to the problem is a set of $k \geq 1$ test configurations that are conform to the FM: $I = \{TC_1, ..., TC_k\}$.

Population. The population P is composed of only one individual: $P = \{I\}$.

Initial Population. The individual of the initial population is initialized by generating randomly a test configuration that is conform to the FM by using a SAT solver.

Fitness Evaluation. The fitness f of an individual I is calculated by evaluating how many mutants are not satisfied by at least one of the test configurations of I. This is called *mutation score*. More formally, if we denote as $M = \{M_1, ..., M_m\}$ the m mutants of the FM, the fitness f of an individual I is evaluated as follows:

$$F(I) = \frac{|\{M_i \in M \mid \exists TC_j \in I \mid TC_j \text{ does not satisfy } M_i\}|}{m} = \text{mutation score},$$

where $|A|$ denotes the cardinality of the set A. It should be noted that all the test configurations considered are satisfying the FM since they belong to I.

Search Operators. The approach makes use of four search operators that operate on an individual I. The operators are divided into two categories: operators that *add* a new test configuration and operators that *remove* a test configuration. The operators are depicted in Figure 3.

Algorithm 1. Generation of SPL Test Configurations

```
 1: Create an initial population P with one individual I : P = {I} containing one test configuration
 2: Evaluate the fitness f of I : f = F(I)
 3: while budget (time, number of generations) do
 4:     Select a search operator with a probability p
 5:     Generate a new individual I' using the selected search operator
 6:     Evaluate the fitness f' = F(I')
 7:     if f' ≥ f then
 8:         I = I'
 9:     end if
10: end while
11: return I
```

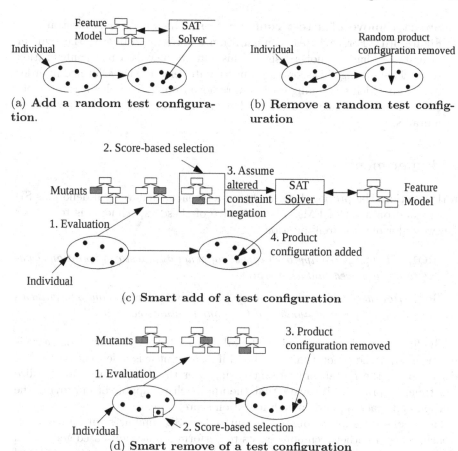

(a) **Add a random test configuration.**

(b) **Remove a random test configuration**

(c) **Smart add of a test configuration**

(d) **Smart remove of a test configuration**

Fig. 3. The search operators used to generate a test configuration set

- **Add a random test configuration.** This operator is presented in Figure 3(a). It adds to the considered individual a test configuration randomly chosen from the space of all the test configurations of the FM .
- **Remove a random test configuration.** This operator is depicted in Figure 3(b). It randomly removes a test configuration from the individual.
- **Smart add of a test configuration.** This operator is presented in Figure 3(c). First, the altered constraints of the mutants are collected. Then, for each constraint, the number of test configurations from I that do not satisfy it is evaluated. This can be view as a mutant constraint score. Then, using this score, a proportionate selection is performed in order to choose one of these constraints. The idea is to promote the constraint that is the less not satisfied by the test configurations of I. Then, the operators tries to select a test configuration which is at the same time satisfying the FM and the negation of the selected constraint. Doing so will result in a test configuration that is able to violate a clause of the mutant and thus do not satisfy it.

- **Smart remove of a test configuration**. This operator is illustrated in Figure 3(d). For each test configuration of I, it is evaluated the number of mutants that are not satisfied. This can be view as a test configuration score. Then, using this score, a proportionate selection is performed in order to choose which test configuration to remove from I. The idea is to promote the removal of test configurations that are not satisfying the less amount of mutants.

4   Experiments

In this section, the proposed search-based approach, that we will denote as SB is evaluated on a set of FMs. The objective of these experiments is to answer the two following research questions:

- [RQ1] *Is the proposed approach capable of generating test configurations leading to an improved mutation score?*
- [RQ2] *How does the proposed approach compare with a random one in terms of mutation score and number of test configurations generated?*

The first research question aims at evaluating whether the mutation score is increasing over the generations of SB and if at a point it is able to converge. We expect to see the mutation score increasing over the generations and stabilize at a time. In practice, it means that the approach is capable of improving the solution and reach a good enough mutation score.

The second question amounts to evaluate how SB compares with a naive approach. Since no other technique exists to perform a mutation-based generation of TCs for SPLs, we compare it to a random one. To this end, two bases of comparison are used. The first one is the evaluation of the mutation score when generating the same number of test configurations with both approaches. The second baseline evaluates the number of configurations required by the random approach to achieve the same level of mutation score as SB. It is expected that a higher mutation score than random for the same number of configurations will be observed and we expect a random generation to necessitate more configurations than SB to achieve a given mutation score.

In order to answer these two questions, an experiment is performed on 10 FMs of various size taken from the Software Product Line Online Tools (SPLOT) [19], which is a widely used repository in the literature. The FMs used in the experiments are described in Table 1. For each FM, it presents the number of features, the number of constraints, the number of possible products and the number of mutants used. The mutants have been created using the mutants operator presented in Table 2 and taken from [20,21]. The mutants leading to an invalid FM formula (e.g., $a \wedge \neg a$) and equivalent mutants (mutants that can never be detected because they are always satisfied by any test configuration) are not considered in this work. Finally, in order to generate random configurations from the FM and the mutants, the PicoSAT SAT solver [22] is used.

Table 1. The feature models used for the experiments

Feature Model	Features	Constraints	Possible products	Mutants
Cellphone	11	22	14	119
Counter Strike	24	35	18,176	208
SPL SimulES, PnP	32	54	73,728	291
DS Sample	41	201	6,912	1,086
Electronic Drum	52	119	331,776	664
Smart Home v2.2	30	82	3.87×10^9	434
Video Player	71	99	4.5×10^{13}	582
Model Transformation	88	151	1.65×10^{13}	851
Coche Ecologico	94	191	2.32×10^7	1,030
Printers	172	310	1.14×10^{27}	1,829

Table 2. Mutation operators used in the experiments in order to alter feature models

Mutation Operator	Action
Literal Omission (LO)	A literal is removed
Literal Negation (LN)	A literal is negated
OR Reference (OR)	An OR operator is replaced by AND

4.1   Approach Assessment (RQ1)

Setup. SB has been performed 30 times independently per FM with 1,000 generation with an equal probability $p = 0.25$ to apply one of the four operators.

4.2   Results

The results are recorded in Figure 4 and Table 3. The figure presents the evolution of the mutation score averaged on all the FM and all the 30 runs while the table presents detailed results per FM. With respect to Figure 4, one can see the ability of the approach to improve the mutation score over the generations and stabilize around 0.8. With respect to Table 3, one may observe that the approach is able to improve the mutation score for each of the considered FM, with improvements of 68% in average for the DS Sample FM. Besides, there are very small (0.03) or non-existent variations among the different final mutation score achieved over the 30 runs, fact demonstrating the ability of SB to reach a good solution at each execution of the approach. Finally, it should be noticed that SB achieves the above-mentioned results using only a small number of generations (1,000 generations). This is an achievement since search-based techniques usually require thousands of executions in order to be effective [18].

4.3   Answering RQ1

The results presented in the previous section demonstrate the ability of SB to both improve the mutation score over the generations and converge towards

Table 3. Comparison between the initial and final mutation score achieved by the proposed search-based approach on the 30 runs for 1,000 generations

Feature Model \ Mutation score	Generation 1			Generation 1,000		
	min	max	avg	min	max	avg
Cellphone	0.39	0.66	0.5	0.79	0.79	0.79
Counter Strike	0.37	0.56	0.45	0.79	0.79	0.79
SPL SimuleES, PnP	0.42	0.62	0.49	0.7	0.7	0.7
DS Sample	0.17	0.27	0.22	0.9	0.9	0.9
Electronic Drum	0.38	0.56	0.44	0.78	0.78	0.78
Smart Home v2.2	0.45	0.66	0.54	0.89	0.89	0.89
Video Player	0.36	0.55	0.45	0.69	0.72	0.71
Model Transformation	0.41	0.61	0.5	0.86	0.86	0.86
Coche Ecologico	0.44	0.57	0.49	0.8	0.8	0.8
Printers	0.35	0.45	0.41	0.74	0.75	0.75

an acceptable mutation score. Indeed, some mutants may not be detectable if they are either leading to an invalid formula or an equivalent to the original FM formula (i.e., there is no test configuration that cannot satisfy it), thus limiting the maximum score achievable by the approach. In this work, we only focus on the process of generating the test suite to maximize the mutation score. Finally, we observe improvements in the mutation score of over 60% and a quick convergence, with very small variations between each of the 30 runs, thus giving confidence in the validity of the search approach.

4.4   Comparison with Random (RQ2)

Setup SB has been performed 30 times independently per FM with 1,000 generation allowed. An equal probability $p = 0.25$ to apply one of the four operators has been set. For each run of SB, a random one has been conducted in order to

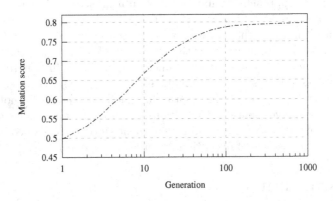

Fig. 4. Evolution of the mutation score over the 1,000 generations of the proposed approach averaged on all the feature models for the 30 runs

Table 4. Comparison between the search-based approach (SB) and a random one on the following basis: (a) same number of test configurations and (b) same mutation score (MS). Each approach has been performed 30 times independently. #Conf denotes the number of test configurations. The execution time is in seconds.

Feature Model	30 runs	SB approach			Rand. same #Conf		Rand. same MS	
		#Conf	MS	Time	MS	Time	#Conf	Time
	min	3	0.79	2	0.48	0	4	0
Cellphone	max	4	0.79	3	0.79	0	42	0
	avg	3.46	0.79	2.66	0.67	0	12.4	0
	min	7	0.8	9	0.68	0	22	0
Counter Strike	max	11	0.8	11	0.75	1	109	2
	avg	9.53	0.8	10.6	0.72	0.16	43.73	0.56
	min	3	0.7	11	0.61	0	4	0
SPL SimulES, PnP	max	5	0.7	13	0.7	1	30	1
	avg	4.36	0.7	11.9	0.66	0.1	9.66	0.16
	min	16	0.9	46	0.56	0	32	1
DS Sample	max	17	0.9	49	0.77	1	114	8
	avg	16.03	0.9	46.8	0.70	0.2	60.26	2.9
	min	5	0.78	22	0.66	0	9	0
Electronic Drum	max	8	0.78	27	0.77	1	29	1
	avg	6.83	0.78	24.8	0.72	0	15.46	0.3
	min	7	0.88	26	0.79	0	13	0
Smart Home v2.2	max	11	0.88	30	0.88	1	43	2
	avg	8.36	0.88	28	0.84	0.1	22.7	0.66
	min	14	0.69	53	0.62	0	161	19
Video Player	max	22	0.72	65	0.65	1	1,000*	532
	avg	18.86	0.71	59	0.64	0.5	518	183
	min	8	0.86	54	0.77	0	15	0
Model Transfo.	max	12	0.86	67	0.85	1	56	4
	avg	9.36	0.86	59.2	0.82	0.2	31.13	1.86
	min	11	0.8	75	0.71	0	17	1
Coche Ecologico	max	14	0.8	89	0.77	1	57	7
	avg	11.76	0.8	80	0.74	0.	31.36	2.9
	min	25	0.74	443	0.67	2	149	110
Printers	max	35	0.75	567	0.72	3	1,000*	4,928
	avg	30	0.75	513	0.70	2.4	481	1,264

*The number of test configurations required by random to achieve the same mutation score as SB has been limited to 1,000.

(a) evaluate the mutation score achieved when randomly generating the same number of TCs as the number proposed by SB, and (b) evaluate the amount of generated TCs required by the random approach in order to achieved the same mutation score. In the latter case, a limit of 1,000 TCs has been set.

Results. The results are recorded in Table 4. It presents the minimum, maximum and average number of TCs, mutation score (MS) achieved and execution time in seconds for the following approaches: SB, random based on the same number of test configurations as SB and random based on the same mutation score as SB. Besides, Figure 5 depicts the distribution of the values over the 30 runs and Figure 6 presents the average values. From these results, one can see that SB is quite stable, with small variations in both the mutation score and number of configurations achieved (5(b) and 5(a)). Compared to random based

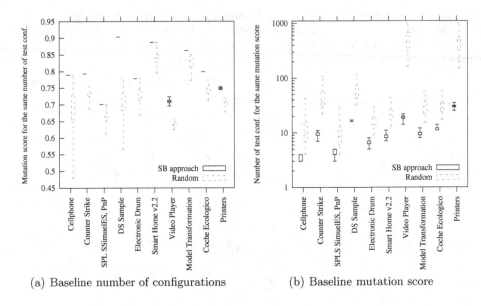

(a) Baseline number of configurations   (b) Baseline mutation score

Fig. 5. Search-based approach VS Random: distribution of the mutation score and number of test configurations on the 30 runs

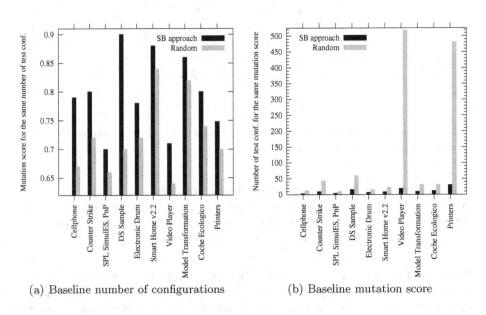

(a) Baseline number of configurations   (b) Baseline mutation score

Fig. 6. Search-based approach VS Random: average values of the mutation score and number of test configurations on the 30 runs

on the same number of configurations, SB always performs better in terms of mutation score. For instance, for the DS Sample FM, there is a difference of 0.34 on minimum mutation score achieved and 0.2 on the average one (Table 4). Regarding the comparison based on the mutation score, the random approach requires much more TCs to achieve the same mutation score. For instance, with respect to the Video Player FM, the random approach requires in average more than 500 TCs to reach a mutation score of 0.71 while SB only needs less than 20 (Figure 6(a)). In addition, there were some cases, e.g., the Printers FM where the random approach was not able to achieved the same mutation score as the one reached by SB, requiring more than 1,000 TCs and more execution time than SB.

Answering RQ2. Our results show that SB outperforms the random approach. We observed a difference between random and SB of up to 34 % in favor of SB. Additionally, the random technique requires much more test configurations to achieve a given mutation score. In some cases, it is not even able to terminate, requiring more than 20 times more TCs. This shows the ability of SB to generate TCs while at the same time maximizing the mutation score that can be achieved.

4.5   Threats to Validity

The experiments performed in this paper are subject to potential threats towards their validity. First, the FMs employed are only a sample and thus the generalization of theses results to all possible FMs is not certain. In particular, using different models might lead to different results. In order to reduce this threat, we selected 10 FMs of different size and complexity. Thus, we tried to use a diversify and representative set of subjects. A second potential threat can be due to the experiments themselves. First, there is a risk that the observed results happened by chance. To reduce this threat, we have repeated the execution of both the proposed approach and the random one 30 times per FM. Doing so allows reducing risks due to random effects. Another threat can be due to the SAT solver used. Indeed, there is a risk that another solver will lead to different results. We choose the PicoSAT solver as it was easy to modify it to produce random solutions. The same threat holds for the mutation operator used. We tried to employ various mutation operators that are relevant for FM formulas. This paper aims at generating test configurations with the aim of detecting mutants. The ability of finding faults is not evaluated. Regarding the mutation score achieved, it is expected that giving more time to the search-based approach will provide better results. Even if small differences are observed in the mutation score compared to the random approach, this can be in practice leading to finding more faults [11,17]. Finally, the presented results could be erroneous due to potential bugs within the implementation of the described techniques. To minimize such threats, we divided our implementation into separated modules. We also make publicly available the source code and the data used for the experiments.

5   Related Work

The use of metaheuristic search techniques for the purpose of the automatic generation of test data has been a burgeoning interest for researchers [23]. In this context, several work have investigated the product configuration generation for SPLs using a metaheuristic search. For instance, in [24], Ensan *et al.* aim at generating a test suite with a genetic algorithm by exploring the whole SPL product space, including product that do not fulfill the FM constraints. In this work, we only explore the space of product satisfying the FM, by using a SAT solver. The importance but also the overhead induced by constraint solvers has been shown in [4,25] and used in some work for the purpose of CIT. For instance, in [26], Garvin *et al.* proposed a simulated annealing approach for generating configurations based on CIT. In [27], a multi-objective genetic algorithm in conjunction with a SAT solver was proposed by the authors with CIT as one of the objective to fulfill. There are also work exploring the whole search space to compute the optimal test suite according to CIT, such as [28]. In this work, we propose a simple hill-climbing-based approach in conjunction with the SAT solver. The difference is that we do not consider CIT as an objective. The product configuration generation process is guided by the mutation score. An exact solving technique can only be used for moderate size search spaces. In this paper, we focus on larger SPLs where the product space cannot be fully explored. Finally, there are work focusing on test case generation for each software product [29].

Mutation has been widely used for the purpose of testing and test generation, e.g., [30,31]. With respect to the mutation of models such as FMs for SPL, Henard *et al.* [20] introduced some operators and used mutants of FM in order to evaluate the ability of a given test suite to find them. While the concept of mutation score was used, it was only a way to evaluate a given test suite. In this paper, the mutation score is used to guide the search for generating test suites. Besides, it has been shown that measuring the mutation score of a test suite with respect to a CIT model like FMs rather than measuring the number of interactions covered gives a stronger correlation to code-level faults [11]. In this paper, we used FMs represented as boolean formulas from which we created mutants. There are several work who investigated the mutation of logic formulas. For instance, Gargantini and Fraser devised a technique to generate tests for possible faults of boolean expressions [32]. In this work, the smart add search operator also aims at triggering the fault introduced in the mutant by using a SAT solver. In the context of logic-based testing, Kaminski *et al.* [33] proposed an approach to design tests depending on logical expressions. In this paper, mutation operators are applied on the logic formula of the FM. The objective is only to generate test configurations according to the mutants of the FM formula.

6   Conclusion and Future Work

This paper devised an approach for generating test configurations for SPLs based on mutation. The novelty of the proposed technique is the use of mutation of the

FM to guide the search, thus focusing on possible faulty implementation of the FM that should be tested. To the authors knowledge, it is the first approach that is performing so. The conducted experiments show the benefit of the approach compared to a random one as it is able to both reduce the test suite size while significantly increasing the mutation score. To enable the reproducibility of our results, our implementation and the FMs used are publicly available at:

http://research.henard.net/SPL/SSBSE_2014/.

Future work spans in the three following directions. First, we will investigate the influence of the parameters and study different variants of the algorithm. In particular, we will compare with standard genetic algorithms. Second, we will propose new operators for improving the search process. Finally, we will undertake supplementary experimentations to further validate the presented findings.

References

1. Pohl, K., Böckle, G., van der Linden, F.: Software Product Line Engineering - Foundations, Principles, and Techniques. Springer (2005)
2. Benavides, D., Segura, S., Cortés, A.R.: Automated analysis of feature models 20 years later: A literature review. Inf. Syst. 35(6), 615–636 (2010)
3. Knauber, P., Bermejo, J., Böckle, G., Sampaio do Prado Leite, J.C., van der Linden, F., Northrop, L., Stark, M., Weiss, D.M.: Quantifying product line benefits. In: van der Linden, F.J. (ed.) PFE 2002. LNCS, vol. 2290, pp. 155–163. Springer, Heidelberg (2002)
4. Perrouin, G., Sen, S., Klein, J., Baudry, B., Traon, Y.L.: Automated and scalable t-wise test case generation strategies for software product lines (2010)
5. do Carmo Machado, I., McGregor, J.D., de Almeida, E.S.: Strategies for testing products in software product lines. ACM SIGSOFT Software Engineering Notes 37(6), 1–8 (2012)
6. Engström, E., Runeson, P.: Software product line testing - a systematic mapping study. Information & Software Technology 53(1), 2–13 (2011)
7. da Mota Silveira Neto, P.A., do Carmo Machado, I., McGregor, J.D., de Almeida, E.S., de Lemos Meira, S.R.: A systematic mapping study of software product lines testing. Information & Software Technology 53(5), 407–423 (2011)
8. Nie, C., Leung, H.: A survey of combinatorial testing. ACM Comput. Surv. 43(2), 11 (2011)
9. Kuhn, D.R., Wallace, D.R., Gallo, A.M.: Software fault interactions and implications for software testing. IEEE Trans. Software Eng. 30(6), 418–421 (2004)
10. Petke, J., Yoo, S., Cohen, M.B., Harman, M.: Efficiency and early fault detection with lower and higher strength combinatorial interaction testing. In: ESEC/SIGSOFT FSE, pp. 26–36 (2013)
11. Papadakis, M., Henard, C., Traon, Y.L.: Sampling program inputs with mutation analysis: Going beyond combinatorial interaction testing. ICST (2014)
12. Jia, Y., Harman, M.: An analysis and survey of the development of mutation testing. IEEE Trans. Software Eng. 37(5), 649–678 (2011)
13. Offutt, J.: A mutation carol: Past, present and future. Information & Software Technology 53(10), 1098–1107 (2011)

14. Papadakis, M., Malevris, N.: Mutation based test case generation via a path selection strategy. Information & Software Technology 54(9), 915–932 (2012)
15. Droste, S., Jansen, T., Wegener, I.: On the analysis of the (1+1) evolutionary algorithm. Theor. Comput. Sci. 276(1-2), 51–81 (2002)
16. Lehre, P.K., Yao, X.: Runtime analysis of the (1 + 1) ea on computing unique input output sequences. Inf. Sci. 259, 510–531 (2014)
17. Henard, C., Papadakis, M., Perrouin, G., Klein, J., Heymans, P., Le Traon, Y.: Bypassing the combinatorial explosion: Using similarity to generate and prioritize t-wise test configurations for software product lines. IEEE Trans. Software Eng. (2014)
18. Harman, M., McMinn, P.: A theoretical and empirical study of search-based testing: Local, global, and hybrid search. IEEE Trans. Software Eng. 36(2), 226–247 (2010)
19. Mendonça, M., Branco, M., Cowan, D.D.: S.P.L.O.T.: Software product lines online tools (2009)
20. Henard, C., Papadakis, M., Perrouin, G., Klein, J., Traon, Y.L.: Assessing software product line testing via model-based mutation: An application to similarity testing. In: ICST Workshops, pp. 188–197 (2013)
21. Kaminski, G.K., Praphamontripong, U., Ammann, P., Offutt, J.: A logic mutation approach to selective mutation for programs and queries. Information & Software Technology 53(10), 1137–1152 (2011)
22. Biere, A.: Picosat essentials. JSAT 4(2-4), 75–97 (2008)
23. McMinn, P.: Search-based software test data generation: A survey. Softw. Test., Verif. Reliab. 14(2), 105–156 (2004)
24. Ensan, F., Bagheri, E., Gašević, D.: Evolutionary search-based test generation for software product line feature models. In: Ralyté, J., Franch, X., Brinkkemper, S., Wrycza, S. (eds.) CAiSE 2012. LNCS, vol. 7328, pp. 613–628. Springer, Heidelberg (2012)
25. Cohen, M.B., Dwyer, M.B., Shi, J.: Constructing interaction test suites for highly-configurable systems in the presence of constraints: A greedy approach. IEEE Trans. Software Eng. 34(5), 633–650 (2008)
26. Garvin, B.J., Cohen, M.B., Dwyer, M.B.: Evaluating improvements to a meta-heuristic search for constrained interaction testing 16, 61–102 (2011)
27. Henard, C., Papadakis, M., Perrouin, G., Klein, J., Traon, Y.L.: Multi-objective test generation for software product lines. In: SPLC, pp. 62–71 (2013)
28. Lopez-Herrejon, R.E., Chicano, F., Ferrer, J., Egyed, A., Alba, E.: Multi-objective optimal test suite computation for software product line pairwise testing. In: ICSM, pp. 404–407 (2013)
29. Xu, Z., Cohen, M.B., Motycka, W., Rothermel, G.: Continuous test suite augmentation in software product lines. In: SPLC, pp. 52–61 (2013)
30. Harman, M., Jia, Y., Langdon, W.B.: Strong higher order mutation-based test data generation. In: SIGSOFT FSE, pp. 212–222 (2011)
31. Fraser, G., Zeller, A.: Mutation-driven generation of unit tests and oracles. IEEE Trans. Software Eng. 38(2), 278–292 (2012)
32. Gargantini, A., Fraser, G.: Generating minimal fault detecting test suites for general boolean specifications. Information & Software Technology 53(11), 1263–1273 (2011)
33. Kaminski, G., Ammann, P., Offutt, J.: Improving logic-based testing. Journal of Systems and Software 86(8), 2002–2012 (2013)

Multi-objective Genetic Optimization
for Noise-Based Testing of Concurrent Software

Vendula Hrubá, Bohuslav Křena, Zdeněk Letko, Hana Pluháčková, and Tomáš Vojnar

IT4Innovations Centre of Excellence, Brno University of Technology, Czech Republic
{ihruba,krena,iletko,ipluhackova,vojnar}@fit.vutbr.cz

Abstract. Testing of multi-threaded programs is a demanding work due to the many possible thread interleavings one should examine. The noise injection technique helps to increase the number of thread interleavings examined during repeated test executions provided that a suitable setting of noise injection heuristics is used. The problem of finding such a setting, i.e., the so called test and noise configuration search problem (TNCS problem), is not easy to solve. In this paper, we show how to apply a multi-objective genetic algorithm (MOGA) to the TNCS problem. In particular, we focus on generation of TNCS solutions that cover a high number of distinct interleavings (especially those which are rare) and provide stable results at the same time. To achieve this goal, we study suitable metrics and ways how to suppress effects of non-deterministic thread scheduling on the proposed MOGA-based approach. We also discuss a choice of a concrete MOGA and its parameters suitable for our setting. Finally, we show on a set of benchmark programs that our approach provides better results when compared to the commonly used random approach as well as to the sooner proposed use of a single-objective genetic approach.

1 Introduction

Multi-threaded software design has become widespread with the arrival of multi-core processors into common computers. Multi-threaded programming is, however, significantly more demanding. Concurrency-related errors such as data races [9], atomicity violations [21], and deadlocks [3], are easy to cause but very difficult to discover due to the many possible thread interleavings to be considered [22,8]. This situation stimulates research efforts towards advanced methods of testing, analysis, and formal verification of concurrent software.

Precise static methods of verification, such as model checking [6], do not scale well and their use is rather expensive for complex software. Therefore, lightweight static analyses [2], dynamic analyses [9], and especially testing [26] are still very popular in the field. A major problem for testing of concurrent programs is the non-deterministic nature of multi-threaded computation. It has been shown [22,8] that even repeated execution of multi-threaded tests, when done naïvely, does often miss many possible behaviors of the program induced by different thread interleavings. This problem is targeted by the *noise injection* technique [8] which disturbs thread scheduling and thus increases chances to examine more possible thread interleavings. This approach does significantly improve the testing process provided that a suitable setting of noise injection heuristics

C. Le Goues and S. Yoo (Eds.): SSBSE 2014, LNCS 8636, pp. 107–122, 2014.

is used. The problem of finding such a setting (together with choosing the right tests and their parameters), i.e., the so-called *test and noise configuration search problem* (TNCS problem), is, however, not easy to solve [13].

In this paper, we propose an application of a *multi-objective genetic algorithm* (MOGA) to solve the TNCS problem such that the solutions provide high *efficiency* and *stability* during repeated executions. By *efficiency*, we mean an ability to examine as much existing and important program behavior with as low time and resource requirements as possible. On the other hand, *stability* stands for an ability of a test setting to provide such efficient results in as many repeated test executions as possible despite the scheduling non-determinism. Such requirements on the tests and testing environment (and hence noise generation) can be useful, for instance, in the context of *regression testing* [26], which checks whether a previously working functionality works in a new version of the system under test too and which is executed regularly, e.g., every night.

Our proposal of a MOGA-based approach for testing of concurrent programs aims both at high efficiency as well as stability, i.e., we search for such tests, test parameters, noise heuristics, and their parameters that examine a lot of concurrency behavior in minimal time and that provide such good results constantly when re-executed. With that aim, we propose a multi-objective fitness function that embeds objectives of different kinds (testing time, coverage related to finding common concurrency errors like data races and deadlocks, as well as coverage of general concurrency behavior). Moreover, the objectives also embed means for minimizing the influence of scheduling non-determinism and means emphasizing a desire to search for less common behaviors (which are more likely to contain not yet discovered errors). Further, we discuss a choice of one particular MOGA from among of several known ones—in particular, the *Non-Dominated Sorting Genetic Algorithm II* (NSGA-II) and two versions of the *Strength Pareto Evolutionary Algorithm* (SPEA and SPEA2)—as well as a choice of a configuration of its parameters suitable for our setting. Finally, we show on a number of experiments that our solution provides better results than the commonly used random setting of noise injection as well as the approach of solving the TNCS problem via a single-objective genetic algorithm (SOGA) presented in [13].

2   Related Work

This section provides a brief overview of existing approaches for testing and dynamic analysis of multi-threaded programs as well as of applications of meta-heuristics to the problems of testing and analysis of multi-threaded programs.

Testing Multi-Threaded Programs. Simple *stress testing* based on executing a large number of threads and/or executing the same test in the same testing environment many times has been shown ineffective [23,22,8]. To effectively test concurrent programs, some way of influencing the scheduling is needed. The *noise injection* technique [8] influences thread interleavings by inserting delays, called *noise*, into the execution of selected threads. Many different noise heuristics can be used for this purpose [20]. The efficiency of the approach depends on the nature of the system under test (SUT) and the testing environment, which includes the way noise is generated [20]. A proper choice of *noise seeding heuristics* (e.g., calling `sleep` or `yield` statements, halting selected threads, etc.), *noise placement heuristics* (purely random, at selected statements, etc.), as well as of the values of the many parameters of these heuristics (such as strength, frequency, etc.) can rapidly increase the probability of detecting an error, but on the other hand, improper noise injection can hide it [17]. A proper selection of the noise heuristics and their parameters is not easy, and it is often done by random. In this paper, we strive to improve this practice by applying multi-objective genetic optimization.

An alternative to noise-based testing is *deterministic testing* [12,22,30] which can be seen as execution-based model checking. This approach is based on deterministic control over the scheduling of threads, and it can guarantee a higher coverage of different interleavings than noise-based testing. On the other hand, its overhead may be significantly higher due to a need of computing, storing, and enforcing the considered thread interleavings. Since the number of possible interleavings is usually huge, the approach is often applied on abstract and/or considerably bounded models of the SUT. It is therefore suitable mainly for unit testing.

Both of the above mentioned approaches can be improved by combining them with *dynamic analysis* [9,21,3] which collects various pieces of information along the executed path and tries to detect errors based on their characteristic symptoms even if the errors do themselves not occur in the execution. Many problem-specific dynamic analyses have been proposed for detecting special classes of errors, such as data races [9], atomicity violations [21], or deadlocks [3].

Meta-heuristics in Testing of Concurrent Programs. A majority of existing works in the area of search-based testing of concurrent programs focuses on applying various meta-heuristic techniques to control state space exploration within the *guided (static) model checking* approach [11,27,1]. The basic idea of this approach is to explore areas of the state space that are more likely to contain concurrency errors first. The fitness functions used in these approaches are based on detection of error states [27], distance to error manifestation [11], or formula-based heuristics [1] which estimate the number of transitions required to get an objective node from the current one. Most of the approaches also search for a minimal counterexample path.

Applications of meta-heuristics in deterministic testing of multi-threaded programs are studied in [5,28]. In [5], a cross entropy heuristic is used to navigate deterministic testing. In [28], an application of a genetic algorithm to the problem of unit test generation is presented. The technique produces a set of unit tests for a chosen Java class. Each unit test consists of a prefix initialising the class (usually, a constructor call), a set of method sequences (one sequence per thread), and a schedule that is enforced by a deterministic scheduler.

In [13], which is the closest to our work, a SOGA-based approach to the TNCS problem is proposed and experimentally shown to provide significantly better results than random noise injection. On the other hand, the work also shows that combining the different relevant objectives into a scalar fitness function by assigning them some fixed weights is problematic. For instance, some tests were sometimes highly rated due to their very quick execution despite they provided a very poor coverage of the SUT behavior. Further, it was discovered that in some cases, the genetic approach suffered from degradation, i.e., a quick loss of diversity in population. Such a loss of diversity can unfortunately have a negative impact on the ability of the approach to test different program behaviors. Finally, it turned out that candidate solutions which were highly rated during one evaluation did not provide such good results when reevaluated again. In this paper, we try to solve all of the above problems by using a MOGA-based approach enhanced by techniques intended to increase the stability of the approach as well as to stress rare behaviors.

3   Background

In this section, we briefly introduce multi-objective genetic algorithms, the TNCS problem, and the considered noise injection heuristics. Moreover, we provide an overview of our infrastructure and test cases used for an evaluation of our approach.

Multi-objective Genetic Algorithms (MOGA).   The genetic algorithm is a biology-inspired population-based optimization algorithm [31,7]. The algorithm works in iterations. In each iteration, a set of candidate solutions (i.e., individuals forming a population) is evaluated through a fitness function based on some chosen objective(s). The obtained fitness is then used by a selection operator to choose promising candidates for further breeding. The breeding process employs crossover and mutation operators to modify the selected individuals to meet the exploration and/or exploitation goals of the search process.

In single-objective optimization, the set of candidate solutions needs to be totally ordered according to the values of the fitness function. The traditional approach to solve a multi-objective problem by single-objective optimization is to bundle all objectives into a single scalar fitness function using a *weighted sum of objectives*. The efficiency of this approach heavily depends on the selected weights which are sometimes not easy to determine.

On the other hand, multi-objective optimization treats objectives separately and compares candidate solutions using the *Pareto dominance* relation. A MOGA searches for non-dominated individuals called *Pareto-optimal* solutions. There usually exists a set of such individuals which form the *Pareto-optimal front*. Solutions on the Pareto-optimal front are either best in one or more objectives or represent the best available trade-off among considered objectives. There exist several algorithms for multi-objective optimization that use different evaluation of individuals, but all of them exploit the non-dominated sorting. In this paper, we consider the *Non-Dominated Sorting Genetic Algorithm II* (NSGA-II) [7] and two versions of the *Strength Pareto Evolutionary Algorithm* (SPEA and SPEA2) [31].

The Test and Noise Configuration Search Problem.   The *test and noise configuration search problem* (the TNCS problem) is formulated in [13] as the problem of selecting test cases and their parameters together with types and parameters of noise placement and noise seeding heuristics that are suitable for certain test objectives. Formally, let $Type_P$ be a set of available types of noise placement heuristics each of which we assume to be parametrized by a vector of parameters. Let $Param_P$ be a set of all possible vectors of parameters. Further, let $P \subseteq Type_P \times Param_P$ be a set of all allowed combinations of types of noise placement heuristics and their parameters. Analogically, we can introduce sets $Type_S$, $Param_S$, and S for noise seeding heuristics. Next, let

$C \subseteq 2^{P \times S}$ contain all the sets of noise placement and noise seeding heuristics that have the property that they can be used together within a single test run. We denote elements of C as *noise configurations*. Further, like for the noise placement and noise seeding heuristics, let $Type_T$ be a set of test cases, $Param_T$ a set of vectors of their parameters, and $T \subseteq Type_T \times Param_T$ a set of all allowed combinations of test cases and their parameters. We let $TC = T \times C$ be the set of *test configurations*. The TNCS problem can now be seen as searching for a test configuration from TC according to given objectives.

Considered Noise Injection Heuristics. We consider 6 basic and 2 advanced noise seeding techniques that are all commonly used in noise-based testing [20]. The basic techniques cannot be combined, but any basic technique can be combined with one or both advanced techniques. The basic heuristics are: *yield, sleep, wait, busyWait, synchYield*, and *mixed*. The *yield* and *sleep* techniques inject calls of the `yield()` and `sleep()` functions. The *wait* technique injects a call of `wait()`. The concerned threads must first obtain a special shared monitor, then call `wait()`, and finally release the monitor. The *synchYield* technique combines the yield technique with obtaining the monitor as in the *wait* approach. The *busyWait* technique inserts code that just loops for some time. The *mixed* technique randomly chooses one of the five other techniques at each noise injection location. Next, the first of the considered advanced techniques, the *haltOneThread* technique, occasionally stops one thread until any other thread cannot run. Finally, the *timeoutTamper* heuristics randomly reduces the time-outs used in the program under test in calls of `sleep()` (to ensure that they are not used for synchronisation). These heuristics can be used with different *strength* in the range of 0–100. The meaning of the strength differs for different heuristics—it means, e.g., how many times the yield operation should be called when injected at a certain location, for how long a thread should wait, etc.

Further, we consider 3 noise placement heuristics: the *random* heuristics which picks program locations randomly, the *sharedVar* heuristics which focuses on accesses to shared variables, and the *coverage-based* heuristics [20] which focuses on accesses near a previously detected context switch. The *sharedVar* heuristics has two parameters with 5 valid combinations of its values. The *coverage-based* heuristics is controlled by 2 parameters with 3 valid combinations of values. All these noise placement heuristics inject noise at selected places with a given probability. The probability is set globally for all enabled noise placement heuristics by a *noiseFreq* setting from the range 0 (never) to 1000 (always).

The total number of noise configurations that one can obtain from the above can be computed by multiplying the number of the basic heuristics, which is 6, by 2 reflecting whether *haltOneThread* is/is not used, 2 reflecting whether *timeoutTamper* is used, 100 possible values of noise strength, 5 values of the *sharedVar* heuristics, 3 values of of the coverage-based heuristics, and 1000 values of *noiseFreq*. This gives about 36 million combinations of noise settings. Of course, the state space of the test and noise settings then further grows with the possible values of parameters of test cases and the testing environment.

Test Cases and Test Environment. The experimental results presented in the rest of the paper were obtained using the SearchBestie [19] platform based on the IBM Concurrency

Testing Tool (ConTest) [8] and its plug-ins [16,18] to inject noise into execution of the considered programs and to collect the obtained coverage. The used meta-heuristic algorithms were implemented within the ECJ library [29] which cooperates with the SearchBestie platform as well.

Among our test cases, we include five multi-threaded Java programs used in the previous work on the subject [13]: in particular, the Airlines, Animator, Crawler, Elevator, and Rover case studies (Airlines having 0.3 kLOC, Rover having 5.4 kLOC, and the other programs having around 1.2–1.5 kLOC of code each). Each of these programs contains a concurrency-related error. Moreover, three further multi-threaded benchmark programs, namely, Moldyn, MonteCarlo, and Raytracer, from the Java Grande Benchmark Suite [25], which contain a large number of memory accesses, have been used (their sizes range from 0.8 to 1.5 kLOC). All considered programs have one parametrized test that is used to execute them. All our experiments were conducted on machines with Intel i7 processors with Linux OS, using Oracle JDK 1.6.

4   Objectives and Fitness Function

One can collect various metrics characterizing the execution of concurrent programs. Our testing infrastructure is, in particular, able to report test failures, measure duration of test executions, and collect various code and concurrency coverage metrics [18] as well as numbers of warnings produced by various dynamic analyzers searching for data races [24,9], atomicity violations [21], and deadlocks [3]. In total, we are able to collect up to 30 different metrics describing concurrent program executions. Collecting all of these data does, of course, introduce a considerable slowdown. Moreover, some of the metrics are more suitable for use as an objective in our context than others.

In this section, we discuss our selection of objectives suitable for solving the TNCS problem through a MOGA-based approach. In particular, we focus on the number of distinctive values produced by the metrics, correlation among the objectives, and their stability. By the stability, we mean an ability of the objective to provide similar values for the same individual despite the scheduling non-determinism. Finally, we introduce a technique that allows us to emphasize uncommon observations and optimize candidate solutions towards testing of such behaviors.

Selection of suitable objectives. It has been discussed in the literature [7] that multi-objective genetic algorithms usually provide the best performance when a relatively low number of objectives is used. Therefore, we try to stay with a few objectives only. Among them, we first include the *execution time of tests* since one of our goals is to optimize towards tests with small resource requirements.

As for the goal of covering as much as possible of (relevant) program behavior, we reflect it in maximizing several chosen concurrency-related metrics. When choosing them, we have first ruled out metrics which suffer from a *lack of distinct values* since meta-heuristics do no work well with such objectives (due to not distinguishing different solutions well enough).

Subsequently, we have decided to include some metrics characterizing how well the behavior of the tested programs has been covered from the point of view of finding three *most common concurrency-related errors*, namely, data races, atomicity violations, and

Table 1. Correlation of objectives across all considered test cases

	Time	Error	WConcurPairs	Avio*	GoldiLockSC*	GoodLock*
Time	1	-0.083	0.625	-0.036	-0.038	-0.360
Error	-0.083	1	-0.137	-0.213	-0.221	-0.216
WConcurPairs	0.625	-0.137	1	0.116	0.038	-0.263
Avio*	-0.036	-0.213	0.116	1	0.021	-0.274
GoldiLockSC*	-0.038	-0.221	0.038	0.021	1	0.770
GoodLock*	-0.360	-0.216	-0.263	-0.274	0.770	1

deadlocks. For that, we have decided to use the *GoldiLockSC**, *GoodLock**, and *Avio** metrics [18]. These metrics are based on measuring how many internal states of the GoldiLock data race detector [9] or the GoodLock deadlock detector [3], respectively, have been reached, and hence how well the behavior of the SUT was tested for the presence of these errors. The *Avio** metric measures witnessed access interleaving invariants [21] which represent different combinations of read/write operations used when two consecutive accesses to a shared variable are interleaved by an access to the same variable from a different thread. A good point for *GoldiLockSC** and *Avio** is that they usually produces a high number of distinct values [18]. With *GoodLock**, the situation is worse, but since it is the only metric specializing in deadlocks that we are aware of, we have decided to retain it.

Next, in order to account for other errors than data races, atomicity violations or deadlocks, we have decided to add one more metric, this time choosing a general purpose metric capable of producing a high number of distinct tasks. Based on the results presented in [18], we have chosen the *ConcurPair* metric [4] in which each coverage task is composed of a pair of program locations that are assumed to be encountered consecutively in a run and a boolean value that is *true* iff the two locations are visited by different threads. More precisely, we have decided to use the weighted version *WConcurPairs* of this metric [13] which values more coverage tasks comprising a context switch.

Since *correlation among objectives* can decrease efficiency of a MOGA [7], we have examined our selection of objectives from this point view. Table 1 shows the average correlation of the selected metrics for 10,000 executions of our 8 test cases with a random noise setting. One can see that the metrics do not correlate up to two exceptions. *WConcurPairs* and *Time* achieved on average the correlation coefficient of 0.625 and the *GoodLock** and *GoldiLockcSC** metrics the correlation coefficient of 0.770[1]. However, there were also cases where these metrics did not correlate (e.g., the correlation coeffiecient of *GoldiLockSC** and *Avio** was 0.021). We therefore decided to reflect the fact that some of our objectives can sometimes correlate in our choice of a concrete MOGA, i.e., we try to select a MOGA which works well even under such circumstances (cf. Section 5).

Dealing with Scheduling Nondeterminism. Due to the scheduling nondeterminism, values of the above chosen objectives collected from single test runs are unstable.

---

[1] In this case, only three of the case studies containing nested locking and hence leading to a non-zero coverage under *GoodLock** were considered in the correlation computation.

A classic way to improve the stability is to execute the tests repeatedly and use a representative value [15]. However, there are multiple ways how to compute it, and we now aim at selecting the most appropriate way for our setting.

For each of our case studies, we randomly selected 100 test configurations, executed each of them in 10 batches of 10 runs, and computed the representative values in several different ways for each batch of 10 runs. In particular, we considered median (*med*), mode (*mod*)[2], and the cumulative value (*cum*) computed as the sum in the case of time and as the united coverage in case of the considered coverage metrics. We do not consider the often used average value since we realized that the data obtained from our tests were usually not normally distributed, and hence the average would not repre-

Table 2. Stability of representatives

Case	med	mod	cum
Airlines	**0.033**	0.054	0.051
Animator	**0.012**	0.027	0.092
Crawler	**0.211**	0.261	0.255
Elevator	0.145	0.227	**0.107**
Moldyn	**0.020**	0.025	0.024
MonteCarlo	**0.015**	0.019	0.022
Raytracer	0.022	0.020	**0.016**
Rover	**0.059**	0.100	0.141
Average	**0.065**	0.092	0.088

sent them accurately. We did not consider other more complicated evaluations of representative values due the high computational costs associated with using them. Subsequently, we compared stability of the representative values obtained across the batches. Table 2 shows the average values of variation coefficients of the representatives computed across all the considered configurations for each case study and each way of computing a representative. Clearly, the best average stability was provided by median, which we therefore choose as our means of computing representative values across multiple test runs for all the following experiments.

Emphasizing rare observations. When testing concurrent programs, it is usually the case that some behavior is seen very frequently while some behavior is rare. Since it is likely that bugs not discovered by programmers hide in the rare behavior, we have decided to direct the tests more towards such behavior by *penalizing* coverage of frequently seen behaviors. Technically, we implement the penalization as follows. We count how many times each coverage task of the considered metrics got covered in the test runs used to evaluate the first generation of randomly chosen candidate solutions. Each coverage task is then assigned a weight obtained as one minus the ratio of runs in which the task got covered (i.e., a task that was not covered at all is given weight 1, while a task that got covered in 30 % of the test runs is given weight 0.7). These weights are then used when evaluating the coverage obtained by subsequent generations of candidate solutions.

Selected fitness function. To sum up, based on the above described findings, we propose a use of the following fitness functions, which we use in all our subsequent experiments: Each candidate solution is evaluated 10 times, the achieved coverage is penalized, and the median values for the 4 selected metrics (*GoldiLockSC**, *GoodLock**, *WConcurPairs*, and *Time*) are computed.

---

[2] Taking the biggest modus if there are several modus values.

5   Selection of a Multi-objective Optimization Algorithm

Another step needed to apply multi-objective optimization for solving the TNCS problem is to choose a suitable multi-objective optimization algorithm and its parameters. Hence, in this section, we first select one algorithm out of three well-known multi-objective optimization algorithms, namely, *SPEA*, *SPEA2*, and *NSGA-II* [7,31]. Subsequently, we discuss a suitable setting of parameters of the selected algorithm.

The main role of the multi-objective algorithms is to classify candidate solutions into those worth and not worth further consideration. We aim at selecting one of the algorithms that is most likely to provide a satisfactory classification despite the obstacles that can be faced when solving the TNCS problem. As we have already discussed, these obstacles include the following: (a) Some objectives can sometimes be able to achieve only a *small number of distinct values* because the kind of concurrency-related behavior that they concentrate on does not show up in the given test case. (b) Some of the objectives can sometimes *correlate* as discussed in Section 4. (c) We are working with a *nondeterministic environment* where the evaluation of objectives is not stable. We have proposed ways of reducing the impact of these issues already in Section 4, but we now aim at a further improvement by a selection of a suitable MOGA.

In addition, we also consider the opposite of Issue (a), namely, the fact that some objectives can sometimes achieve rather *high numbers of values*. Dealing with high numbers of values is less problematic than the opposite (since a high number of objective values can be divided into a smaller number of fitness values but not vice versa), yet we would like to assure that the selected MOGA does indeed handle well the high numbers of values and classifies them into a reasonable number of fitness values.

We studied the ability of the considered algorithms to deal with correlation and low or high numbers of distinct objective values using four pairs of objectives. In these pairs, we used the *Avio** metric (based on the Avio atomicity violation detector [21]) and the *GoldiLockSC** metric, which we found to highly correlate with the correlation coefficient of 0.966 in the same kind of correlation experiments as those presented in Section 4 (i.e., they correlate much more than the objectives we have chosen into our fitness functions). As a representative of objectives that often achieve a small number of values, we included the number of detected errors (*Error*) into the experiments, and as a representative of those that can often achieve high values, we take the execution time (*Time*). We performed experiments with 40 different individuals (i.e., test and noise configurations) and evaluated each of them 11 times on the Crawler test case.

Table 3 shows into how many classes the obtained 440 results of the above experiments were classified by the considered algorithms when using four different pairs of objectives. We can see that the *SPEA* algorithm often classifies the results into

Table 3. Pairs of objectives and their evaluation by multi-objective optimization algorithms

Pair of objectives	SPEA	SPEA2	NSGA-II
(Avio*, GoldiLockSC*)	4	366	106
(Time, Error)	7	437	386
(Error, GoldiLockSC*)	8	240	199
(Time, GoldiLockSC*)	30	410	38

a very low number of classes while *SPEA2* into a large number of classes, which is close to the number of evaluations. *NSGA-II* stays in all cases in between of the extremes, and we therefore consider it to provide the best results for our needs.

Next, we discuss our choice of suitable values of parameters of the selected MOGA, such as the size of population, number of generations, as well as the selection, crossover, and mutation operators to be used. Our choice is based on the experience with a SOGA-based approach presented in [13] as well as on a set of experiments with *NSGA-II* in our environment. In particular, we experimented with population sizes and the number of generations such that the number of individual evaluations in one experiment remained constant (in particular, 2000 evaluations of individuals per experiment[3]). Therefore, for populations of size 20, 40, and 100, we used sizes of 100, 50, and 20 generations, respectively. Next, we studied the influence of three different crossover operators available in the ECJ toolkit [29] (called *one*, *two* and *any*) and three different probabilities of mutation (0.01, 0.1 and 0.5). As the selection operator, we used the mating scheme selection algorithm instead of the fitness-based tournament or proportional selection which are commonly used in single-objective optimization but provide worse results or are not applicable in multi-objective optimization [14]. We fixed the size of the archive to the size of the population.

In total, we experimented with 27 different settings of the chosen MOGA (3 sizes of population, 3 crossover operators, and 3 mutation probabilities). For each setting, we performed 10 executions of the MOGA process which differ only in the initial random seed values (i.e., only in the individuals generated in the first generation) on the Airlines, Animator, and Crawler test cases. In general, we did not see big differences in the results obtained with different sizes of populations. On the other hand, low probabilities of mutation (0.01 and 0.1) often led to degeneration of the population within a few generations and to low achieved fitness in the last generation. A high mutation set to 0.5 did not suffer from this problem. Further, the *any* crossover operator provided considerably lower values of fitness values in the last generation, while there were no significant differences among the *one* and *two* crossover operators.

Based on these experiments, we decided to work with 50 generations and 20 individuals in a population (i.e., compared with the above experiments, we decrease the number of generations for the given number of individuals since at the beginning the number of coverage tasks grew up, but after the 50th generation there was not much change). In the breeding process, we use the mating scheme algorithm as the selection operator with the recommended parameters $\alpha = 5$, $\beta = 3$; and we use the crossover operator denoted as *two* in ECJ, which takes two selected individuals (integer vectors), divides them into 3 parts at random places, and generates a new candidate solution as the composition of randomly chosen 1st, 2nd, and 3rd part of parents. Finally, to implement mutation, we use an operator that randomly selects an element in the vector of a candidate solution and sets it to a random value within its allowed range with probability 0.5. The resulting agile exploration is compensated by the *NSGA-II* archive, and so the search does not loose promising candidate solutions despite the high mutation rate.

6   Experimental Evaluation

In this section, four experimental comparisons of the proposed MOGA-based approach with the random approach and a SOGA-based approach are presented. First, we show

---

[3] We used 2000 evaluations because after the 2000 evaluations, saturation used to happen.

that our MOGA-based approach does not suffer from degeneration of the search process identified in the SOGA-based approach in [13]. Then, we show that the proposed penalization does indeed lead to a higher coverage of uncommon behavior. Finally, we focus on a comparison of the MOGA, SOGA, and random approaches with respect to their efficiency and stability. All results presented here were gathered from testing of the 8 test cases introduced in Section 3.

In the experiments, we use the following parameters of the SOGA-based approach taken from [13]: size of population 20, number of generations 50, two different selection operators (tournament among 4 individuals and fitness proportional[4]), the *any-point* crossover with probability 0.25, a low mutation probability (0.01), and two elites (that is 10 % of the population). However, to make the comparison more fair, we build the fitness function of the SOGA-based approach from the objectives selected above[5]:

$$\frac{WConcurPairs}{WConcurPairs_{max}} + \frac{GoodLock^*}{GoodLock^*_{max}} + \frac{GoldiLockSC^*}{GoldiLockSC^*_{max}} + \frac{time_{max} - time}{time_{max}}$$

Here, the maximal values of objectives were estimated as 1.5 times the maximal accumulated numbers we got in 10 executions of the particular test cases. As proposed in [13], the the SOGA-based approach uses cumulation of results obtained from multiple test runs without any penalization of frequent behaviors.

All results presented in this section were tested by the statistical t-test with the significance level $\alpha = 0.05$, which tells one whether the achieved results for Random, MOGA, and SOGA are significantly different. In a vast majority of the cases, the test confirmed a statistically significant difference among the approaches.

Degeneration of the Search Process. Degeneration, i.e., lack of variability in population, is a common problem of population-based search algorithms. Figure 1 shows average variability of the MOGA-based and SOGA-based approaches computed from the search processes on the 8 considered test cases. The x-axis represents generations, and the y-axis shows numbers of distinct individuals in the generations (max. 20). The higher value the search process achieves the higher variability and therefore low degeneration was achieved. The graph

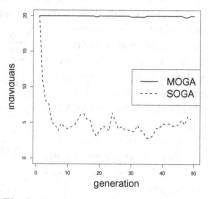

Fig. 1. Degeneration of the MOGA-based and SOGA-based search processes

clearly shows that our MOGA-based approach does not suffer from the degeneration problem unlike the SOGA-based approach.

---

[4] Experiments presented in [13] showed that using these two selection operators is beneficial. Therefore, we used them again. On the other hand, for MOGA, the mating schema provides better results.

[5] In the experiments performed in [13], the fitness function was sensitive on weight. Therefore, we remove the weight from our new fitness function for SOGA.

Degeneration of the SOGA-based approach, and subsequently, its tendency to get caught in a local maximum (often optimizing strongly towards a highly positive value of a single objective, e.g., minimum test time but almost no coverage) can in theory be resolved by increasing the amount of randomness in the approach, but then it basically shifts towards random testing. An interesting observation (probably leading to the good results presented in [13]) is that even a degenerated population can provide a high coverage if the repeatedly generated candidate solutions suffer from low stability, which allows them to test different behaviors in different executions.

Effect of Penalization. The goal of the above proposed penalization scheme is to increase the number of tested uncommon behaviors. An illustration of the fact that this goal has indeed been achieved is provided in Table 4. The table in particular compares results collected from 10 runs of the final generations of 20 individuals obtained through the MOGA-based and SOGA-based approaches with results obtained from 200 randomly generated individuals. Each value in the table gives the average percentage of uncommon be-

Table 4. Impact of the penalization built into the MOGA approach

Test	MOGA	SOGA	Random
Airlines	59.66	**60.61**	19.14
Animator	70.1	**74.31**	44.73
Crawler	**70.73**	66.32	61.19
Elevator	**89.26**	83.96	65.69
Moldy	**68.32**	44.25	39.73
Montecarlo	40.13	**54.52**	28.25
Raytracer	**73.08**	60.49	54.68
Rover	**53.87**	41.45	30.62
Average	**65.52**	60.73	43.00

haviors spot by less than 50 % of candidate solutions, i.e., by less than 10 individuals. Number 60 therefore means that, on average, the collected coverage consists of 40 % of behaviors that occur often (i.e., in more than 50 % of the runs) while 60 % are rare.

In most of the cases, if some approach achieved the highest percentage of uncommon behaviors under one of the coverage metrics, it achieved the highest numbers under the other metrics as well. Table 4 clearly shows that our MOGA-based approach is able to provide a higher coverage of uncommon behaviors (where errors are more likely to be hidden) than the other considered approaches.

Efficiency of the Testing. Next, we focus on the efficiency of the generated test settings, i.e., on their ability to provide a high coverage in a short time. We again consider 10 testing runs of the 20 individuals from the last generations of the MOGA-based and SOGA-based approaches

Table 5. Efficiency of the considered approaches

Case	Metrics	MOGA	SOGA	Random
Airlines	C/Time	**0.06**	**0.06**	0.04
	S/Time	**3.73**	3.29	2.98
Animator	C/Time	0.07	**0.29**	0.19
	S/Time	0.33	**1.01**	0.65
Crawler	C/Time	0.21	**0.22**	0.12
	S/Time	**4.15**	3.84	2.05
Elevator	C/Time	0.03	**0.04**	0.02
	S/Time	2.69	**3.64**	1.28
Moldy	C/Time	**0.01**	**0.01**	**0.01**
	S/Time	11.73	**16.83**	2.56
Montecarlo	C/Time	**0.01**	**0.01**	**0.01**
	S/Time	9.52	**9.66**	0.01
Raytracer	C/Time	**0.01**	**0.01**	**0.01**
	S/Time	**7.16**	5.13	0.69
Rover	C/Time	**0.11**	0.10	0.08
	S/Time	**5.17**	2.49	2.18
Avg. impr.			2.01	2.11

and 200 test runs under random generated test and noise settings. Table 5 compares the efficiency of these tests. In order to express the efficiency, we use two metrics. Namely, *C/Time* shows how many coverage tasks of the *GoldiLockcSC** and *GoodLock** metrics got covered on average per time unit (milisecond). Next, *S/Time* indicates how many coverage tasks of the general purpose *WConcurPairs* coverage metric got covered on average per a time unit. Higher values in the table therefore represent higher average efficiency of the testing runs under the test settings obtained in one the considered ways. The last row gives the average improvement (*Avg. impr.*) of the genetic approaches against random testing. We can see that both genetic approaches are significantly better than the random approach. In some cases, the MOGA-based approach got better evaluated while SOGA won in some other cases. Note, however, that as shown in the previous paragraph, the MOGA-based approach is more likely to cover rare tasks, and so even if it covers a comparable number of tasks with the SOGA-based approach, it is still likely to be more advantageous from the practical point of view.

Stability of Testing. Finally, we show that candidate solutions found by our MOGA-based approach provide more stable results than the SOGA-based and random approaches. In particular, for the MOGA-based and SOGA-based approaches, Table 6 gives the average values of variation coefficients of the coverage under each of the three considered coverage criteria for each of the 20 candidate solutions from the last obtained generations across 10 test runs. For the case of random testing, the variation coefficients were

Table 6. Stability of testing

Case	MOGA	SOGA	Random
Airlines	**0.06**	0.17	0.29
Animator	**0.02**	0.11	0.12
Crawler	0.38	0.38	**0.26**
Elevator	0.50	**0.48**	0.58
Moldyn	**0.11**	0.20	0.70
Montecarlo	0.13	**0.11**	0.89
Raytracer	**0.16**	0.46	0.76
Rover	**0.08**	0.10	0.32
Average	**0.18**	0.25	0.49

calculated from 200 runs generated randomly. The last row of the table shows the average variation coefficient across all the case studies. The table clearly shows that our MOGA-based approach provides more stable results when compared to the other approaches.

7 Threats to Validity

Any attempt to compare different approaches faces a number of challenges because it is important to ensure that the comparison is as fair as possible. The first issue to address is that of the *internal validity*, i.e., whether there has been a bias in the experimental design or stochastic behavior of the meta-heuristic search algorithms that could affect the obtained results. In order to deal with this issue, Section 5 provides a brief discussion and experimental evidence that supports the choice of the NSGA-II MOGA algorithm out of the three considered algorithms. In order to address the problem of setting the various parameters of meta-heuristic algorithms, a number of experiments was conducted to choose configurations that provide good results in the given context. Similarly, our choice of suitable objectives was done based on observations from previous experimentation [18]. Care was taken to ensure that all approaches are evaluated in the same environment.

Another issue to address is that of the *external validity*, i.e., whether there has been a bias caused by external entities such as the selected case studies (i.e., programs to be tested in our case) used in the empirical study. The diverse nature of programs makes it impossible to sample a sufficiently large set of programs. The chosen programs contain a variety of synchronization constructs and concurrency-related errors that are common in practice, but they represent a small set of real-life programs only. The studied execution traces conform to real unit and/or integration tests. As with many other empirical experiments in software engineering, further experiments are needed in order to confirm the results presented here.

8   Conclusions and Future Work

In this paper, we proposed an application of multi-objective genetic optimization for finding good settings of tests and noise. We discussed a selection of suitable objectives taking into account their usefulness for efficiently finding concurrency-related errors as well as their properties important for the process of genetic optimization (numbers of distinct values, correlation) as well as for stability. We also proposed a way how to emphasize uncommon behaviors in which so-far undiscovered bugs are more likely to be hidden. Further, we compared suitability of three popular multi-objective genetic algorithms for our purposes, which showed that the NSGA-II algorithm provides the best ability to classify candidate solutions in our setting. Finally, we demonstrated on a set of experiments with 8 case studies that our approach does not suffer from the degeneration problem, it emphasizes uncommon behaviors, and generates settings of tests and noise that improve the efficiency and stability of the testing process.

As a part of our future work, we plan to further improve the efficiency and stability of the generated test and noise settings. For this purpose, we would like to exploit the recently published results [10] indicating that searching for a test suite provides better results than searching for a set of the best individuals.

Acknowledgement. We thank Shmuel Ur and Zeev Volkovich for many valuable comments on the work presented in this paper. The work was supported by the Czech Ministry of Education under the Kontakt II project LH13265, the EU/Czech IT4Innovations Centre of Excellence project CZ.1.05/1.1.00/02.0070, and the internal BUT projects FIT-S-12-1 and FIT-S-14-2486. Z. Letko was funded through the EU/Czech Interdisciplinary Excellence Research Teams Establishment project (CZ.1.07/2.3.00/30.0005).

References

1. Alba, E., Chicano, F.: Finding Safety Errors with ACO. In: Proc. of GECCO 2007. ACM (2007)
2. Ayewah, N., Pugh, W., Morgenthaler, J.D., Penix, J., Zhou, Y.: Using FindBugs on Production Software. In: Proc. of OOPSLA 2007. ACM (2007)
3. Bensalem, S., Havelund, K.: Dynamic Deadlock Analysis of Multi-threaded Programs. In: Ur, S., Bin, E., Wolfsthal, Y. (eds.) HVC 2005. LNCS, vol. 3875, pp. 208–223. Springer, Heidelberg (2006)
4. Bron, A., Farchi, E., Magid, Y., Nir, Y., Ur, S.: Applications of Synchronization Coverage. In: Proc. of PPoPP 2005. ACM (2005)
5. Chockler, H., Farchi, E., Godlin, B., Novikov, S.: Cross-entropy Based Testing. In: Proc. of FMCAD 2007. IEEE (2007)

6. Clarke, E., Grumberg, O., Peled, D.: Model Checking. MIT Press (1999)
7. Deb, K.: Multi-Objective Optimization Using Evolutionary Algorithms. Wiley paperback series. Wiley (2009)
8. Edelstein, O., Farchi, E., Goldin, E., Nir, Y., Ratsaby, G., Ur, S.: Framework for Testing Multi-threaded Java Programs. Concurrency and Computation: Practice and Experience 15(3-5) (2003)
9. Elmas, T., Qadeer, S., Tasiran, S.: Goldilocks: A Race and Transaction-aware Java Runtime. In: Proc. of PLDI 2007. ACM (2007)
10. Fraser, G., Arcuri, A.: Whole Test Suite Generation. IEEE Transactions on Software Engineering 39(2) (2013)
11. Godefroid, P., Khurshid, S.: Exploring Very Large State Spaces Using Genetic Algorithms. International Journal on Software Tools for Technology Transfer 6(2) (2004)
12. Hong, S., Ahn, J., Park, S., Kim, M., Harrold, M.J.: Testing Concurrent Programs to Achieve High Synchronization Coverage. In: Proc. of ISSTA 2012. ACM (2012)
13. Hrubá, V., Křena, B., Letko, Z., Ur, S., Vojnar, T.: Testing of Concurrent Programs Using Genetic Algorithms. In: Fraser, G., de Teixeira Souza, J. (eds.) SSBSE 2012. LNCS, vol. 7515, pp. 152–167. Springer, Heidelberg (2012)
14. Ishibuchi, H., Shibata, Y.: A Similarity-based Mating Scheme for Evolutionary Multiobjective Optimization. In: Cantú-Paz, E., et al. (eds.) GECCO 2003. LNCS, vol. 2723, pp. 1065–1076. Springer, Heidelberg (2003)
15. Jin, Y., Branke, J.: Evolutionary Optimization in Uncertain Environments – A Survey. IEEE Transactions on Evolutionary Computation 9(3) (2005)
16. Křena, B., Letko, Z., Nir-Buchbinder, Y., Tzoref-Brill, R., Ur, S., Vojnar, T.: A Concurrency Testing Tool and its Plug-ins for Dynamic Analysis and Runtime Healing. In: Bensalem, S., Peled, D.A. (eds.) RV 2009. LNCS, vol. 5779, pp. 101–114. Springer, Heidelberg (2009)
17. Křena, B., Letko, Z., Tzoref, R., Ur, S., Vojnar, T.: Healing Data Races On-the-fly. In: Proc. of PADTAD 2007. ACM (2007)
18. Křena, B., Letko, Z., Vojnar, T.: Coverage Metrics for Saturation-based and Search-based Testing of Concurrent Software. In: Khurshid, S., Sen, K. (eds.) RV 2011. LNCS, vol. 7186, pp. 177–192. Springer, Heidelberg (2012)
19. Křena, B., Letko, Z., Vojnar, T., Ur, S.: A Platform for Search-based Testing of Concurrent Software. In: Proc. of PADTAD 2010. ACM (2010)
20. Křena, B., Letko, Z., Vojnar, T.: Noise Injection Heuristics on Concurrency Coverage. In: Kotásek, Z., Bouda, J., Černá, I., Sekanina, L., Vojnar, T., Antoš, D. (eds.) MEMICS 2011. LNCS, vol. 7119, pp. 123–135. Springer, Heidelberg (2012)
21. Lu, S., Tucek, J., Qin, F., Zhou, Y.: AVIO: Detecting Atomicity Violations via Access Interleaving Invariants. In: Proc. of ASPLOS 2006. ACM (2006)
22. Musuvathi, M., Qadeer, S., Ball, T., Basler, G., Nainar, P.A., Neamtiu, I.: Finding and Reproducing Heisenbugs in Concurrent Programs. In: OSDI. USENIX Association (2008)
23. Peierls, T., Goetz, B., Bloch, J., Bowbeer, J., Lea, D., Holmes, D.: Java Concurrency in Practice. Addison-Wesley Professional (2005)
24. Savage, S., Burrows, M., Nelson, G., Sobalvarro, P., Anderson, T.: Eraser: A Dynamic Data Race Detector for Multi-threaded Programs. In: Proc. of SOSP 1997. ACM (1997)
25. Smith, L.A., Bull, J.M., Obdržálek, J.: A Parallel Java Grande Benchmark Suite. In: Proc. of Supercomputing 2001. ACM (2001)
26. Spillner, A., Linz, T., Schaefer, H.: Software Testing Foundations: A Study Guide for the Certified Tester Exam, 3rd edn. Rocky Nook (2011)
27. Staunton, J., Clark, J.A.: Searching for Safety Violations Using Estimation of Distribution Algorithms. In: Proc. of ICSTW 2010. IEEE (2010)

28. Steenbuck, S., Fraser, G.: Generating Unit Tests for Concurrent Classes. In: ICST 2013. IEEE (2013)
29. White, D.: Software Review: The ECJ Toolkit. Genetic Programming and Evolvable Machines 13 (2012)
30. Yu, J., Narayanasamy, S., Pereira, C., Pokam, G.: Maple: A Coverage-driven Testing Tool for Multithreaded Programs. In: Proc. of OOPSLA 2012. ACM (2012)
31. Zitzler, E.: Evolutionary Algorithms for Multiobjective Optimization: Methods and Applications. PhD thesis, ETH Zurich (1999)

Bi-objective Genetic Search for Release Planning in Support of Themes

Muhammad Rezaul Karim and Guenther Ruhe

Department of Computer Science
University of Calgary, Canada
{mrkarim,ruhe}@ucalgary.ca

Abstract. Release planning is a mandatory part of incremental and iterative software development. For the decision about which features should be implemented next, the values of features need to be balanced with the effort and readiness of their implementation. Traditional planning looks at the sum of the values of individual and potentially isolated features. As an alternative idea, a theme is a meta-functionality which integrates a number of individual features under a joint umbrella. That way, possible value synergies from offering features in conjunction (theme-related) can be utilized.

In this paper, we model theme-based release planning as a bi-objective (search-based) optimization problem. Each solution of this optimization problem balances the preference between individual and theme-based planning objectives. We apply a two-stage solution approach. In Phase 1, the existing Non-dominated Sorting Genetic Algorithm-II (NSGA-II) is adapted. Subsequently, the problem of guiding the user in the set of non-dominated solutions is addressed in Phase 2. We propose and explore two alternative ways to select among the (potentially large number) Pareto-optimal solutions. The applicability and empirical analysis of the proposed approach is evaluated for two explorative case study projects having 50 resp. 25 features grouped around 8 resp. 5 themes.

1 Introduction

In iterative and incremental development, release planning (RP) is the process of selecting and assigning features of a product to a sequence of consecutive product releases such that the most important technical, resource, budget and risk constraints are met [24]. RP is a cognitively and computationally challenging problem.

Theme-based RP model is a specific form of release planning with the aim of delivering a group of features in a release that are inter-related to each other in a specific context [1]. The motivation for theme-based RP is that certain features would have higher value if they are released along with a set of inter-dependent features, leading to better overall release value and customer satisfaction. With regard to theme-based RP, there have been initial attempts to group features into themes and perform release planning based on those themes [1,14].

Since the creation of individual value and theme-based value are conflicting objectives, maximization of both objectives in RP is a multi-objective optimization

C. Le Goues and S. Yoo (Eds.): SSBSE 2014, LNCS 8636, pp. 123–137, 2014.
© Springer International Publishing Switzerland 2014

problem by nature. In this paper, our first goal is to formulate theme-based RP as a bi-objective optimization problem. We will apply the well proven NSGA-II [9] algorithm as a solution approach and evaluate the solutions based on the presence of features from various themes. To the best of our knowledge, this paper will be the first to propose multi-objective formulation of theme-based RP.

In multi-objective release optimization, the Pareto-front is a set of complementary best solutions which can be used by product managers to select a solution that does a balance between competing objectives. In this paper, our second goal is to assist product managers to identify those solutions that best balance the competing concerns of themes. In line with this goal, we show how the solutions in the Pareto-front can be ranked by taking consideration of product managers' preferences. We conduct case studies on two data sets to validate our approach and to answer the questions about (i) the impact of theme-based considerations on the structure and value of the release plans generated (case study 1) and (ii) the usefulness of theme-based preferences for selecting the final Pareto solution (case study 2).

The rest of the paper is organized as follows: Section 2 discusses existing approaches for RP, while Section 3 gives an introduction to NSGA-II. The bi-objective formulation of theme-based RP and the solution approach including the recommendation approach for how to select the final solution out of the set of Pareto solutions, is described in Section 4. The results of the two explorative case studies are reported in Section 5. The paper concludes in Section 6 with a summary and an outlook to future research.

2   Related Work

Bagnall et al. [4] first suggested the term Next Release Problem (NRP) and described various meta-heuristic optimization algorithms for solving it. It was a single objective formulation of the problem where release planning is defined only for the next release. The objective was to maximize the total number of customers satisfied under a single cost constraint. This approach does not consider the stakeholders priority for a feature. Greer and Ruhe presented EVOLVE, an iterative approach for RP using a genetic algorithm [15]. In this approach, the objectives were to maximize total benefit and minimize the total penalties. These two objectives were combined into a single objective using linear combination. The numbers of releases were not decided a priori. Exact approaches to tackle the single objective formulation of requirements selection problems can be found in Akker et al. [2,3].

Zhang et al. proposed multi-objective formulation of the NRP problem [28] and did experiments with two meta-heuristics: NSGA-II [9] and MOCell [19]. In their formulation, they considered two objectives: maximization of value of features and minimization of cost associated with the features.   Saliu and Ruhe [26] formulated a two-objective RP that balances the tension between user-level and system-level requirements. In [5,7,8,12], several other multi-objective formulation of the RP and NRP problem were proposed. These approaches considered a subset of the objectives: stakeholder's satisfaction, business value, risk or cost associated with implementing various features, for maximization or minimization purpose. Mostly academic and synthetic data sets were used in the case studies conducted. In [5,7,8], feature inter-dependencies were taken into account, while dependency constraints were ignored in [12]. Unlike the other approaches, the approach proposed in [5] can tackle multi-objective formulation in two cases: when the number of releases is known and when it is not known a priori. Over the last few years, several Ant Colony Optimization based approaches were also proposed for NRP and RP [10,11].

Considering theme-based release planning, there have been initial attempts to group features into themes and perform release planning based on those themes [1,14]. In [1], an analytical approach for theme-detection was proposed using existing feature dependencies. Two kinds of feature dependencies (coupling and precedence) were used to construct a feature dependency graph, which was later used to extract clusters using the Chinese Whispers (CW) algorithm [6]. Each cluster represented a theme. In this paper, the terms cluster and theme are used interchangeably. Synergy constraints were formulated between all pairs of features in a cluster, with an increment factor for a pair. Later, EVOLVE II [24] was applied to perform theme-based release planning. It was shown that features belonging to a cluster tend to be released more closely.

In [14], feature trees were proposed for release planning with an industrial case study. Feature trees represented dependencies in the implementation order. AND, OR and REQUIRES relationships between requirements were captured in the feature trees. The AND relationship was specifically exploited to group requirements. In this approach, theme detection and decision making process was mostly manual. From our literature review, we identified that there is no multi-objective formulation of theme-based RP, even though it is intuitive to formulate it in a multi-objective way. In this paper, we will address this gap in the literature and propose a multi-objective formulation of theme-based RP. For simplicity, in our formulation, we will focus on a single (next) release of the RP.

3   Background

3.1   Pareto-Optimal Solutions

We consider a bi-objective maximization problem with two functions $F_1(x)$, $F_2(x)$. For some feasible area X, an n-tuple x' $\in$ X is said to be a Pareto-optimal solution if there is no x $\in$ X such that [16]:

$$\text{(i) } F_i(x) \geq F_i(x') \ \forall i \in \{1, 2\} \text{ and}$$

$$\text{(ii) } F_i(x) \neq F_i(x')$$

Pareto optimal solutions are often referred to as *non-dominated solutions*. The goal of any solution approach is to find as many Pareto-optimal solutions as possible [21]. The Pareto-optimal solutions provide alternatives to decision makers from which one can be finally chosen.

3.2   NSGA-II

NSGA-II is a multi-objective Evolutionary Algorithm (EA) [9]. It was demonstrated
by Zhang et al. [28] and Durillo et al. [12] that NSGA-II shows better performance in
terms of the number of obtained solutions when compared to other techniques. Furthermore, it computes the highest number of solutions which were contained in best
front known for each tested instance [12].

The NSGA-II procedure is shown in Fig. 1. NSGA-II makes use of a population
(P) of N candidate solutions (known as individuals). In this algorithm, a combined
population $R_t = P_t \cup Q_t$ of size $2N$ is formed, where P_t is the first population, Q_t is the
second population generated by conducting crossover and mutation on the first population. Initially, P_t is generated randomly. Once formed, the combined population R_t is
sorted according to non-domination criteria. Then, solutions belonging to the best
non-dominated set F_1 in the combined population are chosen. If the size of F_1 is
smaller than N, remaining members of the population P_{t+1} are chosen from the subsequent non-dominated fronts (F_2, F_3... F_{l-1}). To choose exactly N individuals, solutions
of the last front (say F_l) is sorted in descending order using the crowded-distance
operator [9] and only the required number of solutions is chosen to make the size of
N. The new population P_{t+1} of size N is now used for selection, crossover and mutation to create a new population Q_{t+1} of size N.

```
while not termination criteria do
       Rt  = Pt  ∪  Qt;
       F  =  non-dominated-sort (Rt);
       Pt+1 =  Ø;
       i  = 1;

       while |Pt+1| + |Fi| <=  N do
              compute crowding-distance on Fi;
              Pt+1  =  Pt+1 ∪ Fi ;
                            i  =  i + 1;
       end

       Sort the last front Fi ;
       Rem = Fi  [1 : (N   /Pt+1/)];
       Pt+1  =  Pt+1 ∪ Rem;
       Qt+1  =  make-new-pop(Pt+1);
       t  =  t + 1;
              end
```

Fig. 1. Algorithm for NSGA-II [9]

In NSGA-II, binary tournament selection with crowded-distance operator is used
as an individual selection criterion. To select one individual from multiple individuals
with differing non-domination ranks, the solution with the lower (better) rank is given
preference. If both solutions have the same non-domination ranks, the solution that is
located in a lesser crowded region is preferred.

3.3   Preference Building Based on Lexicographic Ordering

3.3.1   Lexicographical Ordering

For a given set of vectors (being of the same dimension or not), a *lexicographical ordering* is defined (similar to the arrangement of words in a dictionary) as the ordering of all the vectors such that (i) the vectors are in strict decreasing order related to their values of the first vector component), (ii) in case the values are the same for the first component, the decreasing order applies to the second component of the vectors, and (iii) the second principle is applied iteratively up to the component where vectors differ from each other for the first time.

For our purposes, we apply the lexicographical order to a set of vectors representing a set of Pareto solutions and their evaluation in terms of the theme coverage metric M_1.

3.3.2   Theme-coverage Metric

For a given cluster C_j of features representing a theme and a given assignment x of features to the next release, the theme coverage metric $M_1(C_j,x)$ is defined as:

$$M_1(C_j,x) = \frac{T_j}{N_j} *100 \tag{1}$$

Therein, N_j is the total number of features in cluster C_j and T_j is the total number of features of C_j assigned to the next release. This metric expresses the percentage of features of cluster *j* assigned to the next release and was proposed in [1]. We will utilize this metric to provide recommendations to product managers for selecting among Pareto solutions.

3.3.3   Lexicographical Ordering Related to Theme-coverage

Suppose, we have a preference vector $\mathbf{v} = (v_1, v_2,...,v_k)$. Each entry v_j in this vector $\mathbf{v}$ refers to a cluster. The preference vector $\mathbf{v}$ stores different clusters in the order of high preference to low preference.

Now, we form a $m \times k$ matrix $\mathbf{A}$. Each row vector $\mathbf{A}^i \in \mathbb{R}^k$ of the matrix $\mathbf{A}$ represents the ith Pareto-optimal solution. Each entry a_{ij} in the row vector $\mathbf{A}^i$ is formed as follows:

$$a_{ij} = E(i,M_1(C_j,x)) \quad \text{for all i,j} \tag{2}$$

The function E returns the value of metric M_1 for the cluster C_j in the ith Pareto-optimal solution associated with a particular release plan *x*. The resulting matrix $\mathbf{A}$ is:

$$A = \begin{bmatrix} a_{11} & a_{12} & a_{13} & ... & a_{1k} \\ a_{21} & a_{22} & a_{23} & ... & a_{2k} \\ ... & ... & ... & ... & ... \\ a_{m1} & a_{m2} & a_{m3} & ... & a_{mk} \end{bmatrix} \tag{3}$$

Once this matrix $\mathbf{A}$ is formed, row vectors are sorted such that the preference values are in decreasing order. This is achieved using lexicographic ordering as explained in Section 3.3.1. The sorted row vectors give us the rank of the Pareto-optimal solutions.

4   Bi-objective Theme-Based Release Planning

We formulate the balance between planning for maximum value of (semantically unrelated) features (but being of high individual value) and the orientation towards meta-functionalities of semantically related features (called *themes*) as a bi-objective release planning problem.

4.1   Decision Variables

We consider a set of features $F = \{f(1),...,f(N)\}$. The goal of RP is to select a subset of features to be assigned to the next release. The next release plan is represented by a vector of Boolean decision variables $x = (x(1),x(2),...,x(N))$ with

$$x(n) = 1, \text{ if feature } f(n) \text{ is assigned to next release} \tag{4}$$

$$x(n) = 0, \text{ if feature } f(n) \text{ is postponed}$$

4.2   Constraints

The generated release plans must satisfy a set of constraints. These constraints could be related to resources, budget or feature dependencies. Each effort or budget constraint can be represented as:

$$\sum_{n:\ x(n)=1} r(n,t) \leq Cap(k) \text{ for } k = 1...K \tag{5}$$

In (5), $r(n,t)$ represents the consumption of resource type t by feature $f(n)$. The generated release plan must satisfy all the constraints related to different resource types. Next, there can be several types of feature dependency constraints: *precedence, coupling, synergy constraints etc.* If feature $f(n)$ and $f(m)$ is in weak precedence relation R_p, then the following relationship should hold between the respective decision variables $x(n)$ and $x(m)$:

$$x(n) \leq x(m) \text{ for all } (n,m) \in R_p \tag{6}$$

This indicates that the features $f(n)$ needs to be offered before $f(m)$ or in the same release. If feature $f(n)$ and $f(m)$ is in coupling relation R_c, then the following relationship should hold between the decision variables $x(n)$ and $x(m)$:

$$x(n) = x(m) \text{ for all } (n,m) \in R_c \tag{7}$$

This dependency specifies that the features $f(n)$ and $f(m)$ need to be released (or postponed) together. If features $f(n)$ and $f(m)$ have a synergy dependency (belonging to a joint theme), then the value of both of these features increase by a fixed percentage in case they are offered together in conjunction. We can define the synergy as follows:

$$syn(n,m) = (val(n) + val(m))*inc(n,m) \text{ for all } (n,m) \in R_s \tag{8}$$

In (8), $inc(n,m)$ is the increment factor due to a synergy constraint, while $val(n)$ and $val(m)$ represent the values of the features $f(n)$ and $f(m)$, respectively.

4.3   Objectives

4.3.1   Individual Feature Value Objective

For a given release plan x, stakeholders feature points for a feature $f(n)$ is a measure describing the contribution of the feature to the overall satisfaction [24]. This measure is defined as a linear combination of criteria related scores given by a set of stakeholders. The scoring is defined on a nine-point scale $\{1...9\}$. The value of the first objective is defined as the total stakeholders feature points received from all features selected in the next release.

Suppose there are N features, Q planning criteria (e.g. value, time-to-market) and P stakeholders. Now, the first objective function $F_1(x)$ is based on an additive and linear function defined as follows:

$$F_1(x) = \Sigma_{n=1...N} \, x(n)*score(n) \tag{9}$$

where $score(n)$ of feature $f(n)$ is defined as:

$$score(n) = \Sigma_{q=1...Q} \, weight\_criterion(q)*score(q,n) \tag{10}$$

In (10), weight_criterion(q) indicates the weight of planning criterion q, while score(q,n) is the weighted (normalized) average of the stakeholder scores (defined on a nine-point scale) related to this criterion:

$$score(q,n) = \Sigma_{p=1...P} \, weight\_stake(p)*score(n,p,q) \tag{11}$$

In (11), weight_stake(p) refers to the weight of stakeholder p, while score(n,p,q) refers to the value assigned to the feature $f(n)$ by stakeholder p for criterion q.

4.3.2   Objective Based on Theme Synergies

The second objective function is looking at the synergies obtained from delivering features as part of themes. The value of this objective is defined over all pairs of features creating a value synergy:

$$F_2(x) = \Sigma_{(n,m) \in Rs} \, (val(n) + val(m))*inc(n,m) \tag{12}$$

The objective $F_2(x)$ is different from the second objective in [29] which was proposed to analyze requirements interaction. In [29], the second objective was formulated to minimize the sum of the cost associated with individual features as well as the cost incurred due to value and cost related dependencies between features. In our approach, the objective is to maximize $F_2(x)$, to promote offering of features from themes.

4.4   Decision Support for Bi-objective Release Planning

4.4.1   Bi-objective Release Planning

The bi-objective RP tackled in this paper consists of two parts. The first one is to determine a set of Pareto-optimal solutions balancing individual and theme-based consideration of release values:

$$\text{Max } \{(F_1(x), F_2(x)): x \text{ from X defined by (4) - (8)}\} \tag{13}$$

The second part is to look at all the solutions of (13) and to determine the most preferred Pareto solution defined as the one being most strongly aligned with a given preference relation of themes.

4.4.2   Decision Support for Selection of the Most Preferred Pareto Solution

In multi-objective formulation, the Pareto-front contains a set of complementary solutions. The decision-maker needs to decide on a reasonable compromise. This decision-making process is a challenging task since it is a human-centered process with a high level of fuzziness [23]. With more than three objectives, it is also not possible to visualize the Pareto-front to facilitate proper decision making by humans [17]. In addition to that, multi-objective evolutionary algorithms requires a very large number of solutions (e.g. 62500 solutions with four objectives) to approximate the Pareto-front with the increase in the number of objectives [18]. It becomes very difficult to choose a single solution from such a high number of available solutions. For these reasons, it is important to propose new approaches to rank a set of Pareto-solutions.

In this paper, we propose two decision support approaches to rank the Pareto-optimal solutions, which are described below: (i) Ranking based on alignment of solutions with theme preferences, and (ii) Ranking based on weights of themes.

In the first approach, a product manager provides the preference of themes as a preference vector of clusters. Suppose, there are 8 clusters and the provided preference vector is: $\{7, 3, 5\}$. This vector indicates that the product manager prefers highest theme-coverage from cluster 7, followed by cluster 3 and 5. Once the preference is given, the approach described in Section 3.3.3 is used to come up with a ranking of the Pareto-optimal solutions.

Pareto solutions can also be ranked using weight of the themes. Instead of providing partial or total ranking of the themes, a product manager can provide the weight of the themes. The weight of each theme called $weight(C_j)$ can be any value from 0 to 9 (the higher the value, the higher the importance). The score $p(x)$ for each Pareto solution is defined as follows:

$$p(x) = \Sigma_j \, M_1(C_j, x) * weight(C_j) \tag{14}$$

where $M_1(c, x)$ is the value of the metric M_1 for the cluster c under a release plan x and $weight(c)$ is the assigned weight for the cluster c. The higher the score, the higher the rank and attractiveness of the respective solution.

5   Empirical Evaluation

5.1   Case Study Projects

We evaluated the proposed approach for two data sets. The first data set (*data set 1*) [27] is based on Microsoft Word, a word processor. This data set has 50 features, 2 planning criteria, 4 stakeholders, 5 resource types and 81 feature interdependencies. The second data set (*data set 2*) [27] is related to the *ReleasePlanner*™ product development planning tool [22]. *ReleasePlanner*™ is a proprietary decision support system used for the generation of strategic and operational release planning. The related data set has 25 features, 4 planning criteria, 9 stakeholders, 7 resource types and 39 feature inter-dependencies. For the *data set* 1, there are 8 clusters of features, while *data set* 2 has 5 clusters.

In this paper, we did not use any automatic tool to generate any themes or clusters from features. Our experiments and analysis were based on the assumption that features are pre-assigned to clusters and pair wise synergy constraints are available for subset of all possible pairs of features in each cluster. The clusters in the *data set* 1 were generated in [1] using Chinese Whispers (CW) algorithm [6]. The clusters in the *data set* 2, on the other hand, were formed manually. Detail descriptions about the clusters of the used data sets can be found in [27].

5.2 Tuning of Parameters

The proposed approach was implemented in the *jMetal* [13] framework, a widely used tool for conducting multi-objective experiments. We used a simple binary GA encoding in NSGA-II. Each experiment with NSGA-II was executed for 500 generations. To accommodate randomness, each experiment was replicated 50 times. All distinct (in terms of features selected) Pareto-optimal solutions from the overall set of all trials were considered as final solutions.

To select an initial population size we experimented with several values of the size: 100, 250, 500 and single-point crossover with crossover probability P_c of 0.9 and bitwise mutation with mutation probability $P_m = 1/n$ (where n is the number of features). In our experiments, for the *data set* 1 and *data set* 2, we achieved almost the same number of Pareto-optimal solutions with different population sizes. We noticed that with population size 100, the proposed approach generated 43 Pareto-optimal solutions for the *data set* 1, while with the other population sizes 250 and 500, it generated 41 Pareto-optimal solutions in both cases.

The results for the other data set also showed similar trend. For the *data set* 2, with population size 100, the proposed approach generated 7 Pareto-optimal solutions, whereas with population size 250 it generated 6 Pareto-optimal solutions, while with 500 individuals in the population, it generated 4 Pareto-optimal solutions. For both data sets, the computational time was much lower with population size of 100 than with other sizes. In addition, the difference in the number of solutions was not significant. So, to achieve solutions within reasonable computation time, we chose 100 as the population size for our experiments.

Subsequently, we performed several experiments with the selected population size and different values of crossover probability $P_c = 0.9, 0.8, 0.7, 0.6, 0.5, 0.1$ and different values of mutation probability $P_c = 0.9, 0.8, 0.7, 0.6, 0.5, 0.1, 0.01, 1/n$ (where n is the number of features). In the *data set* 1, for all crossover probability settings, the number of Pareto-optimal solutions was high when used with low mutation probabilities like 0.01 and $1/n$. For the *data set* 2, on the other hand, we did not observe any significant differences in terms of the number of solutions found in all the experiments conducted. As our results were not consistent across these two data sets, we chose fairly standard crossover and mutation probability settings $P_c = 0.9$ and $P_m = 1/n$ for all further experiments.

5.3   Case Study Results

First, we analyze the results in terms of the number of Pareto-optimal solutions found. From our results, we notice that for the *data set* 1, there are 43 Pareto optimal solutions, while for the *data set* 2, there are only 7 Pareto-optimal solutions. Fig. 2 shows the Pareto front for the *data set* 1. There is a clear trade-off between the overall value of a solution (objective F_1) and the total increments due to synergy dependencies (objective F_2).

For analysis purpose, we also pick two extreme Pareto-optimal solutions: one that achieves highest value for the stakeholder satisfaction related objective F_1 (Solution A) and one that achieves highest value for the synergy related objective F_2 (Solution B). In Fig. 3, for solution A and B, the assigned features in the next release and the postponed features are represented as two matrices. In both columns of each of the two matrices, features from cluster 1, 2, 7 and 8 are shown in row 2, 3, 4 and 5, respectively. In this figure, we do not show features from those clusters which are postponed in both solutions.

We see that solution A offers features from four different clusters to maximize stakeholder satisfaction. Solution B, on the other hand, mainly focuses on offering features from two clusters, emphasizing a more theme-centric release plan. Since there are 43 Pareto-optimal solutions for the *data set* 1, without proper decision support, it is difficult to decide which one is the best solution in terms of a specific theme-coverage.

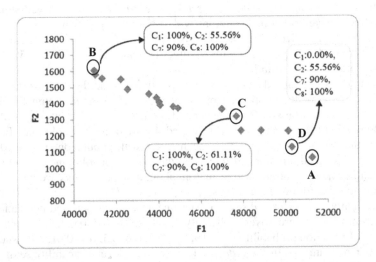

Fig. 2. Pareto-front for the *data set* 1. Each rectangle shows the values for the metric M_1 for different clusters in a solution. C_i refers to the value of M_1 for the ith cluster. A and B represent two extreme solutions: one that achieve maximum value for F_1 and one that achieve highest value for F_2, respectively.

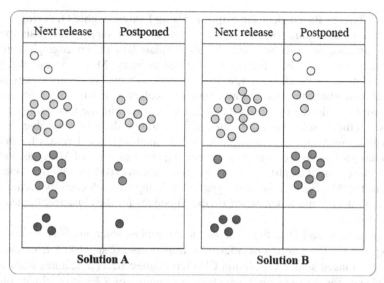

Fig. 3. Release plan without (Solution A) and with (Solution B) theme focus. Features from cluster 1, 2, 7 and 8 are shown in row 2, 3, 4 and 5, respectively. When features from a cluster are postponed in both solutions, that cluster is not shown.

Table 1 shows the objective function values and theme-coverage details for all the Pareto-optimal solutions for the *data set* 2. From F_1 and F_2 values, it is evident that 7 solutions map to three different points in the objective space. The reason is that multiple solutions offering different feature sets map into the same point in the objective space. It is also evident from this table that solution 1 is the most theme-centric as it offers features mainly from cluster 2 and cluster 5. Other solutions are the trade-off between theme-incorporation and stakeholders satisfaction. From our discussion on the Pareto-optimal solutions for the two data sets, we can see that solutions might have varying structures as well as different objective values. This is why, in theme-based bi-objective optimization, it is difficult to choose a single solution.

Table 1. Ranking of solutions for the *data set* 2 using M_1 and theme preference: $C_5 \geq C_2 \geq C_1$

Solution #	F_1	F_2	C_5	C_2	C_1	C_3	C_4
1	64864.00	102.90	83.33	80.00	0.00	0.00	0.00
2	74944.00	74.55	83.33	60.00	20.00	25.00	0.00
3	64864.00	102.90	66.67	80.00	0.00	50.00	0.00
4	67815.00	93.45	66.67	60.00	0.00	0.00	40.00
5	74944.00	74.55	50.00	60.00	20.00	25.00	40.00
6	67815.00	93.45	50.00	60.00	20.00	0.00	60.00
7	74944.00	74.55	50.00	60.00	20.00	25.00	40.00

5.3.1   Theme-Based Decision Support Using Lexicographic Ordering

One of the goals in this paper is to show how decision support can assist product managers in choosing a RP solution. We now explain how the lexicographic ordering of the Pareto-optimal solutions can be performed using the M_1 metric values for each cluster. Suppose for the *data set* 1, a product manager's preference of clusters is: { 7, 8, 2}. This indicates that the product manager prefers to incorporate more features from cluster 7, followed by cluster 8 and 2. To come up with the lexicographic ordering, first, all the 43 solutions were sorted in decreasing order using M_1 values for cluster 7 (most preferred). Several solutions were found with equal values for this metric. So those solutions were sorted in decreasing order in terms of M_1 values for cluster 8, the next preferred cluster. Again, several solutions ended up with the same value for the metric M_1. Finally, the lexicographic ordering was achieved by sorting those solutions in decreasing order, based on the M_1 values for the cluster 2, the least preferred cluster.

Solutions B, C and D in Fig. 2 show the top ranked solutions after lexicographic ordering. All the three solutions offer 90% from cluster 7 and 100% from cluster 8. But the top ranked solution (Solution C) offers highest 61.11% features from cluster 2. In Table 1, for the *data set* 2, we show the ranking of 7 Pareto-optimal solutions obtained using lexicographic ordering, with the preference of clusters as {5, 2, 1}. It is evident that the proposed approach based on lexicographic ordering can assist product managers to rank the solutions and choose one solution.

5.3.2   Theme-based Decision Support Using Weighted Themes

Solutions can be ranked using weight of the themes. Suppose that the assigned weights for cluster 1 to cluster 5 for the *data set* 2 are: w(1)=7, w(2)=8, w(3)=2, w(4)=5 and w(5)=9. Highest weight is given to cluster 5, while the lowest weight is given to cluster 3. The ranking of the 7 Pareto-optimal solutions based on the scores computed using Eq. 14 is given in Table 2. The ranking obtained using this approach is different from the ranking obtained using the lexicographic ordering (see Table 1). We can see that solution 1 and 2 in Table 1 has swapped their places in Table 2. There are changes in the ranking of the other solutions as well. However, the ranking obtained with the two approaches can be made identical. To achieve this, we have to assign weights to the clusters following the product manager's preference order.

Table 2. Ranking of solutions for the *data set* 2 using metric M_1 and weight of clusters: w(1)=7, w(2)=8, w(3)=2, w(4)=5 and w(5)=9

Solution #	C_5	C_2	C_1	C_3	C_4
1	83.33	60.00	20.00	25.00	0.00
2	83.33	80.00	0.00	0.00	0.00
3	50.00	60.00	20.00	0.00	60.00
4	66.67	80.00	0.00	50.00	0.00
5	50.00	60.00	20.00	25.00	40.00
6	50.00	60.00	20.00	25.00	40.00
7	66.67	60.00	0.00	0.00	40.00

In addition, the weights need to be assigned in decreasing order (higher to lower weights). For other clusters not specified in the preference, weight of zero must be used.

5.4   Discussion and Threats to Validity

From our explorative case studies on the two data sets, we can confirm that Pareto-optimal solutions show clear trade-off between overall stakeholder satisfaction and theme incorporation. We also see that lexicographic ordering or theme weight based ranking of the Pareto-optimal solutions can help product managers to pick a solution that best match the given priority of themes.

However, there are some threats to validity: First, the result is based on just two data sets. The proposed approach should be validated with more real world data sets. Second, the scalability of the approach needs to be tested with data sets containing significant number of features and feature inter-dependencies. Third, we used only one theme-coverage metric to come up with ordering of the solutions. Other metrics can be designed to validate the results (see [1] for additional metric suggestions). Fourth, in the two data sets used, following the work in [1], synergy constraints were defined only between pair of features in a cluster. Synergy constraints should be defined involving more than two features in the data sets to be used in future.

6   Summary and Outlook to Future Research

Consideration of themes is a new way to increase the attractiveness and meaningfulness of release planning results. In this paper, we have demonstrated how theme-based RP can be formulated as a bi-objective optimization problem that can be tackled with NSGA-II. We have also proposed two ways of ranking the solutions in the Pareto-front by taking consideration of product managers' preferences of theme-coverage. Our case study results show how multi-objective formulation can identify solutions that balance the competing concerns of theme incorporation and overall value of features selected for the next release.

There are several ideas to conduct future research. In this work, we did not try to evaluate the quality of Pareto-optimal solutions in terms of convergence to the true unknown Pareto-front as well as in terms of the spread of the solutions. In future, these will be taken into account. We generated plans for a single release of the RP. In RP, we usually plan for several releases ahead. In future, this work will be extended to perform RP for more than one release. For our experiments, we relied on the constraint-handling mechanism of NSGA-II as specified in [9]. We believe that the quality of Pareto-optimal solutions in terms of the features offered might be improved if other constraint handling mechanisms are employed. Finally, there is a plan to conduct more empirical investigations to study the acceptance of the proposed solutions in a real-world context.

Acknowledgment. This research was supported by the Natural Sciences and Engineering Research Council of Canada, NSERC Discovery Grant-250343-12. We would like to thank Fazlul Chowdhury for providing access to the *data set* 2 used in the case study. We sincerely thank Jason Ho, Reza Karimpour, S.M. Didar-Al-Alam and the anonymous reviewers for their insightful comments.

References

1. Agarwal, N., Karimpour, R., Ruhe, G.: Theme-based product release planning: An analytical approach. In: Proceedings of the 47th Annual Hawaii International Conference on System Sciences, pp. 4739–4748 (2014)
2. Akker, M.V.D., Brinkkemper, S., Diepen, G., Versendaal, J.: Determination of the next release of a software product: An approach using integer linear programming. In: Proceedings of the 11th International Workshop on Requirements Engineering: Foundation for Software Quality, pp. 247–262 (2005)
3. Akker, M.V.D., Brinkkemper, S., Diepen, G., Versendaal, J.: Software product release planning through optimization and what-if analysis. Information and Software Technology 50, 101–111 (2008)
4. Bagnall, A., Rayward-Smith, V., Whittley, I.: The next release problem. Information and Software Technology 43(14), 883–890 (2001)
5. Brasil, M.M.A., da Silva, T.G.N., de Freitas, F.G., de Souza, J.T., Cortés, M.I.: A multi-objective optimization approach to the software release planning with undefined number of releases and interdependent requirements. In: Zhang, R., Zhang, J., Zhang, Z., Filipe, J., Cordeiro, J. (eds.) ICEIS 2011. LNBIP, vol. 102, pp. 300–314. Springer, Heidelberg (2012)
6. Biemann, C.: Chinese whispers: An efficient graph clustering algorithm and its application to natural language processing problems. In: Proceedings of the First Workshop on Graph Based Methods for Natural Language Processing, Stroudsburg, PA, USA, pp. 73–80 (2006)
7. Cai, X., Wei, O., Huang, Z.: Evolutionary approaches for multi-objective next release problem. Computing and Informatics 31(4), 847–875 (2012)
8. Colares, F., Souza, J., Carmo, R., Padua, C., Mateus, G.R.: A New Approach to the Software Release Planning. In: Proceedings of the XXIII Brazilian Symposium on Software Engineering, pp. 207–215, 5–9 (2009)
9. Deb, K., Pratap, A., Agarwal, S., Meyarivan, T.: A fast and elitist multi-objective genetic algorithm: NSGA-II. IEEE Transactions on Evolutionary Computation 6(2), 182–197 (2002)
10. del Sagrado, J., del Aguila, I.M., Orellana, F.J.: Ant colony optimization for the next release problem: A comparative study. In: Proceedings of the 2nd International Symposium on Search Based Software Engineering, Washington, DC, USA, pp. 67–76 (2010)
11. de Souza, J.T., Maia, C.L.B., do Nascimento Ferreira, T., do Carmo, R.A.F., Brasil, M.M.A.: An ant colony optimization approach to the software release planning with dependent requirements. In: Cohen, M.B., Ó Cinnéide, M. (eds.) SSBSE 2011. LNCS, vol. 6956, pp. 142–157. Springer, Heidelberg (2011)
12. Durillo, J.J., Zhang, Y., Alba, E., Harman, M., Nebro, A.J.: A study of the bi-objective next release problem. Empirical Software Engineering 16(1), 29–60 (2011)
13. Durillo, J.J., Nebro, A.J.: jMetal: A Java framework for multi-objective optimization. Advances in Engineering Software 42(10), 760–771 (2011)

14. Fricker, S., Schumacher, S.: Release planning with feature trees: Industrial case. In: Regnell, B., Damian, D. (eds.) REFSQ 2011. LNCS, vol. 7195, pp. 288–305. Springer, Heidelberg (2012)
15. Greer, D., Ruhe, G.: Software release planning: An evolutionary and iterative approach. Information and Software Technology 46(4), 243–253 (2004)
16. Lin, J.G.: Multiple-Objective Problems: Pareto-Optimal Solutions by Method of Proper Equality Constraints. IEEE Transactions on Automatic Control 21(5), 641–650 (1976)
17. López Jaimes, A., Coello, C.A.C., Urías Barrientos, J.E.: Online objective reduction to deal with many-objective problems. In: Ehrgott, M., Fonseca, C.M., Gandibleux, X., Hao, J.-K., Sevaux, M. (eds.) EMO 2009. LNCS, vol. 5467, pp. 423–437. Springer, Heidelberg (2009)
18. Mkaouer, W., Kessentini, M., Bechikh, S., Deb, K., Cinnelde, M.O.: High Dimensional Search-based Software Engineering: Finding Tradeoffs among 15 Objectives for Automating Software Refactoring using NSGA-III. COIN Report No. 2013002 (2013)
19. Nebro, A.J., Durillo, J.J., Luna, F., Dorronsoro, B., Alba, E.: Mocell: A cellular genetic algorithm for multi-objective optimization. International Journal of Intelligent Systems 24(7), 25–36 (2007)
20. Ngo-The, A., Ruhe, G.: A systematic approach for solving the wicked problem of software release planning. Soft Computing 12(1), 95–108 (2007)
21. Obayashi, S., Sasaki, D., Oyama, A.: Finding Tradeoffs by Using Multi-objective Optimization Algorithms. Transactions of the Japan Society for Aeronautical and Space Sciences 47(155), 51–58 (2004)
22. ReleasePlanner™, https://www.releaseplanner.com/rpApp (last accessed June 02, 2014)
23. Renaud, J., Thibault, J., Lanouette, R., Kiss, L., Zaras, K., Fonteix, C.: Comparison of two multi-criteria decision aid methods: Net flow and rough set methods in a high yield pulping process. European Journal of Operational Research 177(3), 1418–1432 (2007)
24. Ruhe, G.: Product Release Planning: Methods, Tools and Applications. CRC Press (2010)
25. Saliu, O., Ruhe, G.: Supporting software release planning decisions for evolving systems. In: 29th Annual IEEE/NASA Software Engineering Workshop, pp. 14–26 (2005)
26. Saliu, O., Ruhe, G.: Bi-objective release planning for evolving software systems. In: Proceedings of ISEC/FSE, pp. 105–114 (2007)
27. Theme-based Release Planning Data Sets, https://sites.google.com/site/mrkarim/data-sets (last accessed June 02, 2014)
28. Zhang, Y., Harman, M., Mansouri, S.A.: The multi-objective next release problem. In: Proceedings of the 9th Annual Conference on Genetic and Evolutionary Computation, pp. 1129–1137 (2007)
29. Zhang, Y., Harman, M., Lim, S.: Empirical evaluation of search based requirements interaction management. Information and Software Technology 55(1), 126–152 (2013)

Combining Stochastic Grammars and Genetic Programming for Coverage Testing at the System Level

Fitsum Meshesha Kifetew[1,2], Roberto Tiella[1], and Paolo Tonella[1]

[1] Fondazione Bruno Kessler, Trento, Italy
{kifetew,tiella,tonella}@fbk.eu
[2] University of Trento, Italy

Abstract. When tested at the system level, many programs require complex and highly structured inputs, which must typically satisfy some formal grammar. Existing techniques for grammar based testing make use of stochastic grammars that randomly derive test sentences from grammar productions, trying at the same time to avoid unbounded recursion. In this paper, we combine stochastic grammars with genetic programming, so as to take advantage of the guidance provided by a coverage oriented fitness function during the sentence derivation and evolution process. Experimental results show that the combination of stochastic grammars and genetic programming outperforms stochastic grammars alone.

Keywords: Genetic programming; grammar based testing; stochastic grammars.

1 Introduction

Search based test data generation has been the subject of active research for a couple of decades now, and a number of techniques and tools have been developed as a result [1–3]. However, there is still the need for test data generation techniques applicable to programs whose inputs exhibit complex structures, which are often governed by a specification, such as a grammar. We refer to such systems as *grammar based systems*. An example of such systems is Rhino, a compiler/interpreter for the JavaScript language. Test cases to this system are JavaScript programs that respect the rules of the underlying JavaScript grammar specification. Despite some efforts made in recent years in this direction [4–6], there is no solution that is effective in achieving the desired level of adequacy and is scalable to reasonably large/complex grammars.

The challenge in generating test cases for grammar based systems lies in choosing a set of input sentences, out of those that can be potentially derived from the given grammar, in such a way that the desired test adequacy criterion is met. In practice, the grammars that govern the structure of the input are far from trivial. For instance, the JavaScript grammar, which defines the structure of the

C. Le Goues and S. Yoo (Eds.): SSBSE 2014, LNCS 8636, pp. 138–152, 2014.

input for Rhino, contains 331 rules and many of these rules are deeply nested and recursive. One way to deal with this problem is through the use of *stochastic grammars*, where the application of rules is controlled by probability distributions crafted so as to reduce the risk of infinite or unbounded recursion. Such probabilities can also be learned from a corpus, so as to increase the chances of generating sentences that resemble those observed in the field. On the other hand, Genetic Programming (GP) [7] has been used, albeit with relatively simpler structures, to evolve tree structures suitable for a particular objective (e.g., failure reproduction [8]). We propose a novel combination of stochastic grammars and GP that integrates the effectiveness of stochastic grammars, capable of controlling infinite recursion and of generating realistic sentence structures, with the evolutionary guidance of GP, capable of evolving inputs from the grammar so as to achieve high system-level branch coverage. Evaluation on three grammar based systems shows that this combined approach is effective both in achieving high system coverage and in revealing real and seeded faults.

The remainder of this paper is organized as follows: in Section 2 we present basic background on stochastic grammars and evolutionary test case generation. Section 3 presents the proposed approach and its implementation, while experimental results are described in Section 4. Closely related works are discussed in Section 5 and finally Section 6 outlines future works and concludes the paper.

2 Background

This section provides basic background on two topics that are extensively used in the paper: (1) stochastic grammars, and (2) evolutionary algorithms.

2.1 Stochastic Grammars

Notation and definitions: Figure 1 shows a simple context free grammar (CFG) $G = (T, N, P, s)$, with four terminal symbols (contained in set T), one non-terminal symbol (set N), three production rules (π_1, π_2, π_3) and start symbol s. A derivation for the sentence "(n)+n" and the associated parse tree are also shown in Figure 1.

A CFG can be used as a tool to randomly generate strings that belong to the language $L(G)$, expressed by grammar G, by means of the process described in

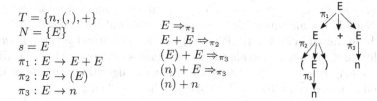

Fig. 1. An simple grammar, a derivation for the string "(n)+n" and its syntax tree

---

Algorithm 1. Generation of a string using a CFG

$S \leftarrow s$
$k = 1$
while $k <$ MAX_ITER and S has the form $\alpha \cdot u \cdot \beta$, where $\alpha \in T^*$ and $u \in N$ **do**
   $\pi \leftarrow$ **choose**(P_u)
   $S \leftarrow \alpha \cdot \pi(u) \cdot \beta$
   $k = k + 1$
end while
if $k <$ MAX_ITER **then**
   return S
else
   return TIMEOUT
end if

Algorithm 1. The algorithm applies a production rule, randomly chosen from the subset of applicable rules P_u (by means of the function **choose**), to the left-most non terminal u of the working sentential form S, so obtaining a new sentential form that is assigned to S. The algorithm iterates until there are no more non-terminal symbols to substitute (i.e., $S \in T^*$, since it does not have the form $\alpha \cdot u \cdot \beta$ with $u \in N$) or a maximum number of iterations is reached. The behavior of Algorithm 1 can be analyzed by resorting to the notion of *Stochastic Context-free Grammars* [9].

Definition 1 (Stochastic Context-free Grammar). *A* Stochastic Context-free Grammar *S is defined by a pair (G, p) where G is a CFG, called the* core CFG *of S, and p is a function from the set of rules P to the interval $[0, 1] \subseteq \mathbb{R}$, namely $p : P \to [0, 1]$, satisfying the following condition:*

$$\sum_{u \to \beta \in P_u} p(u \to \beta) = 1, \textit{ for all } u \in N \tag{1}$$

Condition (1) ensures that p is a (discrete) probability distribution on each subset $P_u \subseteq P$ of rules that have the same non-terminal u as left hand side.

An invocation of Algorithm 1 can be seen as realizing a derivation in a stochastic grammar based on G where probabilities are defined by the function **choose**. The number of iterations that Algorithm 1 needs to produce a sentence depends on the structure of the grammar G and on the probabilities assigned to rules. As a matter of fact, interesting grammars contain (mutually) recursive rules. If recursive rules have a high selection probability p, the number of iterations needed to derive a sentence from the grammar using Algorithm 1 can be very large, in some cases even infinite, and quite likely beyond the timeout limit MAX_ITER.

Consider the grammar in Figure 1, with $p(\pi_3) = q, p(\pi_2) = 0$ and $p(\pi_1) = 1 - q$. The probability that the generation algorithm terminates (assuming MAX_ITER $= \infty$) depends on q. If $q < 1/2$ the probability that the algorithm terminates is less than 1 and it decreases at lower values of q, reaching 0 when $q = 0$.

This example shows that when Algorithm 1 is used in practice, with a finite value of MAX_ITER, the timeout could be reached frequently with some choices of probabilities p, resulting in a waste of computational resources and in a small number of sentences being generated. A method to control how often recursive rules are applied is definitely needed. We discuss two methods widely adopted in practice: the 80/20 rule and grammar learning.

The 80/20 Rule: Given a CFG $G = (T, N, P, s)$, for every non-terminal $u \in N$, P_u is split into two disjoint subsets P_u^r and P_u^n, where P_u^r (respectively P_u^n) is the subset of rules in P_u which are (mutually) recursive (respectively non-recursive). Probabilities of rules are then defined as follows:

$$p(\alpha \to \beta) = \begin{cases} q/|P_u^n|, \text{ if } \alpha \to \beta \in P_u^n \\ (1-q)/|P_u^r|, \text{ if } \alpha \to \beta \in P_u^r \end{cases}$$

so as to assign a total probability q to the non-recursive rules and $1 - q$ to the recursive ones. A commonly used rule of thumb consists of assigning 80% probability to the non-recursive rules ($q = 0.80$) and 20% to the recursive rules. In practice, with these values the sentence derivation process has been shown empirically to generate non-trivial sentences in most cases, while keeping the number of times the timeout limit is reached reasonably low.

Learning Probabilities from Samples: Another approach to assign rule probabilities to a CFG consists of learning the probabilities from an available corpus. If the grammar is not ambiguous, every sentence has only one parse tree and probabilities can be easily assigned to rules by observing how many times a rule is used in the parse tree for each sentence in the corpus. In the presence of ambiguity, learning can take advantage of the *Inside-outside* algorithm [10]. The inside-outside algorithm is an iterative algorithm based on expectation-maximization. Starting from randomly chosen probability values, it repeatedly refines the rule probabilities so as to maximize the corpus likelihood.

2.2   Evolutionary Algorithms

Evolutionary algorithms search for approximate solutions to optimization problems, whose exact solutions cannot be obtained at acceptable computational cost, by evolving a population of candidate solutions that are evaluated through a fitness function. Genetic algorithms (GAs) have been successfully used to generate test cases for both procedural [2] and object-oriented software [3]. GAs evolve a population of test cases trying to maximize a fitness function that measures the distance of each individual test case from a coverage target still to be reached. The genetic operators used for evolutionary test case generation include test case mutation operators (e.g., mutate primitive value) and crossover between test cases (e.g., swap of the tails of two input sequences) [1].

Whole Test Suite Generation: Whole test suite generation [3] is a recent development in the area of evolutionary testing, where a population of *test suites* is evolved towards satisfying *all coverage targets at once*. Since in practice the infeasible (unreachable) targets for a system under test (SUT) are not generally known a priori, generating test data considering one coverage target at a time is potentially inefficient as it may waste a substantial amount of search budget trying to find a solution for infeasible targets. Whole test suite generation is not affected by this problem as it does not try to cover one target at a time. Rather, the fitness of each test suite is measured with respect to *all coverage targets*. That is, when a test suite is executed for fitness evaluation, its performance is measured with respect to all test targets.

Genetic Programming: Genetic programming [7] follows a similar process as GAs. However, the individuals manipulated by the search algorithm are tree-structured data (*programs*, in the GP terminology) rather than encodings of solution instances. While there are a number of variants of GP in the literature, in this work we focus on Grammar Guided GP (GGGP) [7]. In GGGP, individuals are sentences generated according to the formal rules prescribed by a (context free) grammar. Specifically, initial sentences are generated from a CFG and new individuals produced by the GP search operators (crossover and mutation) are guaranteed to be valid with respect to the associated CFG.

An individual (a sentence from the grammar) in the population is represented by its parse tree. Evolutionary operators (crossover and mutation) play a crucial role in the GP search process. Subtree crossover and subtree mutation are commonly used operators in GP. The instances of these operators that we use in our approach are described in detail in Section 3.

3   Combined Approach

Our approach combines grammar-guided genetic programming with a suitable fitness function so as to evolve *test suites* for system-level branch coverage of the SUT. Since we perform whole-test suite optimization, which is more appropriate for system level testing, we evolve both test suites and the test cases inside the test suites. For test suite evolution we use GA, while for test case evolution we use grammar guided GP (see Section 2).

3.1   Representation of Individuals

Individuals manipulated by the GA are *test suites*. Each test suite is composed of *test cases*. A test case is a single input to the SUT. In other words, a test case is a well-formed sentence derived from the grammar of the SUT. Hence, a test suite in the GA is a set of sentences, represented by their parse trees.

3.2   Initialization

The initial population of test suites is obtained by generating input sentences according to the stochastic process described in Algorithm 1 and by grouping them randomly into test suites. Stochastic sentence generation uses either heuristically fixed or learned probabilities, as discussed in Section 2.

3.3   Fitness Evaluation

The GA evaluates each individual (test suite) by computing its fitness value. For this purpose, the tree representation of the test cases in the suite is unparsed to a string, which can be passed to the SUT as input. The GA determines the fitness value by running the SUT with all unparsed trees from the suite and measuring the amount of branches that are covered, as well as the distance from covering the uncovered branches.

During fitness evaluation, branch distances [1] are computed from all possible branches in the SUT, spanning over multiple classes. The fitness of the suite is the sum of all such branch distances. This fitness function is an extended form of the one employed by Fraser et al [3] for unit testing of classes. GA uses Equation 2 to compute the fitness value of a test suite T, where $|M|$ is the total number of methods in the SUT; $|M_T|$ is the number of methods executed by T (hence $|M - M_T|$ accounts for the entry branches of the methods that are never executed); $d(b_k, T)$ is the minimum branch distance computed for the branch b_k; a value of 0 means the branch is covered.

$$fitness(T) = |M| - |M_T| + \sum_{b_k \in B} d(b_k, T) \qquad (2)$$

3.4   Genetic Operators

In our approach, genetic operators work at two levels: at the upper level, GA operators are used to evolve test suites (TS); at the lower level, GP operators are used to evolve the parse trees that represent the input sentences of the test cases contained in a test suite. Evolution at the lower level is regarded as a special kind of mutation (namely, parse tree mutation) at the upper level. Hence, GP operators are activated according to the probability of parse tree mutation set in the upper GA level. In particular, the GP operator *subtree mutation* is applied to a test case that belongs to test suite T with probability $1/|T|$. The GP operator *subtree crossover* is applied with probability α.

GA Operators [3]

TS Mutation: insert new test cases: with a small probability β a new test case is added to T; additional test cases are added with (exponentially) decreasing probability. The new test cases to insert are generated by applying Algorithm 1.

TS Mutation: delete test cases: with a small probability γ a test case is removed from T. The test case which covers the least number of branches is selected for removal, so as to keep the most promising individuals in the test suite.

TS Crossover: Given two parent test suites T_1 and T_2, crossover results in off-spring O_1 and O_2, each containing a portion of test cases from both parents. Specifically, the first $\delta|T_1|$ tests from T_1 and the last $(1-\delta)|T_2|$ tests from T_2 are assigned to O_1; while the first $\delta|T_2|$ tests from T_2 and the last $(1-\delta)|T_1|$ tests from T_1 are assigned to O_2, for $\delta \in [0,1]$.

GP Operators [7]

Subtree mutation: Subtree mutation is performed by replacing a subtree in the tree representation of the individual with a new subtree, generated from the underlying stochastic grammar by means of Algorithm 1. Figure 2 shows an example of subtree mutation applied to a test case.

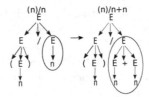

Fig. 2. Subtree mutation: a subtree (circled) is replaced with a new one generated from the grammar using Algorithm 1

Subtree crossover: Figure 3 shows an example of subtree crossover between two test cases in a test suite T. Two subtrees rooted at the same non terminal are selected in the parent trees and swapped, so as to originate two new offspring trees.

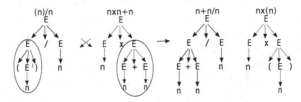

Fig. 3. Subtree crossover: subtrees of the same type (circled) from *parents* are exchanged to create *children*

3.5   Implementation

We implemented the proposed approach in a prototype (hereafter referred to as StGP) by extending the EvoSuite test generation framework [11]. In particular, we extended EvoSuite with: (1) a new parse-tree based representation of individuals; (2) a new initialization method, which resorts to stochastic grammar based sentence derivation; (3) new GP operators which manipulate parse tree representation of individuals. Moreover, the top-level algorithm has been modified to accommodate the two levels (GA and GP) required by our approach. For each SUT, we assume that there is a system level entry point through which it can be invoked. In cases where such entry point is missing, we define one, acting as a test driver for invoking the core functionalities of the SUT.

For learning rule probabilities from a corpus, we extended an existing implementation of the inside-outside algorithm[1], which given a grammar and a set of sentences produces as output a probability for each rule in the grammar.

During fitness evaluation, the tree representation of each individual test case is unparsed to a string which is then wrapped into a sequence of Java statements. These sequences of Java statements are then executed against the instrumented SUT. Figure 4 shows a simplified example of this process.

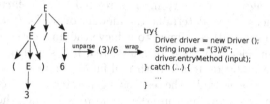

Fig. 4. During fitness evaluation, tree representations are unparsed and wrapped into sequences of Java statements

As recommended by Arcuri et al. [12], we have implemented StGP in such a way that it takes advantage of accidental coverage. If the execution of a test case covers a search target which was not covered so far, such a test case is kept as a solution, regardless of the survival of the test suite it belongs to. At the end of the search, such test cases are merged with the best suite evolved by the search. In this way test cases that exercise uncovered targets but are not part of the final "best" test suite are not lost.

We implemented a random generation technique (RND hereafter) as a baseline for comparing the performance of StGP. RND generates a random test case from the grammar, executes it against the SUT, and collects all covered branches [12]. It stops either when full coverage is reached or search budget is finished.

4   Experimental Results

To evaluate the effectiveness of StGP, we carried out experiments on three open source grammar based systems with varying levels of complexity, and compared its effectiveness with respect to the baseline (RND). Specifically, we formulated the following research questions:

---

[1] http://web.science.mq.edu.au/~mjohnson/Software.htm

RQ1 (combination): Does StGP achieve higher system-level coverage than RND?

RQ2 (grammar learning): Does grammar learning contribute to further increase coverage?

RQ3 (fault detection): What is the fault detection rate of StGP, with and without learning, as compared to RND?

4.1 Metrics

For RQ1 and RQ2, the metrics used to measure the *effectiveness* of the techniques being compared is *branch coverage at the system level*, computed as the number of branches covered by the generated test cases out of the total number of branches in the SUT. In cases where there is no statistically significant difference in coverage, a secondary metrics related to *efficiency* is computed. For measuring efficiency, we determine the amount of *search budget* (number of unique test cases executed) consumed to achieve the final coverage.

For RQ3 we consider two kinds of faults: real faults and mutants, injected into the SUT by a mutation tool[2]. With real faults, we measure the *number of unique faults that are exposed* by the test cases generated by the techniques being compared. With mutants, we measure the *mutation score*, i.e., the proportion of mutants that are *killed* by the generated test cases. A mutant is considered as killed if the original and mutated programs produce different outputs when the generated test cases are executed.

4.2 Subjects

The subjects used in our experiments are open source Java systems that accept structured input based on a grammar. `Calc`[3] is an expression evaluator that accepts an input language including variable declarations and arbitrary expressions. `MDSL`[4] is an interpreter for the Minimalistic Domain Specific Language (MDSL), a language including programming constructs such as functions, loops, conditionals etc. `Rhino`[5] is a JavaScript compiler/interpreter.

Considering the complexity of the input structure (specifically, the associated grammar) they accept, these subjects are representative of small (Calc), medium (MDSL), and large (Rhino) grammar based systems. Table 1 reports the size in LOC (Lines Of Code) of the source code and the number of productions in the respective grammars. Terminal productions, accounting for the lexical structure of the tokens, are excluded. These grammars are far more complex than those typically found in the GP literature and contain several nested and recursive definitions. Hence, they represent a significant challenge for the automated generation of test data.

---

[2] http://www.pitest.org
[3] https://github.com/cmhulett/ANTLR-java-calculator/
[4] http://mdsl.sourceforge.net/
[5] http://www.mozilla.org/rhino (version 1.7R4)

Table 1. Subjects used in our experimental study

Name	Language	Size(KLOC)	# Productions
Calc	Java	2	38
MDSL	Java	13	140
Rhino	Java	73	331

The corpus used for learning stochastic grammars is composed of sentences we selected from the test suites distributed with the SUT (for Calc and MDSL) and from the V8 JavaScript Engine benchmark[6] (for Rhino).

4.3   Procedure and Settings

Since both StGP and RND are based on stochastic grammars, they heavily rely on probabilistic choices. Therefore, we repeated each experiment 10 times, and measured statistical significance of the differences using the Wilcoxon non parametric test.

Based on some preliminary sensitivity experiments, we assigned the following values to the main parameters of our algorithm: population size = 20, crossover rate = 0.75, subtree crossover rate $\alpha = 0.1$, new test insertion rate $\beta = 0.1$, test deletion rate $\gamma = 0.01$. For the other parameters we kept default values set by the EvoSuite tool. Since the subjects used in our experiments differ significantly in size and complexity, giving the same search budget to all would not be fair. Hence, we resorted to the following heuristic rule for budget assignment: we give each SUT a budget of $n * |branches|$, where $|branches|$ is the number of branches in the SUT. Based on a few preliminary experiments, we chose the value $n = 5$.

4.4   Results

Table 2 shows the branch coverage achieved by each technique. Results of the Wilcoxon test of significance are also shown. For subjects MDSL and Rhino StGP achieves statistically significantly higher coverage than RND, both with and without learning. StGP-LRN gave consistently the highest coverage on all subjects. For subject Calc all techniques achieve the same coverage. One possible explanation could be that since this subject is small, both in terms of source code and grammar, it is relatively easy for all techniques to achieve maximum coverage. On the other hand, StGP-LRN consumes on average a substantially lower search budget to achieve such coverage. The difference in budget consumption with the baseline is significant at level 0.1 (p-value = 0.08). If learning is disregarded, we can still notice that StGP outperforms RND by a statistically significant coverage difference, with the exception of Calc, for which no coverage difference can be observed across all test data generation techniques.

In addition, Table 2 also reports the increase in coverage, $\Delta(\%)$ column in the table, which range from 2.19% (56 branches) for MDSL to 36.04% (1218 branches) for Rhino.

---

[6] https://code.google.com/p/v8/

Table 2. Branch coverage with *p*-values obtained from the Wilcoxon test. *Goals* is the total number of coverage goals; *Covered* is the number of covered goals; *Budget* is the amount of search budget consumed. Best values are shown in boldface.

		RND	StGP	Δ(%)	p-val	RND-LRN	StGP-LRN	Δ(%)	p-val
Calc	Goals	439	439			439	439		
	Covered	**334**	**334**	0.00	NA	**334**	**334**	0.00	NA
	Cov(%)	**76.08**	**76.08**			**76.08**	**76.08**		
	Budget	488	502		0.97	614	308		0.08
MDSL	Goals	3673	3673			3673	3673		
	Covered	2571	2627	2.19	2.44E-4	2543	**2661**	4.62	1.08E-5
	Cov(%)	70.00	71.53			69.25	**72.44**		
	Budget	18365	18366			18365	18366		
Rhino	Goals	14763	14763			14763	14763		
	Covered	3380	4598	36.04	1.08E-5	4504	**5076**	12.70	1.08E-5
	Cov(%)	22.89	31.15			30.51	**34.39**		
	Budget	73815	73816			73815	73816		

> We can answer **RQ1** positively. StGP significantly improves coverage over RND in two out of three subjects. When achieving the same coverage, StGP consumes a lower search budget.

As can still be seen from Table 2, learning the probabilities of the stochastic grammar from a corpus further improves the achieved coverage, in particular for the more complex subjects, MDSL and Rhino. Learning improves the coverage achieved by StGP both with respect to the baseline (RND-LRN, with *p*-value < 0.05; see last column of Table 2) and with respect to StGP without learning (with *p*-value equal to 4.35E-04 for MDSL; 1.08E-05 for Rhino).

> We can answer **RQ2** positively. The coverage achieved by StGP is further improved when the probabilities of the stochastic grammar are learned from a corpus in two out of three subjects.

Table 3. Real faults exposed on average by each technique

Subject	RND	StGP	p-val	RND-LRN	StGP-LRN	p-val
Calc	9.1	7.6	0.01	8.4	6.2	0.01
MDSL	6.4	6.6	0.66	7.5	9.5	0.03
Rhino	0	0.3	0.17	1	0.7	0.27

Table 3 reports the real faults exposed by the generated test suites. The reported values are averages over 10 executions. For subject Calc, the technique that exposes the highest number of real faults is RND. This result can be explained by considering that maximum coverage is achieved quite easily by all techniques for this subject (see Table 2). This means that the coverage oriented fitness function used by StGP is not particularly useful in the test data generation process, while the stochastic traversal of the grammar productions produces input data with higher fault exposing capability. Learning is also not particularly beneficial with Calc, the simplest among the experimental subjects. For MDSL, StGP with learning (StGP-LRN) exposes the highest number of faults. The difference with the baseline (RND-LRN) is statistically significant (at level 0.05). For Rhino, both RND-LRN and StGP-LRN expose around 1 fault on average (1 and 0.7, respectively), with no statistically significant difference between them. In the case of Rhino, the most complex among the considered subjects, it is interesting to notice that, without learning, no fault is exposed by RND, and a small number (0.3 on average) by StGP. This is consistent with the results on coverage (see Table 2), where the best performance is reached by techniques that include learning. It seems that with complex subjects, *grammar learning is a strong prerequisite to achieve high coverage and high exposure of real faults.*

Since mutation analysis is resource intensive, we carried out the analysis on a selected subset of classes from each SUT. In particular, we selected classes that are involved in deep computations inside the SUT. This means that to reach these classes the input must be well formed and meaningful. For instance, in Rhino the input JavaScript program needs to pass lexical and syntax checking before reaching the Interpreter or CodeGenerator. Table 4 reports the mutation scores. Similarly to the real faults discussed above, the reported values are averages over 10 executions.

Table 4. Mutation scores achieved on average by each technique

Subject	Class	RND	StGP	p-val	RND-LRN	StGP-LRN	p-val
Calc	CalcLexer	**84.88**	**84.50**	0.11	83.18	**83.49**	0.56
	CalcParser	**56.59**	49.28	0.07	**65.65**	60.14	0.08
MDSL	Dispatcher	**48.69**	48.57	0.94	**62.18**	58.88	0.04
	MiniLexer	**34.20**	32.31	0.14	**37.09**	**37.09**	1.00
	MiniParser	35.34	**35.49**	0.97	48.86	**52.00**	0.10
Rhino	CodeGenerator	45.94	**55.24**	1.77E-04	60.62	**63.40**	1.72E-04
	Interpreter	20.24	**30.94**	1.82E-04	34.91	**36.35**	7.41E-04

Results on mutation analysis, reported in Table 4, are consistent with the results obtained with real faults (see Table 3). With Calc, the role of the coverage oriented fitness function is marginal and actually there is no statistically significant difference between StGP and RND (with or without learning). It seems that on a subject as simple as Calc, fitness guided genetic programming and grammar learning are not useful to increase the mutation score.

On MDSL, a medium complexity subject, the situation is quite different. Learning makes a substantial difference and the highest mutation scores are achieved always when learning is carried out (columns RND-LRN and StGP-LRN in Table 4). On the other hand, the adoption of GP has various consequences on the classes of this subject. In one case, it is beneficial (class MiniParser), in another case it is irrelevant (class MiniLexer) and in another one RND has higher mutation score (class Dispatcher).

On Rhino, the most complex among the analysed subjects, StGP with learning achieves the highest mutation scores in all considered cases (see Table 4). The difference with the baseline is statistically significant.

> We can answer **RQ3** positively for medium-high complexity subjects. Real faults are exposed equally well or better than RND by StGP with learning, on medium-high complexity subjects; the mutation score achieved by StGP is higher than RND on the most complex subject. With medium-high complexity subjects learning plays a fundamental role in the generation of test cases with high fault exposing capability.

From a qualitative viewpoint, the real faults exposed in the subject programs are of type: `NullPointerException`, `ArithmeticException`, `ClassCastException`, `ArrayIndexOutOfBoundsException` and `StackOverflowError`. Furthermore, certain types of faults are exposed only by StGP (`StackOverflowError` in MDSL and Rhino; `ClassCastException` in Rhino).

4.5 Threats to Validity

The main threats to validity for our results are internal and external. *Internal validity* threats concern factors that may affect a dependent variable and were not considered in the study. In our case, different grammar based test data generation techniques could be used, with potentially varying effectiveness. We chose stochastic random generation as a baseline as it is representative of state-of-the-art techniques for random grammar based test generation. Further comparisons with other generators are necessary to increase our confidence in the results.

External validity threats are related to the generalizability of results. We have chosen three subjects representative of small, medium and large grammar based systems (both in terms of size and grammar complexity). Even though these subjects are quite diverse, generalization to other subjects should be done with care. We plan to replicate our experiment on more subjects to increase our confidence in the generalizability of the results.

5   Related Works

The idea of exploiting formal specifications, such as grammars, for test data generation has been the subject of research for several decades now. In the 70s Purdom proposed an algorithm for the generation of short programs from a CFG making sure that each grammar rule is used at least once [13]. The algorithm ensures a high level of coverage of the grammar rules. However, rule coverage does not necessarily imply code coverage nor fault exposure [14].

In a recent work by Poulding et al. [5], the authors propose to automatically optimize the distribution of weights for production rules in stochastic CFGs using a metaheuristic technique. Weights and dependencies are optimized by a local search algorithm with the objective of finding a weight distribution that ensures a certain level of branch coverage.

Symbolic Execution (SE) has been applied to the generation of grammar based data by Godefroid et al. [15] and Majumdar et al. [6]. Both approaches reason on symbolic tokens and manipulate them via SE. The work of Godefroid et al.

focuses on grammar based fuzzing to find well formed, but erroneous, inputs that exercise the system under test with the intention of exposing security bugs. The work of Majumdar et al. focuses on string generation via concolic execution with the intention of maximizing path exploration. As both works employ SE, they are affected by its inherent limitations, for instance scalability. Furthermore, the success of these approaches depends on the accuracy of symbolic tokens that summarize several input sequences into one.

In the context of generating test data from grammars for code coverage, a recent work closely related to ours is that of Beyene and Andrews [4]. Their approach involves generating Java classes from the symbols (terminals and non terminals) in the grammar. The invocation of a sequence of methods on instances of these classes results in the generation of strings compliant with the grammar. In their work, they apply various strategies for generating method sequences, including metaheuristic algorithms and deterministic approaches, such as depth-first search, with the ultimate objective of finding a test suite that maximizes statement coverage of the system under test.

Our approach differs from the aforementioned works in that our approach uses a more guiding fitness function, directed towards high SUT coverage, combined with well established GP operators that evolve the desired input structures. Our fitness function is measured directly on the SUT and is based on the branch coverage achieved with the input data, while existing works use indirect guidance from the execution of the SUT. Furthermore our approach is able to scale easily to large and complex systems with complex grammars.

6 Conclusions and Future Work

In this paper we have presented an approach that combines the power of stochastic grammars with a coverage oriented fitness function for the generation of branch adequate, system-level test data for grammar based systems. Experimental results obtained on three grammar based systems with varying grammar complexities show that the proposed approach is effective, particularly on the most complex subjects. On such subjects, when grammar learning is activated, our approach reaches the highest coverage and fault exposure capability.

To address the main threats to the validity of our results, in our future work we will apply the proposed approach to additional subjects and we will compare it with further grammar based testing techniques available from the literature.

References

1. McMinn, P.: Search-based software test data generation: A survey. Journal of Software Testing, Verification and Reliability (STVR) 14, 105–156 (2004)
2. Pargas, R., Harrold, M.J., Peck, R.: Test-data generation using genetic algorithms. Journal of Software Testing, Verification and Reliability (STVR) 9, 263–282 (1999)
3. Fraser, G., Arcuri, A.: Whole test suite generation. IEEE Transactions on Software Engineering 39(2), 276–291 (2013)

4. Beyene, M., Andrews, J.H.: Generating string test data for code coverage. In: Proceedings of the International Conference on Software Testing, Verification, and Validation (ICST), pp. 270–279 (2012)
5. Poulding, S., Alexander, R., Clark, J.A., Hadley, M.J.: The optimisation of stochastic grammars to enable cost-effective probabilistic structural testing. In: Proceedings of the 15th Annual Conference on Genetic and Evolutionary Computation, GECCO 2013, pp. 1477–1484. ACM, New York (2013)
6. Majumdar, R., Xu, R.G.: Directed test generation using symbolic grammars. In: Proceedings of the 22nd IEEE/ACM International Conference on Automated Software Engineering (ASE), pp. 134–143 (2007)
7. McKay, R.I., Hoai, N.X., Whigham, P.A., Shan, Y., O'Neill, M.: Grammar-based genetic programming: A survey. Genetic Programming and Evolvable Machines 11(3-4), 365–396 (2010)
8. Kifetew, F.M., Jin, W., Tiella, R., Orso, A., Tonella, P.: Reproducing field failures for programs with complex grammar based input. In: Proceedings of the International Conference on Software Testing, Verification, and Validation, ICST (2014)
9. Booth, T.L., Thompson, R.A.: Applying probability measures to abstract languages. IEEE Transactions on Computers 100(5), 442–450 (1973)
10. Lari, K., Young, S.J.: The estimation of stochastic context-free grammars using the inside-outside algorithm. Computer Speech & Language 4(1), 35–56 (1990)
11. Fraser, G., Arcuri, A.: Evosuite: Automatic test suite generation for object-oriented software. In: Proceedings of the 19th ACM SIGSOFT Symposium and the 13th European Conference on Foundations of Software Engineering, ESEC/FSE 2011, Szeged, Hungary, pp. 416–419 (2011)
12. Arcuri, A., Iqbal, M.Z., Briand, L.: Formal analysis of the effectiveness and predictability of random testing. In: Proceedings of the 19th International Symposium on Software Testing and Analysis, ISSTA 2010, pp. 219–230. ACM, New York (2010)
13. Purdom, P.: A sentence generator for testing parsers. BIT Numerical Mathematics 12, 366–375 (1972), doi:10.1007/BF01932308
14. Hennessy, M., Power, J.F.: An analysis of rule coverage as a criterion in generating minimal test suites for grammar-based software. In: Proceedings of the 20th IEEE/ACM International Conference on Automated Software Engineering, ASE 2005, pp. 104–113. ACM, New York (2005)
15. Godefroid, P., Kiezun, A., Levin, M.Y.: Grammar-based whitebox fuzzing. In: Proceedings of the ACM SIGPLAN Conference on Programming Language Design and Implementation (PLDI), pp. 206–215 (2008)

Feature Model Synthesis
with Genetic Programming

Lukas Linsbauer, Roberto Erick Lopez-Herrejon, and Alexander Egyed

Software Systems Engineering
Johannes Kepler University
Linz, Austria
lukas.linsbauer@jku.at, roberto.lopez@jku.at, alexander.egyed@jku.at
http://www.jku.at/isse

Abstract. Search-Based Software Engineering (SBSE) has proven successful on several stages of the software development life cycle. It has also been applied to different challenges in the context of Software Product Lines (SPLs) like generating minimal test suites. When reverse engineering SPLs from legacy software an important challenge is the reverse engineering of variability, often expressed in the form of Feature Models (FMs). The synthesis of FMs has been studied with techniques such as Genetic Algorithms. In this paper we explore the use of Genetic Programming for this task. We sketch our general workflow, the GP pipeline employed, and its evolutionary operators. We report our experience in synthesizing feature models from sets of feature combinations for 17 representative feature models, and analyze the results using standard information retrieval metrics.

Keywords: Feature, Feature Models, Feature Set, Reverse Engineering, Software Product Lines, Variability Modeling.

1 Introduction

Search-Based Software Engineering (SBSE) is an emerging research area that focuses on the application of search-based optimization techniques to problems in software engineering [1]. Examples of these techniques are hill-climbing, simulated annealing, genetic algorithms, or swarm optimization [2]. SBSE has been applied at several stages of the software development life cycle, but most prominently for software testing [3].

Genetic Programming (GP) is a form of evolutionary computation that employs a tree-based representation of computer programs whose fitness is determined on how well the encoded programs solve a computational problem [4]. However, it is also used to solve mathematical problems like symbolic regression where the goal is to find a formula that best explains a set of sample points.

Software Product Lines (SPLs) are families of related software systems where each product has a different combination of features [5]. Most of the industrial applications of SPLs start from a set of system variants, each providing a different

C. Le Goues and S. Yoo (Eds.): SSBSE 2014, LNCS 8636, pp. 153–167, 2014.
© Springer International Publishing Switzerland 2014

set of feature combinations, that must be reverse engineered into a SPL [6]. A crucial step in this reverse engineering effort is obtaining a *feature model* [7] – the de facto standard to represent the valid feature combinations – that denotes all the desired feature combinations. Similarly to the use of GP for symbolic regression, we use GP to find a feature model that best explains a set of product variants.

Feature models are important to model the variability of software systems. They describe which features can be combined and which ones cannot in order to form products. However, often such information is not available, for example when companies maintain portfolios of legacy software product variants that are the result of ad hoc methods like clone and own, where a new product variant is created by copying an existing variant and adapting it to fit another customer's requirements, or by making existing variants highly configurable [8]. Only once the number of variants or possible configurations has become unmanagable companies decide to reverse engineer an SPL from their existing product variants [9]. The first step to this is often the reverse engineering of a feature model. She et al. provide two algorithms to solve this problem, a task that has been shown to be NP-hard [10].

A recent publication by Harman et al. summarizes the developments in the application of genetic programming and genetic improvement for reverse engineering tasks and proposes new research directions where both SBSE techniques could be employed [11]. Among these directions is SPLs for which the authors sketch some potential research venues. In this paper we make, to the best of our knowledge, the first application of genetic programming in the realm of SPLs. We extend our previous work [12] where we employed a genetic algorithm for reverse engineering feature models. We show that genetic programming provides a more accurate representation of the feature models which, provided with more specialized operators, can produce better reverse engineering results.

2   Feature Models and Running Example

Feature models have become the *de facto* standard for modelling the feature combinations for SPLs [7]. They depict features and their relationships collectively forming a tree-like structure. The nodes of the tree are the features denoted as labelled boxes, and the edges represent the relationships among them. Figure 1 shows the feature model of our running example, the *Graph Product Line (GPL)* [13], a standard SPL that has been extensively used as a case study. In GPL, a product is a collection of algorithms applied to directed or undirected graphs.

In a feature model, each feature (except the root) has one parent feature and can have a set of child features. A child feature can only be included in a feature combination of a valid product if its parent is included as well. The root feature is always included. There are four kinds of feature relationships: i) *Mandatory features* are selected whenever their respective parent feature is selected. They are depicted with a filled circle. For example, features GraphType and Algorithms,

Feature	P0	P1	P2	P3	P4
GPL	✓	✓	✓	✓	✓
Driver	✓	✓	✓	✓	✓
Benchmark	✓	✓	✓	✓	✓
GraphType	✓	✓	✓	✓	✓
Directed	✓		✓		
Undirected		✓		✓	✓
Weight		✓	✓	✓	✓
Search	✓	✓	✓	✓	
DFS	✓		✓		✓
BFS		✓		✓	
Algorithms	✓	✓	✓	✓	✓
Num	✓	✓	✓		
CC		✓		✓	✓
SCC			✓		
Kruskal	✓				
Prim				✓	✓
Cycle			✓		✓
Shortest			✓		

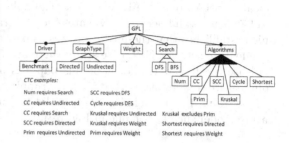

CTC examples:

Num requires Search   SCC requires DFS

CC requires Undirected   Cycle requires DFS

CC requires Search   Kruskal requires Undirected   Kruskal excludes Prim

SCC requires Directed   Kruskal requires Weight   Shortest requires Directed

Prim requires Undirected   Prim requires Weight   Shortest requires Weight

Table 1. Sample Feature Sets of GPL   **Fig. 1.** GPL Feature Model

ii) *Optional features* may or may not be selected if their respective parent feature is selected. An example is feature `Weight`, iii) *Exclusive-or relations* indicate that exactly one of the features in the exclusive-or group must be selected whenever the parent feature is selected. They are depicted as empty arcs crossing over a set of lines connecting a parent feature with its child features. For instance, a graph can be either directed or undirected by selecting either feature `Directed` or `Undirected` respectively, iv) *Inclusive-or relations* indicate that at least one of the features in the inclusive-or group must be selected if the parent is selected. They are depicted as filled arcs crossing over a set of lines connecting a parent feature with its child features. As an example, when feature `Algorithms` is selected then at least one of the features `Num`, `CC`, `SCC`, `Cycle`, `Shortest`, `Prim`, and `Kruskal` must be selected.

Besides the parent-child relations, features can also relate across different branches of the feature model with the so called *Cross-Tree Constraints (CTCs)*. Figure 1 shows the CTCs of our feature model in textual form. These constraints as well as those implied by the hierarchical relations between features are usually expressed and checked using propositional logic in Conjunctive Normal Form (CNF) [14]. For instance, the CTC `Num requires Search` means that whenever feature `Num` is selected, feature `Search` must also be selected. In CNF this CTC is written as $\neg Num \lor Search$.

The following definitions are based on our previous work [12]:

Definition 1. *A feature set is a 2-tuple [sel, $\overline{sel}$] where sel and $\overline{sel}$ are respectively the set of selected and not-selected features of a system variant. Let FL be the list of features of a feature model, such that sel, $\overline{sel} \subseteq FL$, sel $\cap$ $\overline{sel}$ = $\emptyset$, and sel $\cup$ $\overline{sel}$ = FL.*

Definition 2. *A feature set is valid if the selected and not-selected features adhere to all the constraints imposed by the feature model.*

For example, the feature set `fs=[{GPL, Driver, Benchmark, GraphType, Directed, Search, DFS, Algorithms, Num}, {Undirected, Weight, BFS, CC, SCC, Kruskal, Prim, Cycle, Shortest}]` is valid. In fact, it corresponds to feature set P0 in Table 1. As another example, a feature set with features `DFS` and `BFS` is not valid because it violates the constraint of the exclusive-or relation which establishes that these two features cannot appear selected together in the same feature set. For GPL case study there are 73 different valid feature sets.

Please recall that the focus of this paper is on synthesizing feature models from feature sets. In other words, for our running example, starting from a table such as Table 1 that includes all the valid feature sets, our goal is to derive a feature model such as the one in Figure 1.

3   Feature Model Synthesis

This section describes the genetic programming pipeline we followed, the feature model representation we used, and the evolutionary operators that were developed.

3.1   Genetic Programming Pipeline

The genetic programming pipeline that we employed is shown in Figure 2. It consists of a set of operators. The gray operators are problem specific while the white ones are generic. It starts with a *Builder* that produces an initial population of randomized individuals. The *Selection* selects individuals from the current population and either passes them to the *Crossover* operator or to the *Reproduction* operator (depending on the crossover probability). The crossover produces offspring individuals that ideally maintain valuable traits of their parent individuals according to a fitness criterion. The reproduction operator just clones individuals. As a next step the individuals either pass through the *Mutation* operator which performs random mutations on the individuals or again just through the reproduction (based on the mutation probability). The part of the pipeline that produces a new population (i.e. the next generation of individuals) from an old one is called *Breeding*, shown as a box in our figure. Finally the fitness of the new individuals is evaluated and they are put back into the population to constitute the next generation. In most cases the new generation completely replaces the old one possibly with the exception of a select number of elite individuals (the ones with the best fitness) which survive and live on in the next generation.

3.2   Feature Model Representation

For the feature model representation we followed a *Model Driven Engineering (MDE)* approach whereby a *metamodel* defines the structure and semantics of the models that can be derived from it [15]. We choose a simplified version of

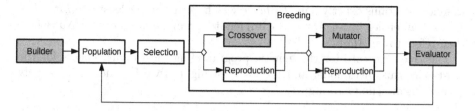

Fig. 2. Genetic Programming Pipeline Overview

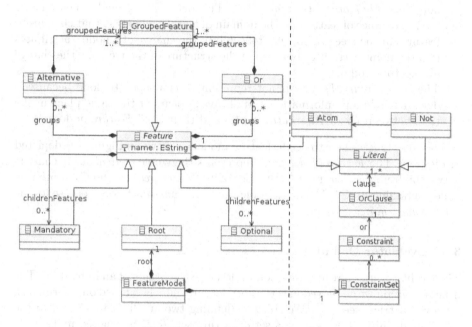

Fig. 3. Feature Model Metamodel

the SPLX metamodel[1], a common standard representation for feature models, which is shown in Figure 3.

This metamodel describes the structure of a feature model individual, represented by the *FeatureModel* meta class. The left part describes the *feature tree*. It has exactly one *Root* feature that, just like any other feature node (i.e. any node that inherits from *Feature*), can have an arbitrary number of *Mandatory* and *Optional* child features as well as an arbitrary number of *Alternative* (i.e. exclusive-or) and *Or* (i.e. inclusive-or) group relations which must have at least one *GroupedFeature* as a child. The right part of the metamodel describes the CTCs of a feature model individual. It has exactly one *ConstraintSet* which describes a propositional formula in CNF. It contains an arbitrary number of *Constraints* which correspond to clauses in a CNF expression. A *Constraint*

---

[1] http://www.splot-research.org/

therefore contains exactly one *OrClause* which must have at least one *Literal*. A *Literal* can either be an *Atom* which refers to a feature directly or a *Not* which then refers to an *Atom*.

The tree structure for the genetic programming individuals reflects for the most part this metamodel and is mostly straightforward to derive. The only exceptions are the following:

- The abstract class *Feature* is represented by its own type of node even though it is an abstract class. This *Feature* node is placed as a child of the inheriting node (e.g. *Mandatory*, *Optional*, etc.). This decision was made to emphasize the importance of features in the domain of feature models so that changes to features in the tree are not just reflected in the change of a node's attributes (i.e. the name attribute) but also in the structure of the tree (i.e. the change of a feature node).
- The class *GroupedFeature* is not represented as a separate node because it does not hold any information and always appears at the same place in the tree: between *Or* or *Alternative* nodes and their child *Feature* nodes.

The tree structure for the GPL feature model as shown in Figure 1 is depicted in Figure 4. The *FeatureModel* node represents the whole *Individual*. It consists of two children: the *Root* node as the root of its *feature tree* and the *ConstraintSet* node containing its CTCs. For example the first *Constraint* node represents the CTC *Num requires Search*.

3.3   Evaluator Definition

The Evaluator uses a fitness function to describe the fitness of an individual. The fitness function we employed in the case of feature models is based on information retrieval metrics (see [16]). We start by defining two auxiliary functions. In the following definitions, let sfs be a set of feature sets (e.g. as denoted in Table 1) which represents our input, and let fm be a candidate feature model individual to be evaluated:

- $\#containedFeatureSets : \mathcal{SFS} \times \mathcal{FM} \rightarrow \mathbb{N}$, returns the number of feature sets received as first argument sfs that are valid according to a feature model fm.
- $\#featureSets : \mathcal{FM} \rightarrow \mathbb{N}$, returns the number of feature sets denoted by a feature model fm.

An ideal candidate feature model describes exactly the feature sets contained in sfs and no more. To express that we use the *precision* and *recall* metrics.

Definition 3. Precision. *The fraction of the retrieved feature sets that are relevant to the search.*

$$precision(sfs, fm) = \frac{\#containedFeatureSets(sfs, fm)}{\#featureSets(fm)}$$

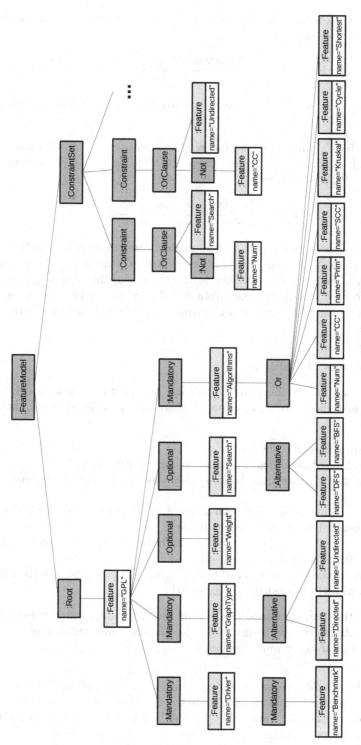

Fig. 4. GPL Feature Model Tree Structure

Definition 4. *Recall*. *The fraction of the feature sets that are relevant to the search that are successfully retrieved.*

$$recall(sfs, fm) = \frac{\#containedFeatureSets(sfs, fm)}{|sfs|}$$

Our Evaluator uses the F_β measure as fitness function which is defined as follows [16]:

Definition 5. *F_β measure*. *It is a weighted measure of precision and recall. The value of β indicates how many times the recall values weigh more in comparison with the precision values.*

$$F_\beta = \frac{(1 + \beta^2) \times precision \times recall}{\beta^2 \times precision + recall}$$

To compute these metrics the feature model representation is executed in the sense that every node is implemented as a function that manipulates a set of feature sets in order to compute the final feature sets that are represented by the whole feature model. For example a *Mandatory* node adds to every feature set in the set its child feature, or a *Constraint* node removes certain feature sets from the set.

3.4   Operators Definitions

Not all semantic constraints can be implicitly conveyed by a metamodel. In the case of our metamodel for feature models there were additional constraints that also apply:

- A feature is identified by its name.
- There is a fixed set of feature names in each feature model.
- Every feature appears exactly once in the feature tree part of a feature model individual.
- CTCs must not contradict each other, i.e. the corresponding CNF of the entire constraint set must be satisfiable.
- CTCs can only be either *requires* or *excludes*, i.e. exactly two literals per clause with at least one being negated.
- There is a maximum number of CTCs (given as a percentage of the number of features) which must not be exceeded.

Based on the tree structures derived from the metamodel and on these domain constraints the necessary operators for genetic programming, namely *Builder*, *Crossover*, and *Mutator* were developed.

Builder. The *Builder* creates random feature trees and random CTCs that conform to the metamodel and also adhere to the additional domain constraints. We implemented it using the tools FaMa [17] and BeTTy [18], which are frameworks written in Java for managing and reasoning about feature models.

Mutator. The *Mutator* makes small random changes to a feature model individual. One of the following mutations is performed randomly on the feature tree with equal probability:

- Randomly swaps two features in the feature tree.
- Randomly changes an *Alternative* relation to an *Or* relation or vice-versa.
- Randomly changes an *Optional* or *Mandatory* relation to any other kind of relation (*Mandatory, Optional, Alternative, Or*).
- Randomly selects a subtree in the feature tree and puts it somewhere else in the tree without violating the metamodel or any of the domain constraints.

The mutations performed on the CTCs, applied with equal probability, are:

- Adds a new, randomly created CTC (i.e. clause) that does not contradict the other CTCs and does not already exist.
- Randomly removes a CTC (i.e. a clause).

Crossover. The *Crossover* takes two individuals from the current population, the parents, and creates two new individuals from them, the offspring. The offspring should maintain desirable traits from both their parents. Just like the other operators the crossover also has to make sure that every offspring still conforms to the metamodel and does not violate any of the additional domain constraints. The following describes how our crossover for feature model individuals works.

1. The offspring is initialized with the root feature of $Parent_1$. If the root feature of $Parent_2$ is a different one then it is added to the offspring as a mandatory child feature of its root feature.
2. Traverse the first parent depth first starting at the *root* node and add to the offspring a random number r of features that are not already contained by appending them to their respective parent feature already contained in the offspring using the same relation type between them (the parent feature of every visited feature during the traversal is guaranteed to be contained in the offspring due to the depth first traversal order).
3. Traverse the second parent exactly the same way as the first one.
4. Go to step 2 until every feature is contained in the offspring.

The second offspring is obtained the exact same way only that the parents are reversed (i.e. the process starts with the second parent $Parent_2$) and the same sequence of random numbers is used.

The crossover for CTCs is performed by building the union of CTCs of both parents and then assigning a random subset to the first offspring and the remaining to the second offspring.

4   Evaluation

This section first presents the process followed for our evaluation and then analyzes its results.

4.1   Process

We implemented the presented approach using ECJ[2], a generic framework for evolutionary computation written in Java. For the evaluation of the approach we used 17 feature models of actual SPLs that are publicly available[3]. They are shown in Table 2.

Table 2. Feature Models Summary

Feature Model Name	NF	NP	Domain
Apache	10	256	web server
argo-uml-spl	11	192	UML tool
BDBFootprint	9	256	database
BDBMemory	19	3,840	database
BDBPerformance	27	1,440	database
Curl	14	1024	data trasfer
DesktopSearcher	22	462	file search
fame_dbms_fm	20	320	database
gpl	18	73	graph algorithms
LinkedList	27	1,344	data structures
LLVM	12	1,024	compiler library
PKJab	12	72	messenger
Prevayler	6	32	object persistence
SensorNetwork	27	16,704	networking
Wget	17	8,192	file retrieval
x264	17	2,048	video encoding
ZipMe	8	64	data compression

NF: Number of Features, **NP**: Number of Products,
***BDB**: prefix stands for Berkeley DataBase.

We computed for each of these feature models the respective sets of valid feature sets which we used as input to our GP pipeline. The parameter values we employed are shown in Table 3. Note that as a fitness function in our Evaluator we use the F_1 measure, putting equal weight on recall and precision. As a base line to compare our results to we used a *Random Search* (RS) that just randomly creates feature models in hopes of finding a good solution. Details can be found in [19]. The number of random tries is set to the product of the maximum number of generations and the population size of our genetic programming problem so that the number of evaluated candidate feature model individuals is the same for both: $maxGenerations \times populationSize = 100 \times 100 = 10000$ performed evaluations. For the generation of random feature models again the tools FaMa [17] and BeTTy [18] were used. Additionally we used the *Genetic Algorithm* (GA)

---

[2] http://cs.gmu.edu/~eclab/projects/ecj/
[3] http://www.fosd.de/fh,http://spl2go.cs.ovgu.de/,http://fosd.de/
SPLConqueror

Table 3. Genetic Programming Parameters

Parameter	Value
Fitness Function	F_1 measure
Crossover Probability	0.7
Feature Tree Mutation Probability	0.5
CTCs Mutation Probability	0.5
Population Size	100
Maximum Number of Generations	100
Number of Elites	1
Selection Method	Tournament Selection
Tournament Size	6
Maximum CTC Percentage* ...	
... for Builder	0.1
... for Mutator	0.5

*(relative to number of features)

approach to feature model reverse engineering from our previous work [12] and extended it to use F_1 as its fitness function to allow for a comparison of the results. Other than the fitness function nothing was changed on that approach.

For every feature model we did 30 independent runs. Table 4 shows for every feature model the average and the best F_1 value as well as the variance for each our Genetic Programming (GP) approach, the Random Search (RS) and our previous Genetic Algorithm (GA) approach. All the runs were performed on a machine with an Intel® Core™ i5 processor with 3.1 GHz and 8 GB of main memory. The total execution time of our genetic programming approach for all the runs (17 feature models times 30 runs = 510 runs) was at around 13 hours with an average time per run of around 1.5 minutes. For our GPL running example a run took on average only roughly 6 seconds.

4.2 Statistical Analysis

We performed the statistical analysis using R[4], an environment for statistical computing.

The *Wilcoxon Signed-Rank Test* [20] determines whether the difference of two data samples is statistically significant (alternative hypothesis) or due to chance (null hypothesis). We performed the test on the average F_1 values to compare our genetic programming approach against the random search baseline which yielded a p-value of 0.00001526 which leads to rejecting the null hypothesis and accepting the alternative hypothesis that there is a significant difference between our genetic programming approach and the random search. Applying this same test to compare our genetic programming approach against the genetic algorithm

---

[4] http://www.r-project.org/

Table 4. F_1 Values per Feature Model over 30 runs for Genetic Programming (GP), Random Search (RS) and Genetic Algorithm (GA)

FM Name	F_1 for GP			F_1 for RS			F_1 for GA		
	Mean	Best	Variance	Mean	Best	Variance	Mean	Best	Variance
Apache	1.00	1.00	0.0000	0.73	0.95	0.0112	0.72	1.00	0.0160
argo-uml-spl	1.00	1.00	0.0000	0.62	0.98	0.0096	0.67	1.00	0.0188
BDBFootprint	1.00	1.00	0.0000	0.78	0.98	0.0103	0.70	1.00	0.0103
BDBMemory	0.29	0.40	0.0048	0.05	0.13	0.0004	0.16	0.32	0.0051
BDBPerformance	0.22	0.33	0.0029	0.02	0.04	0.0000	0.16	0.23	0.0020
Curl	0.77	0.89	0.0148	0.25	0.35	0.0015	0.46	0.87	0.0170
DesktopSearcher	0.29	0.34	0.0010	0.05	0.08	0.0002	0.21	0.42	0.0061
fame_dbms_fm	0.21	0.38	0.0078	0.04	0.08	0.0001	0.13	0.22	0.0019
gpl	0.47	0.57	0.0086	0.09	0.19	0.0009	0.22	0.41	0.0044
LinkedList	0.28	0.34	0.0028	0.02	0.04	0.0001	0.20	0.32	0.0018
LLVM	1.00	1.00	0.0000	0.53	0.70	0.0081	0.70	1.00	0.0080
PKJab	0.97	1.00	0.0048	0.50	0.66	0.0033	0.66	0.80	0.0115
Prevayler	1.00	1.00	0.0000	0.96	1.00	0.0011	0.69	1.00	0.0072
SensorNetwork	0.26	0.33	0.0016	0.02	0.05	0.0001	0.14	0.21	0.0009
Wget	0.72	0.89	0.0164	0.16	0.23	0.0008	0.40	0.61	0.0041
x264	0.47	0.68	0.0093	0.11	0.20	0.0008	0.23	0.45	0.0054
ZipMe	1.00	1.00	0.0000	0.88	1.00	0.0057	0.72	1.00	0.0160

approach resulted in a p-value of 0.0003204 also indicating a significant difference between the two approaches.

The $\hat{A}_{12}$ *Effect Size Measure* [20, 21] represents the probability that using one algorithm (our genetic programming approach) yields better results than using another algorithm (random search and genetic algorithm approach). An $\hat{A}_{12}$ measure of 0.5 would mean both algorithms perform equally well. The value we obtained based on the average F_1 values of our genetic programming approach and the random search is $\hat{A}_{12} = 0.7750865$ which means that the genetic programming approach clearly outperforms the random search, as the probability of achieving better results with it is at 77.5%. Computing this measure for our genetic programming approach and the genetic algorithm approach yielded $\hat{A}_{12} = 0.7474048$ which again means that our genetic programming approach outperforms the genetic algorithm approach.

4.3   Threats to Validity

Following the guidelines in [22] we identified three threats to validity that are relevant to our work. The first is the parameter settings that were used during the evaluation, all of which are given in Table 3. Mostly standard values for genetic programming were used except for the mutation probability where we followed the example of [23] and used an above standard value. The second threat is the correctness of the implementation. To address this threat we provide an overview of our genetic programming pipeline (Figure 2), we used ECJ as a proven framework for evolutionary computation to implement our approach with, and we make the full implementation and data available for replication[5]. The third threat is the selection of the corpus of feature models on which the evaluation was performed. These feature models stem from actual SPLs and we thus believe that they are good representatives of the feature models domain.

5   Related Work

In this section, we briefly summarize the pieces of work that are closest to ours.

Our previous work studied reverse engineering feature models using a genetic algorithm [12]. We encoded feature models based on a depth-first traversal order. The key limitations of that approach were the relative ordering that features should have between them and the heavy performance penalty of detecting and fixing incorrect individuals after mutation and crossover.

The work by Haslinger et al. presents an ad hoc algorithm also to reverse engineer feature models [24]. The main distinction with our work is that it only reverse engineers one feature model, as opposed to potentially many equivalent feature models in our work. The work by She et al. also provides ad hoc algorithms for reverse engineering feature models, however, in contrast with our work, they start from a set of constraints expressed either in CNF or DNF. Work by Acher et al. relies on user-defined domain knowledge to help structure the hierarchy between features [25]. This knowledge helps to eliminate semantically correct (i.e. correct feature combinations) feature models that are hierarchically incorrect (i.e. parent-child relation swapped). These two pieces of work could be respectively leveraged to seed the initial population and guide the search in our approach. These are two issues we plan to explore as part of our future work.

Recent work by Acher et al. presents several feature model composition operators [26]. They provide their semantics and analyze their properties. We believe their work could help our approach to both define other crossover operators as well as put them in a more formal footing. Doing this is part of our future work.

6   Conclusions and Future Work

In this paper we applied genetic programming to the problem of reverse engineering feature models in the context of SPLs. We showed the workflow that we followed along with the resulting representation of feature models and the evolutionary operators used in our genetic programming pipeline. We reported our encouraging experience synthesizing 17 feature models and compared our results to a random search baseline as well as to previous work in the area of feature model reverse engineering and showed that our approach outperforms both.

As future work we plan to investigate the impact of seeding knowledge derived from ad-hoc reverse engineering algorithms into our GP pipeline, as well as other operators for crossover based on feature model composition. Currently the fitness

---

[5] http://www.sea.uni-linz.ac.at/sbse4vm/data/ssbse.zip

of individuals is based on whether feature sets are contained or not. This is rather coarse grain. We want to employ a more fine-grain fitness metric that works on the level of single features instead of complete feature sets. Also we plan to evaluate our approach using more feature models.

Acknowledgments. This research is partially funded by the Austrian Science Fund (FWF) project P25289-N15 and Lise Meitner Fellowship M1421-N15.

References

1. Harman, M., Mansouri, S.A., Zhang, Y.: Search-based software engineering: Trends, techniques and applications. ACM Comput. Surv. 45(1), 11 (2012)
2. Harman, M., McMinn, P., de Souza, J.T., Yoo, S.: Search based software engineering: Techniques, taxonomy, tutorial. In: Meyer, B., Nordio, M. (eds.) Empirical Software Engineering and Verification. LNCS, vol. 7007, pp. 1–59. Springer, Heidelberg (2012)
3. de Freitas, F.G., de Souza, J.T.: Ten years of search based software engineering: A bibliometric analysis. In: Cohen, M.B., Ó Cinnéide, M. (eds.) SSBSE 2011. LNCS, vol. 6956, pp. 18–32. Springer, Heidelberg (2011)
4. Poli, R., Langdon, W.B., McPhee, N.F.: A Field Guide to Genetic Programming. Lulu (2008)
5. Batory, D.S., Sarvela, J.N., Rauschmayer, A.: Scaling step-wise refinement. IEEE Trans. Software Eng. 30(6), 355–371 (2004)
6. Lopez-Herrejon, R.E., Egyed, A.: Sbse4vm: Search based software engineering for variability management. In: Cleve, A., Ricca, F., Cerioli, M. (eds.) CSMR, pp. 441–444. IEEE Computer Society (2013)
7. Kang, K., Cohen, S., Hess, J., Novak, W., Peterson, A.: Feature-Oriented Domain Analysis (FODA) Feasibility Study. Technical Report CMU/SEI-90-TR-21, Software Engineering Institute, Carnegie Mellon University (1990)
8. Laguna, M.A., Crespo, Y.: A systematic mapping study on software product line evolution: From legacy system reengineering to product line refactoring. Sci. Comput. Program. 78(8), 1010–1034 (2013)
9. Krueger, C.W.: Easing the transition to software mass customization. In: van der Linden, F.J. (ed.) PFE 2002. LNCS, vol. 2290, pp. 282–293. Springer, Heidelberg (2002)
10. She, S., Ryssel, U., Andersen, N., Wsowski, A., Czarnecki, K.: Efficient synthesis of feature models. Information and Software Technology (in press, 2014)
11. Harman, M., Langdon, W.B., Weimer, W.: Genetic programming for reverse engineering. In: Lämmel, R., Oliveto, R., Robbes, R. (eds.) WCRE, pp. 1–10. IEEE (2013)
12. Lopez-Herrejon, R.E., Galindo, J.A., Benavides, D., Segura, S., Egyed, A.: Reverse engineering feature models with evolutionary algorithms: An exploratory study. In: Fraser, G., Teixeira de Souza, J. (eds.) SSBSE 2012. LNCS, vol. 7515, pp. 168–182. Springer, Heidelberg (2012)
13. Lopez-Herrejon, R.E., Batory, D.: A standard problem for evaluating product-line methodologies. In: Bosch, J. (ed.) GCSE 2001. LNCS, vol. 2186, pp. 10–24. Springer, Heidelberg (2001)

14. Benavides, D., Segura, S., Cortés, A.R.: Automated analysis of feature models 20 years later: A literature review. Inf. Syst. 35(6), 615–636 (2010)
15. Stahl, T., Völter, M., Bettin, J., Haase, A., Helsen, S.: Model-driven software development - technology, engineering, management. Pitman (2006)
16. Manning, C.D., Raghavan, P., Schütze, H.: Introduction to information retrieval. Cambridge University Press (2008)
17. Benavides, D., Segura, S., Trinidad, P., Cortés, A.R.: Fama: Tooling a framework for the automated analysis of feature models. In: Pohl, K., Heymans, P., Kang, K.C., Metzger, A., eds.: VaMoS. Volume 2007-01 of Lero Technical Report, 129–134 (2007)
18. Segura, S., Galindo, J., Benavides, D., Parejo, J.A., Cortés, A.R.: BeTTy: Benchmarking and testing on the automated analysis of feature models. In: Eisenecker, U.W., Apel, S., Gnesi, S. (eds.) VaMoS, pp. 63–71. ACM (2012)
19. Luke, S.: Essentials of Metaheuristics. Lulu (2009) Available for free at http://cs.gmu.edu/~sean/book/metaheuristics/
20. Arcuri, A., Briand, L.: A hitchhiker's guide to statistical tests for assessing randomized algorithms in software engineering. Software Testing, Verification & Reliability (2012)
21. Vargha, A., Delaney, H.D.: A critique and improvement of the "cl" common language effect size statistics of mcgraw and wong. Journal of Educational and Behavioral Statistics 25(2), 101–132 (2000)
22. de Oliveira Barros, M., Neto, A.C.D.: Threats to Validity in Search-based Software Engineering Empirical Studies. Technical Report 0006/2011, Universidade Federal Do Estado Do Rio de Janeiro. Departamento de Informatica Aplicada (2011)
23. Faunes, M., Cadavid, J.J., Baudry, B., Sahraoui, H.A., Combemale, B.: Automatically searching for metamodel well-formedness rules in examples and counterexamples. In: [27], pp. 187–202
24. Haslinger, E.N., Lopez-Herrejon, R.E., Egyed, A.: On extracting feature models from sets of valid feature combinations. In: Cortellessa, V., Varró, D. (eds.) FASE 2013 (ETAPS 2013). LNCS, vol. 7793, pp. 53–67. Springer, Heidelberg (2013)
25. Acher, M., Baudry, B., Heymans, P., Cleve, A., Hainaut, J.L.: Support for reverse engineering and maintaining feature models. In: Gnesi, S., Collet, P., Schmid, K. (eds.) VaMoS, pp. 20:1–20:8. ACM (2013)
26. Acher, M., Combemale, B., Collet, P., Barais, O., Lahire, P., France, R.B.: Composing your compositions of variability models. In: [27], pp. 352–369
27. Moreira, A., Schätz, B., Gray, J., Vallecillo, A., Clarke, P. (eds.): MODELS 2013. LNCS, vol. 8107. Springer, Heidelberg (2013)

A Robust Multi-objective Approach
for Software Refactoring under Uncertainty

Mohamed Wiem Mkaouer[1], Marouane Kessentini[1], Slim Bechikh[1],
and Mel Ó Cinnéide[2]

[1] University of Michigan, MI, USA
firstname@umich.edu
[2] Lero, University College Dublin, Ireland
mel.ocinneide@ucd.ie

Abstract. Refactoring large systems involves several sources of uncertainty related to the severity levels of code smells to be corrected and the importance of the classes in which the smells are located. Due to the dynamic nature of software development, these values cannot be accurately determined in practice, leading to refactoring sequences that lack robustness. To address this problem, we introduced a multi-objective robust model, based on NSGA-II, for the software refactoring problem that tries to find the best trade-off between quality and robustness. We evaluated our approach using six open source systems and demonstrated that it is significantly better than state-of-the-art refactoring approaches in terms of robustness in 100% of experiments based on a variety of real-world scenarios. Our suggested refactoring solutions were found to be comparable in terms of quality to those suggested by existing approaches and to carry an acceptable robustness price. Our results also revealed an interesting feature about the trade-off between quality and robustness that demonstrates the practical value of taking robustness into account in software refactoring.

1 Introduction

Large-scale software systems exhibit high complexity and become difficult to maintain. It has been reported that the cost of maintenance and evolution activities comprises more than 80% of total software costs. In addition, it has been shown that software maintainers spend around 60% of their time in understanding the code. To facilitate maintenance tasks, one of the widely used techniques is refactoring which improves design structure while preserving the overall functionality of the software [12].

There has been much work on different techniques and tools for refactoring [12], [23], [21], [9]. The vast majority of these techniques identify key symptoms that characterize the code to refactor using a combination of quantitative, structural, and/or lexical information and then propose different possible refactoring solutions, for each identified segment of code. In order to find out which parts of the source code need to be refactored, most of the existing work relies on the notion of design defects or code smells. Originally coined by Fowler [12], the generic term code smell refers to structures in the code that suggest the possibility of refactoring. Once code smells have been identified, refactorings need to be proposed to resolve them. Several automated

C. Le Goues and S. Yoo (Eds.): SSBSE 2014, LNCS 8636, pp. 168–183, 2014.
© Springer International Publishing Switzerland 2014

refactoring approaches are proposed in the literature and most of them are based on the use of software metrics to estimate quality improvements of the system after applying refactorings [23], [21], [9], [17], [20].

The existing literature on software refactoring invariably ignores an important consideration when suggesting refactoring solutions: the highly dynamic nature of software development. In this paper, we take into account two dynamic aspects as follows:

- *Code Smell Severity*: This is the severity level assigned to a code smell type by a developer. It usually varies from developer to developer, and indeed a developer's assessment of smell severity will change over time as well.
- *Code Smell Class Importance*: This is the importance of a class that contains a code smell, where importance refers to the number and size of the features that the class supports. A code smell with large class importance will have a greater detrimental impact on the software. Again, this property will vary over time as software requirements change [15] and classes are added/deleted/split.

We believe that the uncertainties related to class importance and code smell severity need to be taken into consideration when suggesting a refactoring solution. To this end, we introduce in this paper a novel representation of the code refactoring problem, based on *robust* optimization [3], [16] that generates robust refactoring solutions by taking into account the uncertainties related to code smell severity and the importance of the class that contains the code smell. Our robustness model is based on the well-known multi-objective evolutionary algorithm NSGA-II proposed by Deb et al. [8] and considers possible changes in class importance and code smell severity by generating different scenarios at each iteration of the algorithm. In each scenario, the detected code smell to be corrected is assigned a severity score and each class in the system is assigned an importance score. In our model, we assume that these scores change regularly due to reasons such as developers' evolving perspectives on the software or new features and requirements being implemented or any other code changes that could make some classes/code smells more or less important. Our multi-objective approach aims to find the best trade-off between maximizing the quality of the refactoring solution in terms of the number of code smells corrected and maximizing its robustness in terms of the severity of the code smells corrected and the importance of the classes that contains the code smells.

The primary contributions of this paper are as follows:

- The paper introduces a novel formulation of the refactoring problem as a multi-objective problem that takes into account the uncertainties related to code smell detection and the dynamic environment of software development. To the best of our knowledge, and based on recent search-based software engineering (SBSE) surveys [15], this is the first work to use robust optimization for software refactoring, and the first in SBSE to treat robustness as a helper objective during the search.
- The paper reports on the results of an empirical study of our robust NSGA-II technique as applied to six open source systems. We compared our approach to random search, multi-objective particle swarm optimization (MOPSO) [18], search-based refactoring [17], [20] and a refactoring tool [24] not based on heuristic search. The results provide evidence to support the claim that our proposal enables the generation of robust refactoring solutions without a high loss of quality using a variety of real-world scenarios.

2   Multi-objective Robust Software Refactoring

2.1   Robust Optimization

In dealing with optimization problems, including software engineering ones, most researchers assume that the input parameters of the problem are exactly known in advance. Unfortunately, this is an idealization often not the case in a real-world setting. Additionally, uncertainty can change the effective values of some input parameters with respect to nominal values. For instance, when handling the knapsack problem (KP), which is one of the most studied combinatorial problems [3], we can face such a problem. As stated by [3], uncertainty is unavoidable in real problem settings; therefore it should be taken into account in every optimization approach in order to obtain robust solutions. Robustness of an optimal solution can usually be discussed from the following two perspectives: (1) the optimal solution is insensitive to small perturbations in terms of the decision variables and/or (2) the optimal solution is insensitive to small variations in terms of environmental parameters. Figure 1 illustrates the robustness concept with respect to a single decision variable named x. Based on the $f(x)$ landscape, we have two optima: A and B. We remark that solution A is very sensitive to local perturbation of the variable x. A very slight perturbation of x within the interval [2, 4] can make the optimum A unacceptable since its performance $f(A)$ would dramatically degrade. On the other hand, small perturbations of the optimum B, which has a relatively lower objective function value than A, within the interval [5,7] hardly affects the performance of solution B (i.e., $f(B)$) at all. We can say that although solution A has a better quality than solution B, solution B is more *robust* than solution A. In an uncertain context, the developer would probably prefer solution B to solution A. This choice is justified by the performance of B in terms of robustness. It is clear from this discussion robustness has a price, called *robustness price or cost*, since it engenders a *loss in optimality*. This loss is due to preferring the robust solution B over the non-robust solution A. According to Figure 1, this loss is equal to $abs(f(B) - f(A))$. Several approaches have been proposed to handle robustness in the optimization field in general and more specifically in design engineering [16].

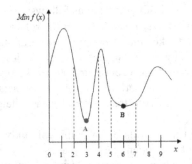

Fig. 1. Illustration of the robustness concept under uncertainty related to the decision variable x. Solution B is more robust than solution A.

2.2   Multi-objective Robust Optimization for Software Refactoring

2.2.1 Problem Formulation

The refactoring problem involves searching for the best refactoring solution among the set of candidate ones, which constitutes a huge search space. A refactoring solution is a sequence of refactoring operations where the goal of applying the sequence to a software system S is typically to minimize the number of code smells in S.

We propose a robust formulation of the refactoring problem that takes class importance and smell severity into account. Consequently, we have two objective functions to be maximized in our problem formulation: (1) the quality of the system to refactor, i.e., minimizing the number of code smells, and (2) the robustness of the refactoring solutions in relation to uncertainty in the severity level of the code smells and in the importance of the classes that contain the code smells. Analytically speaking, the formulation of the robust refactoring problem can be stated as follows:

$$
\begin{aligned}
&\textit{Maximize}\\
&\begin{cases}
f_1(x,S) = NCCS(x,S)/NDCS(S)\\
f_2(x,S) = \sum_{i=1}^{NCCS} [SmellSeverity(CCS_i, x, S) + Importance(CCS_i, x, S)]
\end{cases}\\
&\textit{subject to}\quad x = (x_1,...,x_n) \in X
\end{aligned}
$$

where X is the set of all legal refactoring sequences starting from S, x_i is the i-th refactoring in the sequence x, $NCCS(x,S)$ is the *Number of Corrected Code Smells* after applying the refactoring solution x on the system S, $NDCS$ is the *Number of Detected Code-Smells* prior to the application of solution x to the system S, CCS_i is the i-th Corrected Code Smell, *SmellSeverity*(CCS_i, x, S) is the severity level of the i-th corrected code smell related to the execution of x on S, and *Importance*(CCS_i, x, S) is the importance of the class containing the i-th code smell corrected by the execution of x on S.

The smell's severity level is a numeric quantity, varying between 0 and 1, assigned by the developer to each code smell type (e.g., blob, spaghetti code, functional decomposition, etc.). We define the class importance of a code smell as follows:

$$
Importance(CCS_i, x, S) = \frac{(NC/MaxNC(S)) + (NR/MaxNR(S)) + (NM/MaxNM(S))}{3}
$$

such that *NC/NR/NM* correspond respectively to the *Number of Comments/Relationships/Methods* related to the CCS_i and *MaxNC/MaxNR/MaxNM* correspond respectively to the *Maximum Number of Comments/Relationships/Methods* of any class in the system S. There are of course many ways in which class importance could be measured, and one of the advantages of the search-based approach is that this definition could be easily replaced with a different one. In summary, the basic idea behind this work is to maximize the resistance of the refactoring solutions to perturbations in the severity levels and class importance of the code smells while maximizing simultaneously the number of corrected code smells. These two objectives are in conflict with each other since the quality of the proposed refactoring solution usually decreases when the environmental change (smell severity and/or class importance) increases. Thus, the goal is to find a good compromise between (1) quality and (2) robustness. This compromise is directly related to *robustness cost*, as discussed above. In fact, once the bi-objective trade-off front (quality, robustness) is obtained, the developer can navigate through this front in order to select his/her preferred refactoring solution. This is achieved through sacrificing some degree of solution quality while gaining in terms of robustness.

2.2.2   The Solution Approach

Solution Representation. To represent a candidate solution (individual/chromosome), we use a vector-based representation. Each dimension of the vector represents a refactoring operation where the order of application of the refactoring operations corresponds to their positions in the vector. The standard approach of pre- and post-conditions [12], is used to ensure that the refactoring operation can be applied while preserving program behaviour. For each refactoring operation, a set of controlling parameters (e.g., actors and roles as illustrated in Table 1) is randomly picked from the program to be refactored. Assigning randomly a sequence of refactorings to certain code fragments generates the initial population. An example of a solution is given in Figure 2 containing 3 refactorings. To apply a refactoring operation we need to specify which actors, i.e., code fragments, are involved/impacted by this refactoring and which roles they play to perform the refactoring operation. An actor can be a package, class, field, method, parameter, statement or variable. Table 1 depicts, for each refactoring, its involved actors and its role.

Table 1. Refactoring types and their involved actors and roles

Refactorings	Actors	Roles
Move method	class	source class, target class
	method	moved method
Move field	class	source class, target class
	field	moved field
Pull up field	class	sub classes, super class
	field	moved field
Pull up method	class	sub classes, super class
	method	moved method
Push down field	class	super class, sub classes
	field	moved field
Push down method	class	super class, sub classes
	method	Method
Inline class	class	source class, target class
Extract method	class	source class, target class
	method	source method, new method
	statement	moved statements
Extract class	class	source class, new class
	field	moved fields
	method	moved methods
Move class	package	source package, target package
	class	moved class
Extract interface	class	source classes, new interface
	field	moved fields
	method	moved methods

Inline_Class (Student, Person)
Pull_Up_Method (salary, Professor, Person)
Move_Method (grade, Registration, Student)

Fig. 2. A sample refactoring solution

Solution Variation. For crossover, we use the one-point crossover operator. It starts by selecting and splitting at random two parent solutions. Then, this operator creates two child solutions by putting, for the first child, the first part of the first parent with the second part of the second parent, and vice versa for the second child. This operator must respect the refactoring sequence length limits by eliminating randomly some refactoring operations if necessary. For mutation, we use the bit-string mutation operator that picks probabilistically one or more refactoring operations from its or their associated sequence and replaces them by other ones from a list of possible refactorings. These two variation operators have already demonstrated good performance when tackling the refactoring problem [23][21].

Solution Evaluation. Each refactoring sequence in the population is executed on the system S. For each sequence, the solution is evaluated based on the two objective functions (quality and robustness) defined in the previous section. Since we are considering a bi-objective formulation, we use the concept of Pareto optimality to find a set of compromise (Pareto-optimal) refactoring solutions. By definition, a solution x Pareto-dominates a solution y if and only if x is at least as good as y in all objectives and strictly better than y in at least one objective. The fitness of a particular solution in NSGA-II [8] corresponds to a couple (*Pareto Rank, Crowding distance*). In fact, NSGA-II classifies the population individuals (of parents and children) into different layers, called non-dominated fronts. Non-dominated solutions are assigned a rank of 1 and then are discarded temporary from the population. Non-dominated solutions from the truncated population are assigned a rank of 2 and then discarded temporarily. This process is repeated until the entire population is classified with the domination metric. After that, a diversity measure, called *crowding distance*, is assigned front-wise to each individual. The crowding distance is the average side length of the cuboid formed by the nearest neighbors of the considered solution. Once each solution is assigned its Pareto rank, based on refactoring quality and robustness to change in terms of class importance and smell severity levels, in addition to its crowding distance, mating selection and environmental selection are performed. This is based on the crowded comparison operator that favors solutions having better Pareto ranks and, in case of equal ranks, it favors the solution having larger crowding distance. In this way, convergence towards the Pareto optimal bi-objective front (quality, robustness) and diversity along this front are emphasized simultaneously. The basic iteration of NSGA-II consists in generating an offspring population (of size N) from the parent one (of size N too) based on variation operators (crossover and mutation) where the parent individuals are selected based on the crowded comparison operator. After that, parents and children are merged into a single population R of size $2N$. The parent population for the next generation is composed of the best non-dominated fronts. This process continues until the satisfaction of a stopping criterion. The output of NSGA-II is the last obtained parent population containing the best of the non-dominated solutions found. When plotted in the objective space, they form the Pareto front from which the developer will select his/her preferred refactoring solution.

3   Design of the Empirical Study

3.1   Research Questions and Systems Studied

RQ1: To validate the problem formulation of our approach, we compared our NSGA-II formulation with Random Search.

RQ2.1: How does NSGA-II perform compared to another multi-objective algorithm in terms of robustness cost, etc.?

RQ2.2: How do robust, multi-objective algorithms perform compared to mono-objective Evolutionary Algorithms?

RQ2.3: How does NSGA-II perform compare to existing search-based refactoring approaches?

RQ2.4: How does NSGA-II perform compared to existing refactoring approaches not based on the use of metaheuristic search?

RQ3: Insight. Can our robust multi-objective approach be useful for developers in real-world setting?

In our experiments, we used a set of well-known and well-commented open-source Java projects. We applied our approach to six large and medium sized open source Java projects: Xerces-J, JFreeChart, GanttProject, ApacheAnt, JHotDraw, and Rhino. Table 2 provides some descriptive statistics about these six programs. We selected these systems for our validation because they range from medium to large-sized open source projects that have been actively developed over the past 10 years, and include a large number of code smells. In addition, these systems are well studied in the literature and their code smells have been detected and analyzed manually [17], [20], [21].

Table 2. Software studied in our experiments

Systems	Release	#Classes	#Smells	KLOC
Xerces-J	v2.7.0	991	66	240
JFreeChart	v1.0.9	521	57	170
GanttProject	v1.10.2	245	41	41
ApacheAnt	v1.8.2	1191	82	255
JHotDraw	v6.1	585	21	21
Rhino	v1.7R1	305	61	42

3.2   Evaluation Metrics Used

We use the three following performance indicators [33] when comparing NSGA-II and MOPSO: *Hypervolume (IHV), Inverse Generational Distance (IGD), Contribution (IC).* In addition to these three multi-objective evaluation measures, we used these other metrics mainly to compare between mono-objective and multi-objective approaches defined as follows:

    −Quality: number of Fixed Code-Smells (FCS) is the number of code smells fixed after applying the best refactoring solution.

    −Severity of fixed Code-Smells (SCS) is defined as the sum of the severity of fixed code smells:

$$SCS(S) = \sum_{i=1}^{k} SmellSeverity(d_i)$$

where k is the number of fixed code smells and *SmellSeverity* corresponds to the severity (value between 0 and 1) assigned by the developer to each code smell type (blob, spaghetti code, etc.). In our experiments, we use these severity scores 0.8, 0.6, 0.4 and 0.3 respectively for blob, spaghetti code, functional decomposition and data class.

–*Importance of fixed Code-Smells (ICS)* is defined using three metrics (number of comments, number of relationships and number of methods) as follows:

$$ICS(S) = \sum_{i=1}^{k} importance(d_i)$$

where *importance* is as defined in the previous section.

–*Correctness of the suggested Refactorings (CR)* is defined as the number of semantically correct refactorings divided by the total number of manually evaluated refactorings.

–*Computational time (ICT)* is a measure of efficiency employed here since robustness inclusion may cause the search to use more time in order to find a set of Pareto-optimal trade-offs between refactoring quality and solution robustness.

Our experimental study is performed based on 51 independent simulation runs for each problem instance and the obtained results are statistically analyzed by using the Wilcoxon rank sum test [2] with a 95% confidence level ($\alpha = 5\%$).

For each multi-objective algorithm and for each system (cf. Table 2), we performed a set of experiments using several population sizes: 50, 100, 200, 500 and 1000. The stopping criterion was set to 250,000 fitness evaluations for all algorithms in order to ensure fairness of comparison. Each algorithm was executed 51 times with each configuration and then comparison between the configurations was performed based on *IHV, IGD* and *IC* using the Wilcoxon test. Table 3 reports the best configuration obtained for each couple (algorithm, system).

The MOPSO used in this paper is the Non-dominated Sorting PSO (NSPSO) proposed by Li [18]. The other parameters' values were fixed by trial and error and are as follows: (1) crossover probability = 0.8; mutation probability = 0.5 where the probability of gene modification is 0.3; stopping criterion = 250,000 fitness evaluations. For MOPSO, the cognitive and social scaling parameters c_1 and c_2 were both set to 2.0 and the inertia weighting coefficient w decreased gradually from 1.0 to 0.4. Since refactoring sequences usually have different lengths, we authorized the length n of number of refactorings to belong to the interval [10, 250].

Table 3. Best population size configurations

System	NSGA-II	MOPSO	Mono-EA
Xerces-J	1000	1000	1000
JFreeChart	500	200	500
GanttProject	100	100	100
ApacheAnt	1000	1000	1000
JHotDraw	200	200	200
Rhino	100	200	200

3.5 Results

3.5.1 Results for RQ1
Table 4 confirms that NSGA-II and MOPSO are better than random search based on the three quality indicators IHV, IGD and IC on all six open source systems. The Wilcoxon rank sum test showed that in 51 runs both NSGA-II and MOPSO results were significantly better than random search. We conclude that there is empirical evidence that our multi-objective formulation surpasses the performance of random search thus our formulation is adequate (this answers RQ1).

3.5.2 Results for RQ2
In this section, we compare our NSGA-II adaptation to the current, state-of-the-art refactoring approaches. To answer the second research question, RQ2.1, we compared NSGA-II to another widely used multi-objective algorithm, MOPSO, using the same adapted fitness function. Table 4 shows the overview of the results of the significance tests comparison between NSGA-II and MOPSO. NSGA-II outperforms MOPSO in most of the cases: 13 out of 18 experiments (73%). MOPSO outperforms the NSGA-II approach only in GanttProject, which is the smallest open source system considered in our experiments, having the lowest number of legal refactorings available, so it appears that MOPSO's search operators make a better task of working with a smaller search space. In particular, NSGA-II outperforms MOPSO in terms of IC values in 4 out 6 experiments with one 'no significant difference' result. Regarding IHV, NSGA-II outperformed MOPSO in 5 out of 6 experiments, where only one case was not statistically significant, namely GanttProject. For IGD, the results were the same as for IC. A more qualitative evaluation is presented in Figure 3 illustrating the box plots obtained for the multi-objective metrics on the different projects. We see that for almost all problems the distributions of the metrics values for NSGA-II have smaller variability than for MOPSO. This fact confirms the effectiveness of NSGA-II over MOPSO in finding a well-converged and well-diversified set of Pareto-optimal refactoring solutions.

Next, we use all four metrics FCS, SCS, ICS and ICT to compare three robust refactoring algorithms: our NSGA-II adaptation, MOPSO, and a mono-objective genetic algorithm (Mono-EA) that has a single fitness function aggregating the two objectives. We first note that the mono-EA provides only one refactoring solution, while NSGA-II and MOPSO generate a set of non-dominated solutions. In order to make meaningful comparisons, we select the best solution for NSGA-II and MOPSO using a *knee point* strategy [53]. The knee point corresponds to the solution with the maximal trade-off between quality and robustness, i.e., a small improvement in either objective induces a large degradation in the other. Hence moving from the knee point in either direction is usually not interesting for the developer [50]. Thus, for NSGA-II and MOPSO, we select the knee point from the Pareto approximation having the median IHV value. We aim by this strategy to ensure fairness when making comparisons against the mono-objective EA. For the latter, we use the best solution corresponding to the median observation on 51 runs. We use the trade-off "worth" metric proposed by Rachmawati and Srinivasan [51] to find the knee point. This metric estimates the worthiness of each non-dominated refactoring solution in terms of trade-off between quality and robustness. After that, the knee point corresponds to the solution having the maximal trade-off "worthiness" value. The results from 51 runs are depicted in Table 5(a). It can be seen that both NSGA-II and MOPSO provide a better trade-off between quality and robustness than a mono-objective EA in all six systems. For FCS, the number of fixed code smells using NSGA-II is better than MOPSO in all systems except for GanttProject (84% of cases) and also the FCS score for NSGA-II is better than mono-EA in 100% of cases. We have the same observation for the SCS and ICS scores where NSGA-II outperforms MOPSO and Mono-EA in at least 84% of cases. Even for GanttProject, the number of fixed code smells using NSGA-II is very close to those fixed by MOPSO. The execution time of NSGA-II is invariably lower than that of MOPSO with the same number of iterations, however the execution time required by Mono-EA is lower than both NSGA-II and MOPSO. It is well-known that a mono-objective algorithm requires lower execution time for convergence since only one objective is handled. In conclusion, we answer RQ2.2 by concluding that the results obtained in Table 5(a) confirm that both multi-objective formulations are adequate and outperform the mono-objective algorithm based on an aggregation of two objectives (quality and robustness).

Table 5 also shows the results of comparing our robust approach based on NSGA-II with two mono-objective refactoring approaches [17], [20] and a practical refactoring technique where developers used a refactoring plug-in in Eclipse to suggest solutions to fix code smells. Kessentini et al. [17] used genetic algorithms to find the best sequence of refactoring that minimizes the number of code smells while O'Keeffe and Ó Cinnéide [20] used different mono-objective algorithms to find the best sequence of refactorings that optimize a fitness function composed of a set of quality metrics. In Ouni et al. [21], the authors ask a set of developers to fix manually the code smells in a number of open source systems including those that we are considering in our experiments. It is apparent from Table 5 that our NSGA-II adaptation outperforms mono-objective approaches in terms of smell-fixing ability (FCS) in only 11% of cases. However, our NSGA-II adaptation outperforms all the mono-objective and manual approaches in 100% of experiments in terms of the two robustness metrics, SCS and ICS. This is can be explained by the fact that NSGA-II aims to find a compromise between both quality and robustness however the remaining approaches did not consider robustness but only quality. Thus, NSGA-II sacrifices a small amount of quality in order to improve robustness. Furthermore, the number of code smells fixed by NSGA-II (277) is very close to the number fixed by the mono-objective and manual approaches (the best being Kessentini et al. [17] that fixed a total of 285 code smells), so the sacrifice in solution quality is quite small. When comparing NSGA-II with the remaining approaches we considered the best solution selected from the Pareto-optimal front using the knee point-based strategy described above. To answer RQ2.3 and RQ2.4, the results of Table 5(b) support the claim that our NSGA-II formulation provides a good trade-off between robustness and quality, and outperforms on average the state of the art of refactoring approaches, both search-based and manual, with a low robustness cost.

3.6.3 Results for RQ3

Figure 4 depicts the different Pareto surfaces obtained on three open source systems (Apache Ant, JHotDraw and Gantt Project) using NSGA-II to optimize quality and robustness. Due to space limitations, we show only some examples of the Pareto-optimal front approximations obtained which differ significantly in terms of size. Similar fronts were obtained on the remaining systems. The 2-D projection of the Pareto front helps developers to select the best trade-off solution between the two objectives of quality and robustness based on their own preferences. Based on the plots of Figure 4, the developer could degrade quality in favor of robustness while controlling visually the robustness cost, which corresponds to the ratio of the quality loss to the achieved robustness gain. In this way, the preferred robust refactoring solution can be realized.

One striking feature about all the three plots is that starting from the highest quality solution the trade-off between quality and robustness is in favor of quality, meaning that the quality degrades slowly with a fast increase in robustness up to the knee point, marked in each figure. Thereafter, there is a sharp drop in quality with only a small increase in robustness. It is very interesting to note that this property of the Pareto-optimal front is apparent in all the problems considered in this study. It is likely that a developer would be drawn to this knee point as the probable best trade-off between quality and robustness. Without any robustness consideration in the search process, one would obtain the highest quality solution all the time (which is not robust at all), but Figure 4 shows how a better robust solution can be obtained by sacrificing just a little in quality. Figure 5 shows the impact of different levels of perturbation on the Pareto-optimal front. Our approach takes as input as the maximum level of perturbation applied in the smell severity and class importance at each iteration during the optimization process. A high level of perturbation generates more robust refactoring solutions than those generated with lower variations, but the solution quality in this case will be higher. As described by Figure 4, the developer can choose the level of perturbation based on his/her preferences to prioritize quality or robustness. Although the Pareto-optimal front changes depending on the perturbation level, there still exists a knee point, which makes the decision making by a developer easier in such problems.

Table 4. The significantly best algorithm among random search, NSGA-II and MOPSO (No sign. diff. means that NSGA-II and MOPSO are significantly better than random, but not statistically different).

Project	IC	IHV	IGD
Xerces-J	NSGA-II	NSGA-II	NSGA-II
JFreeChart	NSGA-II	NSGA-II	NSGA-II
GanttProject	MOPSO	No sign. diff.	MOPSO
ApacheAnt	NSGA-II	NSGA-II	NSGA-II
JHotDraw	NSGA-II	NSGA-II	NSGA-II
Rhino	No sign. diff.	NSGA-II	No sign. diff.

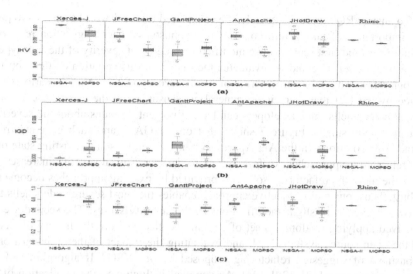

Fig. 3. Boxplots using the quality measures (a) IC, (b) IHV, and (c) IGD applied to NSGAII and MOPSO

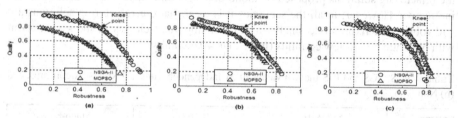

Fig. 4. Pareto fronts for NSGA-II obtained on three open source systems: (a) ApacheAnt (large), (b) JHotDraw (medium) and (c) GanttProject (small)

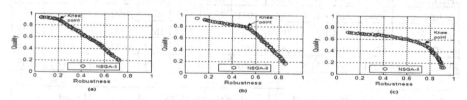

Fig. 5. Pareto fronts for NSGA-II obtained on JHotDraw with different perturbation levels variation (robustness): (a) low, (b) medium and (c) high

Figure 6 describes the manual qualitative evaluation of some suggested refactoring solutions. It is clear that results are almost similar between our proposal and existing approach in terms of the semantic coherence of suggested refactorings. We consider that a semantic precision more than 65% acceptable since most of the solutions should be executed manually by developers and our tool is a recommendation system. Thus, developers can evaluate if it is interesting or not to apply some refactorings based on their preferences and the semantic coherence.

To answer RQ3 more adequately, we considered two real-world scenarios to justify the importance of taking into consideration robustness when suggestion refactoring solutions. In the first scenario, we modified the degree of severity of the four types of code smells over time and we evaluated the impact of this variation on the robustness of our refactoring solution in terms of smell severity (SCS). This scenario is motivated by the fact that there is no general consensus about the severity score of detected code smells thus developers can have divergent opinions about the severity of detected code smells. Figure 7 shows that our NSGA-II approach generates robust refactoring solutions on the Ant Apache system in comparison to existing state of the art refactoring approaches. In fact, the more the variation in severity increases over time the more the refactoring solutions provided by existing approaches become non-robust. Thus, our multi-objective approach enables the most severe code smells to be corrected even with slight modifications in the severity scores. The second scenario involved applying randomly a set of commits, collected from the history of changes of the open source systems [21], and evaluating the impact of these changes on the robustness of suggested refactoring proposed by our NSGA-II algorithm and non-robust approaches [17], [20], [24]. As depicted in Figure 8, the application of new commits modifies the importance of classes in the system containing code smells and the refactoring solutions proposed by mono-objective and manual approaches become ineffective. However, in all the scenarios it is clear that our refactoring solutions are still robust and fixing code smells in most of important classes in the system even with high number of new commits (more than 40 commits).

Table 5. FCS, SCS and ICS median values of 51 independent runs: (a) Robust Algorithms, and (b) Non-Robust algorithms

Systems	NSGA-II				MOPSO				Mono-EA			
	FCS	SCS	ICS	ICT	FCS	SCS	ICS	ICT	FCS	SCS	ICS	ICT
Xerces-J	52/66	31.7	29.3	1h38	48/66	28.4	26.7	1h44	41/66	24.9	24.1	1h21
JFreeChart	49/57	29.3	27.1	1h35	44/57	24.8	21.6	1h42	34/57	21.2	19.3	1h16
GanttProject	36/41	21.6	18.4	1h28	38/41	22.9	19.3	1h26	29/41	19.2	17.5	1h03
ApacheAnt	74/82	39.8	38.1	1h45	72/82	36.2	37.3	1h53	59/82	29.1	34.2	1h27
JHotDraw	17/21	11.3	10.3	1h33	15/21	9.8	8.2	1h47	13/21	8.3	8.2	1h14
Rhino	49/61	28.6	21.3	1h31	46/61	26.1	19.3	1h43	38/61	21.3	17.1	1h05

Systems	Kessentini et al.'11				O'Keeffe et al.'08				Manual			
	FCS	SCS	ICS	ICT	FCS	SCS	ICS	ICT	FCS	SCS	ICS	ICT
Xerces-J	53/66	28.6	27.8	1h24	53/66	26.3	25.3	1h16	54/66	28.4	25.3	N/A
JFreeChart	49/57	25.8	22.3	1h13	48/57	23.6	21.9	1h04	50/57	23.9	21.2	N/A
GanttProject	37/41	19.2	17.1	1h08	37/41	20.2	17.8	1h06	37/41	19.3	16.9	N/A
ApacheAnt	76/82	32.4	33.4	1h25	75/82	33.5	34.1	1h23	71/82	31.2	32.4	N/A
JHotDraw	18/21	9.3	9.1	1h10	17/21	9.1	9.6	1h17	19/21	9.8	8.9	N/A
Rhino	52/61	24.9	16.4	1h01	51/61	23.2	17.6	1h04	51/61	24.2	16.2	N/A

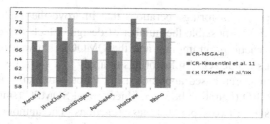

Fig. 6. The qualitative evaluation (CR) of some refactorings   proposed by NSGA-II, [17]   and [20]

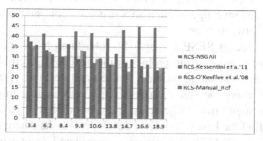

Fig. 7. The impact of code smells severity variations on the robustness of refactoring solutions for ApacheAnt proposed by NSGA-II, [17], [20] and [24]

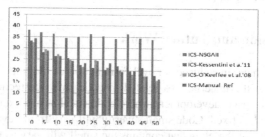

Fig. 8. The impact of class importance variation on the robustness of refactoring solutions for Apache Ant proposed by NSGA-II, [17], [20] and [24]

4   Related Work

The majority of existing work combines several metrics in a single fitness function to find the best sequence of refactorings. Seng et al. [23] propose a single-objective optimization based-approach using genetic algorithm to suggest a list of refactorings to improve software quality. The search process uses a single fitness function to maximize a weighted sum of several quality metrics. Closely related work is that of O'Keeffe and Ó Cinnéide [20] where different local search-based techniques such as hill climbing and simulated annealing are used to implement automated refactoring guided by the QMOOD metrics suite [1]. In a more recent extension of their work, the refactoring process is guided not just by software metrics, but also by the design that the developer wishes the program to have [19]. In recent work, Kessentini et al. [17] propose single-objective combinatorial optimization using a genetic algorithm to find the best sequence of refactoring operations that improve the quality of the code by minimizing as much as possible the number of design defects detected on the source code. They use genetic programming and the QMOOD software metric suite [1] to identify the most suitable set of refactorings to apply to a software design. Harman et al. [14] propose a search-based approach using Pareto optimality that combines two quality metrics, CBO (coupling between objects) and SDMPC (standard deviation of methods per class), in two separate fitness functions. The authors start from the assumption that good design quality results from good distribution of features (methods) among classes. Ó Cinnéide et al. [19] use multi-objective search-based refactoring to conduct an empirical investigation to assess structural cohesion metrics and to explore the relationships between them.

According to a recent SBSE survey [15], robustness has been taken into account only in two software engineering problems: the next release problem (NRP) and the software management/planning problem. Paixao and de Souza propose a robust formulation of NRP where each requirement's importance is uncertain since the customers can change it at any time [10]. In work by Antoniol et al., the authors propose a robust model to find the best schedule of developers' tasks where different objectives should be satisfied [1], [13]. Robustness is considered as one of the objectives to satisfy. In this paper, for the first time, we have considered robustness as a separate objective in its own right.

5   Conclusion and Future Work

In this paper, we have introduced a novel formulation of the refactoring problem that takes into account the uncertainties related to code smell correction in the dynamic environment of software development where code smell severity and class importance cannot be regarded as fixed. Code smell severity will vary from developer to developer and the importance of the class that contains the smell will vary as the code base itself evolves. We have reported the results of an empirical study of our robust technique compared to different existing approaches [17], [20], [24]. Future work involves extending our approach to handle additional code smell types in order to test further the general applicability of our methodology. In this paper, we focused on the use of a structural metric to estimate class importance, but this can be extended to consider also the pattern of repository submits to achieve another perspective on class importance.

References

[1] Antoniol, G., Di Penta, M., Harman, M.: A Robust Search-Based Approach to Project Management in the Presence of Abandonment, Rework, Error and Uncertainty. In: METRICS 2004, pp. 172–183 (2004)

[2] Arcuri, A., Briand, L.C.: A practical guide for using statistical tests to assess randomized algorithms in software engineering. In: ICSE 2011, pp. 1–10 (2011)

[3] Beyer, H.-G., Sendhoff, B.: Robust optimization – A comprehensive survey. Computer Methods in Applied Mechanics and Engineering 196(33-34), 3190–3218 (2007)

[4] Chatzigeorgiou, A., Manakos, A.: Investigating the evolution of code smells in object-oriented systems, Innovations in Systems and Software Engineering. NASA Journal (2013)

[5] Das, I.: Robustness optimization for constrained nonlinear programming problem. Engineering Optimization 32(5), 585–618 (2000)

[6] Deb, K., Gupta, H.: Introducing robustness in multi-objective optimization. Evolutionary Computation Journal 14(4), 463–494 (2006)

[7] Deb, K., Gupta, S.: Understanding knee points in bi-criteria problems and their implications as preferred solution principles. Engineering Optimization 43(11), 1175–1204 (2011)

[8] Deb, K., Pratap, A., Agarwal, S., Meyarivan, T.: A fast and elitist multiobjective genetic algorithm: NSGA-II. IEEE Transactions on Evolutionary Computation 6(2), 182–197 (2002)

[9] Du Bois, B., Demeyer, S., Verelst, J.: Refactoring—Improving Coupling and Cohesion of Existing Code. In: WCRE 2004, pp. 144–151 (2004)

[10] Esteves Paixao, M.-H., De Souza, J.-T.: A scenario-based robust model for the next release problem. In: GECCO 2013 (2013)

[11] Ferrucci, F., Harman, M., Ren, J., Sarro, F.: Not going to take this anymore: Multi-objective overtime planning for software engineering projects. In: ICSE 2013, pp. 462–471. IEEE Press, Piscataway (2013)

[12] Fowler, M., Beck, K., Brant, J., Opdyke, W., Roberts, D.: Refactoring – Improving the Design of Existing Code, 1st edn. Addison-Wesley (1999)

[13] Gueorguiev, S., Harman, M., Antoniol, G.: Software project planning for robustness and completion time in the presence of uncertainty using multi objective search based software engineering. In: GECCO 2009, pp. 1673–1680 (2009)

[14] Harman, M., Tratt, L.: Pareto optimal search based refactoring at the design level. In: GECCO 2007, pp. 1106–1113 (2007)

[15] Harman, M., Mansouri, A., Zhang, Y.: Search-based software engineering: Trends, techniques and applications. ACM Comput. Surv. (2012)

[16] Jin, Y., Branke, J.: Evolutionary optimization in uncertain environments – A survey. IEEE Transactions on Evolutionary Computation 9(3), 303–317 (2005)

[17] Kessentini, M., Kessentini, W., Sahraoui, H., Boukadoum, M., Ouni, A.: Design Defects Detection and Correction by Example. In: Proceedings of ICPC 2011, pp. 81–90 (2011)

[18] Li, X.: A non-dominated sorting particle swarm optimizer for multiobjective optimization. In: GECCO 2003, pp. 37–48 (2003)

[19] Ó Cinnéide, M., Tratt, L., Harman, M., Counsell, S., Moghadam, I. H.: Experimental Assessment of Software Metrics Using Automated Refactoring. In: Proceedings of the ESEM 2012, pp. 49–58 (2012)

[20] O'Keeffe, M., Ó Cinnéide, M.: Search-based Refactoring for Software Maintenance. Journal of Systems and Software, 502–516 (2008)

[21] Ouni, A., Kessentini, M., Sahraoui, H., Boukadoum, M.: Maintainability Defects Detection and Correction: A Multi-Objective Approach. Journal of Automated Software Engineering, 47–79 (2012)

[22] Palomba, F., Bavota, G., Di Penta, M., Oliveto, R., De Lucia, A., Poshyvanyk, D.: Detecting Bad Smells in Source Code Using Change History Information. In: Proceedings of ASE 2013 (2013)

[23] Seng, O., Stammel, J., Burkhart, D.: Search-based determination of refactorings for improving the class structure of object-oriented systems. In: Proceedings of GECCO 2006, pp. 1909–1916 (2006)

[24] http://www.jdeodorant.com/

Towards Automated A/B Testing

Giordano Tamburrelli and Alessandro Margara

Faculty of Informatics. University of Lugano, Switzerland
{giordano.tamburrelli,alessandro.margara}@usi.ch

Abstract. User-intensive software, such as Web and mobile applications, heavily depends on the interactions with large and unknown populations of users. Knowing the preferences and behaviors of these populations is crucial for the success of this class of systems. A/B testing is an increasingly popular technique that supports the iterative development of user-intensive software based on controlled experiments performed on live users. However, as currently performed, A/B testing is a time consuming, error prone and costly manual activity. In this paper, we investigate a novel approach to automate A/B testing. More specifically, we rephrase A/B testing as a search-based software engineering problem and we propose an initial approach that supports automated A/B testing through aspect-oriented programming and genetic algorithms.

1 Introduction

Modern software systems increasingly deal with large and evolving populations of users that may issue up to millions of requests per day. These systems are commonly referred to as *user-intensive* software systems (e.g., Web and mobile applications). A key distinguishing feature of these systems is the heavy dependence on the interactions with many users, who approach the applications with different needs, attitudes, navigation profiles, and preferences[1].

Designing applications that meet user preferences is a crucial factor that may directly affect the success of user-intensive systems. Underestimating its importance can lead to substantial economic losses. For example, an inadequate or distorted knowledge of user preferences in a Web application can lead to an unsatisfactory user experience with consequent loss of customers and revenues.

Domain experts typically provide valuable insights concerning user preferences that engineers can exploit to obtain an effective design of user-intensive applications. Unfortunately, this information could be inaccurate, generic, and obsolete. In practice, it is almost impossible to design applications that accurately capture all possible and meaningful user preferences upfront.

As a consequence, engineers typically design a user-intensive application relying on the initial available knowledge while, at run-time, they continuously monitor, refine, and improve the system to meet newly discovered user preferences. In this context, engineers increasingly rely on *A/B testing* [2] [11] to evaluate and

---

[1] We collectively identify these factors under the term *user preferences*.

[2] A/B testing is also known as randomized experiments, split tests, or control/treatment. In this paper we always use the term A/B testing.

C. Le Goues and S. Yoo (Eds.): SSBSE 2014, LNCS 8636, pp. 184–198, 2014.

improve their applications. In A/B testing, two distinct variants (i.e., variant A and B) of the same application are compared using *live experiments*. Live users are randomly assigned to one of the two variants and some metrics of interest (e.g., the likelihood for a user to buy in an e-commerce Web application) are collected. The two variants are compared based on these metrics, and the best one is selected, while the other is discarded. The iterative development of variants and their comparative evaluation through live experiments allow designers to gradually evolve their applications maximizing a given metric of interest. For example, an e-commerce application may be refactored adopting variants that maximize sales, while a mobile application may be refactored adopting variants that maximize the advertisements' views.

A/B testing is being increasingly adopted by the industry and proved to be effective [3]. Still, it suffers from several limitations. Indeed, conceiving, running, and summarizing the results of A/B tests is a difficult, tedious, error prone, and costly manual activity [5]. This paper tackles this issue laying the foundations of an automated A/B testing framework in which the generation of application variants, their run-time evaluation, and the continuous evolution of the system are automatically obtained by casting the process of A/B testing to a Search-Based Software Engineering (SBSE) [7] problem. This novel viewpoint on A/B testing brings to the table several research challenges defined and discussed in the paper.

The contribution of this paper is twofold. First, it lays the foundations and explores the potential of automated A/B testing as an optimization problem. Specifically, it proposes an initial approach based on aspect-oriented programming [8] and genetic algorithms [13], which can be considered as a primer to demonstrate the feasibility of the concepts introduced in the paper and a first concrete step towards their practical application. Second, it provides the SBSE community with a novel and crucial domain where its expertise can be applied.

The remainder of the paper is organized as follows. Section 2 provides a more detailed introduction to A/B testing and discusses some open issues. Section 3 rephrases the process of A/B testing as an optimization problem. Next, Section 4 reifies the illustrated concepts in the context of user-intensive Web applications with a solution based on aspect-oriented programming and genetic algorithms. Section 5 presents some preliminary results. Finally, Section 6 surveys related work and Section 7 draws some conclusions and discusses future work.

2   Background and Problem Statement

This section introduces A/B testing, partially recalling the definition reported in [11]. Next, it points out some of the existing limitations of A/B testing and discusses the need for automating it.

The diffusion and standardization of Web technologies and the increasing importance of user-intensive software represent a perfect playground to evaluate competing alternatives, ideas, and innovations by means of controlled experiments, commonly referred to as A/B tests in this context. The overall process of A/B testing is exemplified in Fig. 1. Live users are randomly assigned to one

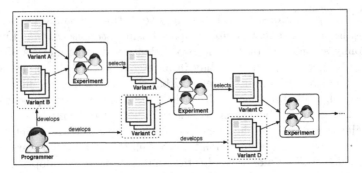

Fig. 1. A/B testing iterative process

of two variants of the system under analysis: variant A (i.e., the *control* variant), which is commonly the current version, and variant B (i.e., the *treatment* variant), which is usually a newer version of the system being evaluated. The two variants are compared on the basis of some metrics of interest related to the user preferences. The variant that shows a statistically significant improvement is retained, while the other is discarded. As previously mentioned, the iterative development of variants and their comparative evaluation through live controlled experiments allow designers to gradually evolve their applications maximizing the metrics of interest.

Even if widely and successfully adopted in industry [3,10], A/B testing is still considered by the majority of developers as a complex and crafted activity rather than a well-established software engineering practice. Indeed, conceiving, running, and summarizing the results of A/B tests is a difficult, tedious, and costly manual activity. More precisely, an accurate and consistent A/B testing demands for several complex engineering decisions and tasks. The most relevant ones are illustrated hereafter.

1. *Development and deployment of multiple variants.* A/B testing requires a continuous modification and deployment of the application codebase to implement and evaluate variants. These variants are deployed and monitored concurrently serving at the same time a certain percentage of users.

2. *What is a variant.* Programs may be customized along different lines. Because of this, a critical choice for developers is the selection of how many and which aspects of the program to change when generating a new variant.

3. *How many variants.* We defined A/B testing as the process of concurrently deploy and evaluate two variants of the system. In the general case, developers may concurrently deploy more than two variants. However, they do not typically have evidences to select this number effectively and to tune it over time.

4. *How to select variants.* As previously mentioned, A/B testing works iteratively. At the beginning of each iteration, developers have to decide which variants to deploy and test. Prioritizing certain variants is critical for quickly finding

better program configurations. However, selecting the most promising variants is also difficult, especially for large and complex programs.

5. *How to evaluate variants.* A sound and accurate comparison of variants in live experiments with users requires mathematical skills (e.g., statistics) that developers do not necessarily have. For example, sizing the duration of tests and the number of users involved is a crucial factor that affects the quality of results.

6. *When to stop.* Usually, A/B testing enacts a continuous adaptation process that focuses on certain specific aspects of a program. Understanding when a nearly optimal solution has been reached for those aspects is critical to avoid investing time and effort on changes that provide only a minimal impact on the quality of the program.

Not only the factors mentioned above represent concrete obstacles for developers, but they also characterize A/B testing as an error-prone process that may yield to unexpected, counter-intuitive, and unsatisfactory results (see for example [9,12]). To facilitate the adoption of A/B testing and to avoid potential errors, we believe it is a crucial goal of the software engineering research to provide the developers with a set of conceptual foundations and tools aimed at increasing the degree of automation in A/B testing. So far, to the best of our knowledge, this research direction has received little attention.

3   A/B Testing as an Optimization Problem

In this section we take a different and novel perspective on A/B testing, rephrasing it as an optimization problem. The conceptual foundations and the notations introduced hereafter are used in the remainder of this paper.

1. *Features.* From an abstract viewpoint a program p can be viewed as a finite set of *features*: $F_p = \{f_1 \ldots f_n\}$. Each feature f_i has an associated domain D_i that specifies which values are valid/allowed for f_i. The concept of feature is very broad and may include entities of different nature and at different level of abstraction. For example, a feature could be a primitive integer value that specifies how many results are displayed per page in an e-commerce Web application. Similarly, a feature could be a string that specifies the text applied to a certain button in a mobile application. However, a feature can also represent more abstract software entities such as a component in charge of sorting some items displayed to the user. The features above are associated to the domains of integers, strings, and sorting algorithms, respectively.

2. *Instantiation.* An instantiation is a function $I_{p,f_i} : f_i \rightarrow D_i$ that associates a feature f_i in F_p with a specific value from its domain D_i. Two key concepts follow: (i) to obtain a concrete implementation for a program p it is necessary to specify the instantiations for all the features in p; (ii) the specification of different instantiations yields to different concrete implementations of the same abstract program p.

3. *Variants.* We call a concrete implementation of a program p a *variant* of p. As a practical example, recalling the features exemplified above, three possible instantiations may assign: (i) 10 to the feature that specifies the number of items displayed per page, (ii) the label *"Buy Now"* to the button, (iii) an algorithm that sorts items by their name to the sorting component. These instantiations define a possible variant of the system.

4. *Constraints.* A constraint is a function $C_{i,j} : D_i \to \mathcal{P}(D_j)$ that, given a value $d_i \in D_i$ for a feature f_i, returns a subset of values in D_j that are *not* allowed for the feature f_j. Intuitively, constraints can be used to inhibit combinations of features that are not valid in the application domains. For example, consider a Web application including two features: font color and background color. A developer can use constraints to express undesired combination of colors. We say that a variant of a program p *satisfies* a constraint $C_{i,j}$ if $I_{p,f_j} \notin C_{i,j}(I_{p,f_i})$. A variant is *valid* for p if it satisfies all the constraints defined for p.

5. *Assessment Function.* An assessment function is a function defined as $o(v) : V_p \to \mathbb{R}$, where $V_p = \{v_1, \ldots, v_m\}$ is the set of all possible variants for program p. This function associates to each and every variant of a program a numeric value, which indicates the goodness of the variant with respect to the goal of the program. The assessment function depends on the preferences of users and can only be evaluated by monitoring variants at run-time. As previously mentioned, the likelihood for a user to buy is a valid assessment function for an e-commerce Web application. Indeed, this metric is evaluated at run-time for a specific variant of the application and concretely measures its goodness with respect to the ultimate goal of the program (i.e., selling goods): higher values indicate better variants.

Given these premises, we can rephrase A/B testing as a search problem as follows. Given a program p characterised by a set of features F_p, a set of constraints C_p, and an assessment function $o(v)$, find the variant $\hat{v} \in V_p$ such that $\hat{v}$ is valid and maximizes $o(v)$:

$$\hat{v} = \arg\max_v o(v)$$

4   Towards Automated A/B Testing

Section 2 identified some difficulties and open issues in the usage of A/B testing, mainly deriving from a limited degree of automation. We claim that, by formulating A/B testing as an optimization problem as shown in Section 3, we can effectively exploit automated search algorithms to investigate and enable automated A/B testing. This section reifies this idea.

In our vision, automated A/B testing can be achieved by combining together two ingredients: (i) an appropriate design-time declarative facility to specify program features, and (ii) a run-time framework in charge of automatically and iteratively exploring the solution space of possible concrete programs by: generating, executing, and evaluating variants. We captured these ideas in a

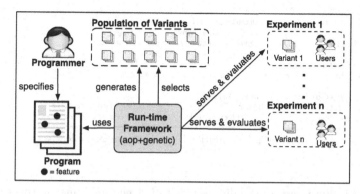

Fig. 2. A reference architecture for automated A/B testing

reference architecture (see Fig. 2) and we implemented it in a prototype tool. The architecture consists of two main steps, summarized below and detailed in the following paragraphs.

Specifying Features. As stated in Section 2, A/B testing requires a significant effort in developing and deploying the conceived variants. To alleviate the developer from this burden, our architecture provides ad-hoc annotations to specify the set of relevant features for a program and their associated domain. In other words, this allows the developer to write a *parametric* program only once, that represents all possible variants that will be automatically instantiated later on at run-time.

Selecting and Evaluating Variants. As stated in Section 2, developers need to take several critical decisions to guide and control the iterative search for better solutions through A/B testing. To overcome these difficulties, our architecture provides a run-time framework that automates the search process by exploiting genetic algorithms. In particular, it creates and iteratively evolves a population of variants by selecting, mutating, and evaluating its individuals. At execution time, the framework instantiates concrete variants from the parameterized program by means of a *dependency injection* mechanism based on aspect-oriented programming [8]. The run-time framework assesses the goodness of instantiated variants by means of an appropriate application-specific assessment function (see Section 2) that measures the preferences of users. Such assessesment function is adopted as fitness function for the genetic algorithm and drives the generation and evolution of new variants at each iteration.

4.1   Specifying Features

In our approach, developers can specify features by means of annotated variable declarations[3]. Variables declared as features cannot be initialized or modified

---

[3] Our prototype is designed for the Java programming language. However, the illustrated concepts and techniques apply seamlessly to other languages and technologies.

```
1 @StringFeature(name="checkOutButtonText",
2   values={"CheckOut", "Buy", "Buy Now!"})
3 String buttonText; // Primitive feature specification
4
5 @IntegerFeature(name="fontSize", range="12:1:18")
6 int textSize; // Primitive feature specification
7
8 Button checkOutButton = new Button();
9 checkOutButton.setText(buttonText); // Primitive feature use
10 checkOutButton.setFontSize(textSize); // Primitive feature use
```

Listing 1.1. Primitive Type Feature Example

since their value is automatically assigned at execution time by the run-time framework. As mentioned in Section 3, the concept of feature is very broad. In particular we distinguish two categories of features: (*i*) *Primitive Type* and (*ii*) *Abstract Data Type* features. The former refers to program features that can be modelled with primitive type (integers, double, boolean, and strings); the latter refers to features implemented through ad-hoc abstract data types. Hereafter we discuss in details both options.

Primitive Type Features. Let us consider the example in Section 3 of a feature of string type that specifies the label of a button in a mobile application. To represent this feature and its domain, developers can declare a string variable annotated with the **@StringFeature** annotation (see Listing 1.1). In this case, the features can assume values in the entire domain of strings. Developers can restrict such domain by specifying a set of valid values in the *values* parameter. Analogous annotations are provided for other primitive types (e.g., **@IntegerFeature**, **@BooleanFeature**, etc.). Differently from string features, the domain of numeric features can be specified as a range of valid values. For example, reasonable values for an integer feature that represents a font size may be in the range (12:18) with a step of 1.

The run-time framework instantiates and serves to users concrete variants of the program that are automatically generated by injecting values to the features declared by the developers. Thus, considering the code in Listing 1.1, a user accessing the system may experience a variant of the program in which the button is labeled with the text *"Buy Now!"* with font size equal to 12, while a different user, at the same time, may experience a different variant of the program with text *"Check-out"* and font size equal to 16.

Generic Data Type Feature. Real-world programs may be characterized by complex features that require ad-hoc abstract data types. We support them by relying on two ingredients: (*i*) an interface that specifies the abstract behavior of the feature and (*ii*) several implementations of the interface that contain the concrete realizations of this feature.

Let us recall the example mentioned in Section 3 of a component in charge of sorting some items displayed to the users. Possible realizations of this feature may sort items by name, price, or rating. Thus, the generic aspect of sorting items can be defined as a feature as shown in Listing 1.2. To do so, developers declare an

```
1  @GenericFeatureInterface(name="sort",
2     values={"com.example.SortByPrice", "com.example.SortByName"})
3  public interface AbstractSortingInterface{
4     public List<Item> sort();
5  }
6
7  public class SortByPrice implements AbstractSortingInterface{
8     public List<Item> sort(){
9        // Sort by price implementation
10    }
11 }
12
13 public class SortByName implements AbstractSortingInterface{
14    public List<Item> sort(){
15       // Sort by name implementation
16    }
17 }
18
19 // ...
20
21 @GenericFeature
22 AbstractSortingInterface sortingFeature; // ADT feature specification
23
24 sortingFeature.sort(..); // ADT feature use
```

Listing 1.2. Generic Data Type Feature Example

interface that includes all the required methods (i.e., *sort(...)* in this example) and implement as many concrete realizations of this interface as needed. The interface must be annotated with the **@GenericFeatureInterface** annotation including the full class name of all its implementations.

Developers can declare variables of the type specified by the interface and annotated with **@GenericFeature**. Analogously to primitive type features, the run-time framework serves to users concrete variants of the program that are automatically generated by injecting an appropriate reference to one of the interface implementations. For example, the invocation to the sort method in the last row of Listing 1.2 may be dispatched to an instance that implements the *SortByName* algorithm or to an instance that implements the *SortByPrice* algorithm, depending on the type of the object injected at run-time.

4.2   Selecting and Evaluating Variants

So far, we explained how developers can declare features in a program and we delegated to the run-time framework the task of generating, executing, and evaluating variants. Now, we explore how the run-time framework actually implements these aspects.

In our prototype, the run-time framework relies on a genetic algorithm that runs online while the system is operating. A genetic algorithm encodes every possible solution of an optimization problem as a *chromosome*, composed of several *genes*. It selects and iteratively evolves a population of chromosomes by applying three main steps (discussed below): (*i*) selection, (*ii*) crossover, and (*iii*) mutation. Each chromosome is evaluated according to a *fitness function*. The algorithm terminates after a fixed number of iterations or when subsequent iterations do not generates new chromosome with significantly improved values of fitness. Solving the problem of searching for variants via genetic algorithms requires to specify an encoding and a concrete strategy for each of the three main steps mentioned above. Next, we provide these ingredients for the specific case of A/B testing.

Encoding. Each feature declared by developers directly maps into a gene, while each variant maps into a chromosome. Analogously, the assessment function, which evaluates variants on live users, corresponds directly to the fitness function, which evaluates chromosomes. Two additional aspects are required to fully specify a valid encoding: the number of chromosomes used in each iteration and the termination condition.

Our framework enables the developers to specify application specific fitness functions. In addition, it accepts a preferred population size, but adaptively changes it at run-time based on the measured fitness values. Furthermore, the framework is responsible for terminating the experiment when the newly generated variants do not provide improvements over a certain threshold.

Selection. Selection is the process of identifying, at each iteration, a finite number of chromosomes in the population that survive, i.e., that are considered in the next iteration. Several possible strategies have been discussed in the literature. For example, the tournament strategy divides chromosomes into groups. Only the best one in each group (i.e., the one with the highest fitness value) wins the tournament and survives to the next iteration. Conversely, the threshold selection strategy selects all and only the chromosomes whose fitness value is higher than a given threshold. Traditional A/B testing, as described in Section 2, corresponds to the tournament strategy when the population size is limited to two chromosomes. Our framework supports several different strategies. This enables for more complex decision schemes than in traditional A/B testing (e.g., by comparing several variants concurrently). At the same time, selection strategies relieve the developer from manually selecting variants during A/B testing.

Crossover & Mutation. Crossover and mutation contribute to the generation of new variants. Crossover randomly selects two chromosomes from the population and generates new ones by combining them. Mutation produces instead a new chromosome (i.e., a new variant) starting from an existing one by randomly mutating some of its genes. One of the key roles of mutation is to widen the scope of exploration, thus trying to avoid converging to local minima. In traditional A/B testing, the process of generating new variants of a program is performed manually by the developers. Thanks to the crossover and mutation steps of genetic algorithms, also this critical activity is completely automated.

The architecture described so far represents a first concrete implementation of an automated solution to the A/B testing problem. This contributes to overcome some of the burdens of manual A/B testing discussed in Section 2. However, it is worth mentioning that some issues still remain open as exemplified hereafter. First, the behaviour of the architecture still needs to be configured by specifying several parameters (e.g., the population size, selection strategy, and the termination condition). Section 5 discusses some relevant scenarios that exemplify their role. Experimental campaigns on real users will be required to further study and tune them appropriately. Second, further investigations are required on the mapping between the automated A/B testing problem and our proposed architecture. As an example let us consider mutation. Its capability are highly dependant from the encoding of features. Currently, we support mutations among different values of primitive types and among different implementations of an interface. In the future we envision more complex forms of mutation that tries to automatically modify the source code (e.g., by swapping the order of some statements). Finally, even if we did not discuss the role of constraints (see Section 3) in our architecture, they can be easily modelled and integrated in genetic algorithms as demonstrated in literature (e.g., [6]).

5   Preliminary Validation

In this section, we provide an initial empirical investigation of the feasibility of automated A/B testing. To do so, we generate a sample program, we simulate different user preferences, and we study to which extent an automated optimization algorithm converges towards a "good" solution, i.e., a solution that maximizes the quality of the program, as measured through its assessment function. In our evaluation, we consider different parameters to model the preferences of users, the complexity of the program, and to configure the computational steps performed by the genetic algorithm.

Experiment Setup. For our experiments, we adopt the implementation described in Section 4. Our prototype is entirely written in Java and relies on JBoss AOP [2] to detect and instantiate features in programs and on the JGAP library [14] to implement the genetic algorithm that selects, evolves, and validates variants of the program at run-time. In our experiments, we consider a program with n features. We assume that each feature has a finite, countable domain (e.g., integer numbers, concrete implementations of a function). Furthermore, for ease of modeling, we assume that each domain D is a metric space, i.e., that we can compute a distance $d_{1,2}$ for each and every couple of elements $e_1, e_2 \in D$. To simulate the user preferences (and compute the value of the assessment function for a variant of the program), we perform the following steps.

1. We split the users into g groups. Each user u selects a "favourite" value $best_f$ for each feature f in the program; users within the same group share the same favourite values for all the features.

2. We assume that the assessment function of a program ranges from 0 (worst case) to 1000 (best case). When a user u interacts with a variant v of a program, it evaluates v as follows. It provides a score for each feature f in v. The score of f is maximum (1000) if the value of f in v is $best_f$ (the favourite value for u) and decreases linearly with the distance from $best_f$. The value of a variant is the average score of all its features.

Table 1. Parameters used in the default scenario

Number of features in the program	10
Number of values per feature	100
Number of variants evaluated concurrently	100
Number of user groups	4
Distance threshold	80% of maximum distance
Number of evaluations for each variant	1000
Stopping condition	10 repetitions with improvement < 0.1%
Selection strategy	Natural selection (90%)
Crossover rate	35%
Mutation rate	0.08%

Table 2. Results for the default scenario

Measure	Average	95% Confidence Interval
Value of the assessment function (Best)	810.9	11.7
Value of the assessment function (Average)	779.2	10.7
Number of Iterations	34.2	5.9

3. We set a distance threshold t. If the distance between the value of a feature and the user's favourite value is higher than t, then the value of the variant is 0.

Intuitively, the presence of multiple groups models the differences in the users' profile (e.g., differences in age, location, culture, etc.). The more the value of features differ from a user's favourite ones, the worse she will evaluate it. The threshold mimics the user tolerance: after a maximum distance, the program does not have any value for her. While this is clearly a simplified and abstract model, it is suitable to highlight some key aspects that contribute to the complexity of A/B testing: understanding how to select the variants of a program and how to iteratively modify them to satisfy a heterogeneous population of users may be extremely difficult. In addition to the issues listed in Section 2, a manual process is time consuming and risks to fail to converge towards a good solution, or it may require a higher number of iterations.

Default Scenario. To perform the experiments discussed in the remainder of this section, we defined a default scenario with the parameters listed in Table 1. Next, we investigate the impact of each parameter in the measured results. For space reasons, we report here only the most significant findings.

Our default scenario considers a program with 10 different features, each one selecting values from a finite domain of 100 elements. At each iteration, we concurrently evaluate 100 program variants, submitting each variant to 1000 random users. Users are clustered into 4 different groups. They do not tolerate features whose distance from their favourite value is higher than 80% of the maximum distance. At each iteration, the genetic algorithm keeps the number of chromosomes (i.e., program variants) fixed. We adopt a natural selection strategy that selects the best 90% chromosomes to survive for the next generation. Selected chromosomes are combined with a crossover rate of 35% and modified using a

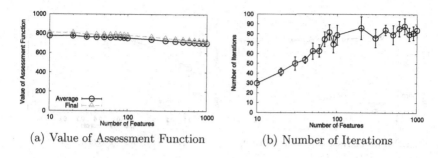

(a) Value of Assessment Function   (b) Number of Iterations

Fig. 3. Impact of the complexity of the program

mutation rate of 0.08%. The process stops when the improvement in fitness value is lower than 0.1% for 10 subsequent iterations.

In each experiment, we measure the number of iterations performed by the genetic algorithm, the value of the assessment function for the selected variant, and the average value of the assessment function for all the variants used in the iterative step. The first value tells us how long the algorithm needs to run before providing a result. The second value represents the quality of the final solution. Finally, the third value represents the quality of the solutions proposed to the users during the iterative process. In A/B testing, this value is extremely important: consider for example an e-commerce Web application, in which the developer wants to maximize the number of purchases performed by users. Not only the final version of the application is important, but also all the intermediate versions generated during the optimization process: indeed, they may be running for long time to collect feedback from the users and may impact on the revenue of the application. We repeated each experiment 10 times, with different random seeds to generate the features of the program, the user preferences, and the selection, crossover, and mutation steps. In the graph below, we show the average value of each measure and the 95% confidence interval.

Table 2 shows the results we measured in our default scenario. Despite the presence of 4 user groups with different requirements, the algorithm converges towards a solution that provides a good average quality. We manually checked the solutions proposed by the algorithm and verified that they always converged to near-optimal values for the given user preferences. The average value of the assessment function during the optimization process is particularly interesting: it is very close to the final solution, meaning that the algorithm converges fast towards good values. Although the average number of iterations is 34.2, the last iterations only provide incremental advantages. As discussed above, this is a key aspect for A/B testing, since developers want to maximize the revenue of an application during the optimization process.

Complexity of the Program. In this section, we analyze how the results change with the complexity of the program, i.e., with the number of specified features. Fig. 3 shows the results we obtained. By looking at the value of the assessment function (Fig. 3(a)), we notice that both the final and the average

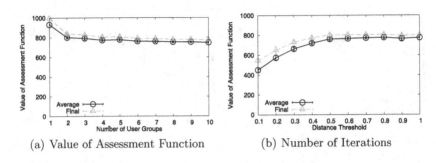

(a) Value of Assessment Function   (b) Number of Iterations

Fig. 4. Impact of the profile of users

quality decrease with the number of features. This is expected, since a higher number of features increases the probability that at least one is outside the maximum distance from the user's preferred value, thus producing a value of 0. Nevertheless, even in a complex program with 1000 features, both values remain above 700. Moreover, the average value remains very close to the final one. Fig. 3(b) shows that the number of iterations required to converge increases with the number of features in the program. Indeed, a higher number of features increases the size of the search space. Nevertheless, an exponential growth in the number of features only produces a sub-linear increase in the number of iterations. Event with 1000 features less than 100 iterations are enough for the genetic algorithm to converge. These preliminary results are encouraging and suggest that automated A/B testing could be adopted with complex program with several hundreds of features.

Profiles of Users. In this section, we analyze how the profile of users impacts the performance of the optimization algorithm. Fig. 4 shows the results we measured by observing two main parameters: the number of user groups and the maximum distance tolerated by users. For space reason, we show only the value of the assessment function: the number of iterations did not change significantly during these experiments. Fig. 4(a) shows that the value of the assessment function decreases with the number of user groups. Indeed, a higher number of groups introduces heterogeneous preferences and constraints. Finding a suitable variant that maximizes the user satisfaction becomes challenging. With one group, the solution proposed by the genetic algorithm is optimal, i.e., it selects all the preferred features of the users in the group. This is not possible in presence of more than one group, due to differences in requirements. Nevertheless, the quality of the solution remains almost stable when considering from 2 to 10 user groups. Finally, also in this case, the average value of the assessment function remains very close to the final one. Fig. 4(b) shows how the selectivity of users influences the results. When reducing the maximum tolerated difference, it becomes more and more difficult to find a solution that satisfies a high number of users. Because of this, when considering a threshold of only 10% of the maximum distance, the final solution can satisfy only a fraction of the users. Thus, the quality of the solution drops below 600.

Discussion. Although based on a synthetic and simple model of the users' preferences, the analysis above highlights some important aspects of A/B testing. First, our experiments confirmed and emphasized some key problems in performing manual A/B testing: in presence of heterogeneous user groups, with different preferences and constraints, devising a good strategy for evolving and improving the program is extremely challenging. Most importantly for the goal of this paper, our analysis suggests that an automated solution is indeed possible and worth investigating. Indeed, in all the experiments we performed, the genetic algorithm was capable to converge towards a good solution. Moreover, it always converged within a small number of steps (less than 100, even in the most challenging scenarios we tested). Furthermore, intermediate variants of the programs adopted during the optimization process were capable of providing good values for the assessment function. This is relevant when considering live experiments, in which intermediate programs are shown to the users: providing good satisfaction of users even in this intermediate phase may be crucial to avoid loss of customs and revenues.

6 Related Work

The SBSE [7] community focused its research efforts on several relevant software engineering challenges covering all the various steps in the software lifecycle ranging from requirements engineering [17], design [16], testing [4], and even maintenance [15]. However, despite all valuable these research efforts, the problem of evolving and refining systems after their deployment – in particular in the domain of user-intensive systems – received very little attention so far and, at the best of our knowledge, this is the very first attempt to introduce this problem in the SBSE community.

Concerning instead the research on A/B testing we can mention many interesting related efforts. For example, Crook et al. [5] discuss seven pitfalls to avoid in A/B testing on the Web. Analogously, Kohavi et al. [9,12] discuss the complexity of conducting sound and effective A/B testing campaigns. To support developers in this complex activity, Kohavi et al. [11] also provided a practical tutorial. Worth mentioning is also [10], which discusses online experiments on large scale scenarios. Finally, worth mentioning is the Javascript project Genetify [1]. The project represents a preliminary effort to introduce genetic algorithms in A/B testing and demonstrates how practitioners actually demand for methods and tools for automated A/B testing as claimed in the motivation of this paper. However, this project is quite immature and does not exploit all the potentials of genetic algorithms as we propose in this paper: it only supports the evolution of HTML pages in Web applications.

7 Conclusions

In this paper we tackled the problem of automating A/B testing. We formalized A/B testing as a SBSE problem and we proposed an initial prototype that relies on aspect-oriented programming and genetic algorithms. We provided two important contributions. On the one hand, we used our prototype to demonstrate the practical feasibility of automated A/B testing through a set of synthetic experiments. On the other hand, we provided the SBSE community with a novel domain where its expertise can be applied. As future work, we plan to test our approach on real users and to refine the proposed approach with customized mutation operators (e.g., changes to the source code) and full support for constraints.

References

1. Genetify, https://github.com/gregdingle/genetify/wiki (accessed February 25, 2014)
2. JBoss AOP, http://www.jboss.org/jbossaop (accessed February 25, 2014)
3. The A/B Test: Inside the Technology Thats Changing the Rules of Business, http://www.wired.com/business/2012/04/ff_abtesting (accessed February 25, 2014)
4. Afzal, W., Torkar, R., Feldt, R.: A systematic review of search-based testing for non-functional system properties. Inf. Softw. Technol. (2009)
5. Crook, T., Frasca, B., Kohavi, R., Longbotham, R.: Seven pitfalls to avoid when running controlled experiments on the web. In: ACM SIGKDD, KDD 2009, pp. 1105–1114. ACM, New York (2009)
6. Deb, K.: An efficient constraint handling method for genetic algorithms. Computer Methods in Applied Mechanics and Engineering 186(2-4), 311–338 (2000)
7. Harman, M., Jones, B.F.: Search-based software engineering. Information and Software Technology 43(14), 833–839 (2001)
8. Kiczales, G., Lamping, J., Mendhekar, A., Maeda, C., Lopes, C., Loingtier, J.-M., Irwin, J.: Aspect-oriented programming. In: Akşit, M., Matsuoka, S. (eds.) ECOOP 1997. LNCS, vol. 1241, pp. 220–242. Springer, Heidelberg (1997)
9. Kohavi, R., Deng, A., Frasca, B., Longbotham, R., Walker, T., Xu, Y.: Trustworthy online controlled experiments: Five puzzling outcomes explained. In: ACM SIGKDD, pp. 786–794. ACM (2012)
10. Kohavi, R., Deng, A., Frasca, B., Walker, T., Xu, Y., Pohlmann, N.: Online controlled experiments at large scale. In: ACM SIGKDD, KDD 2013, pp. 1168–1176. ACM, New York (2013)
11. Kohavi, R., Henne, R.M., Sommerfield, D.: Practical guide to controlled experiments on the web: Listen to your customers not to the hippo. In: ACM SIGKDD, pp. 959–967. ACM (2007)
12. Kohavi, R., Longbotham, R.: Unexpected results in online controlled experiments. ACM SIGKDD 12(2), 31–35 (2011)
13. Koza, J.R.: Genetic programming: On the programming of computers by means of natural selection, vol. 1. MIT Press (1992)
14. Meffert, K., Rotstan, N., Knowles, C., Sangiorgi, U.: JGAP - Java Genetic Algorithms and Genetic Programming Package (2014)
15. O'Keeffe, M., Cinneide, M.O.: Search-based software maintenance. In: Proceedings of the 10th European Conference on Software Maintenance and Reengineering, CSMR 2006, p. 10, 260 (March 2006)
16. Räihä, O.: A survey on search-based software design. Computer Science Review 4(4), 203–249 (2010)
17. Zhang, Y., Finkelstein, A., Harman, M.: Search based requirements optimisation: Existing work and challenges. In: Rolland, C. (ed.) REFSQ 2008. LNCS, vol. 5025, pp. 88–94. Springer, Heidelberg (2008)

Random-Weighted Search-Based Multi-objective Optimization Revisited

Shuai Wang[1, 2], Shaukat Ali[1], and Arnaud Gotlieb[1]

[1]Certus Software V&V Center, Simula Research Laboratory, Norway
[2]Department of Informatics, University of Oslo, Norway
{shuai,shaukat,arnaud}@simula.no

Abstract. Weight-based multi-objective optimization requires assigning appropriate weights using a weight strategy to each of the objectives such that an overall optimal solution can be obtained with a search algorithm. Choosing weights using an appropriate weight strategy has a huge impact on the obtained solutions and thus warrants the need to seek the best weight strategy. In this paper, we propose a new weight strategy called Uniformly Distributed Weights (*UDW*), which generates weights from uniform distribution, while satisfying a set of user-defined constraints among various cost and effectiveness measures. We compare *UDW* with two commonly used weight strategies, i.e., Fixed Weights (*FW*) and Randomly-Assigned Weights (*RAW*), based on five cost/effectiveness measures for an industrial problem of test minimization defined in the context of Video Conferencing System Product Line developed by Cisco Systems. We empirically evaluate the performance of *UDW*, *FW*, and *RAW* in conjunction with four search algorithms ((1+1) Evolutionary Algorithm (EA), Genetic Algorithm, Alternating Variable Method, and Random Search) using the industrial case study and 500 artificial problems of varying complexity. Results show that *UDW* along with (1+1) EA achieves the best performance among the other combinations of weight strategies and algorithms.

Keywords: Uniformly distributed weights, multi-objective optimization, search algorithms.

1 Introduction

A weight-based multi-objective optimization problem requires finding an optimal set of weights for all the objectives, while satisfying the required constraints (e.g., the priority of various objectives defined by users) on weights capturing the complex tradeoff relationships among the objectives with the aim of finding an overall optimal solution for the problem. Such weight-based multi-objective problems have been solved efficiently together with search algorithms (e.g., Genetic Algorithms) in the literature [1-6]. As compared with other types of commonly used techniques (i.e., Pareto-based techniques) [1, 5], weight-based techniques offer the following advantages: 1) These techniques balance all the objectives to find an optimal solution rather than obtaining a set of non-dominated solutions thus eliminating the effort for users to

C. Le Goues and S. Yoo (Eds.): SSBSE 2014, LNCS 8636, pp. 199–214, 2014.
© Springer International Publishing Switzerland 2014

select among the obtained solutions; 2) These techniques are straightforward to implement with computational efficiency; and 3) When objectives have different priorities, weight-based techniques can tackle such situation easily by assigning customized weights to each particular objective.

In the literature [1], the following two weight assignment strategies are commonly used: 1) Assigning fixed weights (equal or unequal) to each objective, termed as *Fixed Weight* (*FW*) strategy in this paper; 2) Assigning random weights to each objective based on a set of pre-defined constraints, coined as *Randomly-Assigned Weights* (*RAW*) strategy. Even though these two strategies have shown promising results [1-4, 6], they still suffer from some limitations. With *FW*, it is rare that all objectives have equal weights and determining appropriate weights usually depends on domain-expertise. A potential solution is to ask users to specify a set of constraints among weights rather than giving exact values. With *RAW*, we observe that it does not guarantee equally-distributed uniformity of selection of weight, i.e., all the potential weights do not have the same probability to be selected. Since one set of fixed weights can determine a specific search direction, there may be no equivalent probability to choose various search directions to find an optimal solution [1].

To reduce the randomness in weight selection using *RAW*, we propose a new weight assignment strategy called *Uniformly Distributed Weights* (*UDW*), which generates weights from a uniform distribution, while meeting a set of user-defined constraints. The strategy gives an equal importance to the generation of weight for each criterion, while preserving the relative importance of criterion. Said otherwise, the goal is to keep the advantages of uniform random generation, while having priorities defined among the various criteria. We evaluate the proposed weight strategy *UDW* as compared with the *FW* and *RAW* using an industrial problem of test minimization for Video Conferencing Systems (VCSs) product line from Cisco Systems. Being specific, this test minimization problem is a multi-objective optimization problem having five distinct objectives: Test Minimization Percentage (*TMP*), Feature Pairwise Coverage (*FPC*), Fault Detection Capability (*FDC*), Average Execution Frequency (*AEF*), and Overall Execution time (*OET*). A fitness function defined on all these five objectives is used in conjunction with the following search algorithms: Genetic Algorithm (GA), (1+1) Evolutionary Algorithm (EA), and Alternating Variable Method (AVM) to compare the three distinct weight assignment strategies. Random Search (RS) is used as the comparison base line. Moreover, inspired by the industrial problem, we created 500 artificial problems of varying complexity to evaluate the three weight assignment strategies in conjunction with all the four algorithms.

The obtained results show that: 1) With *FW*, *RAW* and *UDW*, (1+1) EA significantly outperformed the other search algorithms; 2) With (1+1) EA, *UDW* significantly performed better than *FW* and *RAW*; 3) The performance of (1+1) EA and GA with *UDW* was significantly improved with the increasing complexity of problems.

The rest of the paper is organized as follows: Section 2 provides a relevant background on *FW* and *RAW*. Section 3 presents *UDW* strategy followed by the description of our industrial and artificial case studies (Section 4). Section 5 presents the empirical evaluation with an overall discussion and Section 6 addresses threats to validity. Related work is discussed in Section 7 and Section 8 concludes the paper.

2   Background

Fixed Weights (*FW*) assigns fixed normalized weights (between 0 and 1) to each objective [1]. These weights can be obtained from domain knowledge of experts. For instance, our case requires five weights (w_1, w_2, w_3, w_4, w_5) corresponding to each objective (*TMF, FPC, FDC, OET, AEF*).

    Randomly-Assigned Weights (*RAW*), inspired by Random-Weighted Genetic Algorithm (RWGA) mainly used for weight-based optimization [1], generates a set of distributed normalized weights for each objective while still satisfying the user defined constraints. For instance, we have a constraint $w_2 > w_1$ and using *RAW*, a random distributed value is first generated for w_2 from 0 to 1 and then another distributed value is generated for w_1 from 0 to w_2. At each generation when running search algorithms, each objective is assigned to a distributed normalized weight as above mentioned and meets all the defined constraints, i.e., the weights for each objective are dynamically changed during each generation until the best solution is found or the termination criteria for the algorithms is met. Using *RAW*, multiple search directions can be stipulated by assigning dynamic weights during each generation [1]. However, *RAW* cannot guarantee that each point within the range for weights has the same probability to be selected thus each search directions cannot be reached uniformly.

3   Uniformly Distributed Weights

Inspired by our previous work in [7], the Uniformly Distributed Weights (*UDW*) uniformly selects weights at random when these weights are subject to a set of defined constraints. Notice that solving this problem efficiently is challenging as sampling uniformly tuples of values from an unknown domain is not trivial. More specifically, the tuples of weights generated by *UDW* must satisfy: 1) all the user-defined constraints and 2) an equi-probability selection that guarantee that each search direction has equivalent probability to be reached[1]. Formally speaking, consider a multi-objective optimization problem P involving m optimization objectives $O = \{o_1, o_2, ..., o_m\}$, each objective has a specific weight, corresponding to the set $W = \{w_1, w_2, ..., w_m\}$. Relations among these objectives are captured by a set of n arithmetic constraints $C = \{c_1, c_2, ..., c_n\}$ over the variables in W. Notice that such constraints can be pre-defined by the users based on their particular domain expertise.

    The core idea of *UDW* lies in the pre-computations of subdomains of the input domain (formed by the Cartesian product of each individual weight domain) and consideration of subdomains out of which uniform random sampling is trivial. More precisely, using an arbitrary division parameter k, *UDW* first divides the input domain into k^m equivalent subdomains, where m is the number of weight variables. Second, a systematic refutation is used to eliminate subdomains that do not satisfy the constraints, and finally, uniform random generation of tuples of weights is realized by selecting a remaining subdomain and a tuple at random. Notice that the selected subdomain and tuple may still not satisfy the constraints, and thus rejection may still happen. But, the systematic refutation process would have eliminated most parts of the input domain that do not contain any solution (fully conflicts with the constraints).

The *UDW* algorithm (shown as below) takes as inputs, the set of weights W, the constraint set C, the division parameter k, and the length of the expected sequence of weight tuples (K), i.e., the number of generations during the search[1]. The output of *UDW* is a sequence of K weight tuples for W, called *WK*, such that the sequence is uniformly distributed over the solution set of C. Notice that *UDW* returns fail $(WK = \emptyset)$ when none of the weight tuples satisfy the constraint set C, which shows none of the solutions will be found for the optimization problem based on the defined constraints. The Algorithm works as follows: a weight tuples sequence (WK) is first initialized as empty *(Step 1)* and then the input space is divided into k^m subdomains, i.e., $\{WD_1, ..., WD_{k^m}\}$ *(Step 2)*. The refutation process eliminates a number of subdomains with respect to the constraint set C *(Step 3)*. The remaining subdomains (i.e., $\{WD'_1, WD'_2, ..., WD'_p\}$) are sampled uniformly and from them, uniform tuples of weights are generated at random until K sets are generated *(Step 4)*. Notice that at this step, only the generated tuples that satisfy the constraint set C are kept. The generated set of tuples K is returned and used to assign weights to each objective, in order to guide the search in the search algorithms *(Step 5)*. Notice that despite some similarities with the algorithm presented in [7, 8], our *UDW* algorithm is original in terms of uniformly generating random weights for multi-objective test suite optimization.

Algorithm *UDW*: Uniformly-Distributed Weight Strategy
Input: $W = \{w_1, w_2, ..., w_m\}$, $C = \{c_1, c_2, ..., c_n\}$, division parameter k (Integer)   and length of the expected weight tuples K (Integer)
Output: $W_1, W_2, ..., W_K$ for Objectives O or $\emptyset$
  Step 1: $WK := \theta$
  Step 2: $(WD_1, ..., WD_{k^m}) := Divide(\{w_1, w_2, ..., w_m\}, k)$;
  Step 3: forall $WD_i \in (WD_1, ..., WD_{k^m})$ **do**
      if WD_i is fully unsatisfiable w.r.t. C **then** remove WD_i from $(WD_1, ..., WD_{k^m})$;
  Step 4: Suppose $\{WD'_1, WD'_2, ..., WD'_p\}$ is the remaining list of domains;
  if $p \geq 1$ **then**
    while $K > 0$ **do**
        choose WD'_j uniformly and randomly from $\{WD'_1, WD'_2, ..., WD'_p\}$;
        choose W uniformly and randomly from WD'_j;
        if W satisfies C **then** add W to WK; $K := K - 1$;
  Step 5: return WK for Objectives O.

---

4   Case Studies

Industrial Case Study. Our industrial partner is a product line of Video Conferencing Systems (VCSs) called *Saturn* developed by Cisco Norway [8]. *Saturn* has several products, e.g., C20 (low end product) and C90 (high end product). Test suite minimization for testing a product is essential since it is practically impossible to execute all the test cases developed for the whole product line within the allocated budget [9, 10]. However, such minimization may have descendent impact on the effectiveness of testing (e.g., fault detection capability) when reducing the number of test cases. Thus, this minimization problem can be formulated as a multi-objective optimization

---

[1] Each generation requires assigning a new set of weights to each objective during the search.

problem that is well solved by various search algorithms [1, 5], i.e., we aim at reducing the cost of testing while preserving the effectiveness. We chose this problem to evaluate our proposed weight assignment strategy and such problem can be represented formally as: search for a solution s_k (a subset of the test cases) from the solution space S (all combinations of the test cases for testing a given product) to achieve the following objectives (i.e., maximum effectiveness and minimum cost): $\forall s_l \in S \cap \ s_l \neq s_k$:

$$Effectiveness(s_k) \geq Effectiveness(s_l) \text{ and } Cost(s_k) \leq Cost(s_l)$$

Moreover, three effectiveness measures were previously defined in [6]: *TMP* was used to measure the amount of reduction for the number of test cases as compared with the original test suite; *FPC* and *FDC* were defined to calculate the feature pairwise coverage (each feature represents a testing functionality for VCS testing) and fault detection capability achieved by a potential solution. More detailed definitions and mathematical formulas for these effectiveness measures can be consulted in [6]. Through more investigation with Cisco, an additional effectiveness measure called Average Execution Frequency (*AEF*) was defined to count the average execution frequency for a solution thereby measuring its priority and a cost measure called Overall Execution Time (*OET*) was defined to measure the execution time cost for the potential solution obtained by search algorithms. Moreover, a fitness function based on the cost/effectiveness measures was defined to guide the search. This fitness function converted multi-objective minimization problem into single objective problem based on the weight-based theory [1], which is shown as follows:

$$Fit\_F = 1 - w_1 * nor\ (TMP) - w_2 * nor\ (FPC) - w_3 * nor\ (FDC) - w_4$$
$$* \left(1 - nor(OET)\right) - w_5 * nor\ (AEF)$$

Notice $nor\ (x)$ is a normalization function, which is computed as follows: $x/(x + 1)$. A lower value of fitness function Fit_F (we called such value as Overall Fitness Value (*OFV*)) represents a better solution. Moreover, w_1, w_2, w_3, w_4 and w_5 are a set of weights assigned to *TMP, FPC, FDC, OET* and *AEF* respectively and are required to satisfying a basic constraint $\sum_{i=1}^{5} w_i = 1$ in addition to other constraints capturing tradeoff relationships among the objectives.

We chose four products C20, C40, C60 and C90 from *Saturn* that includes 169 features and each product can be represented by a subset of these features. Each feature can be tested by at least one test case. More specifically, C20, C40, C60 and C90 includes 17, 25, 32 and 43 features respectively and 138, 167, 192 and 230 test cases relevant for testing these products, respectively. Each test case tc_i has a success rate for execution ($SucR_{tc_i}$) for calculating *FDC*, an average execution time (AET_{tc_i}) for measuring *OET* ($OET = \sum_i AET_{tc_i}$) and an execution frequency (EF_{tc_i}) for obtaining *AEF* ($AEF = \frac{\sum_i EF_{tc_i}}{n_s}$, n_s is the number of test cases included in a specific solution). In summary, for *Saturn*, each feature is associated with 5-10 test cases and each test case is associated with 1-5 features with $SucR_{tc_i}$ ranging from 50% to 95%, AET_{tc_i} ranging from 2 minutes to 60 minutes and EF_{tc_i} ranging from 1 time to 50 times per week.

Artificial Problems. We further defined 500 artificial problems to evaluate the performance of *FW*, *RAW* and *UDW*. Notice that the artificial problems are inspired by our industrial case study but with expansion for generality. To achieve this, we first created a feature model containing 1200 features and a test case repository of 60,000 test cases. For each test case tc_i, three key attributes are assigned randomly, i.e., $SucR_{tc_i}$ ranging from 0% to 100%, AET_{tc_i} ranges from 1 minutes to 100 minutes and EF_{tc_i} ranges from 1 time to 100 times per week. Moreover, we created artificial problems with the increasing number of features and associated test cases for each feature, i.e., we used a range of 10 to 1000 with an increment of 10 for features number and each feature can be associated with test cases ranging from 5 to 45 with an increment of 10. Thus, 100*5 = 500 artificial problems were obtained in this way. Notice that such artificial problems are also designed based on the domain expertise of VCS testing and thorough discussions with test engineers at Cisco.

5   Empirical Evaluation

5.1   Experiment Design

Recall that our main goal is to minimize the test suite for testing a product with high effectiveness (*TMP*, *FPC*, *FDC* and *AEF*) while meeting the time budget (*OET*).

To generate suitable weights, it is of paramount importance to provide a set of pre-defined constraints in a given context. In our industrial case study, through the domain analysis and several thorough discussion with test engineers at Cisco, we observed that: 1) *OET* has the highest priority among all the objectives; 2) *FPC* and *FDC* are more important than *TMP* and *AEF*; and 3) *AEF* has the lowest priority among all the objectives. So we came up with five key independent constraints for the test minimization problem, i.e., $w_4 > w_2$, $w_4 > w_3$, $w_2 > w_1$, $w_3 > w_1$ and $w_1 > w_5$. Based on the defined constraints, specific weights for each objective can be generated using different weight strategies for the industrial case study and artificial problems.

Using the experiments, we want to address the following research questions:

RQ1: With each weight strategy (i.e., *UDW*, *FW* and *RAW*), which search algorithm achieves the best performance for each objective and *OFV*?

RQ2: With the best search algorithm, which weight strategy can achieve the best performance for each objective and *OFV*?

RQ3: How does the increment of the number of features and associated test cases influence the performance of the search algorithms along with each weight strategy?

Being specific, our experiment first compares each pair of the four algorithms with each weight strategy to determine which algorithm can achieve the best performance (RQ1). Afterwards, we choose the best algorithm and compare its performance with each weight strategy to evaluate whether *UDW* can outperform the other two weight strategies (RQ2), which also shows which combination of search algorithms and weight strategies can achieve the best performance. Notice that for industrial case study, we evaluate the values for each objective (i.e., *TMP*, *FPC*, *FDC*, *OET* and

AEF) and as for artificial problems, we only evaluate the values of *OFV* to assess the performance and scalability for the selected algorithms with different weight strategies. To address RQ3, Mean Fitness Value for each problem ($MFV_{i,j} = \frac{\sum_{r=1}^{nr} OFV_r}{nr}$) is defined to measure the mean overall fitness value for a certain number of runs *nr* (in our case, $nr = 100$), where *i* is the feature number and *j* is the test case number ($10 \leq i \leq 1000$ with an increment of 10 and $5 \leq j \leq 45$ with an increment of 10). OFV_r is the obtained fitness value after the r_{th} run.

Moreover, Mean Fitness Value for Feature ($MFV\_F_i = \frac{\sum_{j=5}^{45} MFV_{i,j}}{5}$) and Mean Fitness Value for Test Case ($MFV\_TC_j = \frac{\sum_{i=10}^{1000} MFV_{i,j}}{100}$) are further defined to measure the mean fitness function in a given number of features or associated test cases. In this way, a specific MFV_F and MFV_TC can be calculated for each number of features and test cases and RQ3 can be addressed using statistical analysis.

In addition, for all the search algorithms, the maximum number of evaluation for the fitness function is set as 5000 and we collected the optimal solution after the 5000_{th} fitness function evaluation. For GA and (1+1) EA, the mutation of a variable is done with the standard probability $1/n$, where *n* is the number of variables. We used a standard one-point crossover with a rate of 0.75 for GA and set the size of population as 100. RS was used as the comparison baseline to assess the difficulty of the problems [11]. According to the guidelines in [11, 13], each algorithm is run for 100 times to account for random variation inherited in search algorithms.

5.2   Statistical Tests

To analyze the obtained result, the Vargha and Delaney statistics and Mann-Whitney U test are used based on the guidelines for reporting statistical tests for randomized algorithms [11]. The Vargha and Delaney statistics is used to calculate $\hat{A}_{12}$, which is a non-parametric effect size measure. In our context, $\hat{A}_{12}$ is used to compare the probability of yielding higher values for each objective function and overall fitness value (*OFV*) for two algorithms *A* and *B* with different weight strategies. If $\hat{A}_{12}$ is 0.5, the two algorithms have equal performance. If $\hat{A}_{12}$ is greater than 0.5, *A* has higher chances to obtain better solutions than *B*. The Mann-Whitney U test is used to calculate *p*-value for deciding whether there is a significant difference between *A* and *B*. We choose the significance level of 0.05, i.e., there is a significant difference if *p*-value is less than 0.05. Based on the above description, we define that algorithm *A* has better performance than algorithm *B*, if the $\hat{A}_{12}$ value is greater than 0.5 and such better performance is significant if *p*-value is less than 0.05.

To address RQ3, we choose the Spearman's rank correlation coefficient (ρ) to measure the relations between the MFV_F and MFV_TC obtained by the algorithms with different number of features and test cases [12]. More specially, there is a positive correlation if ρ is greater than 0 and a negative correlation when ρ is less than 0. A ρ close to 0 shows that there is no correlation between the two sets of data. Moreover, we also report significance of correlation using $Prob > |\rho|$, a value lower than 0.05 means that the correlation is statistically significant.

5.3   Results and Analysis

Results and Analysis for Industrial Case Study. Notice that due to limited space, all detailed results can be consulted in the technical report [18] (i.e., Table 4 and Table 5). We only present the key findings for each research question (RQ1-RQ2).

Results and Analysis for RQ1. Based on the obtained results (Table 4 in [18]), we concluded that all the three search algorithms (i.e., AVM, GA and (1+1) EA) significantly outperformed RS for each objective and *OFV* with each weight strategy (i.e., *FW, RAW* and *UDW*). Moreover, (1+1) EA achieved significantly better performance than GA and AVM for each objective and *OFV* (RQ1). In addition, AVM had significantly worse performance than GA for each objective and *OFV*. In summary, for each objective and *OFV* for the four *Saturn* products, the performance of the four algorithms can be sorted as (1+1) EA, GA, AVM and RS, from better to worst.

Results and Analysis for RQ2. Based on the results of RQ1, we chose the best algorithm (1+1) EA and compared its performance in conjunction with *FW, RAW* and *UDW* for each objective and *OFV* in the four *Saturn* products (Table 5 in [18]). According to the results, we concluded that (1+1) EA along with *RAW* and *UDW* significantly outperformed (1+1) EA with *FW* for each objective and *OFV*. Moreover, the performance of (1+1) EA with *UDW* was also significantly better than (1+1) EA with *RAW* for *TMP, FPC, FDC, OET, AEF* and *OFV*. Meanwhile, we report the average time used by each algorithm per run, i.e., 2.17 seconds for AVM, 1.78 seconds for GA, 1.55 seconds for (1+1) EA and 1.20 seconds for RS, which shows running search algorithms require similar effort (i.e., time) as compared with RS. In summary, we concluded (1+1) EA along with *UDW* achieved the best performance.

Results and Analysis for Artificial Problems. Recall that the evaluation for artificial problems is based on the overall fitness value (*OFV*) for each of the 500 problems. To answer RQ3, we calculated the spearman's rank correlation using mean fitness values *MFV_F* and *MFV_TC* (Section 5.1) for each algorithm with different weight strategies. The detailed results and analysis are discussed in detail as below.

Results and Analysis for RQ1. Table 1 summarizes the results for comparing the selected search algorithms with *FW, RAW* and *UDW* for the 500 artificial problems. Two numbers are shown in each cell of the table split by a slash. The first number in the column A>B shows the number of problems out of 500 for which an algorithm A has better performance than B ($\hat{A}_{12} > 0.5$), A<B means vice versa ($\hat{A}_{12} < 0.5$), and A=B means the number of problems for which A has equivalent performance as B ($\hat{A}_{12} = 0.5$). The second number after "/" in the column A>B means the number of problems out of 500 for which A has significantly better performance than B ($\hat{A}_{12} > 0.5$ && $p < 0.05$), A<B means vice versa ($\hat{A}_{12} < 0.5$ && $p < 0.05$), and A=B means the number of problems for which there is no significant difference in performance between A and B ($p \geq 0.05$) .We concluded the results as below.

   AVM vs. GA: AVM outperformed GA for on average 40.8% problems   (i.e., $(167+231+214)/3/500*100\% = 40.8\%$), but for 34.94% problems, AVM performed significantly better than GA. AVM performed worse than GA for on average 59.2%

problems and in 52.4% problems, AVM was significantly worse than GA. There were no significant differences between AVM and GA for 12.66% problems.

AVM vs. (1+1) EA: AVM performed better than (1+1) EA for on average 22.92% problems and 17.86% out of these 22.92% problems, AVM significantly outperformed (1+1) EA. On the contrary, for on average 77.06% problems, AVM performed worse than (1+1) EA and for 72.6% problems, AVM performed significantly worse than (1+1) EA. For 9.54% problems on average, there were no significant differences between AVM and (1+1) EA.

Table 1. Results for comparing the algorithms with each weight strategy for artificial problems

Weight Strategy	Pair of Algorithms	A>B	A<B	A=B	Best Algorithm
FW	AVM vs. GA	167/132	333/297	0/71	(1+1) EA
	AVM vs. (1+1) EA	121/98	379/344	0/58	
	AVM vs. RS	377/345	123/101	0/54	
	GA vs. (1+1) EA	134/115	366/348	0/37	
	GA vs. RS	364/331	136/112	0/57	
	(1+1) EA vs. RS	436/408	64/37	0/55	
RAW	AVM vs. GA	231/199	269/238	0/63	(1+1) EA
	AVM vs. (1+1) EA	107/76	393/376	0/48	
	AVM vs. RS	312/267	188/135	0/98	
	GA vs. (1+1) EA	195/164	305/276	0/60	
	GA vs. RS	397/340	103/63	0/97	
	(1+1) EA vs. RS	449/423	51/38	0/39	
UDW	AVM vs. GA	214/193	286/251	0/56	(1+1) EA
	AVM vs. (1+1) EA	116/94	384/369	0/37	
	AVM vs. RS	336/290	164/129	0/81	
	GA vs. (1+1) EA	172/149	328/302	0/49	
	GA vs. RS	369/323	131/105	0/72	
	(1+1) EA vs. RS	427/399	73/54	0/47	

AVM vs. RS: AVM outperformed RS for 68.34% problems with the three weight strategies on average but for 60.14% problems the results were statistically significant. There were no significant differences for 15.54% problems on average.

GA vs. (1+1) EA: For 33.4% problems on average, GA was better than (1+1) EA, but for 29.2% problems, GA was significantly better than (1+1) EA. Moreover, GA was worse than (1+1) EA for 66.6% problems and for 61.74% out of these 66.6% problems, GA was significantly worse than (1+1) EA. There were no significant differences between GA and (1+1) EA for 9.74% problems.

GA vs. RS: There were on average 75.34% problems, for which GA achieved better performance than RS with the selected weight strategies and for average 66.26% problems, GA significantly outperformed RS. Moreover, for 15.06% problems, there were no significant differences between GA and RS.

(1+1) EA vs. RS: In case of (1+1) EA, it performed better than RS for 87.46% problems. Out of these 87.46% problems, on average 82% problems, (1+1) EA was significantly better than RS. For 9.4% problems, there were no significant differences between (1+1) EA and RS.

Concluding Remarks for RQ1: Based on the results, RQ1 can be answered as follows: the performance of AVM, GA and (1+1) EA are all significantly better than RS with all the selected three weight strategies in term of finding an optimal solution for our minimization problem. Moreover, (1+1) EA outperformed GA and GA performed better than AVM together with all the weight strategies. In summary, (1+1) EA achieved the best performance for the three weight strategies in most of the problems.

Results and Analysis for RQ2. Table 2 summarizes the results for comparing *FW*, *RAW* and *UDW* with the best algorithm (1+1) EA for the 500 artificial problems. The data in the columns *A>B*, *A<B* and *A=B* is organized in the same way as in Table 1.

Table 2. Results for comparing the weight strategies along with (1+1) EA for artificial problems

Pair of Weight Strategies	A>B	A<B	A=B
FW vs. RAW	187/165	313/276	0/59
FW vs. UDW	119/91	381/364	0/45
RAW vs. UDW	197/175	303/276	0/49

FW vs. RAW: In conjunction with (1+1) EA, for 37.4% (187/500=37.4%) problems, *FW* outperformed *RAW*, but for 33% of problems, there were significant differences. On the contrary, *RAW* performed better than *FW* for 62.6% problems and for 55.2% problems, *RAW* was significantly better than *FW*. There were no significant differences between *FW* and *RAW* for 11.8% problems.

FW vs. UDW: For (1+1) EA, *FW* performed better than *UDW* for 23.8% problems, but only for 18.2% problems, *FW* significantly outperformed *UDW*. Moreover, the performance of *FW* was worse than *UDW* for 76.2% problems and for 72.8% problems, *FW* was significantly worse than *UDW*. Meanwhile, there were no significant differences between *FW* and *UDW* for 9% problems.

RAW vs. UDW: Combined with (1+1) EA, for 39.4% problems, *RAW* performed better than *UDW* and there were significant differences for 35.2% out of these 39.4% problems. *UDW* outperformed *RAW* for 60.6% problems and *UDW* significantly outperformed *RAW* for 55.2% problems. In addition, there were no significant differences between *RAW* and *UDW* for 9.8% problems.

Similarly, the average time taken by each algorithm is reported per run for the 500 artificial problems, i.e., 4.58 seconds for AVM, 3.96 seconds for GA, 3.41 seconds for (1+1) EA and 3.04 seconds for RS, which shows adapting search algorithms takes similar time as compared with RS.

Concluding Remarks for RQ3: Based on the above results, we can answer RQ3 as follows: along with the best algorithm (1+1) EA, *UDW* achieved the best performance among the three weight strategies and *RAW* outperformed *FW* significantly in most of the artificial problems, i.e., the *UDW* weight strategy in conjunction with (1+1) EA achieved the best performance in our context.

Results and Analysis for RQ3. Table 3 provides the results for Spearman's correlation analysis (ρ) between mean fitness value for feature (*MFV_F*) with the increasing number of features and mean fitness value for test case (*MFV_TC*) with the growth of test cases for the 500 artificial problems. Recall that a lower value of *MFV_F* or *MFV_TC* represents a better performance of an algorithm with a weight strategy.

Increasing Number of Features: For *FW*, *RAW* and *UDW*, we observed that the *MFV_F* values obtained by (1+1) EA and GA decreased significantly with the growth of feature number since all the ρ values were less than 0 and the values of *Prob* > $|\rho|$ were all less than 0.0001 (Table 3), i.e., the performance of (1+1) EA and GA significantly improved as the increasing number of features. For AVM, the *MFV_F* values also decreased when the number of features increases but such decrease was not statistically significant, i.e., AVM also performed better as the increasing number of features but not significantly. Finally, the performance of RS was worse with the growth of the number of features (not significantly) (Table 3).

Table 3. Spearman's correlation analysis for artificial problems

Weight Strategy	Algorithms	Increasing Features		Increasing Test Cases	
		Spearman ρ	*Prob>| ρ|*	Spearman ρ	*Prob>| ρ|*
FW	AVM	-0.07	0.4513	-0.06	0.5436
	(1+1) EA	-0.68	**<0.0001**	-0.13	0.6143
	GA	-0.65	**<0.0001**	-0.12	0.5841
	RS	0.12	0.4870	0.07	0.5323
RAW	AVM	-0.14	0.3764	-0.09	0.5134
	(1+1) EA	-0.71	**<0.0001**	-0.17	0.5670
	GA	-0.64	**<0.0001**	-0.08	0.6537
	RS	0.16	0.5137	0.18	0.5758
UDW	AVM	-0.09	0.6125	-0.10	0.4582
	(1+1) EA	-0.70	**<0.0001**	-0.14	0.4319
	GA	-0.69	**<0.0001**	-0.11	0.5762
	RS	0.09	0.4626	0.15	0.4240

Increasing Number of Associated Test Cases (*Increasing Test Cases* column): The *MFV_TC* values by AVM, (1+1) EA and GA decreased but not significantly with the growth of associated test cases, i.e., the performance of AVM, (1+1) EA and GA in along with all the weight strategies improved (but not significantly) with the growth of associated test cases. On the contrary, RS performed worse (not significantly) when the number of associated test cases increased (Table 3).

Concluding Remarks: Among all the weight strategies, (1+1) EA and GA performed significantly better as the increasing number of features and the performance of AVM and RS were not significantly influenced by the number of features. Moreover, the performance of all the selected search algorithms with the weight strategies are not significantly influenced by the increasing the number of associated test cases.

5.4   Overall Discussion

First, based on the results of RQ1 and RQ2, the reason why *UDW* performs better than *FW* can be explained as follows: 1) *FW* uses fixed predefined weights, meaning that the search space, which is the Cartesian product of all weights, cannot be fully explored. Actually, the optimal solution might not be found in this restricted search space explored in a single direction; and 2) *UDW* uniformly assigns random weights generated during each generation of a search algorithm, which allows the search algorithm to explore multiple directions.

Moreover, with uniformly distributed weights (*UDW*) at each generation, a search algorithm can be guided towards an optimal solution more efficiently than randomly generated weights (*RAW*). This may be because that *RAW* does not permit us to search uniformly at each generation, as the weights cannot be selected with the same probability, due to the presence of constraints. Consider two weights w_1 and w_2 from 0 to 1; for the sake of simplicity, but without losing any generality, we suppose that $w_1, w_2 \in \{0, \frac{1}{N}, \frac{2}{N}, ..., \frac{N}{N}\}$ and the following constraint holds: $w_1 > w_2$. Suppose that we have two distinct candidates for w_1 namely $w_1^0 = \frac{N_1}{N}, w_1^1 = \frac{N_2}{N}$,

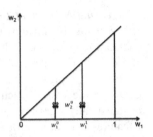

Fig. 1. An example for the probability of selecting weights

where $N_1, N_2 \in \{0,1,...,N\}$ and one candidate for w_2 called w_2^0 (the solution space of the constraint for w_1 and w_2 is represented as Fig. 1). Using *RAW*, if w_1^0 is selected first, the probability of selecting w_2^0 is $Prob(\{w_2^0|w_1^0\}) = \frac{1}{N} * \frac{1}{N_1}$, as the constraint $w_1 > w_2$ holds. If w_1^1 is selected, the probability of selecting w_2^0 is $Prob(\{w_2^0|w_1^1\}) = \frac{1}{N} * \frac{1}{N_2}$. As a consequence, the probability of selecting w_2^0 is not the same in both cases $(\frac{Prob(\{w_2^0|w_1^0\})}{Prob(\{w_2^0|w_1^1\})} = \frac{N_2}{N_1})$, meaning that the couples (w_1^0, w_2^0) and (w_1^1, w_2^0) do not have the same probability to be selected. Hence, there is no equi-probability when it comes to the selection of relevant search directions to find an optimal solution. Unlike *RAW*, *UDW* guarantees the equi-probability selection of w_2^0 whatever be the first weight value selected (i.e., $Prob(\{w_2^0|w_1^0\}) = Prob(\{w_2^0|w_1^1\}) = \frac{1}{\frac{N*N}{2}} = \frac{2}{N*N}$). Thus, each search direction has an equal probability to be reached and thereby, guiding search to find an optimal solution is more equally supported.

Followed by (1+1) EA, GA has significantly better performance than AVM. This can be explained from the fact that both of these algorithms are global search algorithms and thus managed to find global optimal solutions as compared to AVM, which is a local search algorithm. Notice that the performance of (1+1) EA is significantly better than GA and this may be due to the reason that (1+1) EA uses only mutation for exploring the search space as compared to GA which uses both mutation and crossover for exploration and exploitation of search space respectively requiring more generations to find a global optimal solution. By increasing the number of generations (5000 in the current experiment settings), we expect that the performance of GA can be improved, which requires further empirical evaluations.

For the experiments based on the 500 artificial problems, the results were consistent with our industrial case study (RQ1-RQ2). When we looked at the impact of varying number of features (10-1000) and associated test cases (5-45) on the performance of each algorithm along with three weight strategies (RQ3), we observed that (1+1) EA and GA performed significantly better as the increasing number of features, but for AVM and RS, the performance was not significantly influenced with the growth of features. Such interesting behavior can be explained based on the fact that (1+1) EA and GA are global search algorithms, which can still manage to explore the search space and find a global optimal solution even with the increased complexity (more features). On the other hand, AVM's performance (local search) cannot scale with the increased complexity since AVM can be guided towards finding local solutions in the search space but the global optimal solutions might be missed. Moreover, we observed that increasing the number of test cases improved the performance of all search algorithms except RS though not significantly. This phenomenon may be due to the following two reasons: 1) Complexity of test minimization problem for a product is directly related to the number of features and thus increasing the test cases may not affect the performance of the search algorithms; 2) Increased number of test cases means that a feature can be tested with more test cases and thus increases the solution space within the entire search space, i.e., search algorithms can find solutions with better fitness since more solutions are available (though not statistically significant).

In summary, (1+1) EA along with *UDW* weight strategy achieved the best performance in our experiments and thus is suitable for test minimization problem in our industrial context. Moreover, the results suggest weights selected by domain experts might not be accurate to obtain an optimal test minimization solution in practice and thus automated weight strategies such as *UDW* are needed for an optimal solution.

6   Threats to Validity

A prominent construct validity threat is related to the measure used to compare the various algorithms and to avoid such threat we used the measured fitness value, which is comparable across all selected search algorithms. Another common construct threat to validity is the use of termination criterion for the search. In our experiments, we used number of fitness evaluations comparable across all the algorithms.

When using search algorithms, parameter settings may affect the performance of the algorithms (internal validity). In this direction, we used default parameter settings for all the algorithms and these settings have demonstrated promising results [13]. In addition, the complexity of *UDW* in the general case is exponential in the number of weight variables in the problem (i.e., $O(k^m)$) where k is an arbitrary division parameter and m is the number of weight variables). This is a limitation if one wants to consider optimization problem with more than 20 independent objectives ($m > 20$) but our experience with both academic and industrial case studies show that the number of considered objectives never goes up to seven. Consequently, this potential exponential blow-up is not considered as a threat to our approach in practice.

A common conclusion validity threat is due to random variation inherited in search algorithms and thus we repeated our experiments 100 times to reduce the probability that the results were obtained by chance. Moreover, we used appropriate statistical tests for analyzing the data, i.e., Vargha and Delaney, Mann-Whitney U test and Spearman's rank correlation coefficient based on the guideline proposed in [11].

Generalization to new case studies is required to increase the confidence on the results (external validity) and we conducted an empirical evaluation using 500 artificial problems besides an industrial case study and obtained consistent results.

7   Related Works

A comprehensive review for search-based software engineering (SBSE) is available in [5]. In particular, Harman listed a set of potential objectives used for multi-objective test optimization in regression testing [16], which have been extensively studied in the existing literature [14]. In [15], a two-objective problem (i.e., code coverage and execution time) is converted into a single-objective problem for test prioritization using an arithmetical combination of weights for the fitness function. However, there are at least two main differences with our work: 1) The *UDW* approach is not restricted to two criteria and can actually takes any number of test objectives into consideration (e.g., *TMP*, *FDC* and *AEF*) and 2) *UDW* is parameterized by a set of constraints for which it can provide a uniform sampling of weight values, which turns out to be essential when looking at the performance of various search algorithms (e.g., (1+1) EA). As compared with our previous work [6], the motivation in this paper is different. The determination of an appropriate weight assignment strategy using weight-based search algorithms turns out to be crucial to obtain an optimal solution, especially when determining the best possible weights is impossible [1].

In addition, a simple algorithm can be used alternatively to sample values uniformly at random in the presence of constraints. For example, [17] reported on such an algorithm: 1) firstly, it generates tuples of values randomly while ignoring the constraints; 2) secondly, it uses a linear constraint solver (e.g., the Simplex algorithm) to reject the generated tuples that do not satisfy the pre-defined constraints. Even if this approach is appealing by its simplicity, it does not scale up to large dimensions as shown in [7]. In fact, as soon as the constraints become complex (relational, non-linear, mixed integer-real), the number of rejected tuples grows up to a point where the number of calls to the constraint solver is intractable. Note also that using constraint propagation and refutation instead of the Simplex algorithm opens the door to the treatment of non-linear constraints (e.g., $w_1 * w_2 < 1$) but it is also incomplete to determine the exact shape of the solution space.

Moreover, the proposed *UDW* technique is inspired from the Path-Oriented Random Testing (PRT) approach used in the context of code-based testing [7]. Even if the algorithm used to randomly generate uniformly distributed samples is similar to the one used in PRT, we see a main difference, i.e., according to our knowledge, using uniformly random distributed weights when constraints among weights are involved in search-based test minimization has never been explored before. Expressing constraints over weights is a key aspect of the proposed *UDW* technique as it releases test engineers from the tedious task of determining exact values to the weights, while preserving the benefits of *RAW*-approaches of search-based test minimization.

8   Conclusion and Future Work

In this paper, we proposed a new weight assignment strategy called Uniformly Distributed Weights (*UDW*) to generate weights by solving constraints among them with uniform distribution for solving multi-objective optimization problems. *UDW* can guarantee the uniformity for the selection of weights at the same time meeting all the required constraints based on the domain knowledge and expertise. We compared the proposed *UDW* with two commonly-used weight strategies (i.e., Fixed Weights (*FW*) and Randomly-Assigned Weights (*RAW*)) in conjunction with the following search algorithms: (1+1) Evolutionary Algorithm (EA), Genetic Algorithm, Alternating Variable Method, and Random Search based on our industrial problem of test minimization in the context of product lines. For test minimization, a fitness function was defined based on various cost/effectiveness measures (e.g., feature pairwise coverage) identified through our industrial collaboration with Cisco Systems. We performed our empirical evaluation using a Video Conferencing Systems product line provided by Cisco Systems and 500 artificial problems of varying complexity. The results showed that (1+1) EA performs the best among all the algorithms together with *UDW* and thus we conclude that assigning weights based on uniform distribution can significantly improve the performance of (1+1) EA for multi-objective optimization, particularly for multi-objective test minimization in the context of product lines.

In the future, we plan to replicate our experiments in other industrial case studies for assessing the proposed weight strategy *UDW*. We also plan to investigate the effect of uniformly distributed weights on a diverse range of search algorithms.

References

1. Konak, A., Coit, D.W., Smith, A.E.: Multi-objective optimization using genetic algorithms: A tutorial. Reliability Engineering & System Safety (91), 992–1007 (2006)
2. Marler, R.T., Arora, J.S.: Survey of multi-objective optimization methods for engineering. Struct Multidisc Optim. 26, 369–395 (2005)
3. Jin, Y., Okabe, T., Sendhoff, B.: Adapting weighted aggregation for multiobjective evolution strategies. In: Zitzler, E., Deb, K., Thiele, L., Coello Coello, C.A., Corne, D.W. (eds.) EMO 2001. LNCS, vol. 1993, pp. 96–110. Springer, Heidelberg (2001)
4. Murata, T., Ishibuchi, H., Tanaka, H.: Multi-objective genetic algorithm and its applications to flowshop scheduling. Computer & Industrial Engineer. 30(4), 957–968 (1996)
5. Harman, M., Mansouri, S.A., Zhang, Y.: Search Based Software Engineering: A Comprehensive Analysis and Review of Trends Techniques and Applications, Technical Report TR-09-03, King College London (2009)
6. Wang, S., Ali, S., Gotlieb, A.: Minimizing Test Suites in Software Product Lines Using Weighted-based Genetic Algorithms. In: Proceedings of the Genetic and Evolutionary Computation Conference (GECCO), pp. 1493–1500 (2013)
7. Gotlieb, A., Petit, M.: A uniform random test data generator for path testing. The Journal of Systems and Software 83(12), 2618–2626 (2010)
8. Cisco Systems TelePresence codec c90 (2010)
9. Wang, S., Gotlieb, A., Ali, S., Liaaen, M.: Automated Selection of Test Cases using Feature Model: An Industrial Case Study. In: Moreira, A., Schätz, B., Gray, J., Vallecillo, A., Clarke, P. (eds.) MODELS 2013. LNCS, vol. 8107, pp. 237–253. Springer, Heidelberg (2013)

10. Wang, S., Ali, S., Yue, T., Liaaen, M.: Using Feature Model to Support Model-Based Testing of Product Lines: An Industrial Case Study. In: Proceedings of International Conference of Software Quality (QSIC), pp. 75–84 (2013)

11. Arcuri, A., Briand, L.C.: A Practical Guide for Using Statistical Tests to Assess Randomized Algorithms in Software Engineering. In: Proceedings of the International Conference on Software Engineering, pp. 21–28 (2011)

12. Sheskin, D.J.: Handbook of Parametric and Nonparametric Statistical Procedures (2003)

13. Arcuri, A., Fraser, G.: On Parameter Tuning in Search Based Software Engineering. In: Cohen, M.B., Ó Cinnéide, M. (eds.) SSBSE 2011. LNCS, vol. 6956, pp. 33–47. Springer, Heidelberg (2011)

14. Yoo, S., Harman, M.: Regression testing minimization, selection and prioritization: A survey. Software Testing, Verification and Reliability 22(2), 67–120 (2012)

15. Walcott, K.R., Soffa, M.L., Kapfhammer, G.M., Roos, R.S.: Time-Aware Test Suite Prioritization. In: Proceedings of the International Symposium on Software Testing and Analysis, pp. 1–12 (2006)

16. Harman, M.: Making the Case for MORTO: Multi Objective Regression Test Optimization. In: Proceedings of the International Conference on Software Testing, pp. 111–114 (2011)

17. Smith, N.A., Tromble, R.W.: Sampling Uniformly from the Unit Simplex. Technical Report. Johns Hopkins University

18. Wang, S., Ali, S., Gotlieb, A.: Random-Weighted Search-Based Multi-Objective Test Suite Optimization Revisited. Technical Report 2013-01 (2013),
    https://www.simula.no/publications/TR2013-01

A New Learning Mechanism for Resolving Inconsistencies in Using Cooperative Co-evolution Model[*]

Yongrui Xu and Peng Liang[**]

State Key Lab of Software Engineering
School of Computer, Wuhan University, Wuhan, China
{xuyongrui,liangp}@whu.edu.cn

Abstract. Many aspects of Software Engineering problems lend themselves to a coevolutionary model of optimization because software systems are complex and rich in potential population that could be productively coevolved. Most of these aspects can be coevolved to work better together in a cooperative manner. Compared with the simple and common used predator-prey co-evolution model, cooperative co-evolution model has more challenges that need to be addressed. One of these challenges is how to resolve the inconsistencies between two populations in order to make them work together with no conflict. In this position paper, we propose a new learning mechanism based on *Baldwin effect*, and introduce the *learning* genetic operators to address the inconsistency issues. A toy example in the field of automated architectural synthesis is provided to describe the use of our proposed approach.

Keywords: Cooperative co-evolution, Baldwin effect, automated architectural synthesis.

1 Introduction

In many software engineering problems, one aspect of a problem is often related to other aspects [1]. In order to acquire better solutions for these problems, co-evolution mechanism is used to model these problems, and each aspect of the problems corresponds to an independent population. In co-evolutionary computation, there are mainly two different evolution models: one is *predator-prey* model, and the other is *cooperative* model [1]. The main difference between the two models is that each evolving population in predator-prey model evolves to acquire better solutions only for their own populations (e.g., test case population evolves in order to generate better test case only) and the relationship between different populations is competitive. On the contrary, in cooperative co-evolution model, all the populations evolve to acquire better solutions for the whole problem (e.g., in [2], one population represents developers' team staffing, and the other population is responsible for work package scheduling. The two populations co-evolve to achieve minimum completion time for projects).

---

[*] This work is partially sponsored by the NSFC under Grant No. 61170025.
[**] Corresponding author.

C. Le Goues and S. Yoo (Eds.): SSBSE 2014, LNCS 8636, pp. 215–221, 2014.

There are many existing work about predator-prey evolution model, especially in the area of testing, such as [3][4]. However, cooperative co-evolution model is not well explored in Search-Based Software Engineering (SBSE) until very recently [2].

Compared with predator-prey co-evolution model, cooperative co-evolution model has much more challenges when using it. One of these challenges is how to avoid the conflicts between populations that work together to generate the final solutions for the software engineering problems. Here, we take an example to illustrate this challenge briefly. Xu and Liang proposed a cooperative coevolution approach for automated architectural synthesis using patterns [5]. In their approach, there are two populations: one is responsibility population which is used for responsibility synthesis (i.e., how to assign different methods and attributes from requirement specifications to different classes in object-oriented architectural synthesis), and the other is pattern population which is used for architectural pattern synthesis (i.e., how to implement a given pattern in architecture level). When synthesizing the candidate architectural solutions with the individuals from the two cooperative populations, the conflicts may appear. For example, method A and method B belong to the same class in an individual of responsibility population, whilst these two methods belong to different layers in an individual of pattern population (we simply suppose that Layer pattern is used). As methods in the same class should not belong to different layers in Layer pattern, this inconsistency should be resolved before a candidate architectural solution is synthesized with these two individuals. In the above example, the inconsistency occurs when two populations interact cooperatively, and this kind of inconsistency is specific to cooperative co-evolution model. As a consequence, special attention should be paid to resolve inconsistencies in using cooperative co-evolution model.

Recently, the community of SBSE has realized the importance of using Artificial Intelligence (AI) techniques (e.g., machine learning) to solve software engineering problems [6]. In this paper we propose a new learning mechanism, which is based on the Baldwin effect [7] original from the biological evolution field, to address the inconsistency issue in the cooperative co-evolution computation. In our approach, we extend the steps in each generation of evolution procedure with a new kind of genetic operator called **learning operator**, and we define four specific types of learning operators. We further use a specific type of learning operator to resolve the inconsistency issue in the automated pattern-based architectural synthesis as a toy example to show the use and effectiveness of our proposed approach. The contributions of this work are: (1) introduce a new genetic operator for individual learning in each generation, which extends the traditional genetic operators (e.g., selection operator, crossover operator, and mutation operator). This new operator is generic in cooperative co-evolution computation, and AI techniques can be integrated in the search process with this operator; (2) propose a new learning mechanism based on Baldwin effect for cooperative co-evolution computation, which can be used to resolve the inconsistencies between different populations. To our knowledge, it is the first attempt to investigate the learning relationship between different populations in the field of SBSE.

2   Approach

In evolutionary developmental biology, a character or trait change occurs in an organism as a result of its interaction with its environment. In [7], Baldwin proposed a mechanism for specific selection of offspring for general learning ability. Selected offspring would tend to have an increased capacity for learning new skills rather than being confined to genetically coded and relatively fixed abilities. This is a theory of evolutionary process known as Baldwin effect.

In [7], Baldwin observed that there are three different sorts of modifications to organisms which should be distinguished. The first one is rooted in the physical agencies and influences in the environment, which is called "physic-genetic". In nature, physical agencies and influences in the environment include all chemical agents, temperature changes, and so on. This kind of agencies works upon the organism to produce modifications of its form and functions. As far as these forces change the organism peremptorily, they may be considered **accidental**. One of the examples in biology is genetic mutation, and in the field of evolution computation, we can map this kind of modifications into the mutation operators, which are defined to introduce relatively small changes to individual solutions. Second, some "neuro-genetic" modifications arise from the spontaneous activities of the organism itself when it is carrying out of its normal congenital functions [7]. In plants, in unicellular creatures, and in very young children, we can see these variations and adaptations in a remarkable way. The commonality of these changes is that all of them have the **selective** property of the nervous system. In the field of evolution computation, we can map this kind of modifications into the selection operators and crossover operators. In addition, there are a set of "psycho-genetic" modifications which come from the conscious agency of the organism itself [7]. For instance, gregarious influences, maternal instruction, the lessons of pleasure and pain, and experience in the life may change the organism. This kind of modifications has the **intelligent** property, and has great influence on organisms in nature. However, in the field of evolution computation, there is no kind of genetic operators corresponds to this kind of modifications for individuals, which is widespread in nature.

On one hand, for co-evolution computation, each population acts as an external environment for other populations and individuals in one population can learn the experience from individuals of other populations, consequently other populations play a "conscious agency" role [7] of individuals in each population, which further leads to appearance of "psycho-genetic" modifications for individuals. On the other hand, in cooperative co-evolution, close relationships exist between populations, which are the root cause of appeared inconsistencies. Hence we introduce a new genetic operator called learning operator for intelligent learning of individuals, and this new genetic operator can be used to address the inconsistency issue. Fig. 1 illustrates an improved cooperative coevolution procedure, which introduces the new learning mechanism based on Baldwin effect.

Due to space limitation, we omit the details from Step 1 to Step 5, and Step 9, which are widely used in existing SBSE research. In the improved cooperative coevolution procedure, we add Step 6 to Step 8 to implement the learning mechanism for each population in cooperative co-evolution, and the inconsistencies between populations can be resolved in these steps. We introduce these steps (i.e., Step 6, Step 7, and Step 8) in detail in following sub-sections. A toy example in the field of automated architectural synthesis is provided in Section 3.

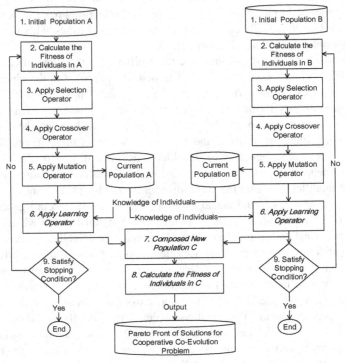

Fig. 1. The improved cooperative co-evolution procedure of our approach

2.1   Apply Learning Operator (Step 6)

In traditional population evolution, when Step 5 is completed, the next generation of each population is produced. But in our approach, the new produced generation of each population is regarded as a change impact for other populations, and each individual in any population should execute certain learning operations with a type of learning operator in Step 6. In this paper, we define four types of learning operators, which are similar to the types of traditional genetic operator (e.g., roulette wheel selection and tournament selection for the selection operator, and one-point and two-point crossover for the crossover operator): (1) *Lazy learning operator*. Similar to human beings that not all the people like learning, some individuals in a population are "lazy" in this step, which means they don't update their genes and remain the same representation. When using this learning operator, it follows the same procedure with traditional evolution for these individuals since no extra learning operation to be conducted; (2) *Localized learning operator*. In a society, people have different interests (e.g., the readers of this paper may be interested in SBSE, but may not be interested in software architecture), and they only care about the knowledge of their interested fields. In this step, some individuals in a population may do localized learning with this operator, which means they update their genes according to the knowledge of only a few individuals in other populations that they are interested. We may use AI techniques (e.g., classification and clustering algorithms) in this learning operator to decide what the "interesting knowledge" that an individual cares about is (e.g., we can define a similarity function to choose the most similar individuals, which possess the "interesting knowledge", in other populations for an individual); (3) *One-to-one learning operator*. Similar to the human communication that some people prefer one-to-one communication, individuals in a population may update their genes according to the knowledge of an individual in other populations, which can also be decided by AI techniques; (4) *Global learning operator*. Some individuals in a population may update their genes according to the knowledge contained in all the individuals in other populations. Statistics or probabilistic methods might be used with this type of learning operator to acquire the collective knowledge of the whole population. In summary, these learning operators are used to adjust and update the genes of individuals according to the knowledge from individuals in other populations except *Lazy learning operator*. Inconsistencies between individuals in different populations can be resolved during this learning step (one exception is that when some "lazy" individuals are composed in the next step, they will make a mistake for their "laziness" because inconsistencies appear. In this situation, these "lazy" individuals only need to re-apply another type of learning operator to resolve the inconsistencies).

2.2   Composed New Population and Calculate the Fitness (Step 7 & 8)

In Step 7, individuals from two population respectively should be composed to a set of new individuals, and these new individuals establish a new population (e.g., for automated pattern-based architectural synthesis problem, it is needed to compose the individuals from responsibility population and pattern population respectively in order to acquire the final solutions. The details can be found in [5]). When this step is completed, we employ the defined fitness function to evaluate the individuals in the new population in Step 8. In our improved cooperative co-evolution procedure, we distinguish the fitness functions in Step 2 and Step 8 explicitly. The former only evaluates an independent aspect of the software engineering problem, but the latter evaluates the problem itself in a cooperative way. For example, in automated pattern-based architectural synthesis [5], both responsibility and pattern populations have an independent fitness function for evaluating their individuals respectively, in which one fitness function measures the quality of responsibility synthesis results (i.e., individuals in responsibility population) and the other measures the quality of pattern synthesis results (i.e., individuals in pattern population), while there is a third fitness function that measures the quality of pattern-based architectural solutions (i.e., individuals in composed population).

3   Example

In this section, we show how to resolve inconsistencies in cooperative co-evolution using our approach with a toy example (a more detailed example can be found in [5] due to space limitation). We use automated pattern-based architectural synthesis that mentioned in the Introduction Section as the application domain of the problem, but our approach is generic for nearly all the software engineering problems using cooperative co-evolution, which is not limited to this specific problem.

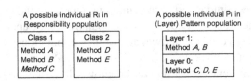

Fig. 2. An example of conflict in automated pattern-based architectural synthesis

As shown in Fig. 2, methods A, B, and C belong to the same class (Class 1) but are not allocated in the same layer (A, B are in Layer 1, and C, D, E are in Layer 0), and consequently the two individuals in responsibility and pattern populations are conflicting. We use the *One-to-one learning operator* to update the genes of the individual in responsibility population according to the knowledge of the individual in pattern population. For instance, in order to generate the next generation solution, R_i should learn the layer allocation information from P_i to update itself (or the other way round). After learning the genes of P_i, R_i knows that methods A and B should not be allocated in a class which contains any of methods C, D, and E. It is then found that the three methods in Class 1 (A, B, and C) of R_i have conflicts. As method C conflicts with both A and B, R_i decides to move C to another class (e.g., Class 2). The result of applying this learning operator to the individuals in responsibility and pattern population is shown in Fig. 3. The conflict is resolved between the two individuals after the learning operation, and we can compose them to an individual for the design problem.

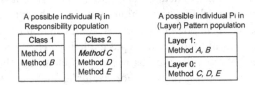

Fig. 3. The result of resolving an inconsistency between individuals using learning operator

4   Conclusions

In this paper, we propose a new learning mechanism for resolving inconsistencies in using cooperative co-evolution model, which is based on Baldwin effect. We extend the traditional genetic operators with the concept of learning operator which includes four types of learning operators. We describe the use of our approach using a toy example in automated pattern-based architecture synthesis. The approach can be applied to various software engineering problems that use cooperative co-evolution.

References

1. Harman, M., Mansouri, S.A., Zhang, Y.: Search-Based software engineering: Trends, techniques and applications. ACM Comput. Surv. 45(1), 1–61 (2012)
2. Ren, J., Harman, M., Di Penta, M.: Cooperative co-evolutionary optimization of software project staff assignments and job scheduling. In: Cohen, M.B., Ó Cinnéide, M. (eds.) SSBSE 2011. LNCS, vol. 6956, pp. 127–141. Springer, Heidelberg (2011)
3. Adamopoulos, K., Harman, M., Hierons, R.M.: How to overcome the equivalent mutant problem and achieve tailored selective mutation using co-evolution. In: Deb, K., Tari, Z. (eds.) GECCO 2004. LNCS, vol. 3103, pp. 1338–1349. Springer, Heidelberg (2004)
4. Arcuri, A.: On the automation of fixing software bugs. In: ICSE, pp. 1003–1006 (2008)
5. Xu, Y., Liang, P.: Co-evolving pattern synthesis and class responsibility assignment in architectural synthesis. In: ECSA (2014)
6. Harman, M.: The role of artificial intelligence in software engineering. In: RAISE, pp. 1–6 (2012)
7. Baldwin, J.M.: A new factor in evolution. The American Naturalist 30(354), 441–451 (1896)

Improving Heuristics for the Next Release Problem through Landscape Visualization

Richard Fuchshuber and Márcio de Oliveira Barros

PPGI/UNIRIO - Rio de Janeiro - Brazil
{richard.fuchshuber,marcio.barros}@uniriotec.br

Abstract. The selection of the requirements to be included in the next release of a software is a complex task. Each customer has their needs, but it is usually impossible to fulfill all of them due to constraints such as budget availability. The Next Release Problem (NRP) aims to select the requirements that maximize customer's benefit, while minimizing development effort. Visualizing the problem search space from a customer concentration perspective, we observed a recurring behavior in all instances analyzed. This work presents these findings and shows some initial results of a Hill Climbing algorithm modified to take advantage of this pattern. The modified algorithm was able to generate solutions that are statistically better than those generated by the original Hill Climbing.

Keywords: heuristics, next release problem, landscape visualization.

1 Introduction

The Next Release Problem (NRP) [2] involves selecting the software requirements to be included in the next release of a software so that benefits (such as customer satisfaction or revenue) are maximized while all constraints (such as budget and development time restrictions) are satisfied. This problem is faced by any company developing large and complex software used by many customers. This is a complex task [7] since each customer has their needs, and it is usually impossible to meet all of them simultaneously, mainly due to resource constraints.

In this work, we explore a novel fitness landscape visualization that has revealed a graphical pattern present in all NRP instances analyzed. We believe that this pattern can contribute to a deeper understanding of the NRP and its characteristics, enabling the creation of more efficient heuristics to find solutions for this problem. We also present a modified Hill Climbing algorithm that uses this knowledge to guide its search by narrowing the search space to a more promising region. Initial experiments have shown that the modified algorithm was able to generate solutions that are statistically better than those generated by the original Hill Climbing. We are not aware of any other work that has used a visualization of the NRP search space as a basis to guide the search process.

C. Le Goues and S. Yoo (Eds.): SSBSE 2014, LNCS 8636, pp. 222–227, 2014.

Besides this introduction, this paper is organized in five sections. Next, we present some background information about the Next Release Problem. The fitness landscape visualization used in this work is explained in Section 3. Then, the modified Hill Climbing algorithm is introduced in Section 4. Section 5 presents the design of the proposed experiment and its results. Finally, future work and conclusions are drawn in section 6.

2   The Next Release Problem

The NRP consists in finding the (close to) optimal subset of candidate requirements which maximize expected profits and whose total cost does not exceed the available budget [3]. The number of choices increases exponentially as the number of customers or requirements grow [2], fact that justifies the use of heuristic methods. There are multiple definitions for the NRP and, in this work, we adopted the mono-objective formulation proposed by Bagnall et al.[2], where the task is to find a subset of customers whose requirements would be included in the next release of a software.

Let S be all the customers related to the requirements R. Let W be the profit gained from satisfying each customer and C be the associated costs. Given a directed acyclic requirements dependency graph $G = (R, E)$, each customer $s_i \in S$ directly requests a set of requirements R_i. The profit of s_i is $w_i \in W$ and the cost of requirement $r_j \in R$ is $c_j \in C$. A predefined budget bound is b. The goal of the NRP is to find an optimal solution X^*, to maximize $w(X)$, subject to $cost(X) \leq b$ [8]. There are other definitions for this problem, with different objectives to be optimized. The NRP was also addressed using multi-objective search algorithms, as shown in Zhang et al.[9].

3   Fitness Landscape Visualization

Visualization is the process of transforming information into a visual form, enabling users to observe the information [4]. The resulting display enables us to perceive visually features which are hidden in the data. In the context of SBSE, it is common to attempt to visualize the fitness landscape of problems, as this visualization can be used to explore the properties of search spaces [5]. The landscape visualization was stated by Harman[5] as one of the open problems in optimization for software engineering. Lu et al.[6] state that fitness landscape characterization shows a lot of promise since it captures the nature of the relationship between the problem and the algorithm employed to solve it.

While investigating the NRP search space, we came across the charts depicted in Fig. 1. These charts were created by generating 100 random solutions for each possible number of customers, from one to the number of customers present in the instance. Each column in the chart is a boxplot representing the fitness values obtained by solutions with a given number of customers. The x axis represents the number of customers satisfied by a solution (i.e. the number of customers whose requirements are included in the solution) and the y axis represents the fitness value of this solution. We can observe an increase in the fitness value while the number of satisfied customers increases, up to a point where only infeasible solutions, represented by negative fitness values, are generated. There is also a transition area, where a mix of feasible and infeasible solutions can be seen.

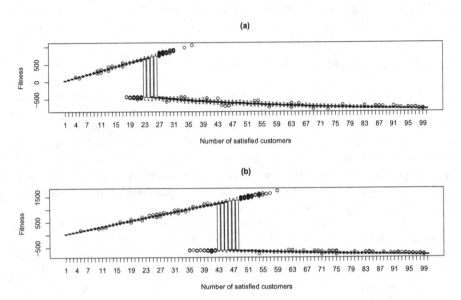

Fig. 1. Random sampling for the nrp-1 instance with a budget of (a) 50% and (b) 70% of the cost of implementing all requirements

The fitness value of each solution was used as input to the R statistical software to generate the boxplots. It is not possible to show other charts due to space constraints, but this interesting graphical pattern was observed in all NRP instances from Bagnall et al.[2] and Xuan et al.[8].

4   Modified Hill Climbing

This section presents a modified Hill Climbing algorithm that uses the graphical pattern shown in the previous section as a way to narrow the search space, focusing on more promising areas. The algorithm is based on the Hill Climbing defined as follows.

The search starts by creating a solution based on a random selection of customers. After the initial selection of customers, the solution fitness is calculated according to Bagnall et al[2]. The solution is stored as the best solution and the main loop of the search follows. The loop tries to find solutions with better fitness by adding or removing a single customer from the current solution at a time. Whenever a solution with higher fitness is found, it becomes the new best known solution and the trials are repeated from the first customer. If no movement is able to improve fitness, a random restart is triggered. The search stops after reaching a predefined number of fitness evaluations.

The proposed modification, named Visual Hill Climbing, differs from the classic Hill Climbing in two ways. First, a phase of random sampling is executed before the Hill Climbing starts. At this phase, several random solutions with S satisfied customers are generated, S ranging from one to the number of customers in the instance. The solution with the highest fitness becomes the best known solution and S is stored as a lower bound to the Hill Climbing algorithm.

After the random sampling is ended, the Hill Climbing is executed with a restriction: it can only visit solutions whose number of satisfied customers is within the range $[S, S+N*\alpha]$, where N is the number of customers in the instance and $\alpha \leq 1$ is a parameter to the algorithm. For example, if the best solution found during the random sampling has 15 satisfied customers and the instance has 100 customers, the modified Hill Climbing will consider only solutions whose number of customers is within the range $[15, 15 + 100 * \alpha]$. This restriction is used to make the algorithm concentrate in a region where, during the random sampling phase, solutions with high fitness values were found.

5 Experiments

To compare the results produced by the classic Hill Climbing with its variation proposed in this work while addressing the NRP, problem instances were optimized according to the problem formulation presented in Bagnall et al[2]. This section conveys the design of the experiment and its results.

5.1 Experimental Setup

For each problem instance under evaluation, the search was executed under four configurations, hereafter referred to as HC, visHC-10, visHC-20 and visHC-40. Configuration HC represents the classic Hill Climbing algorithm described in Section 4. The other configurations are versions from the modified Hill Climbing. They differ from each other by the α value. The α value determines the range of solutions that can be visited, as shown by the formula $[S, S + N * \alpha]$ (described in Section 4). The visHC-10 uses an α of 0.1, while the variations visHC-20 and visHC-40 use 0.2 and 0.4 as α, respectively.

Each configuration was executed 30 times for each instance. Each running cycle resulted in a single best solution whose profit was collected. The search stopped when a predefined budget of 10,000,000 fitness evaluations was consumed. This is the same budget used by Xuan et al.[8] for configuring a genetic algorithm. All configurations were executed in a single computer with an i7 Intel processor running at 3,4 GHz, 4 Gb of RAM, Windows 8.1 Professional, and minimal platform software required to run the Java implementation.[1]

---

[1] Source code available at
https://github.com/richardf/VisualNRP/releases/tag/v.1.0

The experiment was executed upon 15 randomly generated instances previously used by Bagnall et al[2]. Configurations were pair-wise compared in per instance basis. Larger profits denote that the configuration produces more effective results than its competing ones. These values were subjected to the non-parametric Wilcoxon-Mann-Whitney statistical inference test [1] to ascertain whether there was significant difference between configurations.

5.2 Experimental Results

Table 5.2 summarizes profit values observed for the configurations under analysis. The first column indicates the instance name. For each configuration, the fitness of the best solution found and the average fitness among 30 executions are shown. Table 5.2 also show p-values for pair-wise comparison between configurations HC and visHC-40.

Table 1. Results for the randomly generated instances

Instance	HC		visHC-40			visHC-20		visHC-10	
	Best	Avg	Best	Avg	pV	Best	Avg	Best	Avg
nrp1-0.3	1072	1024.47	1081	**1029.03**	0.65	**1088**	1020.17	896	836.43
nrp2-0.3	**3463**	**3237.60**	3331	3164.37	0.01	3301	3106.33	3166	3057.20
nrp3-0.3	**5026**	4710.77	4980	4779.03	0.01	4985	4814.30	4993	**4866.50**
nrp4-0.3	5951	5509.20	5946	5599.63	0.07	5927	5677.27	**5991**	**5759.93**
nrp5-0.3	14116	13797.30	**14355**	**13969.67**	<0.01	13002	12785.10	10198	9903.83
nrp1-0.5	**1732**	1629.53	1714	**1658.50**	<0.01	1651	1578.47	1434	1320.37
nrp2-0.5	6239	5995.37	**6322**	**6094.43**	<0.01	6180	5852.67	5089	4830.00
nrp3-0.5	9030	8893.53	9026	8883.87	0.64	**9187**	**8958.07**	9044	8935.87
nrp4-0.5	11684	11423.43	11841	11400.53	0.72	**12028**	**11490.27**	11724	11386.63
nrp5-0.5	21905	21597.60	**22479**	**22097.70**	<0.01	20873	20424.63	17891	17603.57
nrp1-0.7	2455	2413.63	**2467**	**2416.37**	0.84	2446	2343.57	2244	2107.50
nrp2-0.7	9796	9623.57	**10478**	**10100.33**	<0.01	9477	9093.83	8240	7685.00
nrp3-0.7	13693	13515.90	**13838**	**13661.83**	<0.01	13751	13642.97	13761	13651.43
nrp4-0.7	19390	19152.13	19444	19280.67	<0.01	19443	19237.77	**19501**	**19382.43**
nrp5-0.7	28678	28556.70	**28737**	**28638.37**	<0.01	28703	28632.13	28707	28622.27

The visHC-40 configuration outperformed the other configurations. When considering the best solution, the HC configuration got the best result three times, the visHC-40 configuration seven times, the visHC-20 configuration three times and the visHC-10 only two times. Regarding averages, the HC configuration got the best average only once. The visHC-40 got the best average nine times, visHC-20 twice and visHC-10 three times.

Comparing HC with visHC-40, the former got the best solution five times, while the later got it ten times. In respect to averages, HC won three times, of which only one case was statistically significant with a p-value ≤ 0.01. VisHC-40 outperformed HC for 12 out of 15 instances, nine of these comparisons being statistically significant at 99%.

6   Conclusion

The fitness landscape visualization proposed in this work revealed an interesting graphical pattern that was observed in the NRP instances commonly used by the literature. We believe that this pattern can be used to guide the search to more promising areas of the search space. In order to test this hypothesis, we proposed a modified version of a Hill Climbing that uses a phase of random sampling to narrow the search space. In initial experiments, this modified Hill Climbing was able to obtain solutions that are statistically superior than the solutions obtained by the original Hill Climbing.

Currently, we are investigating whereas this graphical pattern occurs in other NRP instances, indicating that it could be something intrinsical to the problem. We are also trying to determine the best value to the alpha parameter used by the proposed Hill Climbing and investigating other uses of this pattern that could lead us to more effective heuristics. The modification of other heuristics to explore this pattern remains as a future work, as well as comparisons with other algorithms applied in the literature.

References

1. Arcuri, A., Briand, L.: A practical guide for using statistical tests to assess randomized algorithms in software engineering. In: Proceedings of the 33rd International Conference on Software Engineering. ACM (2011)
2. Bagnall, A.J., Rayward-Smith, V.J., Whittley, I.M.: The next release problem. Information and Software Technology 43(14), 883–890 (2001)
3. Barros, M.: An experimental evaluation of the importance of randomness in hill climbing searches applied to software engineering problems. Empirical Software Engineering, 1382-3256 (2014)
4. Gershon, N.D.: From perception to visualization. Computer Graphics 26(2), 414–415 (1992)
5. Harman, M.: The current state and future of search based software engineering. In: 2007 Future of Software Engineering, pp. 342–357. IEEE Computer Society (2007)
6. Lu, G., Bahsoon, R., Yao, X.: Applying elementary landscape analysis to search-based software engineering. In: 2010 Second International Symposium on Search Based Software Engineering (SSBSE), pp. 3–8. IEEE (2010)
7. Sagrado, J., Aguila, I.M., Orellana, F.J.: Ant colony optimization for the next release problem: A comparative study. In: 2010 Second International Symposium on Search Based Software Engineering (SSBSE), pp. 67–76. IEEE (2010)
8. Xuan, J., Jiang, H., Ren, Z., Luo, Z.: Solving the large scale next release problem with a backbone-based multilevel algorithm. IEEE Transactions on Software Engineering 38(5), 1195–1212 (2012)
9. Zhang, Y., Harman, M., Mansouri, S.A.: The multi-objective next release problem. In: Proceedings of the 9th Annual Conference on Genetic and Evolutionary Computation, pp. 1129–1137. ACM (2007)

Machine Learning for User Modeling in an Interactive Genetic Algorithm for the Next Release Problem

Allysson Allex Araújo and Matheus Paixão

Optimization in Software Engineering Group, State University of Ceará
1700 Paranjana Avenue, 60.714-903, Fortaleza, Brazil
{allyssonallex.dpa,mhepaixao}@gmail.com

Abstract. The Next Release Problem consists in selecting which requirements will be implemented in the next software release. For many SBSE approaches to the NRP, there is still a lack of ability to efficiently include the human opinion and its peculiarities in the search process. Most of these difficulties are due to the problem of the human fatigue. Thus, it is proposed the use of a machine learning technique to model the user and replace him in an Interactive Genetic Algorithm to the NRP. Intermediate results are able to show that an IGA can succesfully incorporate the user preferences in the final solution.

Keywords: Interactive Genetic Algorithm, Machine Learning, Next Release Problem, Search Based Software Engineering.

1 Introduction

During an iterative and incremental software development process, there are some complex problems to deal with, such as selecting which requirements will be implemented in the next release. The term *release* is used to describe a stable and executable version of the system to be delivered to the client, in accordance to his preferences. Given this context, it may be mentioned the widely known Next Release Problem (NRP) [1], which is based on the maximization of the client satisfaction while respecting a predefined budget.

The current mono-objective SBSE approaches to the NRP can be considered as decision-making tools, where the requirements' selection for the next release is automatically made, without an effective participation of the requirements engineer. As a consequence, the users present a certain reluctance in accepting such results. Therefore, it seems that an inclusion of the requirements engineer in the search process can result in a proper strategy to handle the NRP, providing a search technique which is guided by his preferences.

Considering the difficulties in including the decision maker in general optimization techniques, one can highlight the Interactive Optimization. Such strategy is able to employ the human as a protagonist in the solution evaluation process, so that his knowledge and other psychological aspects are incorporated

C. Le Goues and S. Yoo (Eds.): SSBSE 2014, LNCS 8636, pp. 228–233, 2014.

in the search process [2]. This level of human interaction is specially needed when it is difficult to capture the evaluation function through mathematical models or when personal judgements are necessary [3].

The Interactive Evolutionary Computation, which is a branch of the Interactive Optimization, is supported by two key components, which are the human evaluation and computational search through Genetic Algorithms [4]. In spite of the fact that GAs are widespread in SBSE, there is still a lack of ability in using the human preferences in the search process. Thus, the Interactive Genetic Algorithm (IGA) is an alternative to handle this problem. The IGA follows the same concepts of a traditional GA, the difference is regarded to the solution evaluation process, where the solution judgement is performed by the user rather than a mathematical function [5].

Regarding the application of IGAs to requirements engineering problems, it can be pointed out the paper by Tonella et al. [6], which examined the use of an IGA in the requirements prioritization process. Its design aims to minimize the number of requirements pairs evaluations obtained from the user, making the approach more scalable and accurate regarding the requirements classification. It is also interesting to point out the work by Simons et al. [7], where it proposes the use the use of an interactive evolutionary approach alongside with intelligent agents to mitigate the difficulties of software design.

Despite the human involvement being interesting and attractive to the search process, it is also the cause of one of the most critical problems in interactive optimization approaches, which is the human fatigue [5]. This exhaustion occurs due to the repeatedly requests for user evaluations, which ends up being a major threat to the IGA evolution.

Therefore, this paper proposes the use of a machine learning technique to model the requirements engineer preferences during the use of the IGA for the NRP. This way, it will be possible to handle the human fatigue and still incorporate the subjective criteria throughout the search process.

The remaining of this paper is organized as follows: Section 2 specifies the proposed IGA and presents results of the empirical study performed to validate it. Section 3 explains the proposed machine learning modeling for the requirements engineer. Finally, Section 4 concludes and discusses future works.

2   An Interactive Genetic Algorithm for the Next Release Problem

Consider $R = \{r_1, r_2, \ldots, r_N\}$ the set of requirements. Each r_i has an importance value v_i and an effort cost c_i. The NRP model proposed in this work is presented next:

$$\text{maximize: } \alpha.score(X) + \beta.she(X) \tag{1}$$
$$\text{subject to: } cost(X) \leq budget \tag{2}$$

$$\text{where, } score(X) = \sum_{i=1}^{N} v_i x_i \tag{3}$$

$$cost(X) = \sum_{i=1}^{N} c_i x_i \tag{4}$$

where *budget* refers to the release available budget. The decision variable is represented by the vector $X = \{x_1, x_2, \ldots, x_N\}$, so that $x_i = 1$ implies that requirement r_i is included in the next release and $x_i = 0$ otherwise. The *score(X)* function (Equation 3) represents the total importance of the release. Similarly, the *cost(X)* function (Equation 4) represents the total effort cost of the release.

In the IGA application to the NRP, each individual is a release. The requirements engineer provides a "grade" for each individual throughout the IGA evolution. This "grade" is called *subjective human evaluation (she)* and represents the user preferences regarding the requirements selection (Equation 1). In this work, this value is given according to a numerical range previously established. When the release fully satisfies the user, the evaluation is maximum.

The approach used in this paper can be considered as a generalization of the work by Baker et. al [8]. When the weights in Equation 1 are configured to $\alpha = 1$ and $\beta = 0$, the classical NRP is reached.

An empirical study was conducted in order to evaluate the proposed IGA for the NRP. The following topics present the settings and results from this study.

2.1   Empirical Study Settings

The set of instances was randomly generated. The number of requirements varies from 50 to 200. There are no interdependencies between requirements and the importance of each requirement takes an integer value between 1 and 5. The effort cost of each requirement also varies from 1 to 5. The instance name is in the format I_R, where R is the number of requirements.

The *score(X)* value is normalized to the same range of *she(X)*. Such normalization is needed in order to avoid a possible overwhelm regarding the functions *score(X)* and *she(X)*. Thus, the only way to prioritize one of the functions is through the weights α and β.

In order to represent the requirements engineer, a simulator was developed. The main purpose of this simulator is not to faithfully simulate a human being, but rather demonstrate the influence of a certain evaluation profile in the search process. Based on the evaluation profile, the simulator defines a "target-individual", which represents what the requirements engineer would consider as an optimal release. The requirements to be included in the target-individual are chosen based on a certain percentage, which in this particular work was defined as 50%. Three differents evaluation profiles were considered: in the **Random** profile, the requirements are randomly defined. In the **Lower Score**, the requirements with least *score* are included. Similarly, in the **Higher Cost**, the requirements with highest cost are included.

Throughout the IGA, the evaluations for each individual are provided according to the similarity to the target-individual. If the individual's requirements are totally different from the target-individual, the evaluation is minimal. In the other hand, when the individual is equal to the target-individual, the evaluation is maximum. The evaluations are proportionally given for the other possibilities. For this empirical study, the minimum $she(X)$ is 0 and the maximum is 10.

Regarding the IGA settings, it was used a fixed amount of 500 individuals, 100 generations, 90% crossover rate, $1/N\%$ mutation rate, an elitism rate of 20% and *budget* equals to 60% of the maximum release cost. All parameters were empirically defined by preliminary tests.

Three weights configurations ($\alpha = 1, \beta = 0$; $\alpha = 0, \beta = 1$; $\alpha = 1, \beta = 1$) were considered. For each weights configuration and instance, the IGA was executed 100 times, collecting the average *similarity degree* of the final solution, which represents how similar is a candidate solution to the target-individual. Consider a set of 6 requirements with a target-individual [100011]. The possible solution [110110], for example, presents 3 equal requirements to the target-individual (r_1, r_3 and r_5), so this solution would present a *similarity degree* of $3/6 = 0.5$. The average of the non-normalized *score(X)* was also collected.

Therefore, the empirical study was conducted in order to answer the following research question:

RQ: What is the influence of the evaluation profile in the search process?

2.2   Results and Analyses

Table 1 shows the average of both *similarity degree* and *score* for each instance, each evaluation profile and different weights settings.

Table 1. Empirical Study Results

Instance	Attributes	RANDOM α, β			LOWER SCORE α, β			HIGHER COST α, β		
		1, 0	0, 1	1, 1	1, 0	0, 1	1, 1	1, 0	0, 1	1, 1
I_50	Similarity Degree	0.48	0.96	0.90	0.30	0.96	0.86	0.30	0.86	0.86
	Score	116.01	71.53	91.55	116.01	60.16	88.96	116.01	63.81	78.21
I_100	Similarity Degree	0.56	0.88	0.81	0.41	0.88	0.79	0.26	0.85	0.80
	Score	230.09	144.63	192.33	230.09	131.84	191.84	230.09	133.56	167.09
I_150	Similarity Degree	0.50	0.79	0.74	0.34	0.79	0.70	0.26	0.76	0.70
	Score	321.55	203.35	307.57	321.60	180.93	287.12	321.50	196.04	260.88
I_200	Similarity Degree	0.46	0.73	0.66	0.29	0.73	0.63	0.26	0.74	0.64
	Score	459.06	299.61	440.65	459.00	259.63	408.31	459.14	266.79	390.04

As can be seen, when the weights are configured to $\alpha = 1$ and $\beta = 0$, all instances present a high *score* value, but a considerably low *similarity degree*. This is due to the fact that only the *score(X)* is considered in the search process.

In contrast, when the weights are configured to $\alpha = 0$ and $\beta = 1$, only $she(X)$ is considered and the *similarity degree* is higher for all instances. Thus, the proposed IGA is able to incorporate the requirements engineer preferences in the solutions. Looking at the I_50 and I_100 instances, with the Random profile, the solutions present a *similarity degree* of 0.96 and 0.88, respectively. In this configuration, it is also clear the *score* values tend to be lower than the previous ones. This is due to the fact that in most cases the solution the requirements engineer considers as good, does not necessarily present a high *score*.

However, the presented approach also allows the configuration $\alpha = 1$ and $\beta = 1$ which aims at optimizing the user preferences and the *score* simultaneously. Such weights configuration can provide valuable insights regarding the trade-offs between *similarity degree* and *score*. This behavior can be seen in the instances I_150 and I_200 for the Lower Score profile, which present a *similarity degree* of 0.70 and 0.63, and *score* of 287.12 and 487.31, respectively.

The Lower Score and Higher Cost profiles are unusual in a real software development environment, but the proposed IGA could still incorporate these preferences in the final solution. Given these results, it is stated the final solutions are considerably influenced by the evaluations profiles, in a way they tend to get closer to the target-individuals, answering the research question.

3   A Machine Learning Approach for User Modeling

As demonstrated in the previous section, the IGA is capable of incorporating the user preferences in the search process. However, as explained earlier, the human fatigue problem makes an interactive approach unfeasible when the number of interactions is high. For an IGA settings with 500 individuals and 100 generations, for example, the requirements engineer would be asked 50000 times.

In order to handle this difficulty, this paper proposes a machine learning technique to model the user evaluation profile. Thus, the learning model would use the individuals, and the respective human evaluations, as a training set, replacing the requirements engineer after a while. The architecture of the proposed machine learning model alongside the IGA can be seen in Figure 1.

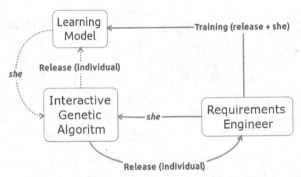

Fig. 1. The Architecture of the Learning Model alongside the IGA

The process is divided into two distinct stages. In the first stage (solid lines), all individuals will be evaluated by the requirements engineer. The IGA is guided by the user's preferences while the learning model learn its behavior. The learning model will be trained until a confidence level is satisfied or a certain number of evaluations is reached. In the second stage (dotted lines), the model would have already learnt the user preferences, and the remaining evaluations will be fully transferred to it, resulting in a significant reduction in human fatigue.

Therefore, when incorporating a learning model to the IGA, it is expected the results remain consistent to the evaluation profile, but with a significant decrease in the number of questions to the requirements engineer.

Currently, the learning model is under development and it is expected to be tested with different learning techniques (Least Means Square, Multilayer Perceptron, etc) which one present a better suiting to the proposal.

4 Conclusion

The requirements selection is a complex task in an iterative and incremental software development project. When search techniques are used to tackle such problems, it becomes difficult to incorporate the user's preferences to the process.

The objective of this work was to develop a feasible Interactive Genetic Algorithm to the Next Release Problem, but in a way it could also deal with the human fatigue. In order to handle this problem, it is proposed a machine learning technique to model the requirements engineer preferences and replace him throughout the search process. Intermediate IGA results show that it is able to incorporate the requirements engineer knowledge in the final solutions.

As future works, it is expected to finalize the implementation and tests related to the learning model; assess different ways in which the requirements engineer can evaluate the solutions; consider interdependencies between requirements; apply the IGA for the multiobjective version of the NRP.

References

1. Bagnall, A.J., Rayward-Smith, V.J., Whittley, I.M.: The next release problem. Information and Software Technology 43(14), 883–890 (2001)
2. Harman, M., Mansouri, S.A., Zhang, Y.: Search based software engineering: A comprehensive analysis and review of trends techniques and applications. Department of CS, Kings College London, Tech. Rep. TR-09-03 (2009)
3. Harman, M., McMinn, P., de Souza, J.T., Yoo, S.: Search based software engineering: Techniques, taxonomy, tutorial. In: Meyer, B., Nordio, M. (eds.) LASER Summer School 2008-2010. LNCS, vol. 7007, pp. 1–59. Springer, Heidelberg (2012)
4. Harman, M.: Search based software engineering for program comprehension. In: 15th IEEE International Conference on Program Comprehension, ICPC 2007, pp. 3–13. IEEE (2007)
5. Takagi, H.: Interactive evolutionary computation: Fusion of the capabilities of ec optimization and human evaluation. Proceedings of the IEEE 89(9), 1275–1296 (2001)
6. Tonella, P., Susi, A., Palma, F.: Using interactive ga for requirements prioritization. In: 2010 Second International Symposium on Search Based Software Engineering (SSBSE), pp. 57–66. IEEE (2010)
7. Simons, C.L., Parmee, I.C., Gwynllyw, R.: Interactive, evolutionary search in upstream object-oriented class design. IEEE Transactions on Software Engineering 36(6), 798–816 (2010)
8. Baker, P., Harman, M., Steinhofel, K., Skaliotis, A.: Search based approaches to component selection and prioritization for the next release problem. In: 22nd IEEE International Conference on Software Maintenance, ICSM 2006, pp. 176–185. IEEE (2006)

Transaction Profile Estimation of Queueing Network Models for IT Systems Using a Search-Based Technique

Shadi Ghaith, Miao Wang, Philip Perry, and John Murphy

School of Computer Science,
University College Dublin, Ireland
shadi.ghaith@ucdconnect.ie

Abstract. The software and hardware systems required to deliver modern Web based services are becoming increasingly complex. Management and evolution of the systems requires periodic analysis of performance and capacity to maintain quality of service and maximise efficient use of resources. In this work we present a method that uses a repeated local search technique to improve the accuracy of modelling such systems while also reducing the complexity and time required to perform this task. The accuracy of the model derived from the search-based approach is validated by extrapolating the performance to multiple load levels which enables system capacity and performance to be planned and managed more efficiently.

1 Introduction

The IT services offered over the internet, and within enterprise premises, increased rapidly over the past few decades. The expectation of a consistent high-quality level of service is growing and becoming more difficult to be met. In the meanwhile, the demand for a cost effective solution to efficiently use computing resources according to workload variations is getting stronger, especially for enterprise service providers.

Predicting enterprise applications service levels under various loads and resources is widely done based on time and cost efficient performance modelling techniques [1]. A Queueing Network Model (QNM) representing the various system resources (such as the CPU and Disk I/O) is built and solved during this process. One input to the QNM solver is the amount of time required to serve each transaction on each resource in all visits to the underlying resource, while excluding the queuing time. This input value is known as the Service Demand.

Obtaining such service demands by measuring the time spent by a single user transaction on each resource faces a major measurement problem due to small service demands. Additionally, some functionality, such as caching, can be only triggered when multiple users access the system, which leads capacity engineers to infer these service demands from multiuser measurements [2] [3] [4]. Such approaches have problems (we will discuss some of them in Section 2)

C. Le Goues and S. Yoo (Eds.): SSBSE 2014, LNCS 8636, pp. 234–239, 2014.

which lead to various approximations and lengthy procedures. This causes a less accurate prediction results which are usually solved by deliberatly increasing the hardware requirments to compensate for this imprecision, resulting in an under-utilized infrastructure. Additionally, the lengthy procedure can easily put an extra pressure on an already busy Capacity Management (CM) projects.

In this paper, we propose a search-based solution to obtain a more accurate service demands from the data obtained from multiuser performance data. This work improves the capacity planning process by enhancing its accuracy and duration. Also, other processes relying on the service demands, such as the performance regression testing technique [5] [6], will also benefit of this work.

2   Queueing Network Models for Capacity Planning

Transactions are created by users of enterprise applications to perform certain functionalities (such as search and buy). These transactions are served by the various system resources (such as the CPU and Disk I/O of each server) to fulfil the user request [1]. The flow of the transaction through the system can be represented by a Queueing Network Model (QNM) [1] such as the one shown in Figure 1. Each node represents a system resource (e.g. CPU, Disk I/O) which consists of a processing unit and a queue for the transaction to wait if the processing unit is busy. Each transaction may visit each resource multiple times and the total time required to serve the transaction on each resource, during all visits and excluding the time in the queue, is called service demand.

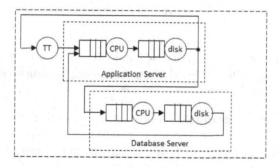

Fig. 1. Queueing Network Model of a Three-Tiered Computer System

The Transaction Response Time (TRT) is the time spent by a certain transaction on all system resources [1] which is the sum of the actual processing time (service demand) along with the time in the queue. The Transaction Profile (TP) is defined as the total series of service demands on all system resources. Thus, the TP is the lower bound of the TRT, or in other words it is equal to the TRT when the transaction is the only one in the system (i.e. no queueing).

Capacity Management (CM) of the system is the process of predicting its performance by solving the QNM (via various known techniques). This provides predictions of TRTs and Resources Utilizations (RUs) for various load and system configurations as depicted in Figure 2. This typically uses the following three inputs:

1. The QNM of the system, similar to the one shown in Figure 1.
2. The load characterization [1] which includes the number of users issuing each transaction and user Think Time (TT).
3. Service demands (TP) for each transaction at each resource. Our focus in this paper is on enhancing the process to obtain the service demands (TPs).

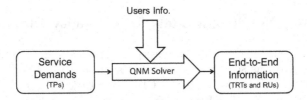

Fig. 2. Solving of Queueing Network Model to Predict System Performance

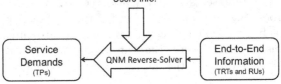

Fig. 3. Presented Approach to Infer TPs From Performance Data (TRTs, RUs)

Estimating the profile of service demands for a given transaction (i.e. the TP) would be most easily achieved by running a single transaction through the system, but this has the following problems:

1. High inaccuracy in measuring service demands due to their small values [3].
2. It is unreliable to measure service demands on virtualised systems [3].
3. Some system behaviours (such as caching) are only triggered under load.

To solve these problems, researchers proposed to focus on measuring the end-to-end parameters, particularly the TRTs and RUs, and to infer the service demands from them [2] [3] [4]. This typically involved running the tests with a number of different load values (time consuming) and simplifying the system to a single node approximation (rarely applicable).

3 Inferring Service Demands

We propose a new method which does not rely on the single node approximation and can use a single multiple user test run at one load level. We propose to

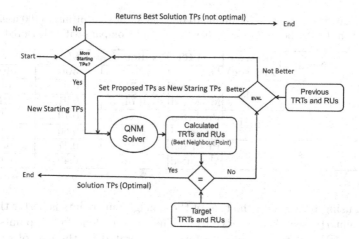

Fig. 4. Reverse-solve QNM by Applying a Search-based Technique

reverse the normal CM process as depicted in Figure 3. The inputs for the QNM reverse-solver are user information, TRTs, RUs while the outputs are the service demands, i.e. the TPs. The QNM reverse-solver is implemented by using the *Repeated Local Search (Continuous Space Hill Climbing)* technique [7] as shown in Figure 4.

The *Local Search* technique is repeated multiple times each with a different starting condition (set of TPs). Given that any TP can have a value ranging from zero to the value of the corresponding TRT, the starting TPs are nominated by evenly dividing the range (0 to TRT) to a predefined number of points. The number is chosen as a compromise between the search time and the accuracy of the result. At the end all the solutions returned by the Local Search (local maximum) are compared, as will be described shortly, and best one is returned.

The quality of the solution (EVal) is defined as the distance between the TRTs (and RUs) and their corresponding target values (ultimate solution) which is calculated as shown below (a smaller value is better):

1. Calculate percentage difference between each proposed and target TRT (RU).
2. For all the TRTs find the average percentage value (Do same for all RUs).
3. Do a weighted summation of the above averages.

The summation of all service demands corresponding to each transaction should equal to the starting TP. Accordingly, the initial service demands are set by dividing the starting TP value among the corresponding service demands either equally or with a predetermined ratio of that transaction. These ratios can be learned by the system and applied to subsequent searches on next releases or similar applications.

The *Local Search* technique loops over all initial service demands. For each one, tests the adjacent points by incrementing (decriminting) that service demand with selected steps. The QNM is solved for all solutions and the outcome is

Table 1. Using the Proposed Technique to Infer TPs from a Multiuser (100 users) Run and Use Them to Predict TRTs at Other Loads and Compare with Measured Values

Transaction Name	Inferred TP (sec)	TRT Predicted and Measured (sec)			
		Users	200	300	400
Home	0.43	Predicted	0.71	0.91	1.05
		Measured	0.74	0.91	1.11
List Products	0.24	Predicted	0.45	0.79	0.95
		Measured	0.48	0.80	1.01
Search for Products	0.26	Predicted	0.39	0.47	0.65
		Measured	0.42	0.49	0.66

evaluated using EVal and if the best of these neighbour points is better than the current point the search will move to it. The same is done for all points in the loop. If the EVal of the proposed solution (generated by the end of the loop) is lower than an epsilon value then the entire search process concludes with a perfect solution. Otherwise, if the proposed solution is better than the previous one, it is set as a new set of starting TPs point and the loop is restarted over all service demands (Local Search still running). This continues until the proposed solution is not better than the current one (local maximum) so the Local Search iteration concludes and a new one is triggerd with new starting TPs.

4   Experimental Evaluation

In order to evaluate our technique, we performed tests on the reference JEE enterprise application (JPetStore) with 4 performance runs of 100, 200, 300 and 400 users. Each run included 10 transactions applied by a load generator tool. Each run took around one hour and the TRTs and RUs were recorded.

We used the presented technique to infer the TPs using the run with 100 users. The TPs corresponding to a subset of the transactions are shown in the second column of Table 1. Then we used these TPs to predict the TRTs at loads of 200, 300 and 400 users using the process in Figure 2. The last three columns of the Table show the TRTs obtained using the prediction process and direct measurements. We can see that the results are close and the error is within normal limits for the QNM based techniques. The search process to obtain the TPs converged in less than 8 minutes, which yields a significant saving of several hours over the existing inference techniques. Finally, we set the number of Local Search repeats to 10 but all cases converged in maximum of three repeats.

5   Related Work

Inferring the service demands (TPs) from TRTs and RUs has been explored because measuring such counters is much easier than measuring the service demands. Casale et al [2] proposed to do a linear regression between the RUs and the service demands. While Kraft et al [3] proposed a similar approach but to use TRTs instead of RUs. These two approaches assume the system can be simplified to one node which does not hold true for most IT systems. In addition, multiple runs with different loads are required which is both time and resource consuming. Liu et al [4] proposed a formulation to estimate the parameters of the QNM using a quadratic programming framework. This requires the end-to-end parameters TRTs, RUs and Throughput from a set of runs which is costly.

6   Conclusions and Future Work

Current techniques to obtain service demands used to solve QNMs in CM projects are inaccurate and time consuming. In this paper, we addressed these concerns by proposing a search-based approach to infer the service demands from end-to-end data (TRTs and RUs) collected from only one performance run. We explained the technique using Local Search accompanied with Restarting techniques. In future, we plan to explore other search alternatives in order to improve the performance of the reverse-solver, mainly when the number of transactions becomes large. Also, we believe that many parameters of the search process can be learned and generalized for various enterprise application (and transaction) categories. In addition, we will show the improvement on CM projects and other fields utilizing service demands, such as the regression testing data analysis.

Acknowledgment. Supported, in part, by Science Foundation Ireland grant 10/CE/I1855.

References

1. Grinshpan, L.: Solving Enterprise Applications Performance Puzzles. John Wiley and Sons, Inc., Hoboken (2012)
2. Casale, G., Cremonesi, P., Turrin, R.: Robust workload estimation in queueing network performance models. In: Proceedings of the 16th Euromicro Conference on Parallel, Distributed and Network-Based Processing, PDP 2008 (2008)
3. Kraft, S., Pacheco-Sanchez, S., Casale, G., Dawson, S.: Estimating service resource consumption from response time measurements. In: Proceedings of the International ICST Conference on Performance Evaluation Methodologies and Tools (2009)
4. Wynter, L., Liu, Z., Cathy, H.X., Zhang, F.: Parameter inference of queueing models for it systems using end-to-end measurements. Performance Evaluation 63(1), 36–60 (2006)
5. Ghaith, S., Wang, M., Perry, P., Murphy, J.: Automatic, load-independent detection of performance regressions by transaction profiles. In: Proceedings of the 2013 International Workshop on Joining AcadeMiA and Industry Contributions to testing Automation, JAMAICA 2013, pp. 59–64. ACM, New York (2013)
6. Ghaith, S., Wang, M., Perry, P., Murphy, J.: Profile-based, load-independent anomaly detection and analysis in performance regression testing of software systems. In: 17th European Conference on Software Maintenance and Reengineering (CSMR 2013), Genova, Italy (2013)
7. Harman, M., Hierons, R., Jones, B., Lumkin, M., Mitchell, B., Mancoridis, S., Rees, K., Roper, M., Clarke, J., Dolado, J.J., Shepperd, M.: Reformulating software engineering as a search problem. In: Software IEE Proceedings (June 2003)

Less is More: Temporal Fault Predictive Performance over Multiple Hadoop Releases[*]

Mark Harman[1], Syed Islam[1], Yue Jia[1], Leandro L. Minku[2],
Federica Sarro[1], and Komsan Srivisut[3]

[1] CREST, University College London, UK
[2] CERCIA, University of Birmingham, UK
[3] Department of Computer Science, University of York, UK

Abstract. We investigate search based fault prediction over time based on 8 consecutive Hadoop versions, aiming to analyse the impact of chronology on fault prediction performance. Our results confound the assumption, implicit in previous work, that additional information from historical versions improves prediction; though G-mean tends to improve, Recall can be reduced.

1 Introduction

Software Fault Prediction is challenging, because of the diverse factors that influence the location and numbers of faults. Such factors vary in strength-of-influence and availability between systems and organisations. Nevertheless, this challenge is important because fault prediction may improve effort targeting and reduce the number of faults that survive into production software [9]. Predictive modelling has thus become an attractive subset of activity for Search Based Software Engineering (SBSE) [1,10]. Search-based approaches have been used to predict effort [7], quality [3], faults [18,19] and performance [14].

Like any prediction system, a fault prediction system is entirely dependent upon the information available to it [9]. One might expect that additional information can only serve to improve predictive performance. Unfortunately, this naïve assumption does not always hold in practice; extra information may be contradictory or misleading and can thereby harm predictive performance.

In this paper, we address the challenge of understanding the way in which information about different versions of the software system impacts upon our ability to define search based fault prediction systems over time. Our previous work has demonstrated that such *project chronology* can be valuable for predictive performance in software effort estimation [15,16]. However, no work has investigated whether chronology is also important in software fault prediction. We extracted and curated[1] data from 8 versions of the Hadoop system, using it to train a search based fault prediction system. Our prediction system [19] uses a Genetic Algorithm to train a Support Vector Machine, which predicts whether a

---

[*] Author order is alphabetical.
[1] All data on which we report here is available at
http://www0.cs.ucl.ac.uk/staff/F.Sarro/projects/hadoop/

C. Le Goues and S. Yoo (Eds.): SSBSE 2014, LNCS 8636, pp. 240–246, 2014.
© Springer International Publishing Switzerland 2014

class is faulty. This is the first time that results have been reported on temporal fault predictive performance, over multiple releases.

Our results reveal that, as expected, overall predictive performance (measured using G-mean) is statistically significantly better when augmented with the data from the entire version history. However, perhaps more surprisingly, we also found that, for half the versions considered, Recall is statistically significantly better using *solely* the previous version. Therefore, this study calls for a fundamental change in the way we view software fault prediction, in order to take chronology into account.

2 Search-Based Temporal Fault Prediction

Problem Formulation: We formulate software fault prediction as a temporal learning problem in which data on a different version of a software system are made available at each *time step*. These data comprise metrics describing all existing classes within the source code of the given version and whether or not faults to be fixed have been found in those classes. Data on all versions up to the current time step are available for building models, even though one may chose not to use all data available. At each time step, faults are predicted in the next version of the system. We refer to the version received at time step t as v_t.

Experimental Objective and Setup: The main objective of our experiments is to analyse how data from different versions of the software system Hadoop impact upon our ability to define search based fault prediction over time. We analysed the following models' performance at predicting faults in version v_{t+1}:

- Models M_t: each model M_t is trained using *all* versions v_0 to v_t;
- Models MP_t: each model MP_t is trained using *only the previous* version v_t.

This allows us to check whether models trained on the most recent version may outperform models trained on all versions so far. In addition, we also investigate the performance of a model MP_t, built from version t, at predicting faults in each and all of the subsequent versions. This will reveal whether the performance of old models always decreases with time, or whether old models can remain useful for prolonged periods of time.

The performance measures analysed are G-mean and Recall. Hadoop denotes a so-called 'imbalanced' learning problem; there are much more non-faulty than faulty examples. We use G-mean because it is usually considered to be more robust than other measures (e.g., the so-called 'Accuracy' and 'F-measure') to the influence of the faulty and non-faulty classes on performance [13]. It is defined as the geometric mean of the Recall and Specificity. Recall is the rate of faulty examples correctly classified as being faulty (i.e., the True Positive Rate), while Specificity is the rate of non-faulty examples correctly classified as being non-faulty (i.e., the False Negative Rate). Recall is particularly important to the software engineer because a good Recall means that few faulty components will be missed. The consequences of low Recall have been argued to be far more important than those of low Precision [17]. This motivates the study of Recall in our analysis.

Technique: Several studies [6,8] have claimed that Support Vector Machines (SVMs) are successful at predicting fault-proneness in software components. However, in order to obtain a more accurate classification, SVMs required a suitable configuration. Previous work has shown that using a Genetic Algorithm (GA) for configuring SVMs enables them to outperform several other techniques, being effective for inter-release fault prediction [5,19]. This motivates the choice of this technique in our experiments. The technique works as follows: a solution to the problem is an SVM configuration consisting of n parameters (with n determined by the SVN kernel function).

As kernel function, we employed the widely used Radial Basis Functions (RBF), which has two parameters C (the soft margin parameter) and γ (the radius of the RBF kernel). The GA chromosome is thus composed by two genes, for C and γ, the values of which vary in the ranges $[0.000001, 0.01]$ and $[8,32000]$ respectively. An initial population of 100 random chromosomes was created. To compute the fitness of a chromosome, representing an SVM configuration, we execute the SVM with the chosen configuration on the training set, thereby obtaining fault predictions. These predictions are evaluated using G-mean as performance criterion (fitness function). Random undersampling [13] of the SVM's training set was used to deal with class imbalance.

To create the new offspring, we use tournament selection with single point crossover and mutation, each with probability of 0.5 and 0.1 respectively. We terminate the search after 300 generations or when best fitness remains unchanged for 30 generations. The GA setting was chosen to be the same to previous work [5,19]. To cope with the stochastic nature of GA, we execute 30 runs and report the boxplots of the performance obtained on the test set, backed up by the results of non-parametric inferential statistical tests, as recommended in the literature [2,12]. As sanity check, we compared our results to those obtained by using a uniformly random classifier that predicts each component in a given test set to be faulty or not-faulty with the same probability (i.e., Random Guessing).

Data Extracted and Preprocessing: We mined the Hadoop JIRA issue repository[2] to extract bug information for each Hadoop Common revision. We filtered out unresolved bugs and only considered fixed bugs with available patches. An issue is deemed to be a 'fixed bug issue' if its type attribute is Bug, its resolution status is Fixed, its status is either Closed or Resolved and the number of attachments is greater than one. We coded this rule as a 'JQL' query, using the JIRA command line tool to extract bug information automatically from the Hadoop JIRA repository. We examined the patches for each bug and located the source files that changed to fix it, considering only the latest patch version for multiply-patched bugs. For each Java class contained in a given revision, we computed the number of bugs found together with the Chidamber-Kemerer metrics [4] and the Lines of Code (LoC) metric using the tool ckjm[3]. The overall data collection and post-processing procedures are described in Algorithm 1.

---

[2] https://issues.apache.org/jira/browse/hadoop
[3] omit.iiar.pwr.wroc.pl/p_inf/ckjm/

We analysed the first 8 versions of Hadoop Common (from 0.0.1 to 0.8.0) containing in total 16 minor releases. From these releases we extracted 626 bug fixes. We filtered out those affecting non java-components and the components contained in the package's tests and examples. This left 509 bug fixes with which we experimented. For each version, we aggregated the data for all the corresponding revisions and considered a class to be faulty if its number of bugs is greater than 1. Considering all revisions together, 81% of the components are non-faulty and 19% are faulty. To save space and support replication, all our data, statistics and results are available on-line [4].

Algorithm 1. The overall data collection and post processing procedures

1. **for** each *released version* **do**
2.   get issue-keys with the JQL query:
      project = "*HADOOP*" **and** *issuetype* = *Bug* **and**
      resolution = *Fixed* **and** *statusin*(*Resolved, Closed*) **and**
      "*Attachmentcount*" ≥ "1"
3.   **for** each *issue-key* **do**
4.   save all information of this issue
5.   get attachment list and find name for the latest patch
6.   download the latest patch
7.   link current issue to files changed in the patch
8.   **end for**
9.   get current version of the source from GIT/SVN
10.   compute the metrics for the source files
11. **end for**
12. merge metrics and bugs for each component together

---

3   Results

Figure 1 presents boxplots for G-mean and Recall values obtained over 30 runs for all models described in Section 2 and for Random Guessing (RG).

We observe that the best among the two models (M_t or MP_t) performs in general better than RG. One-tailed Wilcoxon Sign Rank tests with Holm-Bonferroni corrections (overall $\alpha = 0.05$) revealed that GA+SVM was significantly better than RG (with high effect size: $\hat{A}_{12} > 0.81$) in terms of G-mean on all the considered versions, except for $t = 5$ where there was no statistical difference. The best among the two models is significantly better than RG in terms of Recall on all the considered versions (with high effect size: $\hat{A}_{12} > 0.80$).

We now compare the performance of model M_t, against the corresponding model MP_t, to assess whether models trained on all data outperform those trained solely on the previous version.

Figure 1 reveals that the prediction ability of the models M_t and MP_t varies depending on the version. In particular, M_t provided better G-mean than MP_t on all the versions v_{t+1} except for $t = 1$, while MP_1 provided the best G-mean. This is expected; early versions offer less information. However, M_t provided better Recall values than MP_t only in two cases ($t = 2$ and $t = 6$), similar in one case ($t = 3$), and worse in the remaining ones ($t = 1$, $t = 4$, $t = 5$).

---

[4] http://www0.cs.ucl.ac.uk/staff/F.Sarro/projects/hadoop/

To assess whether these differences are significant we used the Wilcoxon Signed Rank Test with Holm-Bonferroni corrections (overall $\alpha = 0.05$). In particular, we check two null hypotheses: H_0^{G-mean}: "There is no difference between the G-mean provided by M_t and its corresponding MP_t"; and H_0^{Recall}: "There is no difference between the Recall provided by M_t and its corresponding MP_t". The results revealed that we can reject H_0^{G-mean} for all the versions (p-value<0.001), while we can reject H_0^{Recall} for all the models (p-value<0.005), except for $t = 3$ (p-value=0.145). We conclude that (a) there is always statistically significant difference between the G-mean values provided by M_t and MP_t (and with high effect size: $\hat{A}_{12} > 0.80$) and this difference favours M_t, except for $t = 1$ where it favours MP_t; (b) there is statistically significant difference between the Recall values provided by M_t and MP_t (and with high effect size: $\hat{A}_{12} > 0.70$): in three cases ($t = 1$, $t = 4$, $t = 5$) this difference favours MP_t, in two cases ($t = 2$ and $t = 6$) it favours M_t.

These findings from Hadoop indicate that engineers who want to find all faulty components may get better results using models trained solely on the previous version, discarding the extra 'information' present in the version history. Since these results indicate that models MP_t are potentially useful, we now move on to investigate them in more detail.

We investigate the performance of a model, MP_t, built from version t, at predicting faults in each and all of the subsequent versions. Figure 2 shows the median performances. We observe that the G-mean does not always decrease with time (e.g., MP_3 and MP_4), even though earlier models (e.g., MP_0 and MP_1) do tend to become less competitive with time. Once again, Recall is different. We see a lower variation in performance and also, perhaps more importantly, we observe models that remain competitive over many subsequent releases. For instance, MP_0 remains competitive throughout most of the first 8 versions of Hadoop. We also observe that models trained on the most recent version are not always the best fault predictors (e.g., MP_3 outperforms MP_5 for fault prediction in version v_6). This suggests that dynamic adaptive prediction systems [11,10] are required, so that we can automatically recognise the best-suited model for each version.

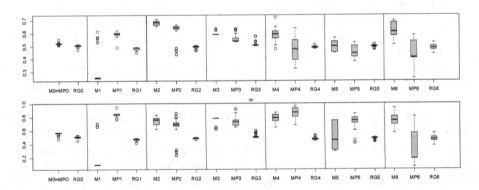

Fig. 1. G-mean (a) and Recall (b) obtained by M_t, MP_t and RG for predicting faults in version v_{t+1}, over 30 runs

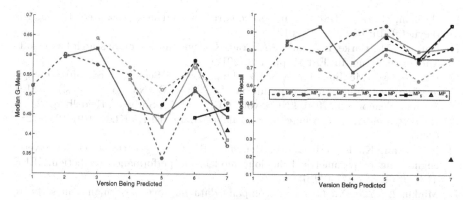

Fig. 2. Median model performance considering 30 runs over time

4   Conclusions

Our analysis of Hadoop showed that using data from all versions is not always needed for prediction. We also found that prediction models trained on early software versions may preferable to those trained on the latest versions. This motivates the further study of dynamic adaptive fault prediction systems.

References

1. Afzal, W., Torkar, R.: On the application of genetic programming for software engineering predictive modeling: A systematic review. Expert Systems Applications 38(9), 11984–11997 (2011)
2. Arcuri, A., Briand, L.: A practical guide for using statistical tests to assess randomized algorithms in software engineering. In: ICSE, pp. 1–10 (2011)
3. Bouktif, S., Sahraoui, H., Antoniol, G.: Simulated annealing for improving software quality prediction. In: GECCO, vol. 2, pp. 1893–1900 (2006)
4. Chidamber, S.R., Kemerer, C.F.: A metrics suite for object oriented design. IEEE TSE 20(6), 476–493 (1994)
5. Di Martino, S., Ferrucci, F., Gravino, C., Sarro, F.: A genetic algorithm to configure support vector machines for predicting fault-prone components. In: Caivano, D., Oivo, M., Baldassarre, M.T., Visaggio, G. (eds.) PROFES 2011. LNCS, vol. 6759, pp. 247–261. Springer, Heidelberg (2011)
6. Elish, K.O., Elish, M.O.: Predicting defect-prone software modules using support vector machines. JSS 81(5), 649–660 (2008)
7. Ferrucci, F., Harman, M., Sarro, F.: Search based software project management. In: Ruhe, G., Wohlin, C. (eds.) Software Project Management in a Changing World, Springer (to appear, 2014)
8. Gondra, I.: Applying machine learning to software fault-proneness prediction. JSS 81(2), 186–195 (2008)
9. Hall, T., Beecham, S., Bowes, D., Gray, D., Counsell, S.: A systematic literature review on fault prediction performance in software engineering. IEEE TSE 38(6), 1276–1304 (2012)

10. Harman, M.: How SBSE can support construction and analysis of predictive models (keynote). In: PROMISE (2010)
11. Harman, M., Burke, E., Clark, J.A., Yao, X.: Dynamic adaptive search based software engineering. In: ESEM, pp. 1–8 (2012)
12. Harman, M., McMinn, P., de Souza, J.T., Yoo, S.: Search based software engineering: Techniques, taxonomy, tutorial. In: Meyer, B., Nordio, M. (eds.) LASER Summer School 2008-2010. LNCS, vol. 7007, pp. 1–59. Springer, Heidelberg (2012)
13. He, H., Garcia, E.A.: Learning from imbalanced data. IEEE TKDE 21(9), 1263–1284 (2009)
14. Krogmann, K., Kuperberg, M., Reussner, R.: Using genetic search for reverse engineering of parametric behaviour models for performance prediction. IEEE TSE 36(6), 865–877 (2010)
15. Minku, L., Yao, X.: Can cross-company data improve performance in software effort estimation? In: PROMISE, pp. 69–78 (2012)
16. Minku, L., Yao, X.: How to make best use of cross-company data in software effort estimation? In: ICSE, pp. 446–456 (2014)
17. Ostrand, T.J., Weyuker, E.J.: How to measure success of fault prediction models. In: SOQUA 2007, pp. 25–30. ACM (2007)
18. Rodríguez, D., Ruiz, R., Riquelme, J.C., Harrison, R.: Subgroup discovery for defect prediction. In: Cohen, M.B., Ó Cinnéide, M. (eds.) SSBSE 2011. LNCS, vol. 6956, pp. 269–270. Springer, Heidelberg (2011)
19. Sarro, F., Di Martino, S., Ferrucci, F., Gravino, C.: A further analysis on the use of genetic algorithm to configure support vector machines for inter-release fault prediction. In: ACM-SAC, pp. 1215–1220 (2012)

Babel Pidgin: SBSE Can Grow and Graft Entirely New Functionality into a Real World System

Mark Harman, Yue Jia, and William B. Langdon

University College London, CREST Centre, UK

Abstract. Adding new functionality to an existing, large, and perhaps poorly-understood system is a challenge, even for the most competent human programmer. We introduce a 'grow and graft' approach to Genetic Improvement (GI) that transplants new functionality into an existing system. We report on the trade offs between varying degrees of human guidance to the GI transplantation process. Using our approach, we successfully grew and transplanted a new 'Babel Fish' linguistic translation feature into the Pidgin instant messaging system, creating a genetically improved system we call 'Babel Pidgin'. This is the first time that SBSE has been used to evolve and transplant entirely novel functionality into an existing system. Our results indicate that our grow and graft approach requires surprisingly little human guidance.

1 Introduction and Backgroud

Despite much progress in software development environments, programming still includes many human activities that are dull, unproductive and tedious. In this paper we propose a new SBSE approach to software development: Grow and Graft, in which a new feature is grown (using genetic programming) and subsequently grafted into an existing system. This grow and graft development approach aims to reduce the amount of tedious effort required by human programmer in order to develop and add new functionality into an existing system.

Our approach is inspired by the recent trend in Search Based Software Engineering (SBSE) called 'genetic improvement' [2,8,10,11,14,15]. Genetic Improvement (GI) uses existing code as 'genetic material' that helps to automatically improve existing software systems. It has been used to repair broken functionality [10,14], and to achieve dramatic scale-ups for sets of small benchmarks [11,15], and also for a 50k LoC genome matching system [8], for graphic shaders [14] and for a CUDA stereo image processing system [7]. Related work on loop perforation has also reported dramatic speed-ups [13]. GI has also been used to port one system to a new version on a different platform [6].

Recently, it has been demonstrated [12] that GI can be used to transplant code [3] from one version of a system to another. In this previous transplantation work [12], code from several versions of MiniSAT (the 'donor') were transplanted into a specific version of MiniSAT using GI. The aim of this transplantation was to improve execution time for a specific task (Combinatorial Interaction Testing).

C. Le Goues and S. Yoo (Eds.): SSBSE 2014, LNCS 8636, pp. 247–252, 2014.
© Springer International Publishing Switzerland 2014

Our approach to software transplantation is to grow code for new functionality, rather than to improve existing non-functional properties of the system (such as execution time). We provide empirical evidence that grow and graft is, indeed, achievable on a large real-world system. Specially, we report on two grafting operations, carried out to insert new functionality into Pidgin, a 200kLoC C/C++ instant messaging system which has several million users worldwide.

In our first illustrative operation, we grafted a simple human-written 'countdown' code fragment. This graft augments Pidgin with the new feature that all the user's messages include the time remaining to the SSBSE 2014 challenge deadline. This example simply serves to illustrate the application of our grafting approach. We then report on a more challenging transplantation, in which we grew and grafted a new feature that augments Pidgin with a 'Babel Fish' that simultaneously translates the user's English language instant messages into Portuguese and Korean. This new functionality is sufficiently anachronistic that we can be relatively sure that no human has hitherto developed it. Nevertheless, it might be useful for improving communications between users who happen to be American, Brazilian and Korean; the general and co-program chairs of SSBSE 2014 and the chair of the SSBSE 2014 challenge track, for example.

1. Grow: First, we use Genetic Programming (GP) to grow, in isolation, fragments of code partly guided by 'suggestions' provided by the developer. The suggestions consist of the names of library functions the developer believes *may* be important and partial ordering constraints on when they should be called. The human may also provide a few necessary conditions for correctness that the programmer knows, from his or her intuition, ought to hold in any correct solution. Our approach thus *does* require a small contribution from the human to capture functionality (with tests) and to constrain the search space with high level humanly-intuitive suggestions; the rest is entirely automated. However the programmer is *not* required to choose any specific variable names, *nor* assignment statements *nor* expressions, *nor* to construct any specific calls, *nor* to determine where any of the statements should reside within the system to be improved.

2. Graft: The working prototype grown by GP is a fragment of code that implements the desired functionality, but which does so entirely in isolation. The remaining challenge is to find a way to incorporate our GP-grown fragment into the larger real-world system. This is the task of the second, 'grafting', phase of our Grow and Graft approach. Grafting the donor fragment involves two activities: finding a viable host insertion location (or locations), and identifying the expressions that serve as parameters between the donor and the host.

This is the first time that either the SBSE or GP community has reported the successful evolution of entirely new functionality in a real world software system. Previous work has either concentrated on improving non-functional properties or repairing existing broken functionality rather than growing genuinely new functional behaviour. We believe that the ability to extend existing real world systems in this way may open many exciting possibilities: Future work can use Grow and Graft to invent software development approaches that blend a small amount of human intuition with a large amount of automated search.

2   Grafting an SSBSE Challenge Deadline Countdown

A small fragment of C code count_down() was written by hand, in complete isolation from Pidgin, and by a programmer unfamiliar with Pidgin. The code fragment takes the current time and returns a string containing the number of days to the SSBSE Challenge Deadline. In this case, the grow phase is trivial, since we need only a single line of code and this is supplied by the programmer. We can thus focus on and explain our fully automated grafting process that transplants [3] the new functionality into Pidgin.

We grafted the countdown into the Pidgin Timestamp 2.10.9 plugin. We used this plugin as a template into which the code is grafted. In the pidgin plugin there is only one variable of type time_t, but there are five variables of type char*. We implemented a simple grafting tool that instantiates each possible value of the template, inserting it before each line of the existing Timestamp 2.10.9 code. There are 14 possible insertion points and 7 possible value substations, so the search space is $7 \times 14 = 98$, of which 69 compiled and ran without error and 2 also passed all test cases. The grafting process took 13 seconds on a 2.66 GHz 2-core machine with 1Gb RAM.

In this case, grafting is an enumerable search problem. However, for larger systems, grafting may, itself, be an SBSE challenge. Grafting was made easier by the Pidgin plugin mechanism, which reduced the graftable search space. We needed only to graft code into the plugin, rather than the whole system. In general, any form of modularity could also be used to reduce the graft space.

3   Growing and Grafting Babel Fish into Pidgin to Create Babel Pidgin

We seek to grow a new functionality (which we christen 'Babel Fish') and then to transplant this into the Pidgin plugin Text Replacement 2.10.9 using grafting, as we did in Section 2.

Growing the Babel Fish requires Genetic Programming (GP). Our GP system is strongly typed and evolves imperative language code statement sequences, the statements of which are either function calls or assignments. The GP system takes a grammar and a source template as input. The grammar specifies a list of data types and functions suggested by the developer as likely to be useful. For growing a Babel Fish we (the programmer in this example) provided the GP with the names of the GoogleTranslate API call for Portuguese and Korean together with the names of string processing library functions (concat and strlen). Of course, this is a significant help to the GP, which could hardly be expected to 'discover' that it should call GoogleTranslate, for example. Nevertheless, such suggestions clearly also denote the most *trivial* application of human intuition.

The GP system applies a single-point crossover operator with a probability of 0.8. After crossover, one of three mutation operators is applied (selected with uniform probability). The three mutation operators are variable replacement, statement replacement and statement swapping.

We use an aggressive elitism selection process that replicates the best individual and inserts it into the new population between 1 and 250 times with a Coupon Collector Distribution (with expected mean of 197 so, typically, 197 insertions). Our approach to elitism aims to ensure sufficient retention of promising code schema in the gene pool. The population size is 500 and the GP terminates when best fitness remains unchanged for 20 generations. All experiments were repeated 30 times to allow for inferential statistical comparison of results.

We experimented with 8 different fitness functions, composed of subsets of 24 equally-weighted fitness components drawn from those defined in Figure 1 on the lefthand side of this page. We do this in order to understand the trade off between human (programmer) effort and automated (GP) effort. In an ideal world, the GP would do all the work. However, since traditional GP has tended to grow only simple and small functions rather than whole programs [5,9] this may be unrealistic. It may also be unnecessary; the programmer need only offer a few simple and (to a human) *naturally intuitive* suggestions of criteria she or he expects to be important in any correct solution. Naturally, we would prefer that the human would be required to provide the least information possible to guide the GP, since we wish to place the least possible software development burden on human shoulders.

#	Category	Description of fitness component
1	Essential	Compiles using gcc
2	Essential	Must not crash
3	Essential	No system warnings appear
4	Essential	Correct output
5	Necessary	Portuguese-trans gets correct string
6	Necessary	Korean-trans gets correct string
7	Necessary	concat gets correct string
8	Necessary	Output contains Portuguese-trans
9	Necessary	Output contains Korean-trans
10	Necessary	Output is different from input
11	Inclusion	Call to Portuguese-trans
12	Inclusion	Call to Korean-trans
13	Inclusion	Call to get text buffer
14	Inclusion	Call to set text buffer
15	Inclusion	Call to buffer start
16	Inclusion	Call to buffer end
17	Inclusion	Call to strlen
18	Inclusion	Call to concat
19	Ordering	buffer start before get text
20	Ordering	buffer end before get text
21	Ordering	Portuguese-trans after get text
22	Ordering	Korean-trans after get text
23	Ordering	Portuguese-trans before set text
24	Ordering	Korean-trans before set text

Fig. 1. The 24 Fitness Components Used

In order to experiment with this human-machine tradeoff, we categorised our fitness functions into four distinct categories: (E)ssential, (N)ecessary, (I)nclusion and (O)rdering. Essential fitness captures the implicit test oracle [4] required by any implementation of any program and therefore requires no human guidance. Necessary fitness consists of properties that the programmer knows will be necessary in any correct solution for the problem in hand. The Inclusion category lists the names of library functions that the programmer believes may prove useful. Finally, the Ordering category is a mechanism through which the programmer specifies partial ordering constraints on the calls made during execution.

Even if the programer were to be asked to provide all of this information, then the (human) effort required would be relatively low. Certainly, human effort would be lower than that required were the human asked to *write* the program extension from scratch, *and* to work out how it should interface to the existing system, *and* to determine where it should be located.

3.1 Results from Growing and Grafting Babel Fishes

Fitness name	Components used (see Fig. 1)	successful growths (p val. compares to E)		mean fitness evaluations ($N = 30$)
E	1..4	0	(p=N/A)	10,500
EI	1..4,11..18	0	(p=N/A)	10,833
EO	1..4,19..24	0	(p=N/A)	11,333
EN	1..4,5..10	2	(p=0.306)	15,483
EIO	1..4,11..24	1	(p=0.500)	13,366
ENI	1..4,5..10,11..18	8	(p=0.030)	16,266
ENO	1..4,5..10,19..24	7	(p=0.044)	14,516
ENIO	1..24	9	(p=0.020)	15,800

Fig. 2. Results for Babel Fish Growth

Figure 2 (on the left) presents the results of our experiments on 8 different fitness functions. In order to more rubustly analyse the results we use a nonparametric two-tailed binomial test to compare the number of successful transplants that we achieved using the essential fitness, E, with each and all of those we achieved using fitnesses EI to ENIO in Figure 2. We use the Hochberg correction in order to account for the fact that we are performing five different inferential statistical tests. With an α level of 0.05, this corrected statistical test indicates that the result for ENIO is significantly different to that for E (with a Vargha-Delaney $\hat{A}_{12}$ effect size 0.64). The p values for ENO and ENI are also smaller than 0.05, but are not considered significant after the Hochberg correction has been applied.

As we expected ENIO, which provides the most guidance to the GP, performs the best: almost a third of its runs result in a successful Babel Fish transplant into Pidgin. This result is statistically significantly better than the results obtained using the essential fitness E alone, which provides insufficient guidance. The results for other fitness choices are also encouraging. They indicate that the grow and graft approach can augment existing real world systems with new functionality, guided by only very modest (and easily obtained) human intuition. Our results provide evidence that the most powerful form of guidance comes from assertions that capture necessary conditions for correctness. Simply adding these simple and intuitive necessity constraints (N) to the essential fitness components (to give EN) leads to successful transplants. However, of all the fitness components with which we experimented, we speculate that defining such necessary constraints would tend to require the most programmer knowledge and effort. It is therefore encouraging that simply using Inclusion and Ordering constraints (EIO fitness in Figure 2) is sufficient to guide the search to a successful transplant. We believe that this result is exciting because it provides an existential proof that a real world systems can be augmented with new functionality with the most meagre of human guidance.

Figure 2 reports results for growth. The graft phase is entirely automated. There are 23 possible insertion points and 2 possible value substitutions, giving a graft space of 46. We use the Babel Fish whose growth was guided by EIO fitness to illustrate graft performance over all our evolved Babel Fishes. Since it was grown with least human effort, it is encouraging that, like all our Babel Fishes, it has at least one successful graft point. Of the 46 graft attempts, 2 failed to compile, 3 crashed, 24 executed without crashing, but failed the functionality test, while 17 were grafted entirely successfully (and thus equally good). The grafting tool enumerated all 46 solutions in 24s. Computationally and conceptually, grafting is surprisingly easy and effective.

4   Conclusions

We have demonstrated that Genetic Improvement can be used to grow code features in isolation, largely oblivious of the system into which they are subsequently to be grafted. Surprisingly little human guidance and domain knowledge is required. Future work will investigate further the minimal human guidance requirement for Grow and Graft Genetic Improvement (GGGI).

Acknowledgement. This work is part supported by the DAASE [1] and GISMO projects [2].

References

1. Harman, M., Burke, E., Clark, J.A., Yao, X.: Dynamic adaptive search based software engineering (keynote paper). In: ESEM, pp. 1–8 (2012)
2. Harman, M., Langdon, W.B., Jia, Y., White, D.R., Arcuri, A., Clark, J.A.: The GISMOE challenge: Constructing the pareto program surface using genetic programming to find better programs (keynote paper). In: ASE, pp. 1–14 (2012)
3. Harman, M., Langdon, W.B., Weimer, W.: Genetic programming for reverse engineering (keynote paper). In: WCRE (2013)
4. Harman, M., McMinn, P., Shahbaz, M., Yoo, S.: A comprehensive survey of trends in oracles for software testing. Tech. Rep. Research Memoranda CS-13-01, Department of Computer Science, University of Sheffield (2013)
5. Koza, J.R.: Genetic Programming: On the Programming of Computers by Means of Natural Selection. MIT Press, Cambridge (1992)
6. Langdon, W.B., Harman, M.: Evolving a CUDA kernel from an nVidia template. In: IEEE World Congress on Computational Intelligence, pp. 1–8. IEEE (2010)
7. Langdon, W.B., Harman, M.: Genetically improved CUDA C++ software. In: EuroGP (to appear, 2014)
8. Langdon, W.B., Harman, M.: Optimising existing software with genetic programming. IEEE Transactions on Evolutionary Computation (TEVC) (to appear, 2014)
9. Langdon, W.B., Poli, R.: Foundations of Genetic Programming. Springer (2002)
10. Le Goues, C., Forrest, S., Weimer, W.: Current challenges in automatic software repair. Software Quality Journal 21(3), 421–443 (2013)
11. Orlov, M., Sipper, M.: Flight of the FINCH through the java wilderness. IEEE Transactions Evolutionary Computation 15(2), 166–182 (2011)
12. Petke, J., Harman, M., Langdon, W.B., Weimer, W.: Using genetic improvement & code transplants to specialise a C++ program to a problem class. In: EuroGP (to appear, 2014)
13. Sidiroglou-Douskos, S., Misailovic, S., Hoffmann, H., Rinard, M.C.: Managing performance vs. accuracy trade-offs with loop perforation. In: FSE, pp. 124–134 (2011)
14. Sitthi-amorn, P., Modly, N., Weimer, W., Lawrence, J.: Genetic programming for shader simplification. ACM Transactions on Graphics 30(6), 152:1–152:11 (2011)
15. White, D.R., Arcuri, A., Clark, J.A.: Evolutionary improvement of programs. IEEE Transactions on Evolutionary Computation (TEVC) 15(4), 515–538 (2011)

Pidgin Crasher: Searching for Minimised Crashing GUI Event Sequences

Haitao Dan, Mark Harman, Jens Krinke, Lingbo Li, Alexandru Marginean, and Fan Wu

CREST, Department of Computer Science,
University College London, Malet Place, London, WC1E 6BT, UK

Abstract. We present a search based testing system that automatically explores the space of all possible GUI event interleavings. Search guides our system to novel crashing sequences using Levenshtein distance and minimises the resulting fault-revealing UI sequences in a post-processing hill climb. We report on the application of our system to the SSBSE 2014 challenge program, *Pidgin*. Overall, our *Pidgin Crasher* found 20 different events that caused 2 distinct kinds of bugs, while the event sequences that caused them were reduced by 84% on average using our minimisation post processor.

1 Introduction

Graphical User Interface (GUI) programs react to non-deterministic event sequences, with the engineering consequence that the functionalities provided by the software may be invoked in unexpected ways, possibly leading to faults. In addition, software engineers need to protect the functionalities from complex user inputs including malicious attacks. This challenges testers to find unusual test sequences that may expose critical defects before they are experienced by users or exploited.

Current GUI testing primarily relies on manual and record-playback techniques [9, 12]. Even with a record-playback tool, GUI testing remains a time consuming procedure, as it is human-centric: testers need to manually search for interesting test sequences. Another problem is that the quality of the tests depends on the testers' experience and understanding of the program. The nature of GUI programs requires testers to explore an exponential number of interleavings of test sequences. This is usually impossible, so testers rely upon assumptions about the way the software will be used to constrain the test sequences that need to be explored.

In this paper we focus on automated search-based GUI testing for the SSBSE Challenge program *Pidgin*. *Pidgin* is a popular instant messaging program [11]. It is developed as an open framework, for which others can develop plugins to enrich its functionalities. Of course, such an open and pluggable architecture may also introduce security vulnerabilities, because plugins could be embedded with malware and exploited by attackers.

C. Le Goues and S. Yoo (Eds.): SSBSE 2014, LNCS 8636, pp. 253–258, 2014.

We introduce and present a system testing tool, *Pidgin crasher*, that is embedded in *Pidgin* and complements existing human-centric GUI testing. *Pidgin crasher* is a GUI testing tool in which search-based algorithms are applied in both on-the-fly test generation and in a post-processing test reduction phase. In order to generate effective crash sequences to reveal potential bugs, *Pidgin crasher* selects the next valid event to send by maximizing the Levenshtein distances to all previously discovered crashing sequences. This selection technique generates shorter sequences that reveal more bugs in *Pidgin* compared to a random sequence generation process.

In order to generate test sequences for *Pidgin*, we use a combination of a *Greedy* search and a simple hill climbing post processing phase. The *Greedy* phase generates incrementally longer test sequences, guided by the measurement of Levenshtein distance to previously encountered sequences. The hill climbing phase is a cleanup operation, similar to those used in Genetic Improvement to reduce the edit sequence [8]. It seeks to minimise the length of the crashing test sequences found in the *Greedy* phase. The overall approach promotes diversity among the set of crashing sequences found by our approach.

We compare our Greedy search with a random approach and a 'tabu random' (that is forbidden to revisit previously encountered sequences, but is not guided by Levenshtein distance). We call this tabu random approach *Blocked* since it is blocked from considering previously encountered sequences.

In our experiments, we run *Pidgin crasher* 1005 times on each of the three different configurations: *Random, Blocked* and *Greedy*. In every execution we found at least one crashing UI sequence. On average, crash sequences generated by our greedy approach are shorter than those generated by the blocked approach (17.5 vs 58.4 UI events).

Overall, we identified 20 different crashing points triggered by 12 different UI events. Further analysis shows that these crashes are caused by two different types of bugs which we term *Type-1* and *Type-2*. *Type-1* faults are those caused by failure to check for NULL pointers passed as actual parameters, while *Type-2* are those faults caused by *Pidgin* requiring the existence of some non-existent resource (e.g. a window or widget). Finally, in our crash sequence reduction experiments, we found that the hill climber reduces crashing sequences with an average reduction factor of 4.88-7.50 (84% on average).

Related Work: To apply the search-based testing, a UI model representing the behaviour of the application under test is usually used to initialise the original tests. Much of the previous work focusses on automating GUI testing [1–4, 7, 10] with a model (manually generated or automatically synthesised), which is used to guide the test generation to follow common user patterns. The closest related work is the EXSYST approach [5]. Like EXSYST we use search-based techniques to find input sequences. However, we target crashing behaviour, whereas EXSYST targets coverage. Furthermore, EXSYST is guided by a state-based model, whereas *Pidgin crasher* does not require a model. In the way that new test sequences are derived from previous crash sequences, our approach is also similar to the concept of test regeneration proposed by Yoo and Harman [13].

2   Test Generation, Execution and Reduction

Pidgin crasher simply targets crashing behaviour, so it does not require a test oracle [6]. It is designed as an automatic testing plugin for *Pidgin* based on GTK+, which is a multi-platform toolkit for creating GUIs used by *Pidgin*. We are using low-level APIs so that the framework not only works on *Pidgin*, but can also be easily adapted to other GTK+ based programs.

On-the-Fly GUI Testing: *Pidgin crasher* conducts testing of GUI programs at the system level. We implement three different on-the-fly UI sequence generation approaches: *Blocked* and *Greedy* search to compare with *Random* search.

In the *Blocked* approach (Algorithm 1), *Pidgin crasher* repeats a procedure of randomly selecting a GTK+ widget (a UI element such as a menu or button from the GTK+ framework) and sending a random but valid signal[1] to *Pidgin* until a crash is observed. The whole process is dynamic, meaning the number of windows varies over time and the window-selecting step adapts to the changing number of windows. In order to avoid previously discovered crashing points, a block list is loaded at the beginning of the random search process. The algorithm records the crashing sequence by writing every emitted signal into a log file.

LoadBlockList();
victim = SelectTopWindow() ;
repeat
  Randomly keep *victim* or execute *victim* = SelectTopWindow() ;
  target = SelectWidget(*victim*) ;
  sig = SelectSignal(*target*) ;
  if *not IsBlocked(*sig*)* **then**
    WriteCrashSequence(*sig*);
    SendSignalByName(*target*, *sig*, ...);
  end
until *a crash*;

Algorithm 1. Random search with block list

The *Greedy* search approach, on the other hand, uses the previously generated sequences to guide the selection of new signals. More specifically, suppose we have a set of signals, S, and a set of crashing sequences previously generated $\mathcal{P} = \{S_1, ...S_n\}$ and each sequence S_i is an ordered string of signals $S_i = s_{i_1} s_{i_2}...$, $s_{i_j} \in S$. When $S_c = s_1...s_k$ is the current sequence of signals we have sent so far (but for which we have yet to encounter a crash), we select the next signal s_{k+1} by computing the furthest Levenshtein distance between the current sequence after the signal is appended and all previous sequence in $\mathcal{P}$. More formally,

$$\forall_{s_i \in S} : M(\mathcal{P}, s_1...s_k s_i) \leq M(\mathcal{P}, s_1...s_k s_{k+1})$$

where $M(\mathcal{P}, S) = \min_{S_i \in \mathcal{P}}\{D(S_i, S)\}$ and where $D(x, y)$ is the Levenshtein distance between x and y.

---

[1] *Events* from the X server are turned into GTK-specific *signals* by GTK.

3   Experiments and Results

In this paper, we answer the following Research Questions (RQs):

RQ1 How effectively can *Pidgin crasher* find potential bugs?
RQ2 What are the coverage of crash points, convergence and redundancy of
the sequences found by each of the three versions of *Pidgin crasher*?
RQ3 What are the kinds of faults found by *Pidgin crasher*?

We use *Pidgin crasher* to generate crashing sequences in each of its three
different modes: *Random, Blocked, Greedy* search. In the *Random* mode, the
next signal to send is randomly selected from all available signals, while the
other two are those approaches described in Section 2.

Pidgin crasher is continuously invoked to produce 201 crashing sequences in
each mode. We repeat the procedure 5 times, so *Pidgin crasher* is run for a
total of 3015 (201 × 5 × 3) times. The sequences so-produced are minimised
by our Hill Climbing process to remove redundancy. In the experiments, we
repetitively send signals to trigger different functionalities via the special API call
`g_signal_emit_by_name(GtkObject *object, const gchar *name, ...)` to
which we pass the selected widget in `object`, the selected signal in `name`, and all
arguments in the variable argument list are passed NULL. All experiments were
run on Ubuntu 13.04 with debug versions of GTK+ 2.24.17 and Glib 2.38.0.

Answer to RQ1: According to the top-right table in Figure 1, the average
lengths of the crashing sequences generated by the *Random, Blocked* and *Greedy*
modes are 14.5, 58.4 and 17.5, respectively. In the same order, the maximum
lengths are 131, 673 and 135. All three modes can find the shortest possible
sequence with length 1 (Column *Min*). In the last column, it is shown that,
on average, *Greedy* mode spends more time to generate 201 crashing sequences
due to the calculations of Levenshtein distance. In summary, *Pidgin crasher* can
effectively crash *Pidgin* in all three modes.
Answer to RQ2 (Coverage): The bottom table in Figure 1 lists the crashing
points found by all runs of *Pidgin crasher*. Of the 9 columns in this table, columns
6, 7 and 8 report the number of times each crash point is discovered. In the
Random approach, 11 out of 20 crashing points are covered, whereas *blocked*
covers 13 and *greedy* covers 19. So both the *Blocked* and the *Greedy* search have
a better coverage than the *Random* approach, while the *Greedy* search achieves
the highest overall coverage, finding all but one of the crashing points found by
all approaches.
Answer to RQ2 (Convergence): Figure 1 top-left shows the growth of the
number of different crashing points found (average of 5 runs). Even though both
Blocked and *Greedy* search find more crashing points than the *Random* approach,
the *Greedy* search clearly converges more quickly than the *Blocked* approach.
Answer to RQ2 (Redundancy): In order to compare the redundancy of
the crashing sequences generated by these approaches, we use the simple Hill
Climbing to remove any irrelevant signals from the sequences. The results show
that the crashing sequences from *Random, Blocked* and *Greedy* search can be

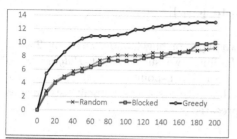

	Avg	Min	Max	Factor	Time (Sec.)
Random	14.5	1	131	4.88	1356
Blocked	58.4	1	673	7.50	2120
Greedy	17.5	1	135	5.91	4650

Crashed Function	Widget	Signal	Crash Location	#Crash			Type
				Rnd	Blk	Grd	
add_room_to_blist_cb	GtkLabel	move-cursor	gtkroomlist.c:250	1	1	3	2
gtk_editable_insert_text	GtkEntry	insert-at-cursor	gtkeditable.c:170	0	2	13	1
gtk_label_activate_link	GtkLabel	activate-link	gtklabel.c:5838	45	116	206	1
gtk_menu_set_child_property	GtkMenu	move-scroll	gtkmenu.c:926	0	1	0	1
gtk_notebook_real_switch_page	GtkNotebook	switch-page	gtknotebook.c:6142	20	39	52	1
gtk_path_bar_scroll_down	GtkMenu	move-scroll	gtkpathbar.c:803	0	0	1	2
gtk_path_bar_scroll_down	GtkButton	clicked	gtkpathbar.c:803	0	0	1	2
gtk_real_menu_item_toggle_size_request	GtkMenuItem	toggle-size-request	gtkmenuitem.c:1452	811	681	435	1
gtk_tree_model_get_valist	GtkTreeView	row-activated	gtktreemodel.c:1470	5	12	11	2
join_button_cb	GtkMenuItem	activate	gtkroomlist.c:265	0	0	1	2
join_button_cb	GtkButton	clicked	gtkroomlist.c:265	0	0	1	2
location_button_toggled_cb	GtkToggleButton	toggled	gtkfilechooserdefault.c:4662	0	0	1	1
menu_add_pounce_cb	GtkMenuItem	activate	gtkconv.c:1169	4	14	41	2
menu_add_pounce_cb	GtkMenuItem	activate-item	gtkconv.c:1169	6	18	51	2
menu_invite_cb	GtkMenuItem	activate	gtkconv.c:1250	12	7	46	2
menu_invite_cb	GtkMenuItem	activate-item	gtkconv.c:1250	12	5	49	2
purple_blist_node_get_type	GtkTreeView	row-collapsed	blist.c	0	0	1	1
purple_blist_node_set_bool	GtkTreeView	row-collapsed	blist.c	0	0	3	2
regenerate_options_items	GtkMenuItem	activate-item	gtkconv.c:3343	49	52	43	2
regenerate_options_items	GtkMenuItem	activate	gtkconv.c:3343	40	57	46	2

Fig. 1. Experimental Results – The upper lefthand subfigure shows convergence of the three approaches. The upper righthand figure reports summary statistics for the average, minimum and maximum sequence length and the average execution time produced by each of the three approaches and, in the fourth column, it reports the reduction in sequence length produced by the post-processing hill climb. The lower, larger, table reports the numbers, types and locations of faults found by each approach.

reduced by a factor of 4.88, 7.50 and 5.91 respectively. The *Blocked* approach generated the longest sequences with the highest redundancy (i.e. the greatest potential for minimisation).

Answer to RQ3: We inspected *Pidgin* to understand the reason for each crash. As a result, we manually categorised all crashing points into two types that reflect two difference classes of reason why *Pidgin* crashes at these points. These two 'types' of fault are reported in the the last column of the lower (larger) table in Figure 1.

A *Type-1* crash happens in the call-back function directly uses a NULL-pointer from the passed arguments to access memory without checking to ensure it is non-NULL. *Type-2* crashes also happen in call-back functions that makes an invalid assumption about the resources available in the current state. For example, function menu_add_pounce_cb opens a conversation window using a pointer fetched from function X which may return NULL. As there is no NULL check in the call-back function, X is assumed to always return a valid pointer, which, however, is violated in some scenarios, where the resource is simply unavailable.

4 Conclusions and Actionable Findings

Using *Pidgin crasher*, we identified two types of bug found caused by 20 different UI signals. According to our findings, we suggest that *Pidgin* return values from any function that may return NULL-pointers should be checked, and that GTK+ signal-emitting APIs that take variable argument lists such as g_signal_emit_by_name should be deprecated.

References

1. Amalfitano, D., Fasolino, A.R., Tramontana, P.: Reverse Engineering Finite State Machines from Rich Internet Applications. In: 15th Working Conference on Reverse Engineering (October 2008)
2. Amalfitano, D., Fasolino, A.R., Tramontana, P., De Carmine, S., Imparato, G.: A toolset for GUI testing of Android applications. In: 28th IEEE International Conference on Software Maintenance (ICSM) (September 2012)
3. Amalfitano, D., Fasolino, A.R., Tramontana, P., De Carmine, S., Memon, A.M.: Using GUI ripping for automated testing of Android applications. In: 27th IEEE/ACM International Conference on Automated Software Engineering (2012)
4. Belli, F., Budnik, C.J., White, L.: Event-based modelling, analysis and testing of user interactions: Approach and case study. Software Testing, Verification and Reliability 16(1) (March 2006)
5. Gross, F., Fraser, G., Zeller, A.: EXSYST: Search-based GUI testing. In: 34th International Conference on Software Engineering (June 2012)
6. Harman, M., McMinn, P., Shahbaz, M., Yoo, S.: A comprehensive survey of trends in oracles for software testing. Technical Report Research Memoranda CS-13-01, Department of Computer Science, University of Sheffield (2013)
7. Jensen, C.S., Prasad, M.R., Møller, A.: Automated testing with targeted event sequence generation. In: International Symposium on Software Testing and Analysis (2013)
8. Langdon, W.B., Harman, M.: Optimising existing software with genetic programming. IEEE Transactions on Evolutionary Computation (TEVC) (to appear, 2014)
9. Memon, A.M.: GUI testing: Pitfalls and process. Computer 35(8) (August 2002)
10. Memon, A.M., Xie, Q.: Studying the fault-detection effectiveness of GUI test cases for rapidly evolving software. IEEE Transactions on Software Engineering 31(10) (October 2005)
11. Pidgin, the universal chat client, http://www.pidgin.im/ (accessed in 2014)
12. Tan, L., Liu, C., Li, Z., Wang, X., Zhou, Y., Zhai, C.: Bug characteristics in open source software. Empirical Software Engineering (June 2013)
13. Yoo, S., Harman, M.: Test data regeneration: Generating new test data from existing test data. Software Testing, Verification and Reliability 22(3) (May 2012)

Repairing and Optimizing Hadoop *hashCode* Implementations

Zoltan A. Kocsis[1], Geoff Neumann[1], Jerry Swan[1], Michael G. Epitropakis[1], Alexander E.I. Brownlee[1], Sami O. Haraldsson[1], and Edward Bowles[2]

[1] University of Stirling, UK
[2] University of York, UK

Abstract. We describe how contract violations in Java[TM] hashCode methods can be repaired using novel combination of semantics-preserving and generative methods, the latter being achieved via Automatic Improvement Programming. The method described is universally applicable. When applied to the HADOOP platform, it was established that it produces hashCode functions that are at least as good as the original, broken method as well as those produced by a widely-used alternative method from the 'Apache Commons' library.

1 Introduction

Every class in the Java[TM] language inherits from Object, which provides default implementations for hashCode and equals. These methods have contractual specifications [8] and in most situations the default implementations need to be overridden. Contractually, equals must conform to the contracts of *Reflexivity, Symmetry, Transitivity, Consistency, Nullity* and *Compatibility*. Reflexivity states that x.equals(x) must always return *true*. Symmetry requires that x.equals(y)== y.equals(x). Transitivity states that x.equals(y)&& y.equals(z) implies x.equals(z). Nullity states that x.equals(null) must return *false*. Compatibility states that x.equals(y) implies hashCode(x)== hashCode(y). Consistency states that (for the same arguments) the results of hashCode and equals must not change on subsequent invocations [9].

Unfortunately, it appears that these contractual obligations are rarely met by the implementers of overridden methods: Vaziri et al. observed [12] that a large number of implementations in widely-used projects (viz. ANT, BCEL, HSQLDB, JAVACUP, JFREECHART, LUCENE, PMD and SHRIKE) are incorrect. It is reasonable to conclude that this is indicative of a systemic problem.

The hashCode method is an integer function of a subset of an object's fields. This paper focuses on two specific requirements: Compatibility and Consistency. To maintain Compatibility, the generated hashCode can depend only on fields used in equals. Breaking the Consistency requirement results in hard-to-diagnose errors: if an object's hashCode changes after it has been placed into a hash container (e.g. HashSet or HashMap) it may become irretrievable. For this reason all fields used in the hashCode method should be immutable.

In addition, an important efficiency objective is minimizing the probability that two different objects return the same hashcode. If every object has an identical

C. Le Goues and S. Yoo (Eds.): SSBSE 2014, LNCS 8636, pp. 259–264, 2014.

hashCode, (e.g. Object's default implementation simply returns 0) then retrieval from hash containers has a complexity of $\mathcal{O}(n)$. By contrast, a perfect hash function (in which every different object has a different hash value) will have a complexity of just $\mathcal{O}(1)$. To meet these objectives, we propose a system for producing contractually correct hashCode methods which use all semantically valid final fields within a class to produce hashcodes with as uniform a distribution as possible. It is well known that software engineers are poor at optimizing hashCode for this purpose. As an alternative we use Automatic Improvement Programming (AIP) to achieve uniformity. AIP is the application of search-based techniques to pre-existing software systems. It has been successfully used to improve 50,000 lines of C++ [7] and also for dynamic (i.e. online) adaptation of Scala source via reflection [11]. To the best of our knowledge, there is no previous work on the integrated correction of hashCodes and their subsequent improvement via AIP.

With further regard to related work, hash functions are ubiquitous in computer science and software engineering. Previous work on generating them has included machine learning [5] and dynamical systems methods [2]. Objectives for constructing hash functions vary, e.g. improving execution speed [3], generalization of the hash function [5] and enforcing the consistency constraint [10]. Techniques and tools for generating hashCode are supported by various independent tools (e.g. *JEqualityGen* [3] and HashCodeBuilder in the 'Apache Commons' library[1]). A semi-automated technique due to Rayside et al. [10] requires only that the programmer give an abstract view of object representation.

2 Methodology

Our analysis centres on HADOOP 2.3.0[2], an open-source Java-based platform for distributed computing. The platform consists of four major components: Hadoop Common, Hadoop Distributed File System, YARN (job scheduling and cluster resource management), and Hadoop MapReduce. Our work focuses on these core parts of the platform, containing 2.4 MLOC.

Initial analysis of HADOOP reveals too many contractually-incorrect implementations of hashCode to list here. As mentioned above, the specific focus of this article is on violations of Compatibility and Consistency. In respect of the latter, we are therefore concerned with mutable fields used in hashCode, viz. those not declared to be final. Denoting a field of a value type (i.e. byte, char, int, long, float or double) to be final ensures immutability. Denoting a reference field (i.e. Object or any of its subclasses) to be final is necessary but not sufficient for immutability: finality ensures that the field cannot be reassigned, but not that the field cannot be mutated if it in turn exposes mutable fields or mutator methods. Discussion of methods to recognize and repair such indirect mutation is beyond the scope of this article.

The methodology we adopt is as follows:

- Search the HADOOP distribution for classes having non-final fields in their hashCode method.

---

[1] http://commons.apache.org/proper/commons-lang/
[2] http://hadoop.apache.org

- Programmatically finalize all non-final fields for which this is a semantics-preserving transformation.
- Generate a new implementation of `hashCode` using only final fields present in `equals`, thus ensuring Compatibility and Consistency.
- Restore (and possibly improve) the quality of `hashCode` distributions via Automatic Improvement Programming.

As a proof-of-concept, the Netbeans IDE was used to determine, via static analysis of HADOOP, all fields which are never actually reassigned. The tool then sets these variables to `final`. The fields used in each `hashCode` implementation were determined via programmatic examination of the source using the Java^{TM} reflection API. We then proceed to enforce the Consistency contract by generating a new `hashCode` that includes only final fields of `equals`. Since the non-final attributes no longer contribute to `hashCode`, it is anticipated that this will degrade the distribution of hash values. In order to compensate, we use Automatic Improvement Programming to evolve a hash function with a highly uniform distribution. The solution representation is in the form of a Koza-tree [6], with field values and random integers uniformly between 0 and 100 (inclusive) as terminals and the functions $\{+, *, XOR, AND\}$ as nonterminals. The search metaheuristic used is iterative improvement [4] with subtree point mutation [6] and random uniform selection of the node to be mutated. The fitness measure seeks to maximize the uniformity (as measured by the χ^2 statistic) over 10,000 randomly-generated instances of the class. We detail the results obtained in three specific cases in the following section.

3 Case Studies

By the method of static analysis described above, an additional 451 fields were safely finalized. While our method is intended to be applicable for all classes containing newly-finalized fields, for the sake of clarity we focus on three classes in the `org.apache.hadoop` package:

1. `hdfs.server.namenode.CheckpointSignature`: the existing implementation violates the Consistency contract for `hashCode`. Our experiment shows that the corrected method generated by our approach has an improved distribution over that generated by `HashCodeBuilder`.
2. `security.token.delegation.AbstractDelegationTokenIdentifier`: the existing `hashCode` implementation violates Consistency and is also likely to return zero. Our approach generates a method that matches the distribution of that generated by `HashCodeBuilder`.
3. `hdfs.server.namenode.startupprogress.Step`: the existing implementation is correct (and is in fact generated by `HashCodeBuilder`), but the hashcodes generated by our method are more uniformly distributed.

Our experiment measures the improvement in the distribution of generated hashcodes gained by using AIP, compared with hashcodes generated by `HashCodeBuilder`, which generates hashCodes either from all `final` fields within the class (or optionally from a user-specified set of fields). In this study, HashCode-Builder used the same set of fields that we identified for use in our own `hashCode`.

Table 1. Experimental results on the uniformity of the hash code distributions generated by the automatic approach, the Apache commons and the original implementation, in terms of the χ^2 statistic

Method	Case study 1			Case study 2			Case study 3		
	m	μ	σ	m	μ	σ	m	μ	σ
automatic	**13.571**	**14.543**	5.307	**14.557**	**14.923**	5.243	**30.115**	**30.852**	10.250
commons	16.698	17.885	7.719	19.512	19.755	6.366	35.709	36.562	12.687
original	15.862	15.789	7.100	N/A			35.709	36.562	12.687
aut. vs com.	p=0.105, $\hat{A}_{12} = 0.636$			p=**0.018**, $\hat{A}_{12} = 0.721$			p=**0.052**, $\hat{A}_{12} = 0.646$		
aut. vs orig.	p=0.792, $\hat{A}_{12} = 0.567$			N/A			p=**0.052**, $\hat{A}_{12} = 0.646$		

The `hashCode` implementations of each of the above classes were tested on 10,000 randomly-generated instances. The χ^2 distribution was used to measure the distance of the computed hashcodes from a uniform distribution (the ideal). This measure was also used to guide the search. Each experiment was repeated 30 times.

4 Results

Table 1 shows the χ^2 statistic for the automatically improved (automatic), `HashCodeBuilder` (commons) and the original implementation (original) if it exists. Specifically, for each case study, we report median (m), mean (μ) and standard deviation (σ) values of the χ^2 statistic. In addition, to assess statistical significance, we utilise the non-parametric Wilcoxon-signed rank test [1] at the 5% level of significance and report the p-value under each test case.

Moreover, to assess the magnitude of an algorithm's performance improvement, we report a non-parametric effect size measure, the $\hat{A}_{12}$ statistic [1]. Intuitively, given a performance measure M, the $\hat{A}_{12}$ statistic measures the probability that algorithm A_1 yields better M values than another algorithm B.

It can be easily observed that the automatic approach is able to enhance the uniformity (as given by the χ^2 statistic) of the hashcode distribution in all cases. In the first case, the automatically produced `hashCode` performs equally well (in significance terms) with the `HashCodeBuilder` and the original implementation. The automatic approach exhibits better average performance in terms of the χ^2 statistic values, but the difference between the three methods is not significant. The effect size is medium in both cases. In the other two cases, our hashcode exhibits significantly better performance, having a large and medium effect size for the second and third cases respectively. The proposed methodology offers a significant improvement over the original method as well, as the second class did not have an effective hash code method to begin with (the original method is likely to return zero).

Generally, we have observed that the automatically evolved hashcodes produce either better or equally good hashcode functions (in terms of their uniform distribution of the produced hash code values) when compared with both `HashCodeBuilder` and the original implementation. The effectiveness and impact of such hash functions is evident in systems where the efficiency of a hash container is a crucial aspect of the system under consideration. Clearly, HADOOP is

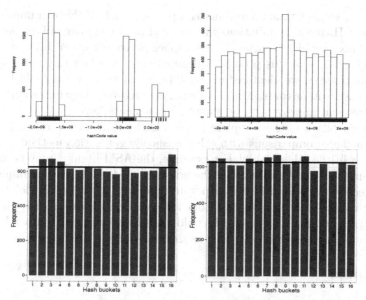

Fig. 1. The distribution of the hashcode values (top) and the distribution of the created objects in hash buckets (bottom), generated by the Apache commons (left) and the evolved function (right)

such a system, which by construction manipulates a huge amount of data that might be stored in hash containers.

In respect of the second case study, Figure 1 shows both the distribution of hash values and how evenly these values are distributed across the buckets of a hash container. This figure compares the automatically generated hashcodes with those from `HashCodeBuilder`. Both techniques appear to be able to evenly fill hash containers, although this is observably less so towards the centre of the range for `HashCodeBuilder`. When the distributions of hash values (in the upper part of the figure) are compared, the superiority of the automatically evolved hash code function can be clearly observed in terms of their uniform distribution.

5   Conclusion and Future Work

We have developed a novel system with which broken implementations of `hashCode` may be repaired so as to enforce contracts and which uses Automatic Improvement Programming to optimise the resulting distribution of hashcodes (which might otherwise be degraded by the repair process). We give case studies in which we fix two classes in the HADOOP library which featured contractually invalid `hashCode` implementations. In both cases, the new methods outperformed those generated by Apache Commons `HashCodeBuilder`.

In the absence of human intervention, code generated by `HashCodeBuilder` does not satisfy Compatibility. Following on from our proof-of-concept, it is possible to create a more fully-automated system able to identify, fix and optimise contractually invalid `hashCode` implementations in a semantics-preserving fashion.

Our findings suggest than an automated approach such as this can improve the efficiency of HADOOP installations that depend on the storage of large amounts of data. This should of course also be applicable to any other Java code. The wider applicability of this project is illustrated by the fact that, in a specific client-code context, we identified over 450 places in which fields could be made final. By augmenting contractual repair with search-based optimization, we anticipate frequent improvement on existing implementations.

This automation of the complete process is the focus of future work, which will also include comparisons with other hashcode generation methods, such as those given in the bibliography. For example, the ASM library[3] may be used to programmatically find and set final the non-final fields by directly manipulating Java bytecode. We could also incorporate functionality to repair violations of the other contracts relating to hashCode and equals, such as symmetry or transitivity. This automated framework could then be incorporated into a broader automatic improvement system such as the Gen-O-Fix system [11].

References

1. Arcuri, A., Briand, L.: A practical guide for using statistical tests to assess randomized algorithms in software engineering. In: Proceedings of the 33rd International Conference on Software Engineering, ICSE 2011, pp. 1–10 (2011)
2. Bahi, J.M., Guyeux, C.: Hash Functions Using Chaotic Iterations. Journal of Algorithms & Computational Technology 4(2), 167–182 (2010)
3. Grech, N., Rathke, J., Fischer, B.: JEqualityGen: Generating equality and hashing methods. In: The Ninth International Conference on Generative Programming and Component Engineering, pp. 177–186 (2011)
4. Hoosand, H.H., Stützle, T.: Stochastic Local Search: Foundations & Applications. Elsevier / Morgan Kaufmann (2004)
5. Kong, W., Li, W.J.: Isotropic Hashing. Technical report (2012)
6. Koza, J.R.: Genetic Programming II: Automatic Discovery of Reusable Programs. MIT Press, Cambridge (1994)
7. Langdon, W.B., Harman, M.: Optimising Existing Software with Genetic Programming. IEEE Transactions on Evolutionary Computation PP(99), 1–18 (2014)
8. Meyer, B.: Applying 'design by contract'. Computer 25(10), 40–51 (1992)
9. Oracle. Java Platform Standard Ed. 7 (2013)
10. Rayside, D., Benjamin, Z., Singh, R., Near, J.P., Milicevic, A., Jackson, D.: Equality and hashing for (almost) free. In: ICSE 2009 Proceedings of the 31st International Conference on Software Engineering, pp. 342–352 (2009)
11. Swan, J., Epitropakis, M.G., Woodward, J.R.: Gen-O-Fix: An embeddable framework for Dynamic Adaptive Genetic Improvement Programming. Technical Report January, Department of Computing Science and Mathematics, University of Stirling, Stirling, UK (2014)
12. Vaziri, M., Tip, F., Fink, S.J., Dolby, J.: Declarative object identity using relation types. In: Ernst, E. (ed.) ECOOP 2007. LNCS, vol. 4609, pp. 54–78. Springer, Heidelberg (2007)

---

[3] http://asm.ow2.org/

Author Index